From Orientalis

From Orientalism to Cultural Capital

The Myth of Russia in British Literature of the 1920s

Olga Soboleva and Angus Wrenn

PETER LANG

Oxford • Bern • Berlin • Bruxelles • Frankfurt am Main • New York • Wien

Bibliographic information published by Die Deutsche Nationalbibliothek.
Die Deutsche Nationalbibliothek lists this publication in the Deutsche Nationalbibliografie; detailed bibliographic data is available on the Internet at http://dnb.d-nb.de.

A catalogue record for this book is available from the British Library.

Library of Congress Control Number: 2016963039

Cover image: Bernard Partridge, 'The Bear Hug', *Punch*, 17 May, 1922.

Cover design: Peter Lang Ltd.

ISBN 978-3-0343-2203-4 (print) • ISBN 978-1-78707-394-4 (ePDF)
ISBN 978-1-78707-395-1 (ePub) • ISBN 978-1-78707-396-8 (mobi)
DOI 10.3726/b11211

Wabernstrasse 40, CH-3007 Bern, Switzerland
info@peterlang.com, www.peterlang.com, www.peterlang.net

This publication has been peer reviewed.

Printed in Germany

Contents

Figures

Preface

How does the marginal become mainstream? And how does the *recherché* become *démodé*? These questions run through the chapters of this book like a red thread, structuring its arguments and provoking the reader to examine some familiar names and some familiar works, as well as a host of more unusual and overlooked material. And they are pertinent and productive questions, too, because they point to the dizzying rapidity with which Russian culture became known (if not always understood) in late nineteenth- and early twentieth-century Britain, as well as the way in which that culture soon became reduced to cliché and myth. Said and Bourdieu structure the argument, as announced in the book's title, but their work is never read reductively. Said's 'Orientalism' is the explicit productive of 'Orientalists', writers and critics keen to paint a picture of Russia as barbaric and 'other'. And Bourdieu's 'literary field' (a concept that has proved as productive as that of 'cultural capital') is one that is populated by agents and actors who are conscious of their choices, if not always of their expertise (or lack thereof). In many ways, however, the ideas presented here are already implicit in Russian culture itself, which has long been aware of both its belatedness and its precocity, and how these seemingly contradictory features structure its relationship with the rest of the world. In his famous *Lettres philosophiques*, written (in French, no less) in the late 1820s and early 1830s, Pyotr Chaadaev announced both Russia's lack of history and its negligible contribution to world culture: 'Alone in the world, we have given it nothing, we have taught it nothing; we have added not a single idea to the multitude of man's ideas; we have contributed nothing to the progress of the human mind and we have disfigured everything we have gained from this process.' Alexander Herzen described Chaadaev's writings as 'a shot that rang out in the dark night', and indeed the mid-century saw a remarkable oscillation between those who defended Russia's place in Europe, and those who sought to situate its riches elsewhere. The idea that self-definition was the product of a dialogue was, moreover, implicit in Herzen's writings, and in words that might have served – in inverted form – as an alternative subtitle to this volume, he claimed that 'we need Europe as an ideal, as a reproach, as a virtuous example; if Europe were not these things, then we should have to invent it.' Both Chaadaev and Herzen might have been surprised to see their diagnoses wholly inverted by the *fin de siècle*, when it was Russia that found itself playing the role of the West's own subconscious, unruly and disruptive, yet also libidinal and highly creative. The interplay between stasis and regeneration, ossification and renewal is also central to the work of the Russian formalists, whose revolutionary ideas on literary theory and history were coterminous with Freud's archaeology of the mind. The language and metaphors employed by the formalists bespeak rupture and revolution. Not for them a direct and unbroken lineage of literary development, but a series of 'knight's moves', of quasi-Oedipal rejections of paternal influence, and the search for alternative genealogies, whether in the form of marginal genres, unfamiliar cultures, or inventive new devices that disrupt the hold of the past over the values of the present. Yet as the formalists were only too aware, one generation's radical innovation becomes the next generation's ossified platitude, and their model of artistic evolution is one that can be applied to patterns of transcultural reception too. The seeming ubiquity of Russian culture in early twentieth-century Britain was an enterprise (and the word is advisedly chosen for its economic associations) that carried with it a highly durable form of canonisation that has proved hard to overcome. Between October 2016 and February 2017, the Fondation Louis Vuitton in Paris staged an exhibition – *Icons of Modern Art* – which reunited the collection of the merchant and patron, Sergei Shchukin. The exhibition attests, of course, to Shchukin's farsightedness (as well as his financial ease), but equally, it shows how the once radical inventive has become part of the cultural heritage of the *homme moyen culturel*. Or consider the incorporation of the scores of Stravinsky, the choreographies of Balanchine, Fokine and Nijinsky, and the designs of Bakst and Benois into the repertoire of the Mariinsky Theatre in St Petersburg, at once effacing both the Soviet *avant garde* and the legacy of socialist realism, and projecting a continuous tradition that runs from Marius Petipa to the present day, as well as a Russian version of Diaghilev's carefully marketed global brand. So how are we to regain a sense of the dynamism that first brought Russian culture to Britain, and create a modern version of the processes described by Olga Soboleva and Angus Wrenn? It may be that Russian culture has an answer. Writing in the wake of the October Revolution, and anxious that the orthodoxy of one age would simply be replaced by conventions of a new one, the Soviet writer and essayist Evgeny Zamyatin proposed a model of permanent and dialectical revolution in which heresy was the guarantee of artistic originality: 'Today is doomed to die, because yesterday has died and because tomorrow shall be born. Such is the cruel and wise law. Cruel, because it dooms to eternal dissatisfaction those who today already see the distant heights of tomorrow; wise, because only eternal dissatisfaction is the guarantee of unending movement forward, of unending creativity.' We may read *From Orientalism to Cultural Capital: The Myth of Russia in British Literature of the 1920s* as an analytical account of a historical phenomenon, yet the dynamic model of literary reception and cultural appropriation that it proposes is one that remains acutely contemporary.

Professor Philip Ross Bullock

Acknowledgements

We are grateful to a large number of colleagues and friends with whom we have had the chance to discuss informally the themes of this book. First and foremost we are immensely grateful to Professor Philip Ross Bullock of Wadham College, Oxford for the benefit of his expertise in this field over many years and especially for kindly agreeing to write the preface to this volume. Professor Rebecca Beasley of Queen's College, Oxford and Dr Matthew Taunton (University of East Anglia), very much the driving forces behind the Russia Research Network which has been meeting regularly in London, deserve special thanks for providing encouragement and direction throughout the past two years. Professor Patrick Parrinder, doyen of Wells scholars, very kindly spoke at LSE at our invitation, and gave invaluable help in relating the period of Wells' life covered in this book to the writer's career overall. We would like to thank Professor Leonee Ormond for her expertise and encouragement in the fields of Barrie and Galsworthy. Dr Alexandra Smith provided very helpful suggestions on D. H. Lawrence. We also thank: Victoria and Albert Museum Collections; *Punch* archives, Tate Britain and Press Association collection for assistance with images. Christabel Scaife, our editor at Peter Lang, has been patient and helpful in equal measure in seeing the project through to completion.

Introduction

Part I: 'They, if anything, can redeem our civilisation'[1]

Knowledge of Russian culture in Britain grew slowly in the nineteenth century, then rapidly in the first decades of the twentieth; this period has, therefore, always been a popular topic of research, conducted largely from a chronological and historical perspective and with regard to its most prominent practitioners. So far little (if any) attention has been paid to the analysis of the deeper structural changes in the reception of Russian culture in Britain brought forth by this wave of Russophilia in the pre-World War I years. Still less effort has been made to reflect upon whether this quantitative growth of interest in and exposure to Russian literature and art facilitated a qualitative shift in the framework of perception, affecting the mode of thinking of the contemporary British cultural elite, as well as the emerging notion of modernist art.

This book moves into that underexplored territory of research, suggesting an interdisciplinary approach to the critical appraisal of the reception of Russia in Britain by examining it through the structural framework of modern socio-political theories of Edward Said and Pierre Bourdieu. The idea of Russia or the Russian myth projected by the British constitutes the main focus of our examination. It will be argued that all the way through to the turn of the twentieth century, the representation of Russia in Britain largely falls within the framework of Orientalism – the concept developed by Edward Said in his eponymous work of 1978, in which he exposes the depiction of non-Western cultures as politically charged fabrications of the

1 Edward Marsh, 'Memoir', in *The Collected Poems of Rupert Brooke: with a Memoir* (London: Sidgwick & Jackson, 1918), pp. xi–clix (p. lxxvii).

European imagination, characterised by an essentially Eurocentric, imperialistic, or civilisatory (in the case of Russia) approach. Following Said's thesis on the significance of literary scholarship in the formation of the Orientalistic viewpoint, we shall look more closely at the post-1910 years with the objective of establishing whether the unprecedented burgeoning of translations from Russian literature in these decades, as well as the exceptional interest in this subject among the British cultural elite, had a crucial impact on and led to a radical change in the configuration of the paradigm of Russian reception. One of the potential effects of this change could be the major shift in the signifying function of the icon: from Russia as the Orientalistic epitome of 'barbaric splendour' towards an emblem deployed to connote British intellectual prestige, a valuable artistic commodity translated into the foreign context, or a fashionable contribution to cultural capital, understood in Pierre Bourdieu's sense of the term.[2]

Some attempt should be made to specify our approach to interpreting this signifying function of the icon, which effectively sheds more light on the way in which the notion of the Russian myth is employed for the purposes of our examination. This approach is rooted in imagology, or representation studies, concerning structural analysis of discursive articulation of national stereotyping – the form of 'literary sociology' in the domain of image making.[3] Recent advances in this area are focused on the so-called constructivist perspective, considering any image of national character as culturally constructed within the framework of the given socio-historical context. This ties in well with modern social studies of national identity that have moved away from the 'realness' of national character as explanatory model, and towards an increasingly pluralistic and culturally mediated projection – a state of mind rather than a deterministic expression

2 Pierre Bourdieu offers the concept of cultural capital to describe how, within a given socio-economic setting, the knowledge of certain literary texts (or art, music and so forth) can be used to assert and communicate one's social and cultural distinctions (*Distinction: A Social Critique of the Judgement of Taste* (London: Routledge, 1984)).

3 Manfred Beller and Joseph Theodoor Leerssen, Introduction to *Imagology: The Cultural Construction and Literary Representation of National*, ed. Manfred Beller and Joseph Theodoor Leerssen (Amsterdam: Rodopi, 2007), pp. xii–xvi (p. xiii).

of the given.[4] The latter includes self-image, as well as the image of the other, which suggests yet another inference to be reviewed. In the light of this constructivist perspective, the representation of 'the other' should be effectively treated as a particular type of 'intertext' – a dynamic product of cultural interference between the 'auto' and 'hetero' image, shaped by the proclivities of a specific historical context. Considering this, as well as the fact that the impact of the context can never be discarded, the very notion of the discursive image turns out to be intrinsically linked to the semantics of a myth (see *Oxford Dictionary*'s definition of myth as a 'widely held but false belief or idea'[5]) – hence, the use of this term adopted in the course of our discussion, which essentially concerns the projection of the myth of Russia constructed by the British.

This work builds on a rich field of previous (albeit in some cases now dated) research which was effective in highlighting a historiographic approach to Anglo-Russian cultural interaction; the reception of canonical Russian authors in Britain; and the distinctive body of relatively recent scholarship which has expanded the study of literary influence on specific modernist authors.[6] It also draws on two newly published interdisciplinary

4 Joep Leerssen, 'Imagology: History and method', in Manfred Beller and Joseph Theodoor Leerssen, eds, *Imagology: The Cultural Construction and Literary Representation of National* (Amsterdam: Rodopi, 2007), pp. 17–32 (p. 25); Hans Manfred Bock, 'Nation als vorgegebene oder vorgestellte Wirklichkeit? Anmerkungen zur Analyse fremdnationaler Identitätszuschreibung', in Ruth Florack, ed., *Nation als Stereotyp: Fremdwahrnehmung und Identität in deutscher und französischer Literatur* (Tübingen: Max Niemeyer Verlag, 2001), pp. 11–36 (p. 34).

5 *Oxford Dictionary of English* <http://www.oxforddictionaries.com/us/definition/american_english/myth> [accessed 2 September 2016].

6 Among others, the first category includes Dorothy Brewer, *East West Passage: A Study in Literary Relationship* (London: George Allen and Unwin, 1954); Gilbert Phelps, *The Russian Novel in English Fiction* (London: Hutchinson's University Library, 1956); Lynn Garafola, *Diaghilev, Ballets Russes* (New York: Oxford University Press, 1989); the second – Royal Gettmann, *Turgenev in England and America* (Urbana: University of Illinois Press, 1941); Glyn Turton, *Turgenev and the Context of English Literature 1850–1900* (London: Routledge, 1992); Peter Kaye, *Dostoevsky and English Modernism, 1900–1930* (Cambridge: Cambridge University Press, 1999); John Burt Foster (Jr), *Transnational Tolstoy: Between the West and the World* (London: Bloomsbury, 2013);

volumes, *A People Passing Rude: British Responses to Russian Culture*, edited by Anthony Cross (Open Book Publishers, 2012) and *Russia in Britain, 1880–1940: From Melodrama to Modernism*, edited by Rebecca Beasley and Philip Ross Bullock (Oxford University Press, 2013), which shifted attention to the contribution of institutions (libraries, publishing houses, theatre) in the promoting and disseminating of Russian literature and art.

This book aims at taking the discussion a step further. Given that the process of cultural representation is determined not by empirical reality (how people 'really are'), but rather by the way in which the discourse regarding it is constructed – on the basis of *vraisemblance* rather than *vérité*, to evoke the neo-Aristotelian juxtaposition, then the ease with which the audience can reciprocate the purport of the projected image should be called into play. In other words, the audience's acceptance of representation as valid plays a cardinal role in the process of image formation; and in this sense, the reputation of the so-called promoters of the image must not be overlooked. This aspect constitutes one of the key points of our study, which focuses attention on those representatives of the British cultural elite whose talent, though not explicitly and consistently devoted to the complex task of doctrinal formulation, nonetheless gained a significant mastery over the minds of their readers, and attained such a degree of public recognition as to turn institutional practices into effective mediators of their personal aesthetics, their cultural theories and artistic points of view.

The reputational currents of the 1920s – the leanings and opinions of contemporary readers were central for the rationale of our literary selection. In 1929, the readers of the *Manchester Guardian* were asked to opine on the 'Novelists Who May Be Read in A. D. 2029' (see Figure 1).[7] Coming out on top in this century hence popularity contest was John Galsworthy, who defeated H. G. Wells (the runner up), Arnold Bennett and Rudyard

---

and the third – George J. Zytaruk, *D. H. Lawrence's response to Russian Literature* (The Hague: Mouton, 1971); Joanna Woods, *Katerina: The Russian World of Katherine Mansfield* (London: Penguin, 2001); Roberta Rubenstein, *Virginia Woolf and the Russian Point of View* (London: Palgrave, 2009).

7 'Novelists Who May Be Read in A. D. 2029', *Manchester Guardian*, 3 April 1929, p. 16.

Kipling by a large margin. J. M. Barrie was in fifth position, followed by a curious for the modern eye medley of authors, which included G. B. Shaw (in eighth place), D. H. Lawrence (twelfth) and Virginia Woolf just about managing to get in 'the first thirty'.

eir fame or their significance. W
g on a simple scheme of P.R.
rrived at the following list of
hich represents the popular ch
he votes are added in each case).

Galsworthy	**1,180**
Wells	**933**
Bennett	**654**
Kipling	**455**
Barrie	**286**
Walpole	**233**

which the only thing worth mark

After these followed a curious medley of authors:

Kaye-Smith	198	Brett Young	25
George Moore	165	"Q"	24
Bernard Shaw	110	Edgar Wallace	21
Conan Doyle	101	Virginia Woolf	21
R. H. Mottram	79	Margaret Kennedy	18
John Buchan	63	Compton McKenzie	16
D. H. Lawrence	61		
Chesterton	60	Ian Hay	16
Aldous Huxley	50	Clemence Dane	15
Hall Caine	48	Belloc	14
Masefield	46	Stephen McKenna	13
Locke	46	Rebecca West	13
Rose Macaulay	41	Baroness Orczy	13
Phillpotts	38	Jeffrey Farnol	12
E. M. Forster	37	H. M. Tomlinson.	10
Philips Gibbs.	26	A. E. W. Mason	10
Warwick Deeping	25		

Figure 1. 'Novelists Who May Be Read in A. D. 2029', *Manchester Guardian*, 3 April 1929.

History does not seem to have been on the side of many of these writers, and certain nominations may now be largely regarded as a sheer whim of literary fashion. This opinion poll, however, did give us a clearer idea for comprising a quintessential (though by no means comprehensive) list of trend-makers in Russian reception. Bearing in mind the evolution of the canon, as well as the authors' impact on the modern cultural perspective, we tried to highlight the individuals who were instrumental for the issues of institutional transmission of Russian culture, who, having secured their position as major socio-cultural opinion-makers, became pivotal for configuring a particular type of the Russian image, shifting attitudes and paving new ways towards canon formation.

The selection includes John Galsworthy and H. G. Wells – two consecutive presidents of the British P. E. N. Club, the oldest human rights and literary organisation, known for its active agitation for freedom of expression; J. M. Barrie, a leading dramatist at the time, whose contribution to the configuration of the institution of the contemporary British theatre of the early twentieth century is difficult to overestimate (today known exclusively for *Peter Pan*, but at the time equally famous for plays addressing class – *The Admirable Crichton*, or gender – *The Twelve-Pound Look*); D. H. Lawrence, Virginia Woolf (one of the key-members of the Bloomsbury group) and T. S. Eliot (in this period editor of *The Criterion*) – pioneers of British modernism, who, being united by an abiding belief in the enlightening mission of arts and culture, exerted a seminal influence on literature and aesthetics, as well as on modern attitudes towards pacifism, sexuality and women's rights. This, of course, is not to say that these writers have ever had a direct impact on or brought about social and political transformation; but it was not uncommon for their contemporaries to see them as the consciousness and spirit of the age: 'The England of today is in part a Shaw-made and a Wells-made democracy', as Lady Rhondda put it in 1930.[8]

Further to the point, the use of the term cultural capital in the title is of considerable significance for the objectives and outcomes of our examination. We aspire to evoke explicitly Pierre Bourdieu's concept, as it provides a crucial mode of understanding not only the general mechanisms of cultural

8 Margaret Rhondda, 'Shaw's Women', *Time and Tide*, 7 March 1930, pp. 300–1.

reception, but also the differential, and in certain respects modernising, function of the Russian paradigm in the cultural space of early twentieth-century Britain. When analysing the configuration of this paradigm within the framework of the British cultural context, we try to go deeper than the simple binaries of the literary and artistic impact, and focus on the conceptual avenues through which the idea of 'the exotic other' was appropriated and internalised in the artistic world of the British authors. The intention is to go into such areas of fictional and poetic creation that may generate other configurations of and perspectives on the notion of 'the real', and to expand the boundaries of one's own familiar self. By taking such a multi-faceted analytical approach to the study of Russian reception in Britain, the book aims not only at placing it in line with the current state of pan-European debate on early twentieth-century culture, but also at casting new light on the British perceptions of modernism, as a transcultural artistic movement, and the ways in which the literary interaction with the myth of Russia shaped and deepened these cultural views.

Olga Soboleva

Part II: 'Prose and verse have been regulated by the same caprice that cuts our coats and cocks our hats'[9]

This study began with reference to Edward Said's seminal work of 1978, *Orientalism*, and it is perhaps appropriate, therefore, to make further reference to this writer, as much in his capacity as editor and literary scholar as cultural theorist. It is fitting that Said, so much associated with the concept of Orientalism, made his name with research on a Slav writer exiled to the West, Joseph Conrad, who then went on to write memorably of the Far East, and especially with the work of Rudyard Kipling. For, although he does not examine the novel in depth in *Orientalism*, Kipling's novel *Kim* (1901) features at length and crucially in Said's later work *Culture and Imperialism* (1993), and in between Said wrote a preface to and edited the same novel in 1987. This work, from the beginning of the twentieth century, conveniently foregrounds a number of the themes covered in the present study. For of course *Kim* not only deals with the coming of age of a white Briton in the Raj, but also culminates in the young hero's involvement in the so-called Great Game, outwitting the agents of Tsarist Russia in their attempts to undermine the British presence in the Indian subcontinent, and in consequence the image of Russia entertained by the West at the turn of the twentieth century comes into play. Moreover, although a Briton, the novel's hero is not English. Christened Kimball O'Hara he is in fact of Irish descent, and furthermore not just Irish but Irish Catholic. As such, just as Conrad was both a victim of Tsarist Russian expansionism in Poland (the reason for his exile in Western Europe) and yet an exponent of British colonialism in Africa and the Far East, Kim likewise has a double identity, as both an instrument of triumphal British imperialism and yet equally a member of the Celtic diaspora, those Irish who were marginalised in Britain after the putting down of the 1798 attempted rebellion led to the

9 Isaac Disraeli, 'Literary Fashions' (1791), in Isaac Disraeli, ed., *Curiosities of Literature* (Boston, MA: Lilly, Wait, Colman and Holden, 1833), III, 35–8 (p. 35).

Act of Union and the imposition of direct rule from Westminster. Said is notable among commentators in emphasising the precise origins of his colonialist: 'Kim, after all, is both Irish and of an inferior social caste; in Kipling's eyes this enhances his candidacy for service.'[10] In Said's work the British Empire is not simply the 'English Empire'. As Said says,

> That Kim himself is both an Irish outcast boy and later an essential player in the British Secret Service Great Game suggests Kipling's uncanny understanding of the workings and managing control of societies. According to Turner [...] societies can be neither rigidly run by 'structures' nor completely overrun by marginal, prophetic, and alienated figures, hippies or millenarians; there has to be an alternation, so that the sway of one is enhanced or tempered by the inspiration of the other. The liminal figure helps to maintain societies, and it is this procedure that Kipling enacts in the climactic moment of the plot and the transformation of Kim's character.[11]

The situation which evolves in *Kim* does not simply involve a distinction between white British colonialists and the 'Oriental' Indians they are ruling. The British themselves are motley, recalling Defoe's reference to a 'mongrel race'.[12] And a fourth force enters the equation. As Said observes,

> The French-speaking Russian agents admit that in India 'we have nowhere left our mark yet', but the British know they have, so much so that Hurree, that self-confessed 'Oriental' is agitated by the Russians' conspiracy on behalf of the Raj, not his own people. When the Russians attack the lama and rip apart his map, the defilement is metaphorically of India itself, and Kim corrects this defilement later.[13]

In terms of the Orientalist categorisation which Said was to bring to such prominence in literary scholarship, here, at the very beginning of the twentieth century Russia is still being depicted as bogeyman, and it is still possible to talk of Russophobia. It is a measure of how prevalent the Russophilia vogue was to become later during the same decade that in a bestseller from 1901 such a depiction could still be offered.

10 Edward Said, *Culture and Imperialism* (London: Vintage, 1994), p. 166.

11 Said, *Culture and Imperialism*, p. 170.

12 Daniel Defoe, *The True Born Englishman* (London: A. Cleugh, 1810), p. 1.

13 Said, *Culture and Imperialism*, p. 193.

The Irish were, of course, not the only participants in the Celtic diaspora under way during the great age of Empire. The Welsh were dispersed by economic forces during the Industrial Revolution (those in the former British Empire today claiming Welsh descent exceed the population of present day Wales.) Scots too were marginalised and dispersed after the Act of Proscription of 1746. In 1745 the Scotch military uprising under Bonnie Prince Charlie against English rule not only rallied the clans against the English presence in Scotland but resulted in an invasion of England itself, repulsed only as far south as Derby before eventual defeat at Culloden the following year. The Scotch threat had been taken so seriously that many of the leaders were executed or sent to the penal colonies overseas, and the wearing of tartan, and even the playing of bagpipes was banned by law. The local Gaelic language used by the clans was marginalised, sent into a decline from which it never recovered. Settlements were given English names, such as Fort Augustus and Fort William. Scotland was even widely referred to in England (and by some Scots) as 'North Britain'. Yet, having been anathematised as a threat within living memory, by the late eighteenth century features of Celtic identity were allowed to reappear, and even became fashionable. The Prince Regent wore tartan at an official visit to Scotland in 1822 stage managed by Sir Walter Scott, whose Waverley novels such as *Rob Roy* (1817) had been sentimentalising and glamourising Scotch identity. By the end of the 1820s Felix Mendelssohn, to become Queen Victoria's favourite among composers of the day, was at work on his *Scottish Symphony*, similarly inspired by a romantic vision of Scotland, and by 1852 Balmoral Castle had been built and become the British Royal Family's preferred holiday residence, though they were arguably just as German as Mendelssohn. In the 1850s one of the first tea plantations to be established in India by the British was the Darjeeling Bannockburn Estate. That it should be named after the most famous battle where the Scots defeated the English, in 1314, and not Culloden, is a measure of the degree to which Scottishness had become something which could be flirted with safely in the realm of image-making, a threat long since neutralised in the real world.

Sir Walter Scott to a large extent was instrumental in bringing to the fore the idea of Scottishness in fiction written in English, and this persisted at a later date in much of the work of Robert Louis Stevenson. In his *The Master of Ballantrae* (1889), the elder of two sons of the laird, a Jacobite, is forced to flee after Culloden, yet subsequently becomes active in India as part of the British Empire. One of the authors in this survey, J. M. Barrie, was writing in the same vein as Stevenson (who reacted to his work), when he produced his novel *The Little Minister* in 1891, and still harking back to it in 1931 with *Farewell Miss Julie Logan*. For that matter, Lydia Lopokova, inspiration for Barrie's *The Truth about the Russian Dancers*, was descended on her maternal side from a Scotch engineer who had several generations before emigrated to St Petersburg.

This trajectory from genuine sense of threat and wild, uncultured otherness in Celtic identity, in the mid-eighteenth century, to 'safe' and 'tamed' yet still thrilling glamour in the early nineteenth century in many ways parallels the transformation of the image enjoyed by Russia in the West in the period from the Crimean War through to the early decades of the twentieth century. Within just a few decades Russia went from being a military enemy of Britain (whether in 1854 in the Crimea, or at the turn of the twentieth century in north-west India) to a country whose literature, music, folk dress and above all ballet caught the British imagination, and became a distinct style, perhaps even *the* national style to be affected in fashionable British society. Tennyson, in *The Charge of the Heavy Brigade*, inspired by Balaklava, referred to the Russian army as 'the dark-muffled Russian crowd', which 'Folded its wings from the left and the right, / And roll'd them around like a cloud' and is described, using a tellingly Oriental word, redolent of the Mongol legacy, as the 'Russian hordes'. Yet even at this date in the Epilogue to the same poem Tennyson anticipated the later change in attitude towards Russia:

> Slav, Teuton, Kelt, I count them all
> My friends and brother souls,
> With all the peoples, great and small,
> That wheel between the poles.[14]

14 Alfred Tennyson, *Poems and Plays* (London, New York and Toronto: Oxford University Press, 1968), p. 529.

That transformation was subsequently helped (but not enabled in the first instance) by political rapprochement. In 1874 Tennyson could make the following declaration, celebrating the marriage of Prince Alfred, Duke of Edinburgh to the Tsar's daughter Maria Alexandrovna:

> The son of him with whom we strove for power
> Whose will is lord thro' all his world-domain –
> Who made the serf a man, and burst his chain –
> Has given our Prince his own imperial Flower,
> Alexandrovna,
> And welcome, Russian flower, a people's pride,
> To Britain, when her flowers begin to blow![15]

Russian culture was in vogue in Britain and in Western Europe considerably before the signing of the Triple Entente in 1908 made the enemies of the Crimean War, Russia, France and Britain allies against contemporary German expansionism. Indeed, this political *rapprochement* with the absolutist Tsarist regime caused difficulties for many on the radical end of the political spectrum (strongly represented in British artistic circles). Russophobia persisted, and surfaced in episodes such as the Dogger Bank Incident of 1904, when the Russian Baltic fleet, en route for Vladivostok, fired on and killed British trawler men, having mistaken them for the Japanese navy. A diplomatic crisis occurred, which briefly threatened to escalate, before being successfully averted.

At times Russophilia could become superficial and lend itself to parody. In Woolf's *Night And Day* Mary is 'dressed more or less like a Russian peasant girl'.[16] And Evelyn Murgatroyd allows her enthusiasm for Garibaldi and the Risorgimento to be transposed onto contemporary Russia in the last years of Tsarism after the 1905 failed revolution (of which she knows next to nothing).[17] In terms of Pierre Bourdieu's analysis, Russian culture, just as had happened with Celtic culture in the previous century, nonetheless became a synecdoche of cultural prestige within literary and other artistic

15 Tennyson, p. 529

16 Virginia Woolf, *Night And Day* (Harmondsworth: Penguin, 1992), p. 302.

17 Woolf, *Night And Day*, p. 132.

circles, and a component of cultural capital. As demonstrated by the ironic reference in Woolf's *Jacob's Room* to the need to come up with an opinion on Chekhov purely for the purposes of polite English society conversation, Russophilia could also become a cliché and an onerous imposition by this period (see Chapter 6).

Was there a significant distinction between the Celtic and the Russian cases? And can the latter be seen as something more than a whim of cultural fashion? On reflection the Celtic vogue concerned fashions in dress and in prose and poetry (Walter Scott and Burns), to a lesser extent music (Beethoven's settings of Burns, Berlioz's works inspired by Scott; Rossini's *La Donna del Lago*; Donizetti's *Lucia di Lammermoor*) or the admittedly synthetic works of the spurious Gaelic bard Ossian. Russophilia in this survey's period, by contrast, involved mainly the novel (Turgenev, Dostoevsky and Tolstoy) and ballet (Diaghilev's company above all), as well as drama (Gorky and Chekhov). Russian poetry was largely absent (Pushkin's influence in Britain is separate and earlier, as well as being on a smaller scale). Neither Scotch nor Russian painters (apart from those who designed for the Ballets Russes) can be said to have played a major part in the vogue abroad for either culture, and there was never really any movement in Scotch drama which was emulated abroad. Nonetheless, as the following chapters will demonstrate, the myth of Russia did prompt sustained and fundamental changes in the type and range of literary work produced by the British writers studied here. But the chief distinction between the Celtic and Russian cases, and of great relevance to the authors considered in this study, is the role played by political ideology.

During the last decades of Tsarism, while the Russophilia vogue was at its height, many authors in Britain were associated with the Friends of Russian Freedom (which expressed solidarity with Russian dissident radicals resident in Britain as well as criticising the perceived excesses of the Tsarist regime at the time of the pogroms), or subsequently with the 1917 Club, set up in London that year by Virginia Woolf's husband Leonard, Ramsay MacDonald and others, to express hopes for a democratic Russian future following Nicholas II's abdication and the coming to power of Kerensky's Provisional Government. The very existence of this institution both confirms the intensity of feelings among British artistic circles and perhaps also indicates an element of what Tom Wolfe was to christen (at the height of the Permissive Sixties later in the twentieth century) 'radical chic'.[18] Yet ultimately the second, Bolshevik Revolution in Russia in October 1917 proved one of the important checks upon the vogue for Russophilia. The 1917 Club continued throughout the 1920s, but the establishment of the Bolshevik regime subsequently formalised as the Soviet Union complicated matters for those otherwise enamoured of Russia. T. S. Eliot did not frequent the 1917 Club, and his right-wing-leaning politics and increasing espousal of Anglo-Catholicism (which dismayed Woolf and others within Bloomsbury) shifted the emphasis as regards his alignment with things Russian. D. H. Lawrence unequivocally rejected the Bolshevik Revolution (after some short-lived flirtation), and so his interest in Russian literature and culture became divorced from contemporary Russia. From the 1920s onwards Virginia Woolf was associated with the Society for Cultural Relations between Peoples of the British Commonwealth and Union of Soviet Socialist Republics (SCR)[19] chaired by her relative Margaret Llewelyn-Davies (who would also have known J. M. Barrie). Woolf, however, declined the opportunity offered by the Bolshevik authorities in 1927, with Leonard Woolf to visit the USSR as guests of the regime in celebration of the tenth anniversary of the Bolshevik Revolution, even while she was inspired to bring Russia into her novel *Orlando*. This would indicate that by this period Russia was becoming something of a conventionalised reference and allusion, in effect a purely literary exercise, a Russia of the mind, which might be made by a contemporary novelist, rather than arising from

18 Tom Wolfe's 'Radical Chic: That Party at Lenny's' (1970) describes 'how culture's patrician classes – the wealthy, fashionable intimates of high society – have sought to luxuriate in both a vicarious glamour and a monopoly on virtue through their public espousal of street politics: a politics, moreover, of minorities so removed from their sphere of experience and so absurdly, diametrically, opposed to the islands of privilege on which the cultural aristocracy maintain their isolation, that the whole basis of their relationship is wildly out of kilter from the start' (Michael Bracewell, 'Molotov Cocktails', *Frieze Magazine*, November–December 2004 <http://www.frieze.com/issue/article/molotov_cocktails> [accessed 20 September 2016]).

19 Maggie Humm, *The Edinburgh Companion to Virginia Woolf and the Arts* (Edinburgh: Edinburgh University Press, 2010), pp. 276–7.

a genuine connexion with Russia in real life. Woolf's diary reveals that she was under no illusions about the repressive realities of Stalin's Russia (at a time when Shaw and the Webbs were busy making light of them) in her remarks when Prince Dmitrii Mirsky, the exiled aristocrat and critic, elected to return to Soviet Russia: 'Has been in England, in boarding houses, "forever". I thought, as I watched his eye brighten and fade – soon there'll be a bullet through your head.'[20]

In such circumstances, continued allusion to the myth of Russia became just that – allusion to a lingering myth very much at odds with the realities of a Stalinist regime of anti-formalism, anti-cosmopolitanism, and enforced conformity with the reactionary tenets of socialist realism now the norm in the Russia of the day. The process by which the Russia craze in the arts ensued upon a period of distrust of and outright enmity towards Russia in Britain, flourished during the first three decades of the twentieth century and then became anachronistic, in the very different conditions which came to apply after 1917, will be outlined in the following chapters.

Angus Wrenn

20 Quoted in *Virginia Woolf*, ed. Robin Majumdar and Allen McLaurin (London: Routledge 2003), p. 346.

CHAPTER 1

The East Wind of Russianness

> There is an east wind coming, Watson [...] such a wind as never blew on England yet. It will be cold and bitter, Watson, and a good many of us may wither before its blast. But it's God's own wind none the less, and a cleaner, better, stronger land will lie in the sunshine when the storm has cleared.[1]

By the time the creator of Sherlock Holmes was writing these words (1917), the East wind had already been tormenting Europe for several years. It was not new, but this time it was indeed much stronger; as Somerset Maugham famously claimed, the Russian virus spread through Europe like a disease:

> Everyone was reading the Russian novelists, the Russian dancers captivated the civilised world, and the Russian composers set shivering the sensibility of persons who were beginning to want a change from Wagner. Russian art seized upon Europe with the virulence of an epidemic of influenza. New phrases became the fashion, new colours, new emotions, and the highbrows described themselves without a moment's hesitation as members of the intelligentsia.[2]

The big stores (Heal's and Harvey Nichols) changed their shop window styles in imitation of Bakst's designs for Diaghilev seasons. Fashionable middle-class ladies acquired fur-trimmed outfit and learned to glide like Russian peasants; while the wife of the British Ambassador sent dresses over from St Petersburg, for the dignitaries to shine at the opulent Slavic theme parties that were spawning all over London.[3]

1 Arthur Conan Doyle, *His Last Bow* (New York: George H. Doran Company, 1917), p. 308.

2 Somerset Maugham, *Ashenden* (New York: Doubleday, Doran, Incorporated, 1928), p. 279.

3 Martin Green and John Swan, *The Triumph of Pierrot* (University Park: Pennsylvania University Press, 1993), p. 65; Garafola, p. 303.

Much has been written recently about the British response to Russian culture during these pre-World War I years, covering a variety of angles and a wide range of areas, including literature, music, craft industries, visual arts and religion. It is difficult to overestimate the degree of insight and the critical value of these thematically orientated studies, which, nonetheless, rarely channel the debate into the field of social theories of cultural reception, aimed at analysing the paradigms of intercultural representation and their re-contextualising and re-shaping in the process of cultural reproduction and transmission. Such an approach seems to be most promising when applied to the analysis of the Russian 'craze' in early twentieth-century Britain, which apart from offering an inexhaustible source of taxonomy and thematic surveys can be equally discussed in terms of the critical mass perspective. The latter draws upon the cumulative effect generated by the almost unprecedented tide of interest in the Russian subject and, consequently, on the potentiality of the so-called 'quantity-to-quality' transition. In other words, the question to ask here is whether a radical shift occurred in the paradigm of stereotyping and representation or, more specifically, in the configuration of the myth of Russia projected by the British. As regards our understanding of this process, the objective is to focus primarily on the issue of the repositioning of the Russian idiom within the British cultural landscape, assuming that, when affected by the dual process of accumulation and recognition, it may acquire a stronger status with a specific differential function, analogous to that of a symbolic artistic cachet or cultural capital, to use the term coined in the social theories of Pierre Bourdieu.[4]

The notion of the Russian myth here constitutes the focal point of our discussion. As explained in the *Introduction*, it is viewed in the light of the constructivist perspective offered by contemporary theories of representation – the science of 'imagology' or image studies.[5] There is a

4 Pierre Bourdieu, *Distinction*, pp. 13–14; Pierre Bourdieu, 'Les conditions sociales de la circulation internationale des idées', *Actes de la recherche en sciences sociales* 145.1 (2002), 3–8 (p. 10).

5 Manfred Beller, 'Perception, Image, Imagology', in Manfred Beller and Joseph Theodoor, eds, *Imagology: The Cultural Construction and Literary Representation of National* (Amsterdam: Rodopi, 2007), pp. 3–16 (p. 13).

distinctive emphasis on the input of pragmatics in the modern imagological approach, which increasingly sees the dynamics of cultural representation in terms of its audience function. Based on the awareness that the cultural sources used in this domain of scholarly research are not merely a record of representation, but rather an artefact of a certain cultural praxis, articulating and even constructing the very notion of the record itself, such an approach aims at problematising the subjectivity of the source-material or historiographic record, and addressing the ways in which the foreign culture is manipulated or distorted in the course of cultural mimesis. It follows that there is always an element of subjective falseness in the very process of cultural representation, which lends a certain mythological quality to the notion of any discursive image.

Within the framework of this modern constructivist perspective, which allows one to move from thematising the constituent elements of representational paradigms to the analysis of their structural makeup, Edward Said's socio-cultural theory of Orientalism (1978), essentially based on the idea of the constructed image of the East, provides an appropriate starting platform for conceptualising various manifestations of the Russian myth projected by the British. The relationship between these two once great colonial Empires has never been perfectly straightforward whether one looks at its political, economic or socio-cultural dimensions. Their opposition has always been predominantly indirect and their geo-political expansion was so widely divergent that such a consummate politician as Bismarck deftly remarked that the confrontation between Russia and England would be impossible in the same way as it was impossible to imagine a war between 'elephants and whales'.[6] Russia has never been treated by Britain as an object of potential colonisation; at the same time neither was it regarded as an equal.

In his seminal work of 1978, Edward Said proposed that the Orient was constructed by the Occident 'as its contrasting image, idea, personality, experience'.[7] It was an image of otherness, which served as 'a Western style

6 Winston Churchill, *A History of the English Speaking Peoples* (London: Bloomsbury, 2015), IV, 178.

7 Edward Said, *Orientalism* (New York: Pantheon Books, 1978), p. 2.

for dominating, structuring, and having authority over the Orient'.[8] And although Russia did not feature in Said's work as one of the major contextual case studies, its image in the European consciousness has been for a long while entangled with the evolving notion of 'the Oriental'. As Larry Wolff points out in his discussion of the emerging idea of 'the European', even in the eighteenth century, 'the geographical border between Europe and Asia was not unanimously fixed, [...] located sometimes at the Don, sometimes further East at the Volga, and sometimes, as today, at the Urals'.[9] Such uncertainty encouraged the construction of the image of Russia as 'a paradox of simultaneously inclusion and exclusion, Europe but not Europe',[10] to the extent that as late as the eve of World War I the Russian territory was still associated (in French scholarship) with what was alternatively termed *l'Europe oriental* and *l'Orient européen*.[11]

Our analysis, therefore, will proceed in a two-fold fashion. Having discussed the British outlook on Russia in view of the Orientalistic perspective, characterised by the West's politically charged, Eurocentric or, in the case of Russia, civilisatory (implicitly condescending) approach, we shall then reflect on the proliferation of Russomania in early twentieth-century Britain to see whether the unparalleled interest in all things Russian among the British cultural milieu resulted in its transformation into a major resource and an essential means for middle class intellectuals in asserting and communicating their cultural distinction.

According to Said's analysis, the backbone of the Orientalistic perspective can be summarised briefly in terms of three quintessential key points, each of which, as will be shown, has a noticeable presence in the British outlook on the Russian image: (1) the tendency towards generalised, non-specific, representation, when the nuanced richness of empirical reality is replaced by a simplified and reductive model; (2) the absence of any

8 Ibid. p. 3.

9 Larry Wolff, *Inventing Eastern Europe* (Stanford, CA: Stanford University Press, 1994), p. 7.

10 Ibid. p. 7.

11 Abel Mansuy, *Le Monde slave et les classiques français aux XVIe–XVIIe siècles* (Paris: Librairie Ancienne Honoré Champion, 1912), pp. 8, 10.

temporal dynamics in these schematic representations; and (3) the politically coloured or politically dependent nature of the discourse. Below we attempt to look at the myth of Russia through the prism of these main characteristics, proceeding from the standpoint of analysis of content and its 'grammar', that is, looking at tendencies and defining patterns rather than performing a qualitative survey of the 'vocabulary', or the full body of literary examples which, when taken in their individual manifestations, may present a counter-case to the dominant trend.

In its very essence, Orientalism is a way of seeing that imagines, underscores, exaggerates and distorts the differences of non-Western cultures as compared to those found in the European tradition. One of the main features of the Orientalistic discourse is the tendency towards generalisations and the use of all-purpose descriptors of 'the other' as an effective means of self-definition (by contrast with the apparently inferior model): there is 'the culturally sanctioned habit', Said claims,

> of deploying large generalisations by which reality is divided into various collectives: languages, races, types, colours, mentalities, each category being not so much a neutral designation as an evaluative interpretation. Underlying these categories is the rigidly binomial opposition of 'ours' and 'theirs', with the former always encroaching upon the latter (even to the point of making 'theirs' exclusively a function of 'ours').[12]

As a result of this long-term opposition and distortion, some stereotypical generic attributes became firmly associated with the notion of the East, and whatever the Occidentals were not, the Orientals infallibly were. This set of attributes can be formulated in terms variously historical (barbarism, primitivism, backwardness), psychological (Asiatic cunningness, cruelty), political (Oriental despotism, servitude, inability of self-governing), and involving gender (femininity, submissiveness) – the entire spectrum of which is traceable in the representation of Russia in English culture from the early accounts of the Elizabethan travellers to the late nineteenth-century writings.

The fact that the first end-of-the-sixteenth-century reports of English visitors from Russia (those of George Turberville, Giles Fletcher, and Sir

12 Said, *Orientalism*, p. 227.

Jerome Horsey) were skewed towards hyperbole and generalisation is, perhaps, not entirely surprising. Considering the long distance and the relatively restricted travelling at the time, the visitors were inevitably struck by the contrast between Muscovites and Europeans; and the image of Russia projected through their impressions was configured almost entirely along the lines of accumulated superlatives and extremes. The country is not just big, but enormous, its wealth is uncountable, the people are gigantic with their bellies so huge 'that [they] overhang the waist';[13] poverty – unspeakable; slavery – all-embracing; and the cruelty of the rulers' 'heavy hand of displeasure' is so unthinkable that one forbears 'to trouble the modest ears and Christian patience of such as shall read it'.[14] The grotesqueness of the portrait was so striking that the first publication of Giles Fletcher's account (1591) was suppressed upon the intervention of Muscovite negotiators, 'fearful of possible Russian reaction and reduction of trade':[15]

13 'The Account of George Turberville', in Lloyd E. Berry and Robert O. Crummey, eds, *Rude and Barbarous Kingdom: Russia in the Accounts of Sixteenth-Century English Voyagers* (Madison: The University of Wisconsin Press, 1968), pp. 71–86 (p. 81); first published in *Tragicall Tales* (1587), and then in Richard Hakluyt's *Principal Navigations* (1589). For the account of the first cultural contacts between English traveller and Russia see Anthony Cross, 'By Way of Introduction: British Perception, Reception and Recognition of Russian Culture', in Anthony Cross, ed., *A People Passing Rude* (Cambridge: Open Book Publishers, 2012), pp. 1–36 (pp. 1–3); Daryl W. Palmer, *Writing Russia in the Age of Shakespeare* (Aldershot: Ashgate, 2004); Anthony Cross, *Peter the Great through British Eyes* (Cambridge: Cambridge University Press, 2000), pp. 1–4; M. P. Alekseev, 'Shekspir i russkoe gosudarstvo XVI–XVII vv', in M. P. Alekseev, ed., *Shekspir i russkaia kul'tura* (Moscow-Leningrad: Akademia nauk, 1965), pp. 784–805; Felicity Stout, *Exploring Russia in the Elizabethan Commonwealth* (Manchester: Manchester University Press, 2015).

14 Sir Jerome Horsey, 'Travels', in *Rude and Barbarous Kingdom*, pp. 262–72 (p. 279); first published in *Russia at the Close of the Sixteenth Century*, ed. Edward A. Bond (London: The Hakluyt Society, 1856).

15 Cross, *Peter the Great through British Eyes*, p. 2.

> And it may be said truly [...] that from the great to the small (except some few that will scarcely be found) the Russe neither believeth anything that an other man speaketh, nor speaketh anything himself worthie to be believed.[16]

In Turberville's report the mythological series of rudeness, wildness and godless idolatry ('The house that hath no god or painted Saint within / Is not to be resorted to, that roof is full of sin') culminated with the portrayal of the most overwhelming drunkenness, which for years to come would become a canonical stereotype, associated with the image of Russia in Western discourse.

> A people passing rude, to vices vile inclin'd,
> Folk fit to be of Bacchus' train, so quaffing in their kind.
> Drinke is their whole desire, the pot is all their pride,
> The sob'rest head doth once a day stand needful of a guide.[17]

As a semantic element of maximal intensity, superlatives or hyperbole correspond to a clear form of cognitive abstraction, offering a distorted (exaggerating certain parts, while blurring the rest) and, therefore, simplified and reductive modality of representation.[18] Such a framework, characteristic of the projected outlook on Russia at the time, ties in well with Said's definition of the Orientalistic perspective, which, according to the scholar, tends to replace 'empiricity' with a set of generalised and schematic constructs.

Moreover, very much in line with Said's analysis of the Orientalistic approach, the established pattern of national stereotyping proved to be remarkably persistent in terms of its temporal and historical manifestations; and for almost three hundred years Russia was inscribed into the construct of Western knowledge as dangerously uncontrolled or weak and

16 Giles Fletcher, 'Of the Russe Commonwealth', in *Rude and Barbarous Kingdom*, pp. 109–248 (p. 245); first published (an abridged version) in Richard Hakluyt's *Principal Navigations* (1599).

17 'The Account of George Turberville', p. 75.

18 Mikhalskaia points out that such a modality corresponds to the early stages of cognitive representation, closely associated with folklore and mythological thinking (N. P. Mikhalskaia, *Obraz Rossii v angliiskoi khudozhestvennoi literature IX–IXX vv* (Moscow: Moskovskii Gosudarstvennyi, Pedagogicheskii universitet, 1995), p. 147).

exotic, cunningly malicious or uncivilised and backward, overwhelmingly rich or dreadfully poor. This could be considered exactly what Said had in mind when he defined Orientalism as a static system of 'synchronic essentialism',[19] implying that the Orient as a place and its reception in the discourse of Orientalism becomes an invariably fixed object – the eternal unchanging reality that remains chiefly the same in any moment of its history and cultural progression.

Here are but a few illustrative examples. The idea of Russia as an embodiment of rough extremes, introduced in the early sixteenth-century accounts,[20] became a formative matrix for all further modifications of its literary portrait, from which the crudeness and savageness of the national character were typically derived – hence the image of the Russian bear as a codifying icon of the country, featuring in Shakespeare's *Macbeth* and *King Henry V*, or in James Thomson's later poem *The Seasons* (1726–30).[21]

19 Said, *Orientalism*, p. 241.

20 'Thus remaining in this haven the space of a weeke, seeing the yeare farre spent, & also very evill wether, as frost, snow, and haile, as though it had beene the deepe of winter, we thought best to winter there', from Richard Chancellor's account of 1553; quoted in Daryl Palmer, 'Jacobean Muscovites: Winter, Tyranny, and Knowledge in *The Winter's Tale*', *Shakespeare Quarterly* 46.3 (1995), 323–39 (p. 323).

21 'Approach thou like the rugged Russian bear' (William Shakespeare, *Macbeth*, in *The Plays of Shakespeare*, 9 vols (London: William Pickering, 1825), IV, 83); and 'Foolish curs, that run winking into the mouth of a Russian bear and have their heads crushed like rotten apples' (William Shakespeare, *King Henry V*, in *The Plays of Shakespeare*, V, 129).

In James Thomson's four-part poem, *The Seasons*, 'Winter' (1726) is emblematised by the Russian landscape:

Hard by these shores, where scarce his freezing stream
Rolls the wild Oby, live the last of Men;
And half enlivened by the distant sun,
That rears and ripens Man, as well as plants,
Here human Nature wears its rudest form.

Deep from the piercing season sunk in caves,
Here by dull fires, and with unjoyous cheer,
They waste the tedious gloom. Immers'd in furs,
Doze the gross race. Nor sprightly jest, nor song,

Another stock trope firmly associated with the idea of extreme Russian roughness was that of mortifying cold and life-threatening frost. One can find it in Sir Philip Sidney's *Astrophel and Stella* (1591), where the notion of 'cold Muscovy'[22] is employed as a metaphor for the enslaving and tyrannous love ignited in Astrophel by Stella:

> Now even that foot-steppe of lost libertie
> Is gone, and now like slave borne Muscovite:
> I call it praise to suffer tyrannie;[23]

or in Shakespeare's *The Winter's Tale*, which, according to the insightful analysis of Daryl Palmer,[24] sends the minds of the audience to Russia more often than through Hermione's famous reference to her Russian extraction ('The Emperor of Russia was my father'[25]). Shakespeare, Palmer argues, modified Greene's *Pandosto* – his original source – to increase the Russian elements in his tale. Following the fashion of the time, it is the whole kingdom of Sicilia that recalls the Northern Empire of Snow, and Leontes appears as an emblem of its ruler, Ivan the Terrible, carrying symbolic cultural associations of 'winter and tyranny'.[26]

Under the reign of Peter the Great (1682–1725) an ambitious programme of Westernisation was embarked upon. Despite that, English literary portrayals of the country still conjured the picture of a backward, sparsely populated territory of nobles and serfs;[27] and the binary of extreme

---

> Nor tenderness they know; nor aught of life,
> Beyond the kindred bears that stalk without.
> (James Thomson, *The Seasons* (London: A. Hamilton, 1793), p. 210).

22 Sir Philip Sidney, *Astrophel and Stella*, in Sir Philip Sidney, *The Last Part of the Countesse of Pembrokes Arcadia: Astrophel & Stella and Other Poems*, ed. Albert Feuillerat (Cambridge: Cambridge University Press, 1922), pp. 241–300 (p. 254); quoted in Stout, p. 3.

23 Sidney, p. 243.

24 Palmer, pp. 323–39.

25 William Shakespeare, *The Winter's Tale*, in *The Plays of Shakespeare*, III, 244.

26 Palmer, p. 324, 332.

27 It is worth highlighting that we are talking about the configuration of Russia's image within the framework of literary sources, which was a much slower process

despotism versus mindless submission to power was retained all the way through seventeenth- and eighteenth-century Russian discourse (as set in George Turberville's story: 'In such a savage soil, where laws do bear no sway / But all is at the king his will to save or else to slay'[28]). Most of the literary sources were centred, unsurprisingly, on the extraordinary figure of Peter the Great. The accounts to mention include Aaron Hill's long narrative poem of 1718 *The Northern Star* (typically based on the rhetoric of eternal winter: 'Eternal Hills of Frost', bounding 'Ambition up in freezing Blood'[29]), Richard Steele's *Letters to The Spectator* (19 April and 9 August 1711[30]), or Daniel Defoe's *An Impartial History of the Life and Actions of Peter Alexowitz, Czar of Muscovy* (1723). Defoe's work was presented as a report by a British officer in the service of the Czar, describing among other deeds Peter's visit to England. The report ends with Peter's Swedish campaign, leaving it to others to continue the story of this Emperor, characterised as the most distinguished of rulers, provided one looks at the Eastern part of the world:

> May some other Pen be honoured with the Narration that the Glories of our August Emperor of Russia may be handed to Posterity in a manner suitable to his Fame and to the Merit of the greatest Prince in all the Eastern Part of the World.[31]

---

as compared to that presented in the first-hand English travellers' stories; the latter, according to Anthony Cross, had been offering a more varied picture of the country by 1725 (Cross, *Peter the Great Through British Eyes*, p. 40). For more detailed accounts see Cross, 'British Awareness of Russian Culture (1698–1801)', pp. 212–35; Anderson, *British Discovery of Russia*.

In this context, one should also mention that the Russian grammar of Henry William Ludolf was published (Oxford University Press) just two years before Peter the Great visited Oxford in 1698, thus marking the start of learning about the country through its literature and language.

28 'The Account of George Turberville', p. 83.

29 Aaron Hill, *The Northern-star: A poem* (London: E. Berington, and J. Morphew, 1718), p. 14.

30 For more detail see Cross, *Peter the Great through British Eyes*, pp. 45–6.

31 Daniel Defoe, *An Impartial History of the Life and Actions of Peter Alexowitz, Czar of Muscovy* (London: W. Chetwood, 1723), p. 420.

As regards the 'bottom' part of the spectrum (the people), in the second part of Defoe's *The Life and Strange Surprising Adventures of Robinson Crusoe* (1717), the famous traveller ventures through Siberia, reporting that the degree of savagery in this land exceeds the wildest expectations of a hard-bitten viewer:

> the inhabitants were mere pagans; sacrificing to idols, and worshipping the sun, moon, and stars, or all the host of heaven; and not only so, but were, of all the heathens and pagans that ever I met with, the most barbarous, except only that they did not eat men's flesh, as our savages of America did.[32]

This, of course, is combined with the slavish devotion to the authority of the Czar, irrefutable even among the 'criminals' in exile, who, despite their misfortune of being banished from the Court, were still 'telling me abundance of fine things of the greatness, the magnificence, the dominions, and the absolute power of the Emperor of the Russians'.[33] In the same vein, the portrayal of Siberia was covered in Oliver Goldsmith's *Citizen of the World* (1762), in which his fictional Chinese correspondents exchanged views on the Russians, highlighting their unchangeable savageness, darkness and 'brutal excess':

> From your accounts of Russia I learn that this nation is again relaxing into pristine barbarity; that its great emperor wanted a life of an hundred years more to bring about his vast design. A savage people may be resembled to their own forests; a few years are sufficient to clear away the obstructions to agriculture; but it requires many, ere the ground acquires a proper degree of fertility: the Russians, attached to their ancient prejudices, again renew their hatred to strangers, and indulge every former brutal excess.[34]

As Macaulay suggested in his *History of England*, Peter's 'singular character, and what was rumoured of his threat designs, excited much curiosity here, but nothing more than curiosity. England had as yet nothing to hope or fear from his vast empire' (Macaulay, *The History of England from the Accession of James the Second*, in *The Works of Lord Macaulay*, ed. Lady Trevelyan, 8 vols (New York: Longmans, Green and Co, 1897), IV, 388).

32 Daniel Defoe, *The Further Adventures of Robinson Crusoe* (Boston and New York: Houghton Mifflin Co, 1908), p. 130.

33 Ibid. p. 153.

34 Oliver Goldsmith, *Citizen of the World*, in *The Works of Oliver Goldsmith*, ed. Peter Cunningham, 4 vols (London: John Murray, 1854), II, 75–487 (pp. 273–74).

The latter, according Goldsmith, had a particularly dreadful effect on those who tried to bring a civilising touch to this country of the savage, but instead only found themselves drowned in the barbarous swamp:

> The great law-giver of Russia attempted to improve the desolate inhabitants of Siberia, by sending among them some of the politest men of Europe. The consequence has shown, that the country was as yet unfit to receive them; they languished for a time with a sort of exotic malady; every day degenerated from themselves, and at last, instead of rendering the country more polite, they conformed to the soil, and put on barbarity.[35]

The ascent to power of Catherine the Great (1762–96) played into the current European ideal of enlightened despotism. This raised some doubts among European onlookers considering whether Russia was ruled by the Oriental despotism of a dictatorial autocrat, or by the progressive regime of a civilised monarch. Russian modernisation was regarded with a mixture of approval and (predominantly) apprehension, and projected the greatly hyped-up prospect of a Russian invasion, as, for instance, in Goldsmith's 'Letters':

> The Russians are now at that period between refinement and barbarity, which seems most adapted to military achievement; and if once they happen to get footing in the western parts of Europe, it is not the feeble efforts of the sons of effeminacy and dissension that can serve to remove them. The fertile valley and soft climate will ever be sufficient inducements to draw whole myriads from their native deserts, the trackless wild, or snowy mountain.[36]

As the Industrial Revolution in Western Europe left Russia behind, the country's backwardness was turned into a prevalent trope. Considering nineteenth-century literary sources, it is sufficient to look at Edward Bulwer Lytton's novel *Devereux* (1829), which contains every single core element of the earlier sixteenth-century model. In this work, Russia, and more precisely its capital St Petersburg, is presented as a land of 'the most terrible climate

35 Ibid. p. 363.
36 Ibid. p. 378.

in which a civilised creature was ever frozen to death',[37] inhabited by the most savage people, who are colossal in size, filthy, and inhumanly ferocious:

> But never, I believe, was there a place which there was so much trouble in arriving at: such winds – such climate – such police arrangements – arranged, too, by such fellows! six feet high, with nothing human about them, but their uncleanness and ferocity! [...] 'It is just the city a nation of bears would build, if bears ever became architects', said I to myself.[38]

Later in the novel, this scheme is complemented by the notion of barbaric subservience in relation to the rulers, which, typically, identifies the Russians as a weak and biddable nation of slaves: 'A Russian [...] bore it [the fearful punishment of the battaog] patiently, and in silence; he only spoke once, and it was to say, "God bless the czar!"'[39]

Six years earlier Byron used a similar axis of mythopoetic superlatives, and employed the metaphor of 'ice' and 'fire' (extreme cold – extreme heat), to contrast Russia with Western civilisation. His poem *The Age of Bronze* (1823) offers a romanticised projection of this binary juxtaposition: the 'ice' of Russian savageness and despotic darkness (evoking such a connotational array as 'stern', 'frozen', 'dense' and 'hard') is seen to be melted by the 'fire' of freedom brought by the advances of the French troops:

> The half barbaric Moscow's minarets
> Gleam in the sun, but 'tis a sun that sets!
> [...] and Moscow was no more!
> Sublimest of volcanos! Etna's flame
> Pales before thine, and quenchless Hecla's tame.[40]

Not much changed in the late Victorian era. *Ivan Ivanovich* (1879), a narrative dramatic idyll of Robert Browning, who had first-hand experience of Russia (where he spent a year of 1834 as a nominal secretary of the Russian

37 Edward Bulwer Lytton, *Devereux A Tale* (Chicago and New York: Belford Clarke & Company, 1887), p. 300.

38 Ibid. p. 300.

39 Ibid. p. 311.

40 George Gordon Byron, *The Works* (London: John Murray, 1837), p. 528.

Consul General, Mr Benckhausen[41]), tells a terrifying story of a peasant woman. On her long sledge-ride through the winter forest she was chased by a pack of wolves. Frantic with despair, she threw her children one-by-one to the hungry beasts, trusting to gain a little time by which those remaining on the sledge might be saved. And although the poet devotes much attention to creating a strong sense of character and historic detail, his narrative largely falls into the same generalised mixture of stereotypes and stock popular clichés. The main female protagonist infallibly manifests all the characteristic traits of a barbaric slave woman, submissive to the absolutism of authority (being brutally executed in the name of God), accustomed to shamanism (performing sacrifices to wolves), and familiar with witchcraft:

> Who knows but old bad Màrpha – she always owed me spite
> And envied me my births – skulks out of doors at night
> And turns into a wolf, and joins the sisterhood.[42]

As regards the narrative and its culturally specific aspects, the action is framed within the outlandishly brutal and hostile setting, concerning both, natural environment (freezing and wild forest) and the barbarism of social habits: as, for instance, the graphic scene of the character's public lynching (by a 'lightning-swift thunder-strong one blow' of an axe[43]), and the crowd's contemplation of her 'dripping' with blood headless body.

Written a decade later, Swinburne's poem *Russia: An Ode* (1890) uses an even darker palette of imagery and tones, comparing the country to an unspeakable hell on Earth that would eclipse the horrors of Dante's infernal journey:

41 Unfortunately, Browning's letters from Russia to his sister were destroyed, and there are only a few sparse reminiscences of this experience. He was 'strangely' impressed by the endless monotony of snow covered pine forests through which they drove for days and nights, and his ear was so good that fifty years later he was still able to hum the Russian tunes to the old prince Gagarin, whom he met in Venice (quoted in Brewster, p. 35).

42 Robert Browning, 'Ivan Ivanovich', in *The Poems of Robert Browning* (Ware: Wordsworth Classics, 1994), pp. 590–5 (p. 593).

43 Ibid. p. 594.

Out of hell a word comes hissing, dark as doom,
Fierce as fire, and foul as plague-polluted gloom;
Ears have heard not, tongues have told not things like these.
Dante, led by love's and hate's accordant spell
Down the deepest and the loathliest ways of hell.[44]

It is, of course, worth bearing in mind that all these rhapsodic artistic sketches came to refer to the image of Russia not as mimetic empirical records, but as shorthand markers for collective literary characterisation, or, to use Foucault's terminology, as the mere *objets discursifs*.[45] And yet, these largely generalised, but colourful and snappy pictures happen to be remarkably effective in projecting the stock of cliché-tropes and associations, which became a synecdoche of the accepted portrait of the nation, configured along the lines of barbarism, despotism and extreme cold.

One must admit that this was not without a certain sense of ambiguity attached to Russia's liminal position. Situated (geographically, as well as in terms of its cultural affiliation) between civilised Europe and the vast stagnation of Asian states, it did baffle the majority of Western observers, whose track of thinking was traditionally streamlined according to the so-called 'cultured West – barbaric East' juxtaposition. The problem was that throughout many decades the idea of Russia was consistently skewed in the direction of the latter; as Rudyard Kipling put it in one of his tales, the biggest British mistake was to treat the Russians as the most Eastern of the European peoples instead of seeing them as the most Western of the Orientals:

Let it be clearly understood that the Russian is a delightful person till he tucks his shirt in. As an Oriental he is charming. It is only when he insists upon being treated as the most easterly of Western peoples, instead of the most westerly of Easterns,

44 Algernon Charles Swinburne, *The Poems*, 6 vols (London: Chatto & Windus, 1911), VI, 366.

45 Michel Foucault, *The Archaeology of Knowledge*, trans. A. M. Sheridan Smith (London and New York: Routledge, 2002), p. 34.

> that he becomes a racial anomaly extremely difficult to handle. The host never knows which side of his nature is going to turn up next.[46]

The great English writer was certainly not alone with regard to this type of interpretative viewpoint. Sir Donald Mackenzie Wallace, one of the major Russian specialists of the 1890s, made a similar remark by saying that the character of the Russians 'corresponds to their geographical position: they stand midway between the laborious, painstaking, industrious population of Western Europe and the indolent, undisciplined, spasmodically energetic populations of Central Asia.' As a result, everything depends on the angle of observation, and to the traveller who comes from the Western side of the globe, the Russians would indeed seem as 'an indolent and apathetic race' akin to the Asian peoples.[47] A much more radical statement was put forward by Emile Dillon, who expressed his views in a series of journalistic essays called 'The Russian Characteristics' and published by the *Fortnightly Review* in 1889 (reprinted as a separate edition later in 1891). A standard set of stereotypical attributes associated with the country was distilled and highlighted in the titles, defining the national character along the lines of 'lying', 'fatalism', 'dishonesty', and 'sloth'. Dillon emphasised a deep rift between Russia and European civilisation, pointing out that its political, social and religious conditions were so barbarically undeveloped that they

> render their possessors as impersonal as the Egyptians that raised Cheops, or the coral-reef builders of the Pacific. In result we have a good-natured, lying, thievish, shiftless, ignorant mass whom one is at times tempted to connect in the same isocultural line with the Weddas of India or the Bangala of the Upper Congo, and who differ from West European nations much as Sir Thomas Browne's vegetating 'creatures of mere existence' differ from 'things of life.'[48]

46 Rudyard Kipling, 'The Man Who Was', in *Life's Handicap* (London: MacMillan and Co, 1891), pp. 84–101 (p. 84). The story first appeared *in Macmillan's Magazine* in April of 1890, and in *Harper's Weekly* in April of 1891.

47 Donald Mackenzie Wallace, *Russia*, 2 vols (London and New York: Cassell and Co, 1905), II, 210.

48 Emile J. Dillon (E. B. Lanin), *Russian Traits and Terrors* (Boston, MA: Benj. R. Tucker, 1891), p. 3; first published in *Fortnightly Review* 52 (1889), pp. 410–32; 573–88; 722–36; 854–68.

The author's radicalised attitude towards the Russians becomes, perhaps, more explicable considering the circumstances of this publication. The political atmosphere of the late 1880s was aggravated by the Great Eastern Crisis, which concerned the Anglo–Russian dispute over territories in Afghanistan. Both countries were on the verge of military conflict; and in such an unsettling situation one could hardly be expected to conjure up a laudatory image of a potential foe. Two decades later, however, this condescending attitude was still widespread all over Britain, to the extent that in 1914 Maurice Baring drew attention to the fact that if one set a question about the Russians to English undergraduates and schoolchildren, the most prevalent answer would be:

> that the Russian was a man got up like a European except in winter, but that if you scratched him you would find a Tartar, and that a Tartar was a man with a yellow skin and a snub nose. I think you might also often get the answer that Russians were Slavs; but that if you asked what a Slav is, you would be told he was a kind of Tartar.[49]

To sum up, just like the idea of the Great Orient, configured within much the same temporal bounds, the image of Russia was contained within and represented by a set of descriptors, typically attached to extra-European peripheral nations, viewed as 'timeless', 'backward', bypassed by progress

49 Maurice Baring, *The Mainsprings of Russia* (London: Thomas Nelson and Sons, 1914), p. 17.
Such a perception can be associated with the saying, popular at the time, attributed either to Napoleon or Mme de Staël: 'Grattez le Russe, vous trouverez un Tartare', also quoted in *Dictionnaire de la langue verte* of 1907, where in the article on the Russians one finds the following citation: 'Grattez le Russe, vous trouverez un Cosaque, grattez le Cosaque, vous trouverez l'ours' with a comment from the author 'fait allusion au vernis de civilisation des Russes, relativement sortie de l'état barbare, s'applique aux gens dont de beaux dehors masquent les vices' (Hector France, *Dictionnaire de la langue verte* (Etoile-sur-Rhône: N. Gauvin, 1990, reprint of the original edn, Paris: Librairie du progrès, 1907), p. 384); quoted in Galina Kabakova, 'Mangeur de Chandelles. L'image du cosaque au XIX siècle', in Katia Dmitrieva and Michel Espagne, eds, *Transferts culturels triangulaires: France-Allemagne-Russie* (Paris: Editions de la maison des sciences de l'homme, 1996), pp. 207–31 (p. 208).

and historical transformation.[50] This view took Europe as a norm and a referential landmark, from which 'exotic' Russia (the term applied condescendingly) deviated. Within the limits of this top-down approach, rooted in a position of Western cultural strength and aimed at affirming a certain distance from the object, nothing but a general panoptical picture of the country was usually required. But to obtain a panoramic view of such a colossal country as Russia, the distance to the vantage point should be sufficiently large. The resulting image turned out to be appropriately reductive. Its topical spectrum was based effectively on a binary two-point model, contrasting 'the power and the people', which corresponded to a qualitative dichotomy involving Oriental ferocity, despotism and violence (also applied to other Eastern empires from Turkey to China, and often coloured by the dazzling luxury of the Imperial court-life) versus submissiveness, massive endurance and compassion.[51] The question of when and in what circumstances each of the binaries was activated and highlighted requires further, more in-depth consideration, for it is linked to the third of the defining features associated with Said's concept of the Orientalistic discourse.

This third important issue, which Said outlines in his study, and which is fully applicable to the British projection of the Russian image, draws a distinction between pure and political interest in, and knowledge of, the subject-matter of the literary discourse.[52] It is important to point out that the term 'political', in Said's work,

> is by no means in direct, corresponding relationship with political power in the raw, but rather is produced and exists in an uneven exchange with various kinds of power, shaped to a degree by the exchange with power political (as with a colonial or imperial establishment), power intellectual (as with reigning sciences like comparative

50 Leerssen, p. 29.

51 Among other literary works that bear witness to this type of dual perception one can mention M. Ropes, *Prince and Page: A Story of Russia*, 1884; F. Barrett, *The Sin of Olga Zassoulich*, 1891; A. E. Barr, *Michael and Theodora. A Russian Story*, 1892; George Gissing's novel *The Crown of Life* (1899); or *Michel Strogoff*, a novel by Jules Verne (1875), widely popular at the time.

52 Said, *Orientalism*, p. 9.

> linguistics or anatomy, or any of the modern policy sciences), power cultural (as with orthodoxies and canons of taste, texts, values), power moral (as with ideas about what 'we' do and what 'they' cannot do or understand as 'we' do).[53]

In other words, what one means here is that the so-called politically coloured discourse is not something related overtly to the ideologically charged politically orientated writing, but rather '*a distribution* of geopolitical awareness into aesthetic, scholarly, economic, sociological, historical, and philological texts',[54] streamed along certain distinct and intellectually predictable lines. Below we shall show that it was this type of politically coloured discourse that effectively shaped the myth of Russia in its British representation.

The graph in Figure 2 presents the number of literary texts related to Russian subject-matter based on the extremely valuable and detailed bibliography compiled by Anthony Cross in his survey of *The Russian Theme in English Literature* (1985).[55]

The temporal boundaries (1820–1920) comprise the period of over a hundred years, leading up to the decade that will constitute the further focus of our examination – the 1920s. In line with Said's thesis, the graph shows a strong correlation between the number of works published on the Russian theme during these years and the changes in the Anglo–Russian political

53 Ibid. p. 12.

54 Ibid. p. 12.

55 Anthony Cross, *The Russian Theme in English Literature from the Sixteenth Century to 1980: An introductory survey and bibliography* (Oxford: W. A. Meeuws, 1985), pp. 84–159.
The trend ties in well with the combined publication statistics (see Figure 3) concerning fiction and first-hand Russia-related travel accounts (1856–1916); the latter is based on a compilation of three sources: Anthony Cross, *In the Land of the Romanovs: An Annotated Bibliography of First-hand English-language Accounts of the Russian Empire (1613–1917)* (Cambridge: Open Book Publishers, 2014); Andrei N. Zashikhin, *Britanskaia rossika vtoroi poloviny XIX-nachala XX veka* (Archangel: Pomorskii pedagogicheskii universitet, 1995) p. 13; and Harry W. Nerhood, *To Russia and Return: An Annotated Bibliography of Travellers' English-Language Accounts of Russia from the Ninth Century to the Present* (Ohio: Ohio State University Press, 1968).

rapport. The first peak coincided with the Crimean War of 1853 to 1856; the second – with the Great Eastern Crisis related to the Anglo–Russian dispute in Central Asia; and the third – with the pre-World War I years and the formation of the Triple Entente, which in 1907 asserted an alliance between Great Britain, the Russian Empire and France. Unsurprisingly, the interest in the Russian theme started to peak after the October Revolution and the Bolsheviks' signing of the separatist Brest-Litovsk treaty with Germany in 1918.

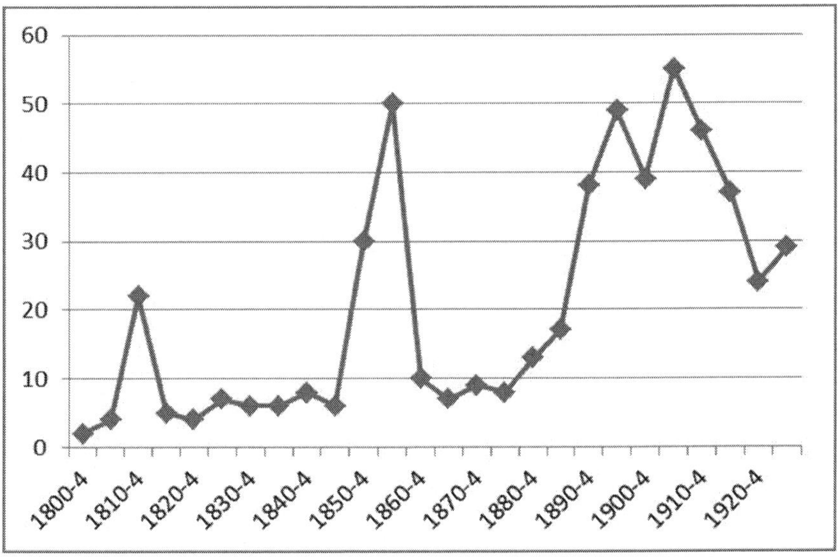

Figure 2. The number of texts (fiction) related to Russian subject-matter based on the bibliography in Anthony Cross, *The Russian Theme in English Literature from the Sixteenth Century to 1980: An introductory survey and bibliography* (1985).

Given that the peak affiliated with the Crimean War was relatively brief, and the reasons for the influx of interest in Russia were fairly uncomplicated and straightforward, we shall move straight on to the discussion of

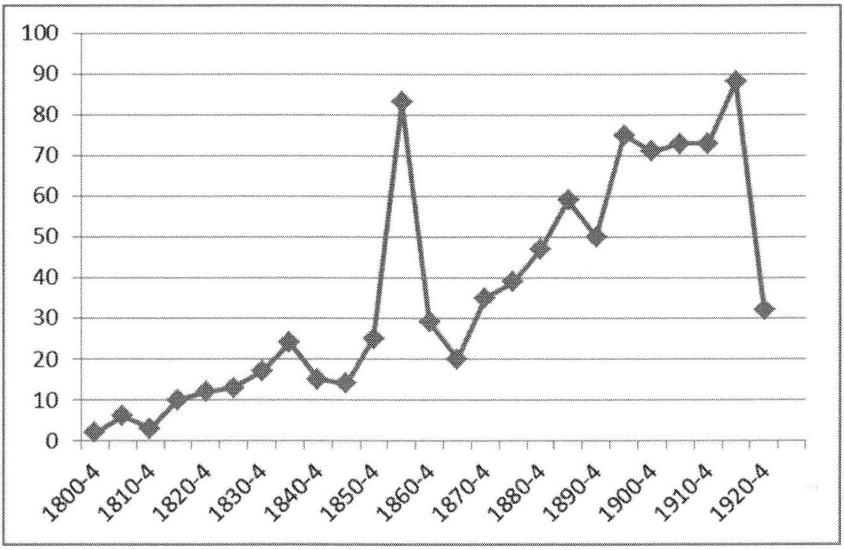

Figure 3. The number of texts (fiction and first-hand travel accounts) related to Russian subject-matter based on collated sources (see List of Figures, p. vii).

the context of the late 1880s. The second peak of interest in the Russian subject came in the wave of the Great Eastern Crisis and in the aftermath of the Russo–Turkish war (1877–8). The conflict brought to a head the rivalry between England and Russia for dominance in Central Asia. By spring 1885 it was descending into a serious threat of Anglo–Russian war, when after the clash of interests on the Afghanistan borders, the British press raised a cry of danger to India. By July 1887 the Boundary Commission was still negotiating the frontiers, the Russians were still advancing into Asian lands; and the closer they came to British India the more attention was given to the study of the threatening northern opponent. A rapid and appreciable interest in Russian culture spread across British society, and people avidly seized at any book that could throw light on the life and customs of the country. Written and published within a week, Charles Marvin's *The Russians at the Gate of Herat* (1885) had sales of 65,000 copies; Smith, Elder, & Co

(London) reprinted Armin Vámbéry's *Central Asia and the Anglo-Russian Frontier Question* (1874), as well as his *Travels in Central Asia* (1864); and other titles during this period included *All the Russians* (1885) by E. C. Phillips, *History of Russia* (1885) by W. K. Kelly, and *The Russian Storm-cloud* or *Russia in Her Relations to Neighbouring Countries* (1886) written by Sergei ('Sergius') Stepniak, one of the leaders of the Russian anarchist movement.

The title of Stepniak's monograph was most telling and revealing with regard to the general vector of contemporary rhetoric on the Russian subject. Russia was seen as a potential threat; consequently, the discourse was focused on the narrative associated with power (emblematised as a 'storm-cloud' in Stepniak's title), ruthlessness and uncontrollable passions, while the opposite polarity, related to compliance and some sort of sympathetic nonchalance, appeared to be blurred. The trend can be further exemplified by the spectrum of proliferating literary translations, including, curiously in such circumstances, the rise to prominence of Lev Tolstoy.

It was only natural that at a time when interest in Russian affairs ran at a very high pitch, the editors started looking for suitable translations from Russian authors. In 1887 the *Fortnightly Review* announced the vogue of 'the Russian novel', which, in the words of the critic, was fully justified and 'well deserved'.[56] Though the new interest embraced Russian literature as a whole, Tolstoy was one of the main attractions. Up until 1885 his name was barely known to the British readership (familiar mainly with the writings of Turgenev) to the extent that *The Contemporary Review* could refer freely to Dmitrii Tolstoy, the Russian Minister of Home Affairs, simply as Count Tolstoy, without any fear that his identity might be mistaken.[57] Henry James' notable essay on Turgenev's literary legacy as well as his *Art of Fiction* of

56 Matthew Arnold, 'Count Leo Tolstoi', *Fortnightly Review* 42 (1887), pp. 783–99 (p. 783).

57 'Contemporary Life and Thought in Russia', *The Contemporary Review* 47 (1885), pp. 727–36. At the end of the 70s there appeared a couple of publications that tried to attract attention to Tolstoy's writings, but they were very sparse: see, for instance, W. E. Henley, 'New Novels', *The Academy* 329 (1878), 186–7; W. R. S. Ralston, 'Novels of Count Leo Tolstoy', *Nineteenth Century* 5 (1879), 650–69; or C. E. Turner, *Studies in Russian Literature* (London: Kessinger Publishing Company, 1882).

1884,[58] also make no mention of Tolstoy's writings, but by 1887 his books were everywhere in the British book-stores: six translations of his works were published between 1885 and 1888, not to mention nineteen American editions which were on sale in Britain. In a short period in the mid-80s, practically everything Tolstoy had written in the preceding thirty-five years was translated and published in English (including W. S. Gottesberger's edition of *War and Peace*, translated from French by Clara Bell in 1886).[59] He was hailed as incomparably the greatest writer who had ever existed, occupying in fiction the same position that Shakespeare occupied with all drama[60] (a highly ironic statement, as some ten years later Tolstoy would become known for his vociferous hatred of Shakespeare).

When viewed in the light of the reception accorded to Tolstoy's writings during the preceding three decades, this sudden tide of interest and fascination appears as an unpredictable, almost capricious whim of literary fashion. And yet, considering the change of the context in the late eighties, one can chart out clearly the undercurrents of this radical turn. From 1860 to 1880, only two of Tolstoy's stories (*Childhood and Youth* in England and *Cossacks* in America[61]) were translated; and only a couple of critical essays (apart from reviews) presented the novelist to the reading public. The critics found Tolstoy's writings 'crudely joined'; the events and settings were

58 Henry James, 'Ivan Turgénieff', *Atlantic Monthly* 53 (1884), pp. 42–55; Walter Besant and Henry James, 'Art of Fiction', *Longman's Magazine* 4 (1884), pp. 502–21.

59 The influx of Tolstoy translations was partly facilitated by the availability of the general body of his works unprotected by intellectual copyright. In 1884 Tolstoy assigned the rights to all of works published before 1881 to his wife, being very generous with the remaining part of his intellectual property, and in 1891 he publicly renounced the copyrights of all he had written after 1881. Free of copyright restriction and royalties, publishing houses around the world issued impressive runs of Tolstoy's works almost immediately upon their official publication in Russia.

60 W. Sharp, 'New Novels', *The Academy* 871 (1889), p. 22. Among the major articles on Tolstoy at the time one should also mention Matthew Arnold's publication 'Count Leo Tolstoi'; W. E. Henley, 'Count Tolstoi's Novels', *Saturday Review*, 1 January 1887; 'Count Tolstoi's Life and Works', *Westminster Review* 130 (1888), pp. 278–93.

61 Leo Tolstoy, *Childhood and Youth* (London: Bell and Dalby, 1862); Leo Tolstoy, *Cossacks*, trans. Eugene Schuyler (New York: Scribner's Sons, 1878 and London: Sampson Low and Co, 1878).

'tolerably life-like', but 'how wild, how primitive and lawless, how ante [...] human', though not 'wholly unpleasant or unclean'.[62] As compared with Turgenev, Tolstoy had more of 'original force', but was not so subtle an artist; he was seen as possessing 'fiercer and freer poetry' than the elder author, but less of the 'contemptuous ennui and arid sophistication'.[63] As a writer, he was certainly out of tune with the mellow, well-tempered aesthetics of these years; so that his stories were met only with indifference, not to say neglect, by readers.[64] Everything changed in less than a decade, and Tolstoy's 'fiercer and freer' tones resonated with the context of the late eighties when the notes of the formidable and wild were foregrounded in the Russian image.

Some sort of comparable context-dependent dynamics can also be traced in the level of activity of the Russian anarchist circle in England. Led by such eminent revolutionaries as Prince Peter Kropotkin, Nikolai Chaikovsky, Felix Volkhovsky and Sergei Stepniak, the initiatives of this circle played a major role in shaping the image of Russia in the eyes of the Western viewers. By the beginning of the 1880s Prince Kropotkin had already become regarded as highly influential in the international political and cultural arena: he worked for the *Arbeiter Zeitung*, *L'Avant-Garde*, *La Justice*, and started his own paper *Le Revolte*. The topics of his articles

62 'Colonel Dunwoddie, and Other Novels', *Atlantic Monthly* 42 (1878), pp. 697–706 (p. 702).

63 Ibid. p. 702.

64 See, for instance, 'Colonel Dunwoddie, and Other Novels', p. 702; 'The Cossacks', *The Observer*, 15 September 1878. *The Times* had literally two lines advertising *Childhood and Youth*, as 'fresh and faithful to a degree that has never been surpassed' ('Count Tolstoi's Childhood and Youth', *The Times*, 20 June 1862, p. 12). *The Saturday Review* found Tolstoy's writing morally corrupt: 'It makes no difference whether a writer is a Russian, or a German, or an Englishman – whether he is or is not like a spring morning, or what may be his noble tendencies. He is not, we think, justified in telling his family history in this way, and in probing the failings of parents in order that he may have the satisfaction of sketching his own childhood' ('Childhood and Youth', *The Saturday Review*, 29 March 1862, pp. 361–2 (p. 362)). Unsigned reviews were published in *The Athenaeum* ('Childhood and Youth: A Tale', 16 August 1862, p. 209), *The Critic* ('The Education of a Russian Noble', 8 March 1862, p. 240) and *The Spectator* ('Childhood and Youth', 8 February 1862, p. 160).

ranged from ideological positions on economics to the debate over the propaganda of the deed.[65] Kropotkin's first attempt to bring about some basic awareness of Russian affairs in London was a dramatic and painful fiasco, forcing him to leave England in October 1882. As he put it in his *Memoirs of a Revolutionist*: 'Better a French prison than this grave.'[66] Not unlike the case of Tolstoy's translations, the context of the late 1880s worked in favour of the anarchists' undertakings. When Kropotkin arrived in London for a second time in March 1886, he was astonished by the complete change of scene: the 'life in London was no longer the dull, vegetating existence that it had been for me four years before', he wrote.[67] Promoted by the tide of political tension and the growing interest in the Russian subject, the anarchists managed to form a pressure group the 'Friends of Russian Freedom' (in 1890 it was turned into the 'Society of Friends of Russian Freedom'), and started publishing *Free Russia* – a monthly newspaper, edited initially by Stepniak and later on by Felix Volkhovsky (till his death in 1914).

Both Volkhovsky and Stepniak paid serious attention to the popularisation and interpretation of Russian literature, which they saw as the most effective way of acquainting foreign audiences with the problems of Russian society. Thomas Hardy attended one of Stepniak's lectures in 1893 and had some vivid recollections of the meeting.[68] It is also worth noting that Constance Garnett, one of the most eminent translators of the Russian classics (seventy-one volumes of the literary works, including Gogol, Turgenev, Goncharov, Tolstoy, Dostoevsky and Chekhov), gained her command of the Russian language in the Russian anarchist circle. She started her lessons under the guidance of Volkhovsky, who was often reproached by his peers (particularly by Nikolai Chaikovsky) for this kind of excessive

65 Later on Kropotkin became highly acclaimed for his major social studies: a comparative analysis of Russian and French prisons (1887), *Memoirs of a Revolutionist* (1899) and *The Great French Revolution, 1789–1793* (1909).

66 Peter Kropotkin, *Memoirs of a Revolutionist* (London: Smith, Elder and Co, 1899), II, 254.

67 Ibid. p. 306.

68 F. E. Hardy, *The Later Years of Thomas Hardy, 1892–1928* (London: Macmillan, 1930), p. 22.

overtures made towards the members of the English literary 'elite' (as they were known among the Russian revolutionary activists in exile). Generally speaking, Volkhovsky, as well as Kropotkin and Stepniak, were very keen on such links with the educated and cultural circles. Through their extensive activities in Britain – numerous press articles and public lectures – they aspired to spread information about Russia, its culture and its problems;[69] and their efforts, carried all the way through the pre-World War I years, made a strong impact on the new wave of interest in Russian affairs.

The pre-World War I decade was marked by widespread and relatively long-lasting attraction to the Russian subject, which yet again was not devoid of the underlying political implications. Following a radical 'u-turn' in Anglo–Russian relations, it resonated with the national propaganda campaign, which now had to justify the alliance of democratic England with autocratic Russia in World War I. The task was uneasy, but not impossible; John Mackail summarised it in one sentence: 'The Russians are different from us, but they are like us, and we have a great deal in common.'[70]

The brief period of Russophobia engendered by the Russo–Japanese War gave way to a new tide of affection for the Russians (especially after the abortive 1905 revolution). The old vision of the country as a 'shapeless mass of barbarism, tyrannised over by a small governing class which itself is half barbarous',[71] was replaced by an encouragingly positive attitude to the newly acquired ally. Far from a clog on or menace to general progress, Russia was now seen as working actively with others towards the needs and ideals of human civilisation. Several factors that contributed to this noticeable reshaping of the Russian image should be outlined.

69 Kropotkin was known for his persuasive and scholarly essays on Russian fiction, collected in the 1915 edition of *Ideals and Realities in Russian Literature*. He also wrote of Tolstoy in the article on anarchism in *The Encyclopaedia Britannica*, naming him one of the prominent representatives of the movement, who based his position on 'the teachings of Jesus and […] the necessary dictates of reason' (Peter Kropotkin, 'Anarchism', in *Encyclopaedia Britannica* (Cambridge: Cambridge University Press, 1910), p. 918).

70 John William Mackail, *Russia's Gift to the World* (London: Hodder and Stoughton, 1915), p. 7.

71 Ibid. p. 6.

The first is related to the extensive imports of Russian culture that marked the turn-of-the-century decades. These years are most often associated with the Diaghilev seasons (1911–14). Leonard Woolf recalls in his autobiography that the British audience was completely enthralled by the performance: 'Night after night we flocked to Covent Garden', he maintains, 'entranced by a new art, a revelation to us benighted British, the Russian Ballet in the greater days of Diaghilev and Nijinsky.'[72] The newspapers and fashionable magazines were full of superlatives and praising comments; and the fact that Diaghilev's premiere in London was scheduled during George V's coronation festivities speaks for itself.

In 1912 the second post-impressionist exhibition, 'British French and Russian Painters' (curated by Roger Fry and Clive Bell[73]), featured two highly successful contemporary artists, Mikhail Larionov and Natalia Goncharova. The latter was to make an unforgettable impression on an even wider audience with her designs for *Le Coq d'or* – Rimsky-Korsakov's opera performed by Diaghilev's company in 1914 (Theatre Royal, Drury Lane). These magnificent productions of Russian opera during the 1913 and 1914 seasons, which appeared as a real celebration of performance art, captured the imagination of the most refined viewers. According to Sir Osbert Sitwell, they raised the standard of music drama to an unprecedented level:

> the Russian operas never before performed in London until these years relieved one suddenly from the Viking world of bearded warriors drinking blood out of skulls, that had been for so long imposed by Germany. They pleased the eye at last, as well as the ear;[74]

while in the words of Rosa Newmarch, these spectacles simply 'rescued' the city's social life in the days just before the assassination of the Archduke:

72 Leonard Woolf, *Beginning Again: An Autobiography of the Years 1911 to 1918* (London: Hogarth Press, 1964), p. 37.

73 Christopher Reed, *A Roger Fry Reader* (Chicago: University of Chicago Press, 1996), pp. 290–6.

74 Osbert Sitwell, *Great Morning* (London: Little and Brown, 1947), p. 263.

> Russian opera, perhaps is the only topic of the hour on which educated people can meet on a common ground of admiration. Ulster, the suffrage, Lloyd-Georgian finance, Mr Winston Churchill, are all dangerous subjects which divide house against house and estrange life-long friends.[75]

In 1916 Macmillan published a very handsome book with an impressive list of British and Russian contributors, entitled precisely *The Soul of Russia*. 'The Soul' was presented in a variety of aspects, covering a wide range of subjects from early icons, peasant crafts and popular folk-songs to the music of Stravinsky and the paintings of Goncharova. There were poems by Briusov and Balmont, and some prose pieces by Sologub, Chekhov and Kuprin – all in an attempt, according to the editor Winifred Stephens, to embrace Russia's 'noble but sometimes unfathomable soul'.[76]

A decade into the twentieth century Britain once again experienced an influx of Russian literary translations; and the general influence of Russian literature during these years can hardly be taken too seriously. Constance Garnett's version of *The Brothers Karamazov*, which appeared in 1912, caused an enormous sensation. John Middleton Murry referred to it as the 'most epoch-making translation of the past', comparable only with Sir Thomas North's *Plutarch*.[77] In the next eight years Garnett followed this work with eleven more volumes of Dostoevsky, triggering a real cult of the author in Britain.[78] First translations of Dostoevsky's novels had been available since the early 1880s, but he was not particularly in favour with the intellectuals during the nineteenth-century decades; and in 1903 the publishers still felt

75 'The Russian Invasion' (a review of Rosa Newmarch's book *The Russian Opera*), *Spectator*, 27 June 1914, p. 1089.

76 Winifred Stephens, preface to *The Soul of Russia* (London: Macmillan, 1916), pp. v–viii (p. vi).

77 Charles A. Moser, 'The Achievement of Constance Garnett', *American Scholar* 57 (1988), 431–8 (p. 435).

78 Harold Orel, 'English Critics and the Russian Novel 1860–1917', *Slavonic and East European Review* 33 (1954), 457–69 (p. 469). 'Constance Garnett's translation of Dostoevsky's major works', her biographer wrote, 'was at least in its immediate effects, one of the most important literary events in modern English literature' (Carolyn G. Heilbrun, *The Garnett Family* (London: Allen and Unwin, 1961), p. 188).

that 'there was no real market for Dostoevsky in England'.[79] Arnold Bennett found *The Brothers Karamazov* very impressive when he read it for the first time in French in 1909, as well as D. H. Lawrence, who was impressed by the French version of *Crime and Punishment* around the same time.[80] In 1910 *Crime and Punishment* (an old translation) was adapted for the stage by Lawrence Irving as *The Unwritten Law*. And although the text underwent some most peculiar alterations (the pawnbroker was replaced by an evil landlord who makes unwelcome advances to Sonia, an innocent maiden; Raskolnikov, a revolutionary student, kills the landlord to protect Sonia's honour[81]), this production, together with a new Everyman edition of the same translation, increased the public recognition of Dostoevsky's name and paved the way for further translations.

The overwhelming interest in reading 'the Russians' was not limited to Dostoevsky's novels. Publishers were quick to reissue old works of the established writers and commissioned new ones. Tolstoy and Turgenev continued to be reprinted (in Constance Garnett's and Louise and Aylmer Maude's translations). Two new versions of Gogol's *Dead Souls* (by Stephen Graham and Charles J. Hogarth), which had long been out of print in English, were relaunched in 1915, followed a year later by the new translation of Aksakov's memoirs.[82] An increasing number of Chekhov's stories had been appearing in the press since 1897. In July 1902 they were thoroughly reviewed by R. E. C. Long for the *Fortnightly Review*;[83] and as soon as the

79 Phelps, p. 156. The first English translation of Dostoevsky's major novels (*Notes from The House of the Dead*) was published in 1881; followed in a couple of years by *Crime and Punishment* and *The Insulted and Injured* (Moser, p. 435).

80 For more detail see Chapter 5 in this book.

81 Walter Neuschäffer, *Dostojewskijs Einfluss auf englischen Roman Anglistische Forschungen* (Heidelberg: Carl Withers Universitätsbuchhandlung, 1935), p. 6.

82 For a detailed account of Russian literary translations see Rachel May, *The Translator in the Text: On Reading Russian Literature in English* (Evanston, IL: Northwestern University Press, 1994), pp. 27–36.

83 R. E. C. Long, 'Anton Tchekhoff', *Fortnightly Review* 72 (1902), 103–18. For the review of the first English translations of Chekhov see also Victor Emeljanow, Introduction to *Chekhov: The Critical Heritage*, ed. Victor Emeljanow (London: Routledge and Paul Kegan, 1981), pp. 1–56 (pp. 1–4).

Dostoevsky craze started to abate (by 1920), a passion for Chekhov steadily took over, inspired yet again by a stream of Garnett's publications (sixteen volumes between 1916 and 1923). Literary journals in England (and in the United States) clamoured for translations and critical articles on Russian literary masters; and the book reviews of the pre-War decades spoke with an informed air of Goncharov, Chekhov, Gogol and Turgenev, presenting it as a matter of particular 'importance that Englishmen should understand the Russian mind.'[84] Russia had become to the young intellectuals 'of today', wrote Rebecca West in 1915, what Italy was to the Victorians:

> as their imaginations, directed by Turner and the Brownings, dreamed of the crumbling richness of Rome and Venice, so we to-day think of that plain of brown earth patterned with delicate spring grass and steel-grey patches of half-melted snow and cupped in a round unbroken sky-line, which is Russia. We are deeply and affectionately familiar with Russian life.[85]

The assertiveness of this and similar statements, which came to be regarded as something tantamount to '*bon ton*' among the socialites of the middle-class milieu, was, in fact, profoundly ironic, given that contemporary Russian literature, with the exception of Gorky and, to a certain extent, Leonid Andreev,[86] remained far less known to English readers than the nineteenth-century classics of the past.

84 'An Impertinent Substitution', *New Statesman* 5 (1915), 628–9 (p. 629). According to certain observers, the proliferation of Russian translations owed much to a completely different factor. Julius West linked it to the sheer pragmatism of the publishing industry and its economic considerations – a typical 'catch-as-catch-can' process: 'International copyright does not apply to Russia', he claimed, 'therefore it is unnecessary either to obtain permission to translate or to pay the Russian author a royalty' (Julius West, 'Translated from the Russian', *New Statesman* 5 (1915), 447–8 (p. 447)).

85 Harold Orel, 'The Victorian View of Russian Literature', *Victorian Newsletter* 51 (1977), 1–5 (p. 5).

86 By 1910 Gorky was much better known among the English public than Chekhov (the situation has since been reversed), and surveys of British (and French) magazines put him first in their list of Tolstoy's younger successors, followed by Korolenko, Potapenko and only then, in fourth position, by Chekhov (*Anton Chekhov's Life*

A somewhat more up-to-date outlook on Russia was offered by a different set of writings, which should not be overlooked when discussing the pre-War configuration of the Russian image. This is the endeavour of the young British 'intermediaries' – journalists and literary scholars, whose active enthusiasm for the Russian subject-matter was buoyed up by the Anglo–Russian political tide. In their numerous articles and analytical surveys, Bernard Pares, Maurice Baring, Harold Williams, Stephen Graham and others, who were all fascinated with Russia in their own special way, tried to create a positive image of the country in the eyes of their readers, and to facilitate the study of Russia in England. One of the platforms for their aspirations was the *Russian Review* journal, founded in 1912 under the initiative of Bernard Pares and intended as 'a centre for the growing movement towards a better understanding between Britain and Russia'.[87] Bernard Pares was one of the founding fathers of Russian studies in Britain, being associated with both the first School of Russian Studies at Liverpool University inaugurated in 1907, and the School of Slavonic Studies, set up in 1915 at King's College London. He also made a considerable contribution to raising the profile of Anglo–Russian political relations by organising the 1909 visit to Britain of a Duma delegation, as well as the reciprocal visit to Russia of British politicians in 1912.[88]

Along with Pares, Maurice Baring was one of several 'ambassadors' for Russia, who were highly acclaimed by the British public. Baring covered the Russo–Japanese War as a correspondent for the *Morning Post*, and had several long stays in the country between 1900 and 1917. Three of his books on the Russian subject, *Landmarks in Russian Literature* (1910), *The Russian People* (1911) and *The Mainsprings of Russia* (1914),

---

and Thought: Selected Letters and Commentary, ed. Simon Karlinsky, trans. Michael Henry Heim (Evanston, IL: Northwestern University Press, 1997), p. 334). Leonid Andreev's plays were quite popular at this time: fourteen of his plays came out in translation between 1907 and 1923; and Bunin's stories also went through several printings.

87 Charlotte Alston, *Russia's Greatest Enemy?: Harold Williams and the Russian Revolutions* (New York: Tauris, 2007), p. 80.

88 Ibid. p. 80.

were very popular among contemporary readers for their picturesque and colourful descriptions, their vivid examples drawn from the life of ordinary people; for the author's gripping enthusiasm concerning the cause of Anglo–Russian understanding, and his astonishing ability to subvert the stereotyped patterns of thinking, so that, for instance, most clichéd Russian vices looked almost like incontestable national virtues. 'The charm of Russian life', wrote Baring,

> lies in its essential goodness of heart, and in its absence of hypocrisy, and it is owing to this absence of hypocrisy that the faults of the Russian character are so easy to detect. It is for this reason that in Gogol's realistic and satirical work, as in The Inspector and Dead Souls, the characters startle the foreign observer by their frank and almost universal dishonesty. The truth is that they do not take the trouble to conceal their shortcomings; they are indulgent to the failings of others, and not only expect but know that they will find their own faults treated with similar indulgence. Faults, failings, and vices which in Western Europe would be regarded with uncompromising censure and merciless blame, meet in Russia either with pity or good-humoured indulgence.[89]

In this context, some words should also be said about the works of Stephen Graham, whose main interest lay in the domain of pilgrimages and peasants. For Graham, as for Baring and Pares, Russia was a life-long commitment; and he tried to bring it closer to the English-speaking readers through the framework of John Ruskin's ideals (a strong sense of community and the dignity of labour). 'The Russians are an agricultural nation, bred to the soil'; it is not the land of 'bomb-throwers'[90] and 'intolerable

89 Maurice Baring, *Landmarks in Russian Literature* (London: Methuen and Co, 1910), pp. 70–1.

90 Such an attitude was widespread after the Greenwich Observatory bombing in 1894. The Greenwich Observatory was the target of an attempted bombing on 15 February 1894. This was possibly the first international terrorist incident in Britain. The bomb was accidentally detonated while being held by twenty-six-year-old French anarchist Martial Bourdin in Greenwich Park, near the Observatory building. Joseph Conrad used the incident in his novel *The Secret Agent* (1907): the plot line turns around an agent-provocateur, who acts within an anarchist cell in London on behalf of a foreign embassy, the latter evidently meant to be Russia, though it is never actually named.

unhappiness', he argued. The Russians 'are strong as giants, simple as children, mystically superstitious by reason of their unexplained mystery. They live as Ruskin wished the English to live.'[91] Through a series of books, produced before and during World War I (*Undiscovered Russia*, *Changing Russia*, *The Way of Marpha and the Way of Mary*, *With the Russian Pilgrims to Jerusalem*), Graham affirmed his reputation as a knowledgeable and thorough researcher, who, in the words of *Russian Review*,

> understands Russia and the Russian people. He writes from the standpoint of modest sympathy, and not from that of patronising superiority. He understands the soul of the Russian. He understands how deeply the Russian is rooted in reality.[92]

Speaking about the vast volume of Russia-related literature circulated in England during these pre-War years, one cannot possibly miss the aura of affectionate sympathy which was prevalent in the majority of these editions. Neither can one characterise the tone of these works as exploitive or authoritatively imperialistic. Moreover, due to the positive vector of the socio-political context, the expression of sympathy projected by the authors sometimes took the form of the most obvious overstatement. The examples were manifold and could be drawn from various domains, including national character, history, psychology, culture and even language. Thus, for instance, Charles Sarolea, a reputable specialist on the Russian subject and the author of a sound study *Europe's Debt to Russia* that was published in 1916, put forward an idea of Russian racial superiority, deduced on the basis of Darwin's teachings. According to Sarolea's thesis, the Russians should occupy the top position on the survival of the fittest scale, because, as a nation, they have been thoroughly tempered by the ruthless severity of the country's geographic and social conditions:

> They have survived a struggle for life of ruthless severity. They have resisted the continued pressure of hunger, war, plague, of a cruel climate, and a more cruel Government.

91 Stephen Graham, *Undiscovered Russia* (London: John Lane the Bodley Head, 1912), p. ix.

92 'Notes on Current Books: *Undiscovered Russia* by Stephen Graham', *Russian Review* 1.1 (1912), 98.

> The Russians have got a splendid physique, they have a capacity of endurance which is surpassed by no other race.[93]

The distinguishing grandeur, spirituality and superiority of the Russian soul was highlighted by several English scholars. William Phelps related it to the extreme vastness of the Russian spaces:

> The immense size of the country produces an element of largeness in the Russian character that one feels not only in their novels, but almost invariably in personal contact and conversation with a more or less educated Russian [...] Bigness in early environment often produces a certain comfortable largeness of mental vision.[94]

In the same vein, Maurice Baring, who took it upon himself to examine the main traits of the national character, opined, apparently without irony, that the Russians were the most naturally humane, as compared to all other inferior, in this sense, European peoples:

> the Russians are more broadly and widely human than the people of other European or Eastern countries, and being more human their capacity of understanding is greater, for their extraordinary quickness of apprehension comes from the heart rather than the head. They are the most humane and the most naturally kind of all the peoples of Europe.[95]

Amusingly, some pages later in the same book Baring cautions against the risk of rushing into 'broad generalisations', which, he affirms, 'bring with them a certain element of exaggeration' to be discounted in a serious analytical survey.[96] It seems, perhaps unsurprisingly, that these exceedingly bold postulations, though born out of sheer enthusiasm, interest and even affection, were characteristic of those who happened to be most closely involved in the area of Russian Studies. Thus, Edward Garnett, husband of the translator Constance Garnett and himself the author of several

93 Charles Sarolea, *Europe's Debt to Russia* (London: Heinemann, 1916), p. 7.

94 William Lyon Phelps, *Essay on Russian Novelists* (New York: Macmillan Co, 1911, reprinted New York: Snova Books, 2004), p. 5.

95 Baring, p. 2.

96 Ibid. p. 51.

books on Russian subjects, also argued for the exclusive pre-eminence of the Russian mind. 'Every reader of Russian literature, from Gogol to our day', he maintained,

> cannot fail to recognise that the Russian mind is superior to the English in its emotional breadth and flexibility, its eager responsiveness to new ideas, its spontaneous warmth of nature. With all their faults the Russian people are more permeated with humane love and living tenderness, in their social practice, than those of other nations.[97]

It is worth giving credit to the vivid expressiveness of Garnett's explorations, which, flattering as they were, suggested yet another example of a supererogatory motion. The pendulum swung to the opposite side of the spectrum: one extremity was replaced by another; and the array of pejorative epithets, associated with all things Russian in the 1890s, was eclipsed by another set of superlatives with a markedly positive slant. This did not mean that the old descriptors were immediately abrogated and forgotten, but rather 'relieved' from their operational function *pro tem*. They remained subliminally present in the 'vocabulary range' connected to the Russian discourse, to be reactivated later, should the chance or opportunity arise. This, in fact, was the case when in 1918 the Bolsheviks signed the separate Brest-Litovsk treaty with the Germans, thus deserting the Allied Forces on the World War I Eastern Front. After two decades of centring the Russian imagery on the spiritual and the refined, the rhetoric of 1917 to 1918 (after the Bolshevik Revolution) effortlessly reactivated the notion of the 'cruel barbarians' of the eighteenth-century vintage. The latter was exemplified by Emile Dillon's new publication, which was released in 1918. One of the leading figures of the earlier anti-Russian campaign (all the way through the 1890s), he came up with another monograph on the subject, asserting (straight in the opening statement) the profound ethnic incompatibility between Saxons and Slavs:

97 Edward Garnett, *Turgenev. A Study* (London: W. Collins Sons and Co, 1917), p. 157.

> Between Slav and Saxon, in particular, there yawns a psychological abyss wide enough in places to sunder two different species of beings, not merely two separate races. And of all Slav peoples the Russian is by far the most complex and puzzling.[98]

Having gone through the full variety of these stages of hostility, sympathy, and benevolent condescension, the lexical spectrum of the Russian discourse became noticeably wider by the early 1920s. It was certainly more nuanced and less schematic. The question of whether the years of extensive Russophilia resulted in dismantling the Orientalistic dichotomy of 'the civilised' and the 'savage' – 'us' and 'them' – is a slightly different matter, which requires further scrutiny and examination. True, the crude image of 'the barbarians' was no longer dominating the palette; however, it gave way to the myth of an 'admirably exotic other', which, when analysed within the framework of the Orientalistic perspective, may prove to be nothing but a somewhat subtler variation on the old tune (a subtle form of condescension); as D. H. Lawrence put it in one of his letters: 'It amazes me that we have bowed down and worshipped these foreigners as we have [...] But it is characteristic of a highly developed nation to bow down to that which is more gross and raw and affected.'[99]

In representing exotic others, Orientalism works as a conceptual and metaphoric 'grid' of interpretation, which helps the mind to intensify its own sense of self, and guarantees a 'positional superiority' for the European (not necessarily political and imperialistic).[100] Even if this grid is flexible, Said argues, the encounter with an exotic other cannot but affirm the

> sovereign Western consciousness out of whose unchallenged centrality an Oriental world emerged, first according to general ideas about who or what was an Oriental, then according to a detailed logic governed not simply by empirical reality but by a battery of desires, repressions, investments, and projections.[101]

98 Emile J. Dillon, *The Eclipse of Russia* (New York, George B. Doran, 1918), p. 1.

99 D. H. Lawrence, Letter to Catherine Carswell, 27 November 1916, in James T. Boulton et al., eds, *The Letters of D. H. Lawrence*, 8 vols (Cambridge: Cambridge University Press, 1979–2001), III (1984), 41.

100 Said, *Orientalism*, p. 7.

101 Ibid. p. 8.

It follows that the representation of non-Western 'others' has necessarily made an implicit contribution to their 'exploitation', defined in terms of complicit affirmation of the desired perspective on the constructed identity of this group:

> The construction of identity [...] involves establishing opposites and 'others' whose actuality is always subject to the continuous interpretation and reinterpretation of their differences from 'us'. Far from a static thing then, identity of self or of other is a much worked-over historical, social, intellectual, and political process [...] What makes [this] difficult to accept is that most people resist the underlying notion: that human identity is not only natural and stable, but constructed, and occasionally even invented outright.[102]

One may still argue that representation as such is always exterior. The author always takes up a position of control vis-à-vis his *objet discursif*, and therefore is immune to any kind of dialogical influence from this object. In the Orientalist mode of reproduction, however, this exteriority acquires a very specific nuance of gradation, for it concerns precisely the degree to which the referent is eclipsed or even obliterated by the productive power of the discourse. In other words, the question is to what extent the autonomous reality is replaced by a purposeful abstraction, by a construct of the Western imagination – a generalised and virtual scheme.

To give an example of this Western aberration with regard to the myth of Russia configured over the pre-War years, one can look at the practices and trends in literary translations that continued to shape the viewpoint of British readers. As already mentioned, Constance Garnett acquired her knowledge of Russian in the anarchist revolutionary circles. Volkhovsky was her first Russian tutor and later on she took up translating Russian literature under the direction of Stepniak. This explains Garnett's noticeable emphasis on social and political undertones that coloured her interpretations of the Russian classics.[103] Similarly, one has to bear in mind that it was not just a cult of Dostoevsky that seized Britain after the launch of *The Brothers Karamazov* (1912) translation, but the cult of Dostoevsky in Garnett's

102 Ibid. p. 332.

103 Edward Garnett, *The Golden Echo* (London: Chatto & Windus 1953), p. 10.

rendition. As pointed out by Rachel May in her analysis of contemporary tendencies in translation, Garnett, undoubtedly, was a highly competent and talented translator: her works were not only by far the best available at the time, but also able to stand comparison with a number of modern translations. Without disregarding the remarkable value of her work, May, nonetheless, draws attention to the fact that Garnett's success lay partly in domesticating the originals and adapting them to the receptive consciousness of the English reader.[104] 'Dostoevsky is so obscure', she wrote, 'and so careless a writer that one can scarcely help clarifying him–sometimes it needs some penetration to see what he is trying to say.'[105]

Such clarification was, perhaps, not unwelcome at the time, and according to *The Times Literary Supplement*: 'English readers, embarking on the huge tract of Dostoevsky's fiction', needed all the help they could get 'in the way of clarity and comfort'.[106] On the other hand, one main result of Garnett's 'clarification' was smoothing the narrative voice of the author, which in this way happened to be passed through the filter of the translator's perception. Often abrupt, subjectively uncertain, with a number of formal imperfections these 'deliberate prevarications and mutterings on the part of the narrator' were, nonetheless, characteristic of Dostoevsky's style; they gave an air of intrigue and rumour and were organic to the contextual aspects of the work.[107] The difference from the original was highlighted by some notorious bilingual experts, including Vladimir Nabokov or Josef Brodsky; both were quite critical of Garnett's translations for her inattentive and even reductive approach to the refined qualities of the authors' narration: 'The reason English-speaking readers can barely tell the difference between Tolstoy and Dostoevsky is that they aren't reading the prose of either one. They're reading Constance Garnett.'[108]

104 May, p. 32.

105 Constance Garnett, 'Russian Literature in English', *The Listener*, 30 January 1947, p. 195.

106 *The Times Literary Supplement*, 4 July 1912, p. 269; quoted in May, p. 32.

107 May, p. 32.

108 David Remnick, 'The Translation Wars', *The New Yorker*, 7 November 2005.

The selection of translations available at the time also made its mark on the 'constructed' image of the Russians. When making their choices, translators had to think about the marketable value of the editions. Group psychology and collective expectations were a significant consideration in these matters. On the one hand, the work should not grate on the eye in terms of the established canon of literary reception (the main reason for all Garnett's alterations). At the same time, it would be desirable for the piece of fiction to produce a stronger (or at least memorable) impact on its readers through, perhaps, arresting imagery, haunting characters and bewildering plot. All of this imposed a certain restriction on the process of filtering and selection, resulting in a tendentious, often grotesquely lopsided image of the Russians, configured largely in response to, and mediated by, the feedback from the marketing prescriptions. Gerald Gould, who published a considerable volume of literary criticism on the Russian subject, commented on this flagrant distortion in one of his articles written for the *New Statesman*. 'I am constantly puzzled by a discrepancy between Russian fiction and what little I know of Russian fact', he maintained,

> I do not like the personal note in criticism, which, like any other art should be objective; but I am bound to use it here to illustrate my objective point. My Russian friends are, if they will allow me to say so, without exception perfectly sane; yet almost all the Russians that I read about in the books are as mad as hatters. Whence the discrepancy? Does Russian literature specialise in insanity, or is it merely that only the madder books are translated?[109]

Gould's comment, apparently, had some wider implications than those related to the domain of literary reception. The impact of Russian fiction happened to be so manifestly pronounced at the time that the audience was inclined to perceive ordinary Russians as no different from those portrayed in Tolstoy's and Dostoevsky's writings. Given that this generalised perception often remained on the surface level of the plot-line, the impression persisted that Russia was populated by Raskolnikov-type neurotic killers, emancipated Turgenev women and sinful, but enticingly charming, transgressors *à-la* Mme Karenin. Even those who happened to have first-hand

109 Gerald Gould, 'New Novels', *New Statesman* 7 (1916), 17–18 (p. 17).

knowledge of the field did not seem to be fully immune from this sort of 'suspension of disbelief' syndrome. On the one hand, Maurice Baring tried to warn his readers against falling into a trap of representational conventionalities and artistic distortions, pointing out that all these famous literary figures looked like ordinary Russians no more than Goethe's Faust embodied a German, and a common Englishman could be equated with King Lear.[110] On the other hand, he himself used these literary archetypes as landmark references for his socio-anthropological postulations. His ideal model of the Russian character, for instance, was presented as a basic combination of Peter the Great, Prince Myshkin (from Dostoevsky's *The Idiot*), and Khlestakov (from Gogol's *Inspector General*):

> What three Russian types, in history and fiction, would [...] sum up the Russian character? I for one would answer Peter the Great, Prince Myshkin, and Khlestakov. And I would add that in almost every Russian you will find an element of all these three types.[111]

For the sake of poetic justice, it is worth pointing out that when stereotyping the English national character, Baring chose a similar politico-mythological combination, made up of John Milton, Mr Pickwick and Henry VIII.

Further to the point, one should say that alongside all the praiseworthy factors related to the import of Russian culture, which at the time overwhelmed the minds of the British educated and cultural circles, the side-effect of this rapid cultural propagation consisted in widening the gap between the referent and its imaginary construct. Russia was seen largely through the prism of its cultural achievements; and its 'empiricity' found a substitute in the generalised archetypes of literary models. The

110 Baring, *The Mainsprings of Russia*, pp. 157–8.

111 Maurice Baring, *The Russian People* (London: Methuen and Co, 1911), p. 55. In his explorations of identity issues, Baring divided all Russians into two types: Lucifer and Ivan the Fool (Baring, *Landmarks in Russian Literature*, p. 80, 95); the latter, characteristically, was largely drawn from Dostoevsky's novels and related to the prime ideal of Tolstoy's teachings. (On the figure of a holy fool in Dostoevsky see Sarah Hudspith, *Dostoevsky and the Idea of Russianness* (London: Routledge, 2004), p. 147).

outcome was similar to that produced by the Diaghilev Ballets' seasons when Bakst's artistic experiment with the sets for *Schéhérazade* became linked to what was widely regarded as a typical *à-la-Russe* style; and the Russian theme-parties in London appeared to be frequented by women in huri garb, turbans and ropes of massive pearls *à-la* Nijinsky.[112] (This offers a telling example of an inadvertent Orientalisation of the Russian image – profoundly ironic in the context of our examination.)

Considering the general atmosphere of critical, or more precisely uncritical overstatement in response to Russian literature and art during these culturally dynamic decades, one imagines that it must have exerted unavoidable pressure on the formation of the artistic world of British authors, whose literary careers were developing in this newly changed cultural context, when exaggerated praise for things Russian was the rule rather than the exception. The point of interest here is to see whether the cumulative effect of Russophilia resulted in an overall paradigmatic shift in the projection of the Russian image, moving away, if at all, from the deep-seated Orientalistic perspective. When proceeding with such an examination, however, it is worth taking into account that apart from the impact of the socio-political climate, the overall cultural landscape of the time was strongly affected by the changes in the metaphysical angle, which had a significant bearing on the *modus operandi* of creative minds, and which was explored and approached through the adoption of innovative, often termed modernist, aesthetic techniques.

As a movement, modernism was brought about by a widespread realisation that Western civilisation was entering an era of bewildering change. New modes of communication, new technologies, and new scientific discoveries combined to challenge perceptions of reality and to generate dramatic new forms of artistic expression. What once were perceived as astounding absolutes relating to the physical universe dissolved under the pressure of scientific advances; and the very solidity of the real vanished in a mist of doubt about the truth of the objective. This led to the deep crisis of consciousness, as Husserl defined it later in the thirties in his Vienna lecture

112 Green and Swan, p. 65.

on the crisis of European existence.[113] Commonly linked to its radical aesthetic innovations, modernism, no doubt, subjected artistic competence to minute scrutiny and reflective examination. However, one misses the point of the modern by interpreting it only as a novel style and an avant-garde form. Behind the apparently formal strategies in the poetics of the movement, behind its proclamation of a historical licence for the new, lay a stimulating sense of existential crisis, which resulted in a new cultural phenomenology and revaluation of the projected image of the self. The former and the latter were, evidently, interconnected. But what is more important in this context is that both used the myth of Russia (at least partly) as one of their structural standpoints, thus endowing it with the dimension of a valuable resource or 'cultural asset', understood and employed in Pierre Bourdieu's sense of the term.[114]

Regarding the first aspect, the crisis of consciousness, as mentioned, was intimately related to the collapse of Cartesian rationalism and the overall materialistic frame of causal thinking. Superimposed on this was the proliferation of interest in the Russian viewpoint, much of which was considered to reflect a temperamental disposition towards the anti-pragmatic, meditative and even mystical mode. This, in a way, filled in the expanding metaphysical void, providing a referential source and a model for self-reflexivity and artistic engagement; and in terms of Western interest in and appropriation of this new perspective it was certainly different from the time-honoured cult of the exotic.

When reflecting on the European crisis of consciousness, Husserl saw 'the reason for the failure of a rational culture' not so much in the essence of rationalism itself, but in its schematic exteriorisation, and its entanglement with 'naturalism' and 'objectivism'.[115] According to the philosopher, the latter should be understood only as a primitive modality of intellectual endeavour – a 'naive external orientation [of the mind]', which, he asserts, lacks

113 Edmund Husserl, 'The Vienna Lecture. Philosophy and the Crisis of European Humanity' (10 May 1935), in *Phenomenology and the Crisis of Philosophy*, trans. David Carr (Evanston, IL: Northwestern University Press, 1970), pp. 269–300.

114 Bourdieu, *Distinction*, pp. 13–14.

115 Husserl, p. 299.

'the ultimate, true rationality made possible by the spiritual world-view'.[116] Genuine rationality, in contrast, can be achieved only through inward-orientated self-reflexive thinking, capable of resolving 'man's now unbearable lack of clarity about his own existence and his infinite tasks'.[117] Given that, as Husserl put it,

> there are only two escapes from the crisis of European existence: the downfall of Europe in its estrangement from its own rational sense of life, its fall into hostility towards the spirit and into barbarity; or the rebirth of Europe from the spirit of philosophy [...] that overcomes naturalism once and for all.[118]

A ready-made platform for this spiritual rebirth was provided by the Russian tradition, which promoted (through its cultural legacy, for instance) a distinctly anti-naturalistic, intuitive and inward-orientated epistemological path. For many in the West, cognition was commonly associated with knowledge in the intellectual or Cartesian sense of the term. Russian culture offered a somewhat different projection of the concept, within which knowledge had an extra dimension of spiritual connection, something akin to the familiarity with a person, rather than with a series of empirical facts. One might say that the Russians had not so much a specific perception of aesthetics as an aesthetic perception of the reality of life – a perception with several important inferences for the Russian mode of cognition. As Leonid Uspensky, an eminent Orthodox philosopher, put it, 'beauty, as it is understood by the Orthodox church [...] is a part of the life to come, when God will be all in all', and this beauty 'can be a path or a means of bringing us closer to God'.[119] Charting a diagram of such a path, dissecting it in parts and analysing its progress through the mysteries of life would be, in the Russian cultural tradition, not merely futile, but potentially detrimental. The end does not justify the means in such a process, for when insisting

116 Ibid. p. 297.

117 Ibid. p. 297.

118 Ibid. p. 299.

119 Leonid Uspensky, 'The Meaning and Content of the Icon', in Daniel B. Clendenin, ed., *Eastern Orthodox Theology: A Contemporary Reader* (Grand Rapids, MI: Baker, 2000), pp. 33–63 (p. 42).

on the analytical examination of an object one does not come to a greater knowledge of its essence, but rather loses sight of this deeper essence altogether. In other words, the chief intention of the Russian approach was not to plunge into the complex analysis of the objective, not to explain or to theorise, but rather to render it more accessible, more immediate, and thereby more real.

Unsurprisingly, in their attempt to respond to the changing metaphysical matrix, to move away from the rational and the objective, and to escape the confinement of the mimetic, the new generation of British authors was keen on translating this Russian idiom into their artistic approach. Accordingly, one can read the key strategy of their aesthetics in transferring the emphasis onto the intuitive and the suggestive, and in regarding self-reflexivity as the main attribute of creative engagement, or, to coin Husserl's expression, as 'the phoenix of a new life-inwardness and spiritualisation'.[120] Examples are manifold;[121] the best one, perhaps, refers to Virginia Woolf's well-known statement in 'Modern Fiction' (written in 1919, published in 1921), in which the Russian cultural oeuvre was presented as a signifier of the new literary aesthetics, as well as the best means of grasping its conceptual

120 Husserl, p. 299.

121 The scope of this book does not allow us to present the large volume of contemporary polemics regarding the mystery of the Russian soul (see Catherine Brown, 'The Russian Soul Englished', *Journal of Modern Literature* 36.1 (2012), 132–49). It is worth, however, saying some words about the original theories of Ellen Jane Harrison, whose contribution to the psychology of the Russian people caused a real sensation at the time. The scholar saw the origin of Russian spirituality in the dominance of imperfective structures in the Russian language, arguing that this implies the psychological emphasis on *how* (the quality of action) rather than on *when* (the temporal limits): 'Time is order; the Latin languages love order and are precise as to time. To the Russian quality of action is of higher importance, so he specialises in aspects' (Jane Ellen Harrison, *Russia and the Russian Verbs: A Contribution to the Psychology of the Russian People* (Cambridge: W. Heffer & Sons, 1915), p. 10). For a more detailed account see Alexandra Smith, 'Jane Harrison as an Interpreter of Russian Culture in the 1910s–1920s', in Anthony Cross, ed., *A People Passing Rude* (Cambridge: Open Book Publishers, 2012), pp. 175–88.

difference from the established canonical mode (as Woolf puts it: the contrast between 'spiritual' and 'materialistic' fiction[122]):

> Whether we call it life or spirit, truth or reality, this, the essential thing, has moved off, or on, and refuses to be contained any longer in such ill-fitting vestments as we provide [...] The most elementary remarks upon modern English fiction can hardly avoid some mention of the Russian influence, and if the Russians are mentioned one runs the risk of feeling that to write of any fiction save theirs is waste of time. If we want understanding of the soul and heart where else shall we find it of comparable profundity? If we are sick of our own materialism the least considerable of their novelists has by right of birth a natural reverence for the human spirit.[123]

By suggesting the Russian as an exponent of the modern (in Woolf's words: 'no one but a modern, no one perhaps but a Russian, could have written a story like "Gusev"'[124]), the Russian ideal was lodged, or translated, at the very centre of the English tradition as both a symbolic and phenomenological asset – a sort of *cachet* that expedites a meaningful artistic progression. Moreover, an implied added value to this asset consisted in triggering the cultural process of auto-reflection, for the very course of this aesthetic transposition exposed the struggle to make the English idiom fit the patterns of the Russian ideal. One can say that this Russian paradigm was yet again employed mainly as an effective means of self-definition by contrast, for everything that the Russian irrationality was the Western analytical mentality was not. However, this was no longer a merely Orientalistic binary of 'us' and 'them', and a juxtaposition with the apparently inferior model, but a privileged point of reference and reflection, and a means of configuring a new artistic and phenomenological stance:

> It is the saint in them [Russian writers] which confounds us with a feeling of our own irreligious triviality, and turns so many of our famous novels to tinsel and trickery

122 Virginia Woolf, 'Modern Fiction', in Virginia Woolf, *The Common Reader* (London: Vintage Classics, 2003), I, 146–54 (p. 149, 151).

123 Ibid. pp. 149–53.

124 Ibid. p. 152.

> [..] They are right perhaps; unquestionably they see further than we do and without our gross impediments of vision.[125]

The revaluation of self-image was also an integral part of the process. In this context it is worth recalling that the modernist self was an entity constructed with an inscribed will to differ in itself. Strictly speaking, the modernist revolt against the burden of convention was largely based on the rejection of the notion of Englishness, shaped and solidified in the Victorian era. It can be best illustrated by Virginia Woolf's drawing the line between the 'Georgian' and 'Edwardian' authors,[126] and thus describing the incipient shift in fiction by invoking specifically English dynastic-historical terms. Consequently, there was nothing the English modernists were more anxious about than the insufficient sense of and aptitude for the modern, which, in their view, was fully missing in the aesthetics of the established national tradition. It is not incidental, therefore, that through its conceptual engagement with the idea of the modern, the English literary branch often seemed to question the very notion of 'Englishness', and vice versa.

A process of image making rarely takes place without a reference to the external marker. This also includes the representation of the self; and the process of national auto-characterisation commonly draws on the juxtaposition with the 'other' – on the dynamic tension that the 'auto-image' and 'hetero-image' tend to put on display in the course of this reflective process.[127] Similarly, the tension between modernity and national traditionalism is rarely resolved without a third element – a conduit that serves to channel much of the anxiety onto the third external 'other', through which contemporary cultural unease can be more easily expressed. In the early decades of the twentieth century, that third term, arguably, was provided by the Russian discourse, which happened to perform a dual function of problematising the validity of the self-image, as well as serving as an

125 Ibid. p. 153.

126 Virginia Woolf, *Mr Bennett and Mrs Brown* (London: Hogarth Press, 1924).

127 Leerssen, p. 27.

'objective correlative' (to use T. S. Eliot's term[128]) for the new artistic and socio-philosophical concerns.

Some mention in this regard should be made concerning terminology and periodisation. Although modernism continues to be used as a descriptive label defining a specific historical period of literary innovation, between the 1890s and 1930s (with high modernism being associated mainly with the early inter-War years), this period, as already mentioned, was intrinsically connected with the authors' existential involvement – their often disregarded artistic commitment to respond to the major crisis of consciousness rooted in rationality and the logic of causal thinking. This response had a much broader cultural scope than the high modernist avant-garde aesthetics, and concerned a wider spectrum of authors, who were sensitive enough to feel the phenomenological impasse of the realist canonical mode and to look for the new resources, or certain new cultural assets, to effectuate this artistic and cultural change.

For many, this response was successfully negotiated through the impact of the proliferating Russian tradition. The examples include John Galsworthy internalising Turgenev's method for his own modality of artistic expression, or D. H. Lawrence rooting his socio-cultural concepts in the theories of Lev Shestov, or J. M. Barrie problematising the notion of Englishness by refracting it through the aesthetics of Diaghilev's Ballets Russes. In all these cases, discussed in the following chapters, Russian literature and art performed a modernising function within the framework of the English artistic canon, and were put on display as a form of cultural capital for those engaged in the area of aesthetic production.

The fact that not all authors in question are commonly affiliated with the high modernist avant-garde culture is, arguably, not of great significance in this context. Within the framework of Bourdieu's theories (of cultural capital and canon formation), their contribution to raising the profile of the Russian paradigm should be connected to their status as the major opinion makers of the day. Bourdieu underlines that the formation of cultural capital is inseparable from the issues of its circulation and transmission, which

128 T. S. Eliot, 'Hamlet and His Problems', in T. S. Eliot, *The Sacred Wood: Essays on Poetry and Criticism* (New York: Alfred A. Knopf, 1921), pp. 87–94 (p. 92).

makes the reception of the new idiom highly dependent on the reputation of the authors, who turn out to be the agents and the promulgators of these emerging cultural views. As John Guillory (who based his study of canonicity on the theories of Bourdieu) points out: 'canonicity is not a property of the work itself, but of its transmission, its relation to other works in a collocation of works;'[129] and a failure to recognise the narrative of reputations as a major factor in image formation would be a lapse in any examination of this cultural process.

We are therefore reluctant to make a definitive link between the reconfiguration of the Russian myth (from Orientalism to cultural capital) and the modernist formal innovations. The process, as will be shown, started quite a bit earlier and was refracted through the prism of the whole variety of artistic modes of expression. The heterogeneity of the latter is yet another factor that complicates the projection of the Russian image; for as Bourdieu put it, 'the ways in which symbolic capital circulates are rarely the same;' but 'thereby the imported text acquires its new mark;' and 'often the importance lies not in what foreign authors are saying, but in what one actually urges them to say.'[130] An attempt to account for the configuration of the image of Russia in the hands of multiple and artistically diverse literary agents is evidently a more challenging, but also a more rewarding undertaking, for it lends a surplus value of multifacetedness and depth to the projection, thus getting closer to a hologram rather than a flat imprint of the myth of Russia constructed by the British.

129 John Guillory, *Cultural Capital: The Problem of Literary Canon Formation* (Chicago: University of Chicago Press, 1993), p. 54.

130 Bourdieu, 'Les conditions sociales de la circulation internationale des idées', pp. 3–8 (p. 6, 5) (translated by the authors).

CHAPTER 2

John Galsworthy: Is It Possible to 'De-Anglicise the Englishman'?

> It is still for us to borrow from Russian literary art, and learn, if we can, to sink ourselves in life and reproduce it without obtrusion of our points of view.[1]

Galsworthy's contribution to shaping the image of Russia in British culture is difficult to overrate. In his 1927 essay 'Twelve Books – and Why?', he named *Anna Karenina* and *War and Peace* among the best pieces in the world's fiction and quoted the observation of Arnold Bennett, who was convinced that 'the twelve best novels of the world were all written by Russians'.[2] Given Galsworthy's unrivalled influence and fame at the time, such a statement was of certain significance for the British public, who for more than two decades were willing to absorb almost everything that Galsworthy published and said. By the time of Galsworthy's death in 1933, general opinion had accorded him first place among British novelists, and his most memorable creations, the Forsytes, were as warmly considered and discussed as if they had been people of flesh and blood.[3] In 1929, the readers of the *Manchester Guardian* were asked to opine on the 'Novelists Who May Be Read in A. D. 2029'. Sitting at the top of this century-hence

1 John Galsworthy, 'Englishman and Russian', in John Galsworthy, *Another Sheaf* (London: Heinemann, 1919), pp. 64–8 (p. 67).

2 John Galsworthy, 'Twelve Books – and Why?', *The Saturday Review of Literature* 6 (1927), 363–4 (p. 364).

3 When in 1922 the hard copy of the Forsyte trilogy was released in London and New York, the sales on both side of the Atlantic 'rapidly topped the million mark' (Catherine Dupré, *John Galsworthy. A Biography* (London: Collins, 1976), p. 246).

summit of popularity was John Galsworthy (defeating Wells, Bennett and Kipling by a large margin).[4]

After the resounding success of *The Man of Property* in 1906, followed by the even higher acclaim given to the premiere of *The Silver Box* (at the Court Theatre in September 1906) Galsworthy was regarded as an embodiment of the wintry conscience of the Edwardian age and 'there was a ready market for anything he wrote'.[5] Numerous public lectures that he gave struck exactly the right chord and were delivered to large and enthusiastic audiences in England and abroad: as Ada Galsworthy described their trip to the USA in 1919, 'there was, nineteen times in twenty, an immense overflow audience to whatever sized hall had been taken for him.'[6] As his fame and popularity grew, he became an eminent and highly influential man of letters. He declined a knighthood, but accepted the highest British honour, the Order of Merit, in 1929, as well as honorary doctorates from many universities. He was awarded the Nobel Prize for Literature in 1932, and characteristically he donated the award money to the P. E. N. Club, the international fellowship of writers of which he was the first President (and one of the founders in 1921), remaining in post for more than a decade. Apart from fiction, Galsworthy wrote twenty full-length plays and a number of short ones, and published numerous volumes of verse, essays and lectures. His narrative art, according to the Presentation Speech of the Nobel Committee, 'has always gently influenced contemporary notions of life and habits of thought', while his dramas showed 'an unusual richness of ideas combined with great ingenuity and technical skill in the working out of scenic effect'.[7]

This mention of gentle influence was, perhaps, a bit of an understatement, particularly with regard to the British reception of Russian authors. Due to his considerable influence on the reading public of the

4 'Novelists Who May Be Read in A. D. 2029', p. 16.

5 Dupré, p. 134.

6 Quoted in 'Galsworthy's Memories', *The Age*, 29 January 1938, p. 27; Dupré, p. 242.

7 Presentation Speech by Anders Österling, Member of the Nobel Committee of the Swedish Academy, on 10 December 1932 <http://www.nobelprize.org/nobel_prizes/literature/laureates/1932/press.html> [accessed 2 September 2016].

time, Galsworthy played a key role in the formation of the contemporary literary canon, in opening and expanding it to include the best examples of Russian writing and, thus, shaping the attitude to and the contours of what was widely looked upon as the Russian myth.

His contribution to this task can be best described as two-fold. In his extensive commentaries on the works of Turgenev and Tolstoy, Dostoevsky, Kuprin and Chekhov, he not only praised the merits of the Russian authors, but emphasised their specific impact on the evolution of Western fiction, thus creating a wave of close interest in and scrutiny of the Russian approach and according it the notion of an artistic *cachet* for those who aspired to excel in the field. 'Just as one cannot see or paint like Whistler by merely wishing to', he argued,

> so one cannot feel or write like Tchehov, because one thinks his is a nice new way [...] Tchehov appeared to be that desirable thing, the 'short cut,' and it is hardly too much to say that most of those who have taken him have never arrived [...] Writers may think they have just to put down faithfully the daily run of feeling and event and they will have a story as marvellous as those of Tchehov. Alas! Things are not made 'marvellous' by being called so, or there would be a good many 'marvellous' things to-day.[8]

Concerning his own writing, Galsworthy found inspiration in the Russian mode of literary expression; and as he had always been very open about his creative process and his narrative techniques, the Russian method gained a firm reputation on the strength of the popularity of Galsworthy's writings. Moreover, by merging the Russian aesthetics with the British literary canon, he thereby solicited certain shifts in the culturally embedded patterns of perception, preparing grounds for better understanding and aesthetic reciprocity, and paving the way for more elaborate and wider cultural interactions.

Galsworthy's attraction to Russian literature and culture predated, and was much deeper than that of many, who, as Maugham famously remarked, were 'infected' by the Russomania virus, 'hung an icon on the wall, read

8 John Galsworthy, 'Four Novelists in Profile', *English Review* 4 (1932), 485–500 (pp. 488–9).

Chekhov and went to the ballet'.[9] Ironically, a fair example of this type of 'infected fiction' can be found in Maugham's own writings of the time. Following his trip to St Petersburg in the summer of 1917, where he was introduced to political circles through Princess Alexandra (Sasha) Kropotkin, a sequence of mystically enthralling Russian duchesses proliferated in his *Ashenden* papers: 'that illusive spirit of romance ... fine eyes and a good ... voluptuous figure, high cheek bones and a snub nose ... In her dark melancholy eyes Ashenden saw the boundless steppes of Russia.'[10] Galsworthy's response to the Russian theme was in all respects different from this sentimentalised compliment to the exotic.

Galsworthy also made a trip to Russia in his mid-twenties, arranged by his father to exert a settling influence on his son's failing legal career.[11] In 1917, he produced a rather unremarkable poem, *Russia-America*, infused by the war-time patriotic spirit:

A wind in the world! O Company
Of darkened Russia, watching long in vain,
Now shall you see the cloud of Russia's pain
Go shrinking out across a summer sky.

A wind in the world! And we have come
Together, sea by sea; in all the lands
Vision doth move at last, and Freedom stands
With brightened wings, and smiles and beckons home![12]

9 Maugham, p. 273.

10 Ibid. p. 274.

Maugham met Sasha in London prior to 1914. She made a striking impression on the writer; the two even had a brief affair, and Sir Gerald Kelly, a friend of Maugham, painted Sasha's portrait. Apart from appearing as Anastasia Aleksandrovna Leonidov, in *Mr Harrington's Washing* (1928), some other instances include: the Grand Duchess Anna Aleksandrovna in the unpublished play *The Road Uphill* (1924); the Archduchess Anastasia in *Jack Straw* (1912); and another Archduchess Anastasia in *Penelope* (1912).

11 Dupré, p. 47.

12 *A Treasury of War Poetry: British and American poems of the world war, 1914–1917*, ed. George Herbert Clarke (Boston, MA and New York: Houghton Mifflin Company, 1917), p. 53.

Apart from that, neither Russia nor the Russians as such ever featured in his writings. Russian fiction was a different matter altogether. Galsworthy's engagement with it spans more than three decades; and the Russian cultural perspective, seen through the prism of the works of the Russian authors, became a persistent subject of his critical essays and reviews: 'Vague Thoughts on Art' (1911), 'A Note on Edward Garnett' (1914), 'Englishman and Russian' (1919), 'Six Novelists in Profile' (1924), and quite a few others. Offering his incisive judgement of style, narrative techniques and literary methods, he frequently invoked and interpreted the works of the Russian authors in a broader cosmopolitan cultural context, thereby highlighting the links with the European tradition and assisting in translating the Russian idiom into Western literary art. When analysing the impact of the Russian narrative on the British discourse, Galsworthy saw its contribution primarily in terms of bringing in 'the fullness of sensation' and 'intellectual honesty'[13] characteristic of the Russian approach: 'those great Russian novelists in whom I have delighted', he wrote,

> possess, before all other gifts, so deep a talent for the revelation of truth [...] The Englishman has what I would call a passion for the forms of truth [...] but has little or no regard for the spirit of truth. Quite unconsciously he [the Englishman] revels in self-deception and flies from knowledge of anything which will injure his intention to 'make good', as Americans say.[14]

It is in this deep-seated spirituality, and in this fearless sincerity that he saw the main distinction between the English and the Russian realist modes ('to the Russian it is vital to realise at all costs the fullness of sensation and reach the limits of comprehension'[15]), The latter, in his view, was more powerful in terms of its engagement with the real, revealing a broader panorama of the human condition:

13 Galsworthy, 'Englishman and Russian', p. 65, 67.

14 Ibid. pp. 64–5.

15 Ibid. p. 65.

> It is still for us to borrow from Russian literary art, and learn, if we can, to sink ourselves in life and reproduce it without obtrusion of our points of view, except in that subtle way which gives to each creative work its essential individuality. Our boisterousness in art is too self-conscious to be real, and our restraint is only a superficial legacy from Puritanism.[16]

Galsworthy himself was a keen reader of the Russian authors and helped to shape his contemporaries' taste and responses to their oeuvre. For some reason, he was of the belief that Chekhov's plays were 'never adequately performed on the English stage', and their inimitable atmosphere ('which makes the work of Tchehov memorable') could never be appropriately rendered.[17] With regard to Chekhov's prose, however, he referred to him as 'the most potent magnet to young writers' characterised by 'intense and melancholy emotionalism', and a lucid understanding of human nature.[18] Over the years Galsworthy changed his vision of Dostoevsky. In 1911, in his 'Vague Thoughts on Art', he praised his works by saying: 'no more deeply fantastic writer can I conceive than Dostoevsky'.[19] However, three years later in 'A Note on Edward Garnett', he already rated him lower than Tolstoy,[20] affirming the change of opinion in his private correspondence with Garnett (5 April 1914):

16 Ibid. pp. 67–8.

17 Galsworthy, 'Four Novelists in Profile', pp. 490–1.

18 Ibid. p. 488.

19 John Galsworthy, 'Vague Thoughts on Art', in John Galsworthy, *The Inn of Tranquillity* (New York: Charles Scriber's Sons, 1912), pp. 254–76 (p. 272).
The same opinion is conveyed in Galsworthy's letters at that time. He expressed a wish (24 April 1910) to read Dostoevsky's *The Idiot*, *The Possessed*, and *The Brothers Karamazov* (which he read in French the same year – a present from Constance Garnett (12 May 1910)) and agreed 'that Tolstoy and Dostoevsky reach places which Turgenev doesn't even attempt.' He also praised *The Dead House* as 'splendid' (1 May 1910) (John Galsworthy, *Letters from John Galsworthy 1900–1932*, ed. Edward Garnett (London: Jonathan Cape, 1934), pp. 177–9). For a more detailed account of Galsworthy's perception of Dostoevsky, see Kaye, pp. 169–74.

20 John Galsworthy, 'A Note on Edward Garnett', in *Forsytes, Pendyces and Others* (New York: Charles Scribner's Sons, 1935), pp. 185–7 (p. 186).

> I am reading *The Brothers Karamazov* a second time; and [...] I'm bound to say it doesn't wash. Amazing in places, of course; but my God! – what incoherence and what verbiage, and what starting of monsters to make you shudder.[21]

In 1932, shortly before his death, there came another cold note on the Russian author. Galsworthy remarked that he kept reading Dostoevsky, finding him 'an interesting (and in some sort irritating) writer', inferior to Tolstoy both as a philosopher and an artist. He doubted Dostoevsky's universality and importance, but acknowledged his overall contribution to the development of literary endeavour: 'His insight was deep and his fecundity remarkable. I think he will live.'[22]

Among the group of Russian realists, to whom Galsworthy lent particular significance, Tolstoy and Turgenev stood out: the former as a major subject of Galsworthy's critical commentaries; the latter – as a prime inspiration of his own artistic method.

The first reference to Tolstoy is in Galsworthy's debut novel *Jocelyn* (1898). When the main character, Giles Legard, enters his wife's bedroom, his sight falls on 'the little table by the couch': there 'were the books she had been reading – Tolstoy's *The Kingdom of God is Within You* – three roses, a medicine glass and a bottle'.[23] Galsworthy must have read *The Kingdom of God* before 1898, in French translation, or probably in Constance Garnett's version from 1893. His knowledge of and esteem for the Russian author are apparent from his letters. To give but a few examples, it is worth noting the letter to Constance Garnett (10 May 1902) concerning her translation of *Anna Karenina* (Heinemann 1901), in which he remarks: 'I'm inclined to think that Tolstoy will go down to posterity on the same mark

21 Galsworthy, Letter to Edward Garnett, 5 April 1914, *Letters from John Galsworthy 1900–1932*, p. 217.
In another letter to Garnett, criticising the young D. H. Lawrence's *Sons and Lovers*, he remarks 'PS – Confound all those young fellows; how they have gloated over Dostoevsky' (Galsworthy, Letter to Edward Garnett, 13 April 1914, *Letters from John Galsworthy*, p. 219).

22 Harold V. Marrot, *The Life and Letters of John Galsworthy* (London: Heinemann, 1935), p. 804.

23 John Galsworthy, *Jocelyn* (New York: Holt, Rinehart and Winston, 1977), p. 79.

as Shakespeare', and quotes Edward Garnett as saying that Tolstoy's art 'touches a new and deeper degree of self-consciousness and therefore of analysis'.[24] In the same letter, as well as in his subsequent correspondence (6 April 1903, 18 July 1908, 3 April 1914), he conveys his keen interest in Tolstoy's works (*The Cossacks*, *War and Peace*, the open 'Letter on Executions'), emphasising the depth of Russian spirituality, especially as compared to the Naturalist mode: 'The body's never worthwhile [...] the men we swear by, Tolstoy, Turgenev, Chekhov [...] knew that great truth; they only use the body, and that sparingly, to reveal the soul.'[25]

As regards his critical essays, Tolstoy is often presented as the utmost embodiment of the Russian tradition – 'the greatest of the Russians'.[26] Galsworthy saw in him a unique mixture of a philosopher and an artist – a fascinating (and even puzzling) amalgamation of a strictly defined ideological platform and intense sincerity unequalled in the British canon:

> Tolstoy is a fascinating puzzle. So singular an instance of artist and reformer rolled into one frame is not, I think, elsewhere to be found [...] About his work, in fact, is an ever present sense of spiritual duality. It is a battlefield on which we watch the ebb and flow of unending conflict, the throb and stress of a gigantic disharmony.[27]

This combination resulted in the striking breadth and depth of social analysis, on the one hand, and in the unparalleled intimacy and freshness of expression – on the other:

24 Galsworthy, Letter to Constance Garnett, 10 May 1902, *Letters from John Galsworthy*, p. 36.

25 Galsworthy, Letters to Edward Garnett, 6 April 1903, 18 July 1908, 3 April 1914, *Letters from John Galsworthy*, p. 48, 166, 218. This letter (3 April 1914) concerns specifically D. H. Lawrence's novel *Sons and Lovers*.

26 Galsworthy, 'A Note on Edward Garnett', p. 186. In his letter to Edward Garnett, he places Tolstoy much higher than Dostoevsky, whose fame at the time was on the rise (Galsworthy, Letter to Edward Garnett, 5 April 1914, *Letters from John Galsworthy*, p. 217).

27 John Galsworthy, 'Six Novelists in Profile', in *Castles in Spain and other Screeds* (London: Heinemann, 1927), pp. 145–71 (p. 157).

> Tolstoy a stylist; for no author, in his story-telling, produces a more intimate feeling of actual life. He is free, in fact, from the literary self-consciousness which so often spoils the work of polished writers. Tolstoy was carried away by his impulses, whether creative or reformative.[28]

This is not to say that Galsworthy always agreed with Tolstoy's track of thinking and ideas. He was very dismissive of Tolstoy's interpretation of the value and *raison d'être* of art ('What is Art?', 1898) as something drawn exclusively from popular appreciation, 'raising up the masses of mankind', as Galsworthy put it, 'to be a definite new Judge'. 'This, at all events', he argued, 'is as far as I dare go in defining what Art is.'[29] He also failed to relate to Tolstoy's later works, impregnated with 'religious fanaticism' and moral preaching,[30] observing regretfully that 'the preacher in him [Tolstoy], who took such charge of his later years, was already casting a shadow over the artist-writer of *Anna Karenina*'.[31]

Despite these differences, however, Tolstoy's works always featured in Galsworthy's critique as the best examples of realist writing, which, he believed, were particularly close to the sensibility of British readers, due to their similarities with the novels of Dickens. Among others, Galsworthy clearly viewed Tolstoy as the most 'English' of the Russian authors, and the parallels with Dickens, regarding captivating plotlines, psychological insights and the depth of social analysis, were persistently underscored in his reviews. Thus, in the 1912 'Introduction to *Bleak House*', Galsworthy remarked that 'the sort of passion that Dickens inspired in him was matched by only seven other novelists', among whom Tolstoy was listed;[32] and later, in 'Six Novelists in Profile', he claimed that Tolstoy's

28 Galsworthy, 'Six Novelists in Profile', p. 158.
29 Galsworthy, 'Vague Thoughts on Art', p. 256.
30 Galsworthy, 'A Note on Edward Garnett', p. 186.
31 Galsworthy, 'Six Novelists in Profile', p. 157.
32 John Galsworthy, 'Introduction to "Bleak House"', in *Forsytes, Pendyces and Others* (New York: Charles Scribner's Sons, 1935), pp. 199–201 (p. 199).

> native force is proved by the simple fact that, taking up again one of his stories after the lapse of many years, one will remember almost every paragraph. Dickens and Dumas are perhaps the only other writers who compare with him in this respect.'[33]

Tolstoy's *War and Peace* was described by Galsworthy as the 'greatest novel ever written':

> The secret of his triumph lies in the sheer interest with which his creative energy has invested every passage. The book is six times as long as an ordinary novel, but it never flags, never wearies the reader, and the ground – of human interest, and historical event, of social life and national life – covered in it, is prodigious.[34]

Such a choice, as well as such an accolade are, perhaps, not entirely surprising, for there are major typological and thematic parallels between Galsworthy's *The Forsyte Saga* and Tolstoy's epic novel. Both works are largely conceived as tantamount to an *'Iliad'* of their time, exploring the questions of national and personal identity, as well as those related to the deeper insights in human nature put to the test in trying circumstances of man's own making: war-torn Russia in *War and Peace*, and the pragmatic world of property in *The Forsyte Saga*. As Galsworthy put it in his preface to the first complete edition of the novel, 'the Forsytean tenacity' with possessive instincts and the sense of property 'is still in all of us'.[35] Moreover, curious as it may seem, both works, commonly attributed to realist prose, essentially put forward the notion of the irrational as the only way to withstand the dehumanising pressure of the practical and the collective (through such characters as Pierre Bezukhov and Natasha in Tolstoy; and Irene and young Jolyon Forsyte in Galsworthy). Could this, to a certain extent, be seen as an attempt to conduct a dialogue with the Russian author? This is hard to answer without indulging in speculation, but one can certainly refer to Galsworthy's keen interest in and affiliation with the Russian cultural tradition of privileging the security of subconscious knowledge and the

33 Galsworthy, 'Six Novelists in Profile', pp. 160–1.

34 Ibid. p. 157.

35 John Galsworthy, Preface to *The Forsyte Saga* (London: Heinemann, 1922), pp. ix–x (p. ix).

comfort of intuitive perception (a cornerstone in the philosophical writings of Tolstoy).

A number of other typological similarities that spring to mind when comparing Tolstoy's and Galsworthy's writings include an attempt to depict the panoramic socio-historical layers through the microcosm of a family saga (such as the Rostovs and the Bolkonskies in *War and Peace*), and to show social degradation and corruption by means of generational juxtapositions. The latter can be best exemplified by Tolstoy's story *Two Hussars* (1856), portraying the old Count Turbin and his son. Twenty years apart, they enact the same sequence of card playing, drinking, and philandering in the same small town. Their characters, however, differ drastically: the father is gallant, generous, honourable and charming; the son is mean, cold, cowardly and scheming. The father's temperament is natural and open (giving his last pennies to the coachman, saving the life of the young cornet Il'in); the son's is devious and pragmatic ('You must look on life in a practical way, or else you will always be a fool'[36]). In Galsworthy's saga, the same juxtaposition is reflected in the figures of old Jolyon and Soames Forsyte; and in the same vein, the author's allegiance lies with the hopelessly generous and the awkwardly authentic.

From a thematic angle, it is worth highlighting such intertextual echoes as the failed marriage of Irene to Soames Forsyte, and her difficulties in obtaining a divorce, which refer to the circumstances of Anna and Karenin.[37] Shelton's 'moral conversion' in *The Island Pharisees* invites a comparison with Nekhludov's epiphany after Katiusha's trial in *Resurrection*: in both cases a powerful inner protest against the falseness of the middle-class world is triggered by a seemingly incidental, but extremely high-pitched emotive encounter. Finally, one ought to mention the big oak tree at the Robin Hill house – a spiritual compass for its inhabitants:

36 Lyof Tolstoï, 'Two Hussars', in *The Russian Proprietor and Other Stories*, trans. Nathan Haskell Dole (New York: Thomas Crowell, 1887), pp. 190–286 (p. 274).

37 These circumstances also resonated in Galsworthy's personal situation: his wife, Ada, had difficulties in obtaining a divorce from her first husband.

> Trees take little account of Time, and the old oak on the upper lawn at Robin Hill looked no day older than when Bosinney sprawled under it and said to Soames: 'Forsyte, I've found the very place for your house',[38]

bringing to mind the iconic oak tree of the Bolkonskies' family estate – a symbolic mouthpiece for Prince Andrei's inner commotions:

> As he passed through the forest Prince Andrew turned several times to look at that oak, as if expecting something from it [...] 'Yes, the oak is right, a thousand times right', thought Prince Andrew. 'Let others – the young – yield afresh to that fraud, but we know life, our life is finished!'[39]

Given all these parallels and thematic echoes, Galsworthy's later attempt to distance himself from the influence of the Russian author sounds somewhat disingenuous, not to say odd. 'I still do read Tolstoy', he wrote not long before his death in 1932, 'and I wish I had more time to do so. But I read him as a master novelist, not as a preacher. I do not think his art or his ethics have ever influenced me.'[40] Such a remark grates on the ear as a blatant understatement, some sort of self-deception or even a pose; and yet there was a lot of penetrating truth in Galsworthy's confession. As much as he admired Tolstoy's achievement and guided British readers to absorb this new type of fiction into their reading experience and their literary world, Tolstoy's artistry *per se* hardly produced any formative effect on Galsworthy's aesthetics, either on his creative pursuits or on his mode of expression. Tolstoy's method, as Galsworthy described it,

> is cumulative – the method of an infinity of facts and pictorial detail: the opposite to Turgenev's, who relied on selection and concentration on atmosphere and poetic balance. Tolstoy fills in all the space and leaves little to the imagination; but with such vigour; such freshness, that it is all interesting.[41]

38 John Galsworthy, *The Forsyte Saga* (London: Heinemann, 1922), p. 458.

39 Leo Tolstoy, *War and Peace*, trans. Louise and Aylmer Maude (Chicago and London: William Benton, 1952), p. 236.

40 Marrot, p. 803.

41 Galsworthy, 'Six Novelists in Profile', p. 159.

This method, largely based on intimacy and directness, and on breaking the barriers of self-consciousness in the flow of the writer's thought, had, in Galsworthy's opinion, a revitalising impact on the development of Western prose. However, being an example of work that 'bears the impress of a mind more concerned with the thing said than with the way to say it',[42] it did not offer much in terms of new narrative paradigms and aesthetic innovation, and in this sense did not present a radical enough departure from the established realist literature of fact. In his formative years as an emerging literary figure, Galsworthy was looking for a more suggestive and intuitive approach.

The author who did become the major building stone of Galsworthy's own development as a writer was Ivan Turgenev, whose artistic viewpoint, style and poetics found their deepest reflection in Galsworthy's creativity and literary explorations. To describe this as mapping the Russian paradigm onto British writing would be, perhaps, too plain an expression, for it was a truly appropriated and internalised concept of Turgenev's aesthetics that was transmitted to the British readership through Galsworthy's work.

In order to look into this in more detail, it is worth going back to Galsworthy's early years – to the time when no-one could possibly have seen in him a world-famous writer or indeed any kind of writer at all.

Late nineteenth-century Britain was a culture transformed by mass production, sweeping waves of immigration and scientific theories that rent asunder the stasis and security of older beliefs.[43] The phenomenal rise in England's national income, expansion of its trade, emergence of a capital class, and a widespread growth of the towns – were some of the visible effects of the industrial revolution. At the same time simmering anger and resent-

42 Ibid. p. 159.

43 By the end of the 1880s such works as Nietzsche's *Gay Science* (1882–7) with his contention that God is dead, and Richard von Krafft-Ebing's revolutionary texts on sexuality (1886) had already been published. Darwin's *On the Origin of Species* appeared in 1859 and *Essays and Reviews* (edited by J. W. Parker), which questioned the Bible as revealed history, in 1860. In the period from 1865 to 1870, Karl Marx began publishing *Das Kapital*, Alfred Nobel invented dynamite, the foundations of quantum physics were laid in the works of Michael Faraday and Heinrich Herz – all challenging the absolutist theories of truth.

ment stirred up gradually in people's minds concerned with the pragmatic rationalism and dehumanisation of the age. With the loss of monolithic certainty formerly derived from such sources as the myth of national unity, religion and art, the expansion of historical and progressive knowledge (the so-called march of the mind) led to the crisis in faith.[44] As William James observed in 1909, looking back at these turn-of-the-century years:

> 'The same returns not, save to bring the different.' Time keeps budding into new moments, every one of which presents a content which in its individuality never was before and will never be again. Of no concrete bit of experience was an exact duplicate ever framed.[45]

The emerging conflict between humanistic aesthetics and the force of an ascendant materialism in ideology and science brought to light the crisis of the traditional realist literature of fact and the morality of action, which could no longer reflect the developments in contemporary thinking, the changing ethos and the shifts in the socio-cultural field. The realist approach found its most defiant opponents in the aesthetic decadence of Oscar Wilde. As keen explorers of the human spirit, the Aesthetes, grouping around the Rhymers' Club (1890–5)[46] and *The Yellow Book* journal (1894–7), saw nineteenth-century progress, pragmatism and prosperity as forces destructive to humanism and imagination; and even indulgence in the abominable and the forbidden became a proof of man's superiority to the natural condition. In the words of Karl Beckson, who traced the history of the movement: 'The courage to do this was considerable [...] and the danger of failure made life a perilous, though extraordinary, adventure.'[47]

44 Frank M. Turner, 'The Victorian Crisis of Faith and the Faith that Was Lost', in Richard J. Helmstadter and Bernard Lightman, eds, *Victorian Faith in Crisis* (Stanford, CA: Stanford University Press, 1990), pp. 9–38 (p. 10).

45 William James, *Some Problems of Philosophy* (Longmans: Green and Co, New York, 1911), pp. 147–8.

46 The members of the Club included Ernest Dowson, Lionel Johnson, Arthur Symons, Richard Le Gallienne, and Yeats, who had helped to found it.

47 Karl Beckson, Introduction, in *Aesthetes and Decadents of the 1890s: An Anthology of British Poetry and Prose*, ed. Karl Beckson (Chicago: Academy Chicago Publishers, 1981), pp. xxi–xliv (p. xliv).

And although the turn of the century saw the movement fading away, its attempt 'to resist a civilisation intent on debasing the imagination' made a strong impact on the new emerging cohort of literary authors.[48]

By the time Galsworthy's generation made their entrance on the literary scene (the end of the 1890s), Wilde's interest in the mysterious uncertainty of the visible, the phenomenal and the real was considerably heightened by the progress of theoretical and quantum physics which questioned the causal model of the world. Developments in medical and social psychology, especially the work of Freud, and Jung and Sir James Frazer's *The Golden Bough* (1890), stressed the active role of the unconscious, turning it into thematic material for literature and art.

The framework of the traditional realist novel appeared to be considerably disrupted. The relationship between the internal and external gained in complexity, blurring the ways in which realist literature used to project its general idea of the moral. The notion of morality as related to and expressed through one's actions – in its straightforward Aristotelian sense:[49] the person is defined by what he does – had lost its clarity, as well as its relevance to the late nineteenth-century ethos. As one of Thomas Hardy's characters claimed (*Tess of the D'Urbervilles*, 1891): 'The beauty or

48 Ibid. p. xliv.
According to Beckson, 'the Imagist Movement (launched before World War I by T. E. Hulme, Ezra Pound, Richard Aldington, and others), the work of James Joyce and T. S. Eliot, and the development of the New Criticism have all felt the influence of late nineteenth-century Aestheticism' (p. xliv).

49 In *Nicomachean Ethics* it is made particularly clear that morality cannot be achieved without action: 'the things we have to learn before we can to do, we learn by doing, e.g. men become builders by building and lyre players by playing the lyre; so too we become just by doing just acts, temperate by doing temperate acts, brave by doing brave acts' (Aristotle, 'Nicomachean Ethics', in *Complete Works of Aristotle*, ed. Jonathan Barnes (Princeton, NJ: Princeton University Press, 1995), II, 1729–867 (p, 1743)). In this context, one can also recollect Yeats' definition of the 'character isolated by a deed' (W. B. Yeats, 'The Circus Animals' Desertion', in Richard J. Finneran, ed., *The Collected Works of W. B. Yeats* (New York: Scribner's Sons, 1997), I, 356). For a more detailed study of this subject see Stefanie Markovits, *The Crisis of Action in Nineteenth-century English Literature* (Columbus: The Ohio State University Press, 2006).

ugliness of a character lay not only in its achievements, but in its aims and impulses; its true history lay, not among things done, but among things willed.'[50]

Inaction – both frustrated external action (with its considerable potential for character building), and heightened mental aspiration – fascinated the new generation of realist authors, who, being more interested in the internal psychological experience rather than in the outward surrounding reality, were trying to find their way in exploring the notion and the mechanisms of consciousness as the morality of thought. What exactly constitutes the sense of self, if action has lost its ability to be the prime signifier of one's ethos? Does a literary work have the means to articulate and to connect to this inner thinking; and what indeed would a narrative shaped by such concerns look like?

This increased emphasis on the human psyche, on the importance of the irrational and the subconscious, drew attention to the avenues of the Russian realist tradition, which was characteristically embedded in the idea of the so-called emotional 'inner knowledge', in the juxtaposition of desire and ethos, and in the analysis of internalisation, sensation, and repression (prominent in the works of Dostoevsky and Tolstoy). As Lev Shestov, an eminent Russian philosopher of the time, argued in his essay on Dostoevsky (1903), 'knowledge and reason had not brought man to freedom, but had only succeeded in delivering man to his fate; after all, 'hope had not been supported by doctrine, but vice versa, doctrine, by hope'.[51]

No single case in the 1890s represents a stronger predilection for this Russian viewpoint than that of Galsworthy. In his attempt to go deeper beyond the visible and the external, to develop a more suggestive and

50 Thomas Hardy, *Tess of the D'Urbervilles* (Peterborough and London: Broadview Press, 1985), p. 343.

51 Lev Shestov, 'Dostoevsky and Nietzsche: The Philosophy of Tragedy', in Lev Shestov, *Dostoevsky, Tolstoy and Nietzsche*, ed. Bernard Martin (Columbus: Ohio State University Press, 1969), pp. 141–322 (p. 174). Shestov viewed Dostoevsky's *Notes from the Underground* as a bona fide critique of pure reason, which established that man's freedom lay not in the kingdom of reason but in its abdication: 'there ends for man the thousand-year reign of "reason and consciousness"; a new era begins – that of "psychology"' (Shestov, p. 174).

evocative approach, Galsworthy saw the examples of the Russian authors as a catalysing stimulus for the evolution of Western prose. 'Under Jane Austen, Dickens, Balzac, Stendhal, Scott, Dumas, Thackeray and Hugo', he wrote,

> the novel attained a certain relation of part to whole; but it was left for one of more poetic feeling and greater sensibility than any of these to perfect its proportions, and introduce the principle of selection, until there was that complete relation of part to whole which goes to the making of what we call a work of art. This writer was Turgenev, as supreme in the art of the novel as Dickens was artless.[52]

Not unlike Henry James, who called Turgenev 'the novelists' novelist',[53] Galsworthy found his true inspiration in Turgenev's writings, which were instrumental for his formation as a writer and remained central for his lifelong literary pursuits. As Ford Madox Ford colourfully described it,

> I must have asked myself a hundred times in my life, if there had been no Turgenev, what would have become of Galsworthy? [...] Or, though that is the way the question was always put to me, it might be truer to the thought I want to express to say: What would Galsworthy have become?[54]

According to Galsworthy's own account, he began reading Turgenev (in English) at the very outset of his literary career, at the time when his first attempts at fiction (a collection of stories *From the Four Winds* and the novel *Jocelyn* published under the pseudonym of John Sinjohn) caused him great dissatisfaction, and were met only with a lukewarm polite reception from Edward Garnett – a renowned contemporary critic, who as a publisher's reader (Fisher Unwin, Gerald Duckworth and Jonathan Cape), exercised over literature a far greater influence than might be surmised from his own

52 Galsworthy, 'Six Novelists in Profile', p. 150.

53 Henry James, *The House of Fiction. Essays on the Novel*, ed. Leon Edel (London: Rupert Hart-Davis, 1957), p. 170.

54 Ford Madox Ford, *Portraits from Life* (London: Houghton Mifflin Company, 1937), p. 124.

fiction and critical publications.[55] Garnett's reader reports on Galsworthy at the time drew attention to the lack of artistry, awkwardness of style and ineptitude of literary form.[56] In this sense of deficiency, Galsworthy recalls in *Glimpses and Reflections*, he turned to the works of Maupassant and Turgenev, which led to a major breakthrough in his command of narrative techniques:

> I had been writing four years, and had spent about a hundred pounds on it. About that time I began to read the Russian Turgenev (in English) and the Frenchman Maupassant in French. They were the first writers who gave me at once real aesthetic excitement, and an insight into proportion of theme and economy of words. Stimulated by them I began a second novel *Villa Rubein*.[57]

It is worth pointing out that Galsworthy's acceptance of Edward Garnett as his first critic and literary mentor owed much to their shared appreciation of Turgenev's writing as an example of mastery and a standard by which one might judge his own literary work.[58] The effect was one of succinctness, temperance and harmony – the qualities that Garnett valued above all in Turgenev's style and highlighted in Galsworthy's *Villa Rubein* by saying that the novel showed 'the disciple's devotion to the master on every page.'[59] Galsworthy's *Villa Rubein* does indeed refer most strikingly to this particular source of inspiration, noted repeatedly by a number of scholars specialising in Turgenev's impact on the European literary world. Thus, Glyn Turton observed that in its plot structure, characterisation and narrative tone, the novel's similarities with *On the Eve* were difficult to overlook:

55 Through extensive reading, Garnett developed a nearly unerring ability to recognise genuine and original literary talent. Among the authors he discovered or befriended were Joseph Conrad, D. H. Lawrence, John Galsworthy, Ford Madox Ford, and W. H. Hudson (Cedric Watts, 'Edward Garnett's Influence on Conrad', *The Conradian* 21.1 (1996), 79–91).

56 George Jefferson, *Edward Garnett. A Life in Literature* (London: Jonathan Cape, 1982), pp. 109–10.

57 John Galsworthy, *Glimpses and Reflections* (Leipzig: Tauchnitz, 1937), p. 154.

58 Dupré, *John Galsworthy*, p. 80.

59 Edward Garnett, Introduction, *Letters from John Galsworthy 1900–1932*, ed. Edward Garnett (London: Jonathan Cape, 1934), pp. 5–16 (p. 8).

> the love of Christian, the heroine, for the artist-anarchist, Harz, maintained in the face of her family's opposition resembles that of Elena for Insarov: Harz himself and the thinly characterised Dawney resemble, in the contrasting types which they represent, the much more substantially realised Shubin and Bersenev.[60]

Along the same lines, Gilbert Phelps[61] drew attention to the thematic framework of Galsworthy's stories, largely borrowed, in his view, from Turgenev's *Torrents of Spring* (1871) and *The First Love* (1860): an elderly man recalls the most memorable emotional experience of his past, and the use of 'flash-back' technique in each case heightens the aching sense of the irrevocable loss. Not unlike Sanin (*The Torrents of Spring*), the conditioning of his class causes Swithin (*The Salvation of Swithin Forsyte*, 1900) to abandon his beloved Rozsi, realising at the end that he had turned his back on what, perhaps, mattered most in his existence ('aloud in his sleep, Swithin muttered: "I've missed something"'[62]). Swithin's fascination with Rozsi evokes Sanin's chivalrous courtship of Gemma, and Count Kasteliz's jealousy of Swithin brings to mind that of Herr Klüber. The same matrix is reiterated in 'The Apple Tree' of 1916 – the story of an upper-class undergraduate Frank Ashurst and a simple girl Megan, where Galsworthy yet again drew chiefly on the pattern of Turgenev's novellas:

> he had stumbled on a buried memory, a wild sweet time, swiftly choked and ended. And, turning on his face, he rested his chin on his hands, and stared at the short grass where the little blue milkwort was growing [...] And this is what he remembered.[63]

The description of Frank Ashurst's emotional climax after his first rendezvous with Megan clearly reproduces the experience of the young narrator of Turgenev's *First Love*; and, in the same way as Sanin, he feels 'to the full the sensations of chivalry and passion. Because she was not of his world, because she was so simple and young and headlong, adoring and defenceless,

60 Turton, p. 170.
61 Phelps, p. 116.
62 John Sinjohn, 'The Salvation of a Forsyte', in John Sinjohn, *A Man of Devon* (Edinburgh and London: W. Blackwood and Sons, 1901), pp. 109–86 (p. 184).
63 John Galsworthy, 'The Apple Tree', in *Five Tales* (London: William Heinemann, 1918), pp. 187–260 (p. 190).

how could he be other than her protector.'[64] Ashurst too leaves his beloved on what is intended to be a temporary absence in order to make necessary arrangements for the marriage, during which, yet again in a fashion similar to Sanin, he meets an old friend belonging to 'his world', which marks the turning point leading to the betrayal.[65]

The parallels are numerous, wide-ranging and extensive; it is not unlikely after all that Irene Forsyte gets her name from one of the main characters in Turgenev's *Smoke*, Irina Osinin. Galsworthy's long-term admiration for Turgenev was discussed by many of his contemporaries and scholars, mainly in terms of point-for-point comparison of plot, theme and characterisation.[66] What remains largely outside these keen and thoroughly conducted studies are the reasons for and the deeper implications of these intertextual associations, as well as those of Galsworthy's profound interest in engaging with and drawing from the aesthetics of Turgenev's works. This interest evidently exceeded the loyalty of an impressionable disciple. As Gilbert Phelps insightfully observed, Turgenev's influence goes far beyond the patterns of Galsworthy's early stories: it is equally traceable all the way through his mature writings when the literary fashion was largely dominated by the newly burgeoning fever for the works of Dostoevsky and Tolstoy.[67] Ada Galsworthy also substantiated the claim of Turgenev's authority over her husband's fiction, remarking (in a letter to Scribner's in 1936) that Galsworthy was 'unconscious of any other influence on his style of work, apart from *Turgenev* and *Maupassant*, his only schoolmasters'.[68]

64 Galsworthy, 'The Apple Tree', pp. 221–2.

65 Boleskey, the Hungarian nationalist (and Rozsi's father in *The Salvation of Swihin Forsyte*), recalls the Bulgarian revolutionary Insarov; while Rozsi's devotion to her father's cause has something in common with the selfless dedication of Elena. Boleskey's quarrel with the Austrian officer in the café suggests Insarov's argument with the Germans during the excursion to Tsaritsino; and the exact mood and atmosphere of his fist encounter with Elena is echoed in Ashurst's and Megan's rendezvous in the moonlit orchard (Phelps, p. 116).

66 Gettmann, pp. 112–25; Turton, pp. 170–3; Kaye, p. 169.

67 Phelps, p. 123.

68 James Gindin, *John Galsworthy's Life and Art* (London: Macmillan, 1987), p. 98.

In his pioneering work on Turgenev's reception in America and England, Royal Gettmann attempted to link Galsworthy's fascination with Turgenev to the likeness of their social affiliations. He noted that both were

> cultivated gentlemen, formally educated, fond of sports, and possessed of an inheritance. But neither were in spiritual accord with the class whence he came, for Turgenev shunned the government service and Galsworthy gave up the legal profession. At the same time they could not throw themselves into a cause, though they were extremely sensitive to the plight of the oppressed, and fearful of the future.[69]

Although largely true in biographical details, this explanation is not entirely convincing. Firstly, because Galsworthy's reverence for Turgenev had come to prominence before he inherited his father's fortune, thereby acquiring financial freedom comparable to that of the Russian author. It was not until *The Island Pharisees* (1904) that, owing to the death of his father, Galsworthy began publishing under his own name. Secondly, as regards their common sensitivity to the plight of the oppressed, Gettmann himself affirms further in his study that this sentiment was not one of the undisputed strengths of Galsworthy's novels. In distinction to Turgenev's sense of utmost desperation, masterfully conjured in *Mumu* or *A Sportsman's Sketches*, it has an element of false pretence in Galsworthy's setting, where pity is squandered on much better off middle-class subjects, such as, for instance, Bossiney and Irene Forsyte. 'Often his subject was out of proportion to the volume and pitch of the emotion', which, in Gettmann's view, 'is sentimentality'.[70] To enhance the point he grounds his observation in Frank Swinnerton's claim that 'Turgenev was at bottom a poet [whereas] Galsworthy was at heart a gentleman.'[71]

69 Gettmann, pp. 178–9.

70 Ibid. p. 179.
This must also have been Conrad's impression when, in writing to Galsworthy about *Fraternity*, he compared Turgenev's misfits Rudin and Nezhdanov, to Hilary, and found the latter essentially contrived: 'One asks oneself what that unfortunate creature was afraid of losing' (Marrot, p. 233).

71 Frank Swinnerton, *The Georgian Scene* (London: Farrar & Rinehart, 1934), p. 194.

Swinnerton, in fact, was one of the first to point out back in the 1930s that Galsworthy turned to Russia, and specifically to Turgenev, for his literary inspiration; and described their kinship as 'a kind of trembling emotion' permeating the works of both authors.[72] It is, perhaps, worth dwelling on this comment a while longer, for it was indeed this element of spiritual, almost irrational affinity that Galsworthy persistently put forward when describing his intimacy with Turgenev's writings. In *The Inn of Tranquillity* he claimed that 'no greater poet [Turgenev] ever wrote in prose;'[73] and in *Castles in Spain and other Screeds* he went on to say that he owed a great debt to Turgenev for his 'spiritual and technical apprenticeship [...] and the deep kinship in spirit'.[74] What Swinnerton, arguably, termed as a commonality of the 'trembling emotion' was a holistic unison of aesthetics, and a shared understanding of the literary craft as an exploration of human psychology and 'spirit', to coin the term favoured later by British modernist authors.[75]

As a man of letters, Galsworthy developed his career in an era of cultural transition. In an attempt to find his own path within the network of competing trends of the 1890s, he was ready to adopt (more likely intuitively than through rational considerations) the Russian author's viewpoint, his method and his mode of expression, because he saw in it a framework of viable responses – for him, the only meaningful responses to the shifting values of realist art. To discuss this framework in greater detail, the main features of Turgenev's (and, as will be shown, Galsworthy's) writing should be considered from a closer perspective. They include: the absence of an action-driven plotline; the representativeness and typicality of characters;

72 Swinnerton, p. 194. Swinnerton remarked perceptively that Galsworthy's early works were written 'directly in imitation of the novels of Turgenev' (Swinnerton, p. 192; see also Gettmann, p. 178).

73 John Galsworthy, *The Inn of Tranquillity* (London: Heinemann, 1927), p. 272.

74 Galsworthy, 'Six Novelists in Profile', pp. 152–3.

75 The term was introduced by Virginia Woolf in her essay of 1923 *Mr Bennett and Mrs Brown*, where she condemned writers of the previous generation (including Galsworthy, H. G. Wells and Arnold Bennett) for being profoundly materialistic – concerned 'not with the spirit, but with the body', spending 'immense skill and immense industry making the trivial and the transitory appear the true and the enduring' (Woolf, *Mr Bennett and Mrs Brown*, p. 22).

impersonal narrative, lacking a clearly defined moral message, and the unity of background with characters' emotional state and theme.[76]

Firstly, it is worth pointing out that Turgenev's novels are not based on a strongly defined plotline. In an attempt to render the content of *Smoke* (1867), *Virgin Soil* (1877), *A Nest of Gentlefolk* (1859), or even *Fathers and Sons* (1862), the reader is struck by the complete absence of chains of causality that in any realist novel are traditionally regarded as the main means of binding the plot. One realises, paradoxically, that in Turgenev all elements that constitute the plotline are cemented not by the governing principle of formal logic, but by a series of chances, some kind of fortuitous coincidence and, in some cases, even the irony of fate. This is, partly, why Yuri Lotman, a major Russian structuralist scholar, argued that the works of Turgenev brought in a strong demythologising trend in the old realist novelistic schemes available at the time; they operated contrary to the commonly adopted myth structure, for the function of myth consists in rising above 'the chaotic accidentality of empirical life, sublimating it to a logically thought-through model'.[77]

In this sense, Turgenev's novels present vivid examples of a viable alternative to what Stephanie Markovitz calls a traditional 'myth-type' or 'action based' novel (typical, for instance, of Dickens), which, according to her study, was developed in response to the 'crisis of action' in realist end-of-the-nineteenth-century prose.[78] The decade of the 1890s, she points out, was the period when the outward actions stopped being the ultimate

76 Turgenev's writing made a strong impact on the development of the European novel of the 1890s; and the main features of his prose are also traceable in the works of Flaubert, Zola and Henry James.

77 Yuri M. Lotman, 'Siuzhetnoe prostranstvo russkogo romana XIX stoletiia', in Yuri M. Lotman, *Izbrannye stat'I* (Tallinn: Aleksandra, 1993), III, 91–106 (p. 105).

78 Markovits, pp. 1–2. As Markovitz puts it, the writers were responding to, and frequently reversing the familiar dictum set out by Aristotle in his *Poetics*: 'All human happiness or misery takes the form of action, the end for which we live is a certain kind of activity, not a quality. Character gives us qualities, but it is in our actions – what we do – that we are happy or the reverse. In a play accordingly they do not act in order to portray the Characters; they include the Characters for the sake of the action' (Ibid.).

indicator of the moral, focusing attention on the interplay of consciousness and ethos, the inner desires and the morality of life. This is how Henry James (a great admirer, not to say a follower, of Turgenev's method) explains his idea of *The Portrait of the Lady* (1881), which, according to the author's Preface of 1908, was prompted by his decision to replace external action with 'an exciting' inward life, marking an 'ado' out of fairly little to do, and producing 'the maximum of intensity with the minimum of strain'.[79]

Morality and ethos in Turgenev's novels are in no way related to the action; on the contrary, the meaningful lives and laudable deeds of his characters are most commonly crowned by their inconsequential and useless deaths.[80] Turgenev shifts the emphasis to the story of inaction – the story of character, built on the assumption that a frustrated action, or inaction, has a stronger connection with human consciousness; and that the growth of imagination is likely to be stimulated when the chances for outward action are curbed. As Markovitz points out, 'on some level, in literature at least, if not in life, we are who we are, not by virtue of what we do, but by what we have failed to do'.[81]

That is, partly, the reason why Turgenev's novels feature a recurrent juxtaposition of a strong-minded man of action and the one inherently prone

79 Henry James, Preface to *The Portrait of a Lady*, in Henry James, *The Art of the Novel. Critical Prefaces* (New York: Charles Scribner's Sons, 1934), pp. 40–59 (p. 42, 48, 56).

80 As Lotman observes: 'As soon as Kister's life [in 'Bretter'] acquires some kind of meaning though his love for Masha, he is immediately sacrificed to Luchkov's whim [...] Not to mention Bazarov's death, but that of Rudin on the barricades, it too looks utterly senseless for it is not derived from his flow of life, but emphasises its failure' (Lotman, p. 105).

81 Markovitz, p. 6. Markovitz argues that excess of action can, in a way, endanger the input of consciousness in characterisation. Taking Dickens' novels as an example (apart from his later novels which are not representative in this regard), she observes that 'his highly engaged and active plots can be seen to result in his famously flat characters'. The 'round exceptions, such as Arthur Clennam in *Little Dorrit* (1857) or Pip in *Great Expectations* (1861), tend to be marked by their passive, will-less natures' (Markovitz, p. 6; the notion of 'flat' and 'round' characters was introduced by E. M. Forster, *Aspects of the Novel* (San Diego, New York and London: Harcourt, 1985), p. 67).

to inaction and reflection – the one who is sensitive to social injustice, but completely incapable of throwing himself wholeheartedly into its cause. All authorial sympathies (perhaps not without some auto-referential perspective) tend to go to the latter. Thus in Turgenev's seminal article *Hamlet and Don Quixote* of 1860, it is Don Quixote who wins the accolade of rational appreciation, but the author clearly sides with Hamlet, with his passivity, his emotional turmoil, and the complexity of his thoughts. Similarly, in *On the Eve*, the authorial sympathies are evidently on the side of socially inept and timid Shubin, while the gratifying lot – the moral pathos, the loyalty of the beloved – is bestowed on the revolutionary Insarov, who, in fact, is a fairly flat and unexciting figure, evoking nothing but bemusement among present-day readers of the work.

Largely in the same vein, Galsworthy's discourse rarely falls into the category of the action-based story; and the character's proactive life strategy is rarely shown as an incontestable manifestation of the good. Not unlike Bazarov, Ferrand in *The Island Pharisees* (1904) has the power of disturbing other people's peace of mind, and his presence in the Denmant household (modelled on Bazarov's visit to Mar'ino) has much the same disruptive effect. The novel (dedicated to Constance Garnett in gratitude for her translations of Turgenev[82]), however, is far from being a typical Edwardian saga. In many ways it is not a novel at all, but a series of episodes or literary sketches, each of which demonstrates some particular aspect of social hypocrisy and the corruption of the middle-class world – the Country House, the University, the Army, the Indian Civil Service. Concerning an overarching plotline, similarly to *Fathers and Sons*, *The Island Pharisees* does not offer much of an action. Bazarov's traits are also quite noticeable in Lord Miltoun from Galsworthy's *The Patrician* of 1911. Although repositioned in a different social setting, the stubbornness, the pride, and the force of personality are apparently in place. As regards the series of events propelling the story, yet again, nothing much happens in this novel,

82 Phelps, p. 117.

in which the characters 'seem not so much [to] act and react upon each other, as jostle each other', as Joseph Conrad once insightfully observed.[83]

The absence of a strong, well-constructed plotline consequently leads to three other characteristics of Turgenev's, and Galsworthy's, novels. The first is the social representativeness of their literary figures, supported by the high-pitched actuality of the content, which is typically centred on the most pressing up-to-date questions and contemporary concerns. Partly, one can see it as a kind of compensatory discursive mechanism, employed by the authors. As Robert Caserio argues in his study *Plot, Story, and the Novel*, 'when writers and readers of novels lose interest in plot and story, they appear to lose faith in the meaning and the moral value of acts'.[84] The only way to win back the faith and interest of such a reader, brought up on the captivating well-defined plots of Dickensian tales, is to present him with a story of himself – to anchor it in the actuality of the current moment and to articulate the subject-matter that would be most relevant to the present-day anxieties and debates . Looking at the spectrum of Turgenev's novels, one can see that all of them are characteristically tied in with the major Russian socio-political issues: *Rudin* (1857) draws upon the emerging generation of revolutionary democrats; the dying class of the landed-gentry is portrayed in *A Nest of Gentlefolk* (1859); Russia on the eve of liberal reforms (the 1861 Emancipation of the Serfs) is conjured in *On the Eve* (1860); social manifestation of the growing ideological schism among the liberals – in *Fathers and Sons* (1862); disillusionment and ideological stagnation is traced in *Smoke* (1867); and the first ever depiction of the populist revolutionaries is in *Virgin Soil* (1877).

In other words, speaking of Hamlet's mirror, which art is supposed to hold up faithfully to nature, this 'mirror' operates with great efficiency in Turgenev's novels; but to describe Turgenev and Galsworthy as keen social reformers, who aimed at exposing injustice and devising ways of helping

83 Joseph Conrad, Letter to John Galsworthy, March 1911, in Frederick R. Karl and Laurence Davies, eds, *The Collected Letters of Joseph Conrad* (Cambridge: Cambridge University Press, 1990), IV, p. 425.

84 Robert Caserio, *Plot, Story, and the Novel* (Princeton, NJ: Princeton University Press, 1979), p. xiii.

the deprived, is to miss the point of their oeuvre. Social controversy and the actuality of settings hardly constitute the *raison d'être* of their novels. They are chiefly explored, or exploited, as effective discursive and structural devices, which made contemporary readers devour each and every one of Turgenev's plotless tales, including examples of his later prose (*Smoke* and *Virgin Soil*), where action *per se* plays an extremely peripheral role. This also explains both the vast popularity of Galsworthy's fiction, when the Forsytes were discussed by his contemporaries as real flesh and blood people, and the subsequent decline of his fame, when the social immediacy of his writing was no longer in tune with the changed cultural references of the post-World War II generation.

Another feature relevant to Turgenev's novel of 'inaction' is the absence of a prevalent didactic message, tied in traditionally with the development of the storyline or the main character of the realist plot. In a way it was a definitive step forward towards a modernist understanding of the relationship between ethics and aesthetics, which denies any ever-present objective order and, in turn, any prevalent style of artistic perception and expression. Very much in line with this tenet, the ideological platform in Turgenev's novels is characteristically undefined or left deliberately vague. This, in turn, is reflected in the highly impersonal or inter-subjective mode of narration, when the authorial voice is hardly an imposition and is dissolved in the polyphony of his fictional selves. To give but a few examples, Insarov (*On the Eve*) is strongly committed to his revolutionary ideals, but the author never comes to back up his righteous aspirations, and, more importantly, to tell the reader what exactly constitutes his worthwhile and laudable cause. The same concerns would be applicable to Bazarov. The information about his motives and persuasions is astonishingly sparse: he considers experimenting with frogs useful, and has an aversion to reading Pushkin; but, with all respect, these interests and habits can hardly make up a coherent ideological stance.

In Galsworthy, Harz (*Villa Rubein*) is a defiant libertarian. In many ways he displays the same qualities as Insarov. Not unlike Elena, Christian shows her selfless loyalty to his supposedly worthy cause and aspirations, which, nonetheless, cannot be described with more clarity than as a hazy pursuit of the bohemian lifestyle. Similarly, in both *The Island Pharisees* and *The Patrician*, we are presented with Bazarov-type figures, whose views are made invariably even less explicable and less defined. Ferrand scornfully resists conformity, and he too, Galsworthy highlights, 'signified rebellion, the subversion of law and order' and his whole figure 'stood for discontent with the accepted'.[85] He seems to be slightly softer than Bazarov, but as regards his social position, he emerges as a simple vagabond without convictions – an anarchist, which means a Nihilist (Bazarov) without a purpose. In *The Patrician*, Lord Miltoun's capacity for shocking the conventional is in evidence whether it concerns friends or foes, but the exact reason why he turns so violently against his own kind, completely escapes even the most attentive reader. As Conrad described him, writing just after the publication of the novel: 'He is to my mind more sombre than Bazarov, and almost as plebeian, with his temperamental asceticism, his nonconformist conscience, and his passion [...] He is a strange bird to come out of that nest.'[86]

This paves the way to the third notable feature that unites Turgenev's and Galsworthy's viewpoint – the rejection of moral pragmatism and an acute sense of uncertainty, inherent to and indivisible from the human condition. Such an approach, yet again, can be largely interpreted along the lines of modernist aesthetics, centred on subjectivity as a necessary and sufficient condition of artistic reflection. It occurs that the only conclusion that one can draw from Galsworthy's and Turgenev's stories consists in an uncanny realisation that human happiness is linked to some entirely subjective and impractically quixotic choices, unsupported by moral credibility or a well-defined ethical appeal. Thus in Turgenev the worthiness of his so-called 'strong' protagonists, like Bazarov or Insarov, is implicitly put into question through the accidental and essentially pointless death

85 John Galsworthy, *The Island Pharisees* (London: William Heinemann, 1904), p. 85.

86 Conrad, Letter to John Galsworthy, March 1911, *The Collected Letters of Joseph Conrad*, IV, p. 425.
The fact that Lord Miltoun's character is contrived was highlighted by Joseph Conrad, who pointed out in his letter to Galsworthy: 'You mean him to be typical. He's a bigger creation than the others, but I should not say a greater. He is above right enough but the reader (this reader) somehow feels that he is what he is because you *will him* to be so' (Conrad, Letter to John Galsworthy, March 1911, *The Collected Letters of Joseph Conrad*, IV, p. 426).

that brings to culmination the lives of these super-heroes. The lucky lot, on the other hand, is bestowed on charismatically inept Nikolai Petrovich Kirsanov, who whatever happens, keeps playing the cello in the middle of his utterly chaotic and badly managed manor, surrounded by his beloved Fenechka and a beautiful child. In like fashion, it is 'hopeless' young Jolyon and impractical Irene who, in contrast to the rest of the Forsytes, manage to find happiness with each other. And as regards the reason and justification, the answer most probably rests in the symbolic gesture of Turgenev's Uvar Ivanovich (*On the Eve*), who, when probed further with these questions, invariably flourishes his fingers and fixes 'his enigmatical stare into the far distance'.[87]

Given that action was no longer considered as the main means of discursive progression, Turgenev's aesthetics also offered some new avenues in the area of character delineation, drawing largely upon merging it with the setting and turning the latter into a so-called emotional compass of the theme. Galsworthy perceptively remarked that Turgenev 'had a perfect sense of line moulding and rounding his themes within himself before working them out in written words; and, though he never neglected the objective, he thought in terms of atmosphere rather than in terms of fact'.[88] Heightened by the writer's refined sensibility and his inner predilection for the intuitive and the suggestive, Turgenev's unprecedented mastery in portraying literary landscapes was a point of admiration, not to say envy, among many of his fellow authors. As Tolstoy once claimed: 'after him [Turgenev] one simply feels like giving up rendering the beauties of nature altogether – just two or three odd words, and it really "smells"'.[89] Turgenev reached an exceptional degree of impressionistic vividness in merging his narrative descriptions with the characters' emotional gradations (often employed as a device for characterisation in his writings). To give but a few

87 Ivan Turgenev, *On the Eve*, trans. Constance Garnett (London: William Heinemann, 1920), p. 290.

88 Galsworthy, 'Six Novelists in Profile', p. 150.

89 Lev Tolstoy, Letter to A. Fet, 11–12 March 1877, in Lev Tolstoy, *Polnoe sobranie sochinenii*, ed. V. G. Chertkov, 90 vols (Moscow: Goslitizdat, 1928–1958), LXII (1956), p. 312 (translated by the authors).

examples, one can mention Elena's tormenting feeling for Insarov, tuned into a cloudy and windy evening:

> She went on, not noticing that the sun had long ago disappeared behind heavy black clouds, that the wind was roaring by gusts in the trees and blowing her dress about her, that the dust had suddenly risen and was flying in a cloud along the road ... Large drops of rain were falling, she did not even notice it; but it fell faster and heavier, there were flashes of lightning and peals of thunder.[90]

or a little sketch of a mellow hot summer weather resonating with Bersenev's leaning towards reveries and philosophical musings:

> Beyond the river in the distance, right up to the horizon, all was bright and glowing. At times a slight breeze passed over, breaking up the landscape and intensifying the brightness; a sunlit vapour hung over the fields. No sound came from the birds; they do not sing in the heat of noonday; but the grasshoppers were chirping everywhere, and it was pleasant as they sat in the cool and quietness, to hear that hot, eager sound of life; it disposed to slumber and inclined the heart to reveries.[91]

Being fascinated by Turgenev's artistic plasticity, combined with his insights into human nature, Galsworthy followed in his steps, exploring the illustrative power of portraying 'through atmosphere' rather than through 'fact'.[92] Perhaps one of the most vivid examples presents itself in the closing sequence of the *Indian Summer of a Forsyte* (1918), depicting old Jolyon in the Robin Hill garden, surrounded by his grandchildren playing somewhere at a distance. Impregnated with the aura of Bossiney and Irene's love, the garden is charged with the poignancy of loss, resonating in old Jolyon's reminiscences and reflections. He is overwhelmed with quiet resignation, his mind faint with regrets, his heart scarred with the moments of unrealised happiness and expectations. There is no melodramatic quality in the flow of his emotions, save for the feeling of acceptance – this almost irrational sense of appeasement of the coming end.

90 Turgenev, *On the Eve*, p. 151.

91 Ibid. pp. 8–9.

92 Galsworthy, 'Six Novelists in Profile', p. 150.

> He was waiting for the midges to bite him, before abandoning the glory of the afternoon. [...] This weather was like the music of 'Orfeo', which he had recently heard at Covent Garden. A beautiful opera [...] 'almost worthy of the old days' – highest praise he could bestow. The yearning of Orpheus for the beauty he was losing, for his love going down to Hades, as in life love and beauty did go – the yearning which sang and throbbed through the golden music, stirred also in the lingering beauty of the world that evening.[93]

Galsworthy was one of the first to appreciate that Turgenev's unison of psychology and setting (especially with regard to nature) had some deeper implications than those concerning the framework of narrative and stylistic innovations. Considering that one's emotional response to nature is irrational *per se*, Turgenev's use of it as a mediator of the human psyche, essentially exposed and explored the irrational dimension of the latter. In Galsworthy's works the same type of experience is often rendered through the medium of music. It is hardly a coincidence, for instance, that in *The Forsyte Saga* the characters who are above all alien to pragmatism and possessive instincts (Irene, old and young Jolyon Forsyte) happen to be most sensitive to music. Moreover, with regard to Irene's piano playing, it not only serves as an outlet for her sensations, but constitutes a key element of her inner portrait. She is not metaphorically compared to music, she is perceived as its embodiment and its manifestation:

> She began to play again. This time the resemblance between her and 'Chopin' struck him [old Jolyon]. The swaying he had noticed in her walk was in her playing too, and the Nocturne she had chosen and the soft darkness of her eyes, the light on her hair, as of moonlight from a golden moon.[94]

93 Galsworthy, *The Forsyte Saga*, pp. 379–82.
The intense lyricism of tone and the highly charged description of the scene bring to mind Turgenev's portrayal of Lavretsky, resting on a bench upon his return to Lisa's old house, with a group of young people running merrily in the background (Ivan Turgenev, *A House of Gentlefolk*, trans. by Constance Garnett (London: William Heinemann, 1922), pp. 390–91).

94 Galsworthy, *The Forsyte Saga*, p. 395.

Galsworthy's attraction to the uncharted avenues of the human psyche, to its allusive elasticity and its ultimate inconclusiveness was a prominent feature of his artistic viewpoint and expression. As he claimed in one of his essays,

> the finality that is requisite to Art [...] is not the finality of dogma, nor the finality of fact, it is ever the finality of feeling – of a spiritual light, subtly gleaned by the spectator out of that queer luminous haze which one man's nature must ever be to others.[95]

And it was precisely in 'that queer luminous haze' of the irrational that he saw the true expression of the real. In like fashion to Turgenev, he displayed an outstanding mastery in the field of what one can term the art of literary impressionism: merging his *object discursif* with the experience of its perception, and aspiring to capture and portrayal the texture and the very process of emotional and aesthetic interaction. This may also explain why many of Galsworthy's admirers saw him not so much as a realist prose writer, but as a philosopher and a mystic poet, concerned with 'the deeper spiritual reality' concealed from the eyes of an idle viewer:

> He [Mr Galsworthy] is a philosopher and a poet, a mystic poet, yet the most precise and systematic of realists. I write this last word without any idea of labelling him as belonging to a school; I am not thinking of his manner, but of the object of his art, determined by his point of view. It is that of all great artists possessed by the desire to seize and express complete reality, not only that which ordinary eyes perceive, but the deeper spiritual reality, the mystery of which haunts them, the power or the idea they divine beneath the appearance of a being or a thing, and try to reveal to us by their interpretation of that appearance.[96]

It was somewhat surprising that such a refined, and in many ways modernist understanding of the art of prose remained unappreciated by the younger generation of British authors, and more specifically by Virginia Woolf, who notoriously claimed that Galsworthy's manner of writing (similar to that of Arnold Bennett and H. G. Wells) had 'laid an enormous stress

95 John Galsworthy, 'Meditations on Finality', in John Galsworthy, *The Complete Essays of John Galsworthy* (Charleston, SC: BiblioBazaar, 2006), pp. 129–33 (p. 129).

96 André Chevrillon, *Three Studies in English Literature: Kipling, Galsworthy, Shakespeare* (Port Washington, NY: Kennikat Press, 1922), p. 155.

upon the fabric of things',[97] but failed to reveal 'the perplexed liquid, this cloudy, yeasty, precious stuff, the soul'.[98] 'No prophet is accepted in his hometown,' and indeed, Woolf somehow missed in Galsworthy everything that she found so refreshingly appealing in Turgenev's novels. She praised the Russian author's use of detail, his ability to construct a scene from meticulous observations, as well as his success in achieving an impersonal inter-subjective vision: 'He [Turgenev] used the other self, the self which has been so rid of superfluities that it is almost impersonal in its intense individuality.'[99] The only thing that one, perhaps, should note in an attempt to explain Woolf's position, is that the writings of Turgenev came under her close scrutiny at a later stage in her career; and it is about a decade that separates her detailed essay on Turgenev (1933)[100] from her criticism of the Edwardians in the early 1920s – the time when she was infatuated with the works of Dostoevsky and Tolstoy. As Royal Gettmann perceptively remarked, Turgenev's (and Galsworthy's) 'net was, perhaps,

97 Virginia Woolf, *Mr Bennett and Mrs Brown*, p. 18. For Woolf's criticism of the Edwardian authors, see also her essay 'Modern Fiction' (1925)

98 Virginia Woolf, 'The Russian Point of View', in Virginia Woolf, *The Common Reader* (London: Vintage Classics, 2003), I, pp. 173–82 (p. 180).

99 Virginia Woolf, 'The Novels of Turgenev', in Virginia Woolf, *The Captain's Death Bed and Other Essays* (San Diego, New York and London: Harcourt, Brace, 1950), pp. 53–61 (p. 61). The essay was first published in *The Times Literary Supplement*, 14 December 1933.

100 Woolf's brief review of Turgenev's fiction appeared in 1921 ('A Glance at Turgenev'), followed by her commentaries on the new biography of the writer in 1927. Woolf's deeper interest in the writings of Turgenev in the early 1930s is mentioned in her diary entries and her letters. Thus in August 1933 she puts in the diary that 'T [Turgenev] wrote and rewrote to clear the truth of the unessential [...] T's idea that you the writer states the essential & lets the reader do the rest'. (Virginia Woolf, *The Diary of Virginia Woolf*, ed. Anne Olivier Bell, 5 vols (London: Hogarth Press, 1977–84), IV, pp. 172–3); in the letter to Helen McAfee (November 1933), she remarks that she 'was greatly impressed by Turgenev, reading him again after many years', and expresses a hope that she 'may lead some of the younger generation to look at him again' (Virginia Woolf, *The Letters of Virginia Woolf*, ed. Nigel Nicolson, 6 vols (London: Hogarth Press, 1975–80), V, p. 246).

too neatly arranged' to display the grip of the subconscious;[101] the latter led modernist sensibility directly to the works of Dostoevsky, in which Russian psychological turmoil and irrationality acquired far more definitive and striking tones.

As regards the apparent controversy involving Galsworthy's interest in the ineffable mystery of feeling and the realist framework of artistic expression, these, in fact, are not as incompatible as they may seem at first glance. There may exist some revealing connections between the former and the latter, for as John Stokes observed in his study of the writings of Oscar Wilde, the reason why the defiant aesthete loved mystery so much was, paradoxically, 'that he was at heart a rationalist', willing to accept that science could offer an increasingly adequate account of the visible world; 'religions die when they are proved to be true', he wrote, 'science is the record of dead religions.'[102] For Galsworthy, this connection between the inner world of the 'spirit' and the manifestation of the real was rooted first and foremost in Russian aesthetics. In an attempt to respond to the clash of humanistic values with the pragmatism of the age, and to chart his median path between Wilde's aestheticism and the extreme realism of Zola and Gissing, he adopted and became a great proponent of the Russian viewpoint (in particular that of Turgenev), centred on the analysis of 'inner action' (or most frequently inaction) and the exploration of the link between the irrational and the humane.

Galsworthy's engagement with the Russian aesthetics was profound and intense, leaving indelible traces in his literary sensibility and his expression. One can say that it is largely owing to the Russian method that he turned his social archetypes into three-dimensional living people, softening the outlines by a penumbra of the atmospheric, and giving them depth by setting them against the backdrop of the mysterious and the suggestive. Considering more general principles of the art of fiction, on the one hand, this type of aesthetic experimentation allowed him to present differently and afresh the structure, the connections and the experience of life,

101 Gettmann, p. 180.

102 John Stokes, *Oscar Wilde: Myths, Miracles and Imitations* (Cambridge: Cambridge University Press, 1996), p. 3.

projected onto the inner reality of human consciousness. On the other, given that these formal innovations could be seen as both the consequence and the cause of the need for greater psychological realism in *belles lettres*, they exposed generic doubts about the philosophical basis of the realist doctrine, or, more specifically, led to an expansion of one's understanding of what was meant by realism *per se*.

Further to the point, a significant socio-cultural aspect of Galsworthy's outlook on the myth of Russia is germane to the discussion. Galsworthy keenly observed that human consciousness (one's spiritual inner self – to use the modernist wording) was evidently bounded by a particular idea of culture as an autonomous activity, with its own self-generated system of determinants and values; so that, as he wittily remarked, it was 'almost impossible to de-Anglicise an Englishman'.[103] One, nonetheless, can hardly overestimate his own contribution to this task. While the Russians undoubtedly influenced his aesthetics, he in turn affected British sensibilities and the framework of cultural perception. It was, of course, a different influence from that exerted through the astute judgement of a critic, as well as from that instilled by an enthusiast of the exotic. It is no exaggeration to say that Galsworthy's contribution to configuring the Russian myth is invaluable in terms of transplanting the Russian paradigm into British aesthetics; and that through this type of internal mediation a significant step was made towards a new, essentially modernist, perspective of cognition – one that exceeds the limitations of cultural rationality and the barriers of self-conscious cultural tradition. As Galsworthy put it in his essay,

> When one says that the Russian novel has already profoundly modified our literature, one does not mean that we have now nearly triumphed over the need for ink, or that our temperaments have become Russian; but that some of us have become infected with the wish to see and record the truth and obliterate that competitive moralising which from time immemorial has been the characteristic bane of English art.[104]

103 Ibid. p. 68.
104 Ibid. p. 67.

CHAPTER 3

H. G. Wells: Interpreting the 'Writing on the Eastern Wall of Europe'

H. G. Wells' obituary in *The Times* stated that he was 'never anything but successful as a writer, and at one time he was possibly the most widely read author in the world':

> Wherever there were visions of a new world in the making, wherever there were schemes for a more rational ordering of human affairs, there also was H. G. Wells [...] Novelist, fantasist, analyst of society, amateur of science, populariser of ideas, his profuse and astonishing literary career exhibits the constant and guiding passion of a single-minded personality.[1]

And indeed, as one of the leading voices of his time, Wells was simultaneously applauded by both his admirers and his political critics, for decades remaining one of the biggest intellectual influences in the English-speaking world. Verbal parallels to his writings may be traced in the speeches of Winston Churchill, who was known to read everything that Wells published and to correspond with the writer, commenting on certain aspects of his political views. As Churchill remarked in his essay of 1931: 'When I came upon The Time Machine, that marvellous philosophical romance [...] I shouted with joy. Then I read all his books.'[2]

1 'Obituary. Mr H. G. Wells', *The Times*, 14 August 1946, p. 7.
His obituary in *The Times Literary Supplement* described him as an 'educator', who 'spoke more clearly than any other man to the youth of the world'.

2 Winston Churchill, 'H. G. Wells', *Sunday Pictorial*, 23 August 1931, in Michael Wolff, ed., *The Collected Essays of Sir Winston Churchill*, 4 vols (London: Library of Imperial History, 1976), III, 50–4 (pp. 52–3).
On Churchill-Wells correspondence see Richard Toye, 'The Great Educator of Unlike People: H. G. Wells and the Origins of the Welfare State', in Roger E. Backhouse and

In the 1920s Wells was at the height of his social and literary fame. According to the survey conducted by *The Manchester Guardian*, he came second (losing only to Galsworthy) among the writers who were considered likely to be read in 100 years' time.[3] He was a passionate believer in progressive politics and his success as a writer turned him into an international celebrity. His essays were widely read and his views made a strong impact on the minds of the generation of his contemporaries, as J. B. Priestley put it, 'Wells dominated the world in which I grew up.'[4]

Among prominent British writers of his time, H. G. Wells had perhaps the closest and the most animated contacts with pre- and post-revolutionary Russia. A friend of Maxim Gorky and Fedor Chaliapin, he made three trips to the country (in January 1914, September to October 1920 and in July 1934), two of which were marked by his conversations with such state figures as Lenin and Stalin.[5]

In 1914 Wells returned from Russia as a staunch Russophile, revealing his impressions of the country in a documentary 'Russia and England: A Study of Contrasts' (published by *Daily News*, 1 February 1914), and in the novel *Joan and Peter* (1918). During war-time Russia became one of

---

Tamotsu Nishizawa, eds, *No Wealth but Life: Welfare Economics and the Welfare State in Britain, 1880–1945* (Cambridge: Cambridge University Press, 2010), pp. 161–88 (pp. 171–2).

At his death Churchill had a substantial collection of Wells' novels, although *Men like Gods* (1923), in which he was satirised as 'Rupert Catskill', was missing (Toye, p. 171).

3 'Novelists Who May Be Read in A. D. 2029', p. 16.

Patrick Parrinder affirms that at that time Wells' 'intellectual, political and literary impact was at its height. During this time, he himself could easily be regarded as a European rather than merely an English writer. He travelled widely, and gave public lectures in the major European capitals' (Patrick Parrinder, Introduction to *The Reception of H. G. Wells in Europe*, ed. Patrick Parrinder (London: Continuum, 2005), pp. 1–13 (p. 1)).

4 S. Winsten, ed., *G. B. S.* (London: Hutchinson, 1946), p. 50.

5 Matthew Taunton, 'Russia and the British Intellectuals. The Significance of *The Stalin-Wells Talk*', in Rebecca Beasley and Philip Ross Bullock, eds, *Russia in Britain, 1880–1940: From Melodrama to Modernism* (Oxford: Oxford University Press, 2013), pp. 209–24.

the main topics of his articles and journalistic essays. Wells' perspective on the subject, including the alliance against Germany and the anti-monarchy February revolution, was largely buoyed up by the British government's official line; and he started to be regarded as an established authority on the Russian theme. The beginning of the 1920s was marked by a high level of tension between the newly formed Soviet Russia and the Western powers; and the cultivation of a more 'informed' vision of the country was taken up by the liberal press, as well as by some experts and opinion formers, including Sir Donald Mackenzie Wallace, Maurice Baring, Harold Williams and Stephen Graham. It was not surprising that Wells also should become interested in the issues surrounding new Russia's image and was willing to make his contribution to this field.

Wells' personal perspective on Russia, as well as his reflections on the socio-political outcomes of the 1917 Russian Revolutions (both the February Revolution and the October uprising), formed a substantial part of his *The Outline of History* volume, a treatise on the development of human civilisation, first serialised in 1919.[6] On 11 February 1920 Wells sent extracts of the monograph to Maxim Gorky, asking whether it would be appropriate to discuss the possibility of a Russian translation.[7] Gorky turned out to be in favour of the idea, thus providing some context for Wells' prospective Moscow visit. The trip followed from September to October 1920: Wells spent a couple of weeks in Russia with his son Gip (who spoke a bit of Russian) at the invitation of Lev Kamenev, one of seven members of the first Bolshevik Politburo, founded in 1917 to manage the Revolution.

Russia in the Shadows, the literary outcome of Wells' 1920 stay in Russia, discussing the country's recovery from total social collapse, was published in a series of five articles in *The Sunday Express* (31 October–28 November 1920),

6 The illustrated version of the book appeared in twenty-four fortnightly instalments, starting 22 November 1919, and was published in book format in 1919/20.

7 Maxim Gorky, *Pis'ma*, ed. F. F. Kuznetsov, 24 vols (Moscow: Nauka, 1997), XIII, 209; Kornei Chukovsky, *Polnoe sobranie sochinenii. Dnevnik 1901–1921*, ed. E. Chukovskaia (Moscow: Terra, 2013), XI, 541.

summarised later in book format.[8] The work fell immediately under the spotlight of public attention: Wells' articles increased the circulation of the paper by 80,000 copies;[9] and the extensive controversy surrounding the writer's viewpoint made a strong contribution to the re-configuration of the British outlook on the Russian myth.

Quite a few laid great expectations on Wells' account of his journey: the general reader was keen to get a trustworthy opinion from an authority in the field. The Russian anti-Bolshevik opposition was persuaded that the picture of extreme social chaos and economic deprivation would cure Wells of his socialist illusions, and his statement on the Russian question could then be used for their political manipulations. The majority, however, largely shared Churchill's conviction (Wells' affirmation would have been a nicety in this case) that the country was being devoured by the 'cancer' of communism, and as such was not in a position to join the rest of the civilised world.[10]

Like much of his writing. Wells' report went largely against the general trend of contemporary opinion. He returned from Russia believing that the Western world should accept the Revolution and should be prepared to come to terms with the new regime. While delineating a grim picture of the country's physical collapse, economic chaos and degradation, he argued that this was the result of the 'unintelligent foreign intervention', and 'the complete internal disorder' – the Civil War, rather than inept actions of the Bolshevik Politburo.[11] To add to the point, his disparagement of political boycotts was supported by a conviction that the Bolsheviks were the only reliable force which could pull the country out of the crisis – the backbone and the hope of 'a new, renascent Russia':

8 Chapter V 'The Petersburg Soviet' was added later, and featured only in the book format.

9 Quoted in Melitsa Krivokapich, *In Pursuit of the Ideal Society* (Montreal: McGill University Press, 1994), p. 55.

10 'We see the Bolshevist cancer eating into the flesh of the wretched being; we see the monstrous growth swelling and thriving upon the emaciated body of its victim' (quoted in 'Churchill and Merejkovsky Reply to Wells', *Current Opinion* 70 (1921), p. 217).

11 H. G. Wells, *Russia in the Shadows* (London: Hodder and Stoughton, 1920), pp. 34–5.

> I have also tried to get the facts of Bolshevik rule into what I believe is their proper proportions in the picture. The Bolsheviks, albeit numbering less than five percent of the population, have been able to seize and retain power in Russia because they were and are the only body of people in this vast spectacle of Russian ruin with a common faith and a common spirit. I disbelieve in their faith, I ridicule Marx, their prophet, but I understand and respect their spirit. They are – with all their faults – the only possible backbone now to a renascent Russia.[12]

It is essentially a limitless task to analyse the entire volume of public response to Wells' account. The papers printed countless letters on the topic, not to mention numerous reviews that appeared in periodicals and weekly journals. *New Statesman*, for instance, described Wells' report as that of a rigorous observer: 'There is nothing at all, we believe, that has been written about Soviet Russia during these three years of Bolshevism that is worthy of comparison with the analysis which Mr H. G. Wells has just published', it wrote,

> He had every qualification; the faculty of keen and curious observation, the sense of the value of big movements, the natural sympathy with anything that was recognisably a genuine human effort, and that profound yet tolerant disillusionment which comes of long association with the Socialist movement of Europe.[13]

The majority, however, saw the English writer as a 'hoodwinked'[14] outsider, who assumed that a fifteen-day trip to Russia was long enough to see through the threat of Bolshevism. Among others, Henry Arthur Jones and Winston Churchill were the most unforgiving in their comments. Jones referred sarcastically to *Gulliver's Travels*, comparing Wells to those Laputan philosophers, who had to be brought down to earth by persistent slapping in the face with a blown bladder: 'Being impressed with your striking resemblance to the Laputan Philosophers I resolved that I would put aside less urgent business and constitute myself your flapper, in the Laputan sense.'[15] As regards Churchill's opinion, although he had always been a great

12 Wells, *Russia in the Shadows*, p. 88.

13 'Russia As It Is', *New Statesman*, 11 December 1920, pp. 296–7 (p. 296).

14 'Mr Wells's Visit to Russia', *The Spectator*, 25 December 1920, pp. 854–5 (p. 854).

15 Quoted in Vincent Brome, *Six Studies in Quarrelling* (London: Cresset Press, 1958), p. 58.

enthusiast of Wells' writing, their positions could not be further apart on the question of Lenin's government and the new regime. Churchill was an outspoken anti-Bolshevik, firm in his belief that

> There has never been any work more diabolical in the whole history of the world than that which the Bolsheviks have wrought in Russia. Consciously, deliberately, confidently, ruthlessly – honestly, if you will, in the sense that their wickedness has been the true expression of their nature – they have enforced their theory upon the Russian towns and cities; and these are going to die.[16]

He was very quick to disparage Wells' account, maintaining with a considerable degree of irony that in a very small period of time the author had managed to become an authoritative 'specialist in Russian affairs.'[17]

Unsurprisingly, the attitude of the Russian émigré circles, who, arguably, had even more grounds for accusing Wells of being superficially 'hoodwinked', was equally hostile. One of the first critical responses to his views – 'Russia in the eyes of an Englishman: naiveties of Mr Wells' – appeared in the pages of *The New Russia*[18] (edited by Nikolai Miliukov, the former Minister of Foreign Affairs for the Provisional Government) as early as 21 October 1920, ten days before Wells' first article was published by *The Sunday Express*. It was then reinforced by a series of more detailed accounts, including 'The Narrow-mindedness of Mr Wells', 'Dilettantism of Mr Wells' or 'Mr Wells' Wrath', in which the titles speak for themselves.[19]

16 Quoted in 'Churchill and Merejkovsky Reply to Wells', p. 216.

17 Winston Churchill, 'Mr Wells and Bolshevism', *The Sunday Express*, 5 December 1920.

18 'Rossiia glazami anglichanina: naivnosti g-na Uellsa', *The New Russia* 38 (1920), p. 250. The report of Wells' talk in the Petersburg Soviet (7 October 1920) was published in *Pravda* (12 October 1920), in the *Daily Herald* (13 October 1920) and in the *New York Times* (14 and 16 October 1920). Wells' speech is quoted in Yurii Kovalev, 'G Uells v Peterburge i Petrograde', *Vtorzhenie v Persei*, ed. E. Brandis and V. Dmitrievskii (Leningra: Lenizdat, 1968), pp. 415–34 (p. 425).

19 'Uzost' vzgliadov g-na Uellsa' (*The New Russia* 40 (1920), p. 289, 309–11); 'Dilettantism g-na Uellsa' (*The New Russia* 42 (1920), p. 357); 'Gnev g-na Uellsa' (*The New Russia* 43 (1920), p. 394). Wells' articles provoked a long-term critical resonance in the émigré circles: N. S. Trubetskoi published a sarcastic foreword to his Russian translation

Among others, Wells' vision of Russia was severely criticised by Ivan Bunin, one of the most prominent émigré writers (to become a Nobel Prize laureate in 1936), who felt obliged to express his poignant indignation at the profound misconception which shaped the tone of Wells' report:

> Dear fellow, we certainly shall not forget your claim that we are worthy exclusively of those scoundrels with whom you stayed for 15 days, and that our Wrangels are just nothing but raiders. I am writing these lines at the time of our greatest sufferings and the deepest dejection. But our sun shall rise – and there is nobody among us who would stop believing in that.[20]

Almost immediately he was joined by Dmitrii Merezhkovsky, an illustrious Russian Silver Age author, condemning Wells' short-sightedness and appealing for a sensible reconsideration of his views:

> And finally, Mr Wells, let me quote yourself. Do you know what Bolsheviks are? They are neither men nor beasts, not even devils, but your Martians. This is happening today, and not only in Russia, but throughout the world, this is precisely what you have so brilliantly predicted in *The War of the Worlds*. The Martians descended on Russia openly, but one feels already that they are proliferating everywhere from inside.
>
> What is the most frightening regarding the Bolsheviks – is that they are creatures belonging to a different world; their bodies are not ours; their souls, not ours. They are strangers to us, us children of the earth, of all the strange transcendence of nature.
>
> You know, Mr Wells, better than anyone. Do you know what the triumph of the Martians means? The loss not only of my country as well as yours, but of the whole planet. Would you therefore side with them against yourself?[21]

The publication of *Russia in the Shadows* also resulted in Wells losing some friends from his London Russophile circle. One of them was Harold

---

of *Russia in the Shadows* (N. S. Trubetskoi, Preface to G. D. Uells, *Rossiia vo mgle* (Sofiia: Rossiisko-bolgarskoe kn-vo, 1921), pp. iii–xvi).

20 Ivan Bunin, 'Some Words to the English Writer', *Obshchee delo* 132 (1920), p. 2 (translated by the authors).

21 Dmitrii Merezhkovsky, 'Pis'mo Uellsu', *Svoboda-Varshava* 125 (1920); 'Lettre ouverte à Wells', *Révue hébdomadaire* 1 (1921), p. 132 (translated by the authors).

Williams – a leader writer (1921) and, from May 1922, an appointed foreign editor for *The Times*. Harold Williams and his wife Ariadna Tyrkova-Williams played a key role in hosting Wells during his 1914 Russian visit, when he stayed at the Tyrkovs' family estate in the Novgorod region. Mrs Tyrkova-Williams had no hesitation in confronting Wells publicly regarding his stance on the Russian question: 'Even H. G. Wells, with his sharp intelligence and restless imagination', she claimed,

> had no intuition of what Communism is. He thought it merely a Russian affair. We argued with him. I am afraid my hot temper was to blame. I insisted that directly, or indirectly, Bolshevism would affect everyone, even his own children. He asserted that the Russian Revolution concerned nobody but Russia. Let the Russians manage their own affairs according to their own lights. He was absolutely sure that revolution or no revolution, his country house at Dunmow would always be full of roses and strawberries. He was partly right. People like H.G. Wells maintain their standard of comfort even in the midst of a world crisis. But what about the crowd of smaller men?[22]

Harold Williams was equally dismayed by Wells' publication. And although he preferred to avoid challenging Wells publicly or in the press, the first draft of his talk at the Institute of International Affairs on 7 December 1920 (written, probably, under a certain degree of emotional tension) contains some distinctly negative references to Wells' opinions.[23] Frank Swinnerton, a mutual friend of both the Williamses and the Wellses, was quick to realise how deeply everybody was distressed by Wells' position. 'I can quite imagine that the Russian articles are worse than exasperating to you',[24] he wrote

22 Ariadna Tyrkova-Williams, *Cheerful Giver* (London: P. Davies, 1935), pp. 218–19. Tyrkova also played a significant role in instigating the Bunin-Wells polemics. Her visit to the Bunins in Paris is recorded in Vera Bunina's diaries on 14 November 1920 with a note: 'She is enflamed by the desire to fight', a week later (21 November) Bunina comments on retyping her husband's 'article against Wells' (Vera Muromtseva-Bunina, *Ustami Buninykh*, ed. Militsa Grin (Moscow: Posev, 2005), II, p. 18).

23 These references were excluded from the final text of the talk. Ariadna Tyrkova-Williams Papers, Box 8; quoted in Irene Zohrab, 'From New Zealand to Russia to Britain: a comment on the work of Harold W. Williams and his relations with English writers', *New Zealand Slavonic Journal* 1 (1985), pp. 3–15 (p. 10).

24 Letter of 9 November 1920; Ariadna Tyrkova-Williams Papers, Box 12; quoted in Zohrab, p. 10.

in a private letter to Williams. In an attempt to moderate a considerable strain in relations and moral damage, he then tried to attribute everything to Wells' eccentricity and emotional affectation:

> We know what originality H. G. has, and how impossible it is for him not to see things with a very eccentric *parti pris*. For anybody who knows a subject thoroughly he must be a cause of gnashing despair. Marvellous man.[25]

Swinnerton's merely tactical remark on Wells' alleged tendency to see 'things with a *parti pris*', or, in other words, to be dominated by his mental schemes and preconceptions, happens to be highly pertinent and revealing. Swinnerton knew Wells well enough to understand that his trip to Russia served essentially as a lens through which the English author was refracting his own socialist models.

Not unlike his fellow Fabians, Sidney and Beatrice Webb, who formulated their tract on the outcomes of the socialist venture (*Soviet Communism. A New Civilisation?*[26]) two weeks before their visit to the country in May 1932, Wells' image of Russia had been largely configured in his earlier writings. Owing to his scientific background and education, his mind-set was that of a modeller and a planner; and on his so-called 'field-trip' in 1920 he arrived already on the lookout for certain things he was expecting to see. It is sufficient to consider the Russian sections of *The Outline of History* volume (published just a year earlier), to realise that Wells' framework of references had already been defined and cemented, and that a fairly unaltered version of his tenets was mapped onto his commentaries on the Russian tour. The examples are manifold and concern, for instance, Wells' lauding of Bolshevik leaders as far-seeing and progressive statesmen, of whom he believed that

> in all the evil they did, they were honest in intention and devoted in method. Manifestly they were attempting to work out an experiment of great value to mankind

25 Letter of 9 November1920; Ariadna Tyrkova-Williams Papers, Box 12; quoted in Zohrab, p. 10.

26 In the second (1941) and third (1945) edition of the book, the question mark was removed from the title.

> and should have been left in peace [...] But they were not left to themselves [...] They were universally boycotted, and the reactionary governments of France and Great Britain subsidized and assisted every sort of adventurer within and without Russia to assist them;[27]

as well as his rather shocking justification of the Bolshevik terror: 'There was a phase of Terroristic government', he argues in *The Outline of History*, 'Thousands of men were seized and shot, and it is doubtful if Moscow could have been restored to even a semblance of order without such violence.'[28] The same disconcerting remark reappears in *Russia in the Shadows*, when he says that 'apart from individual atrocities it [the Red Terror] did on the whole kill for a reason and to an end.'[29] And although Wells claimed now and again that he was extremely alert not to be 'dry-nursed' by the hosts on his visit,[30] he could not help fitting facts into the framework set out in his mind. His perception of Russia was shaped some time before the 1920s, and it is in his earlier encounters with the country that one has to search for an explication or, more precisely, an understanding of the way in which his Russian impressions were moulded into a specific point of view.

As a prominent man of letters Wells was keenly aware of his popularity in Russia, where his novels were translated as early as the end of the 1890s.[31] Even Lev Tolstoy (no admirer of Shakespeare or Milton) was moved enough by his fiction to ask through Aylmer Maude, their mutual friend, to send him a copy of Wells' stories. Wells dutifully obliged, acknowledging the honour (in an accompanying letter of 21 November 1906):

> I never sent you my books, because I assumed that you were inundated with a flow of volumes, supplied by every single debutant-writer of Europe and the US. Now I am

27 H. G. Wells, *The Outline of History* (London: Cassell, 1951), p. 1119.

28 Ibid. p. 1117.

29 Wells, *Russia in the Shadows*, p. 64; the similarities were pointed out in William Harrison, 'H. G. Wells's View of Russia', *Scottish Slavonic Review* 7 (1986), pp. 49–68 (p. 57).

30 'Mr Wells's Visit to Russia', p. 854.

31 Gervert Dzhordzh Uells, *Bor'ba mirov*, trans. K. K. Tolstoy, *Novyi zhurnal inostrannoi literatury*, pp. 6–9 (1898); Gervert Dzhordzh Uells, *Bor'ba mirov*, trans. Z. Zhuravskaya (St Petersburg: Izd. I. N. Skorokhodova, 1898).

> sending you my story 'Love and Mr Lewisham'; a collection of sketches 'The Plattner story', the novel 'The War of the Worlds', and a volume of sociological reflections 'A Modern Utopia', which Mr Maude specifically advised me not to send you, because you are not a utopia fan. But, firstly, this one is quite dissimilar to all others; secondly it is better if you get to know me from the bad side straightaway. I very much hope that this 'hail' of books would not bore you to the slightest degree.[32]

Regarding the influence of Russian literature on Wells' own writing, one can hardly make a strong case for any definitive impact, apart from mentioning a general encouragement 'to use the novel as a platform for a wide range of social, political and moral issues'.[33] As Wells put it in one of his letters in the mid-1920s: 'I have never written any articles on Russian authors. I've a great affection for things Russian & the Russian atmosphere.'[34] The latter was certainly the case; the former turns out to be not quite so, because in his early article 'The Novels of Mr George Gissing', published in 1897 in *The Contemporary Review*, Wells did make some perceptive comments on the writings of Turgenev, characteristically focusing on their social rather than aesthetic merits and seeing them as a prototype of a 'new structural conception' in literature, based on 'the grouping of characters and incidents, no longer about a lost will, a hidden murder, or a mislaid child, but about some social influence or some far-reaching movement of humanity'.[35] This new and broader 'conception of the novel construction', he claimed,

> finds its most perfect expression in several of the works of Turgenev, in 'Smoke', and 'Virgin Soil', each displaying a group of typical individuals at the point of action of

32 H. G. Wells, letter to Lev Tolstoy, 21 November 1906, in Tolstoy, *Polnoe sobranie sochinenii*, LXXVI (1956), pp. 251–2 (translated by the authors).
Tolstoy responded on 2 December: 'Dear Sir, I have received your letter and your books and thank you for both. I expect great pleasure in reading them. Yours truly Leo Tolstoy' (Ibid.).

33 Phelps, p. 146.

34 H. G. Wells, letter dated 1922–26, in H. G. Wells, *The Correspondence of H. G. Wells*, ed. David C. Smith (London: Pickering and Chatto, 1998), III, p. 167.

35 H. G. Wells, 'The Novels of Mr George Gissing', *Contemporary Review* 72 (1897), 193.

> some great social force, the social force in question and not the 'hero' and 'heroine' being the real operative interest of the story.[36]

In the same vein, drawing attention to the social aspects rather than its expressive sensitivity and colours, Wells defended Diaghilev's ballet *Les Noces*, which was disparaged by the majority of critics after its London premiere on 14 June 1926.[37] The ballet, in which Stravinsky showed his increasing propensity for stripped down, clear, and mechanistic sound (created by pianos and unpitched percussion), was based on the traditional Russian rituals of peasant wedding. As so often the critics were much slower to appreciate *Les Noces* than the public. It was quickly passed over, and for a long time its contribution to the development of modern ballet was largely overlooked.[38] Wells, who, in opposition to the majority, loved the ballet-cantata, was moved to write an open letter to the *Dancing Times* (perhaps not without Diaghilev's gentle nudge), which was later printed out and distributed at the performances as an attachment to theatre programmes. Wells cursorily praised the ballet's striking décor, choreography and setting, and placed his main emphasis on its valuable representation of the institution of marriage. 'I have been very much astonished at the reception of *Les Noces* by several of the leading London critics', he wrote,

> Writing as an old-fashioned popular writer, not at all of the high-brow set, I ought to bear my witness on the other side [...] The ballet is a rendering in sound and vision of the peasant soul, in its gravity, in its deliberate and simple-minded intricacy in

36 Ibid. p. 193.

37 Hannen Swaffer, '*Les Noces* filled my cup of bitterness to overflowing', *Daily Express*, 16 February 1926; 'If that was the way the Russian peasant got married [...] no wonder the things have happened as they have', *The Times*, 15 June 1926; 'Nothing but ugliness and aimless noise', *Daily News*, 15 June 1926.

38 Susan Jones, *Literature, Modernism, and Dance* (Oxford: Oxford University Press, 2013), p. 94, 118–19.
In its London premiere it was conducted by Eugene Goossens and the four pianists included Auric, Poulenc, Rieti and Dukelsky (Rieti thought it was an unsuccessful 'stunt' of Diaghilev's to employ four composers instead of four professional pianists, and Stravinsky was 'far from happy about it' (Richard Buckle, *Diaghilev* (New York: Atheneum, 1979), p. 471).

> its subtly varied rhythms, in its deep undercurrents of excitement, that will astonish and delight every intelligent man or woman who goes to see it.[39]

In her account of the interaction between literary modernism and dance in the 1920s, Susan Jones lists Wells as a dedicated literary patron of Diaghilev ballets (together with Richard Aldington, Rebecca West, John Middleton Murry, Katherine Mansfield, the Sitwells, T. S. Eliot and Aldous Huxley).[40] Wells' personal correspondence, however, shows that he was relatively unaffected by the pre-war unrelenting fascination with the Russian Ballets seasons, as well as with the all-embracing vogue for Russian fiction proliferating at the beginning of the century on the British literary scene. The first time Wells mentions reading Dostoevsky's *The Grand Inquisitor* is as late as October 1931, when the book was given to him as a present by Samuel Koteliansky: 'I have read *The Grand Inquisitor* with great pleasure and excitement. It is not my way of approaching these matters, but that makes it all the more interesting. The book was my nicest birthday present.'[41]

Concerning his appreciation of Tolstoy's writings, Wells, as it happens, was not an unreserved admirer of the Russian author. He had an extensive knowledge of Tolstoy's oeuvre, having read a substantial number of his works. 'I read about eighty works of yours – everything which one could get in English', he wrote in a letter to the patriarch of Russian prose, '"War and Peace" and "Anna Karenina", in my view, are the greatest and the most comprehensive of those that I was fortunate to read.'[42] In his *Experiment in Autobiography*, Wells showed more appreciation of *War and Peace*, as a novel where one may 'find a justification for the enhancement and animation of history by fictitious moods and scenes.'[43] In 1922 he joined the

39 H. G. Wells, letter to the editor, *Dancing Times*, June 1926, *The Correspondence of H. G. Wells*, III, p. 213.

40 Jones, p. 94.

41 Wells, letter to Samuel Koteliansky, 1 October 1931, *The Correspondence of H. G. Wells*, III, p. 377; for more on Samuel Koteliansky see Chapter 5 in this book.

42 Wells, letter to Lev Tolstoy, 21 November 1906, in Tolstoy, *Polnoe sobranie sochinenii*, LXXVI, 251–2.

43 H. G. Wells, *Experiment in Autobiography* (London: Faber and Faber, 1934), II, p. 504.

group of British luminaries, including Shaw, Maugham, Jerome K. Jerome and Thomas Hardy, campaigning for a complete Tolstoy edition in English (an open letter by Shaw appeared 28 February 1922 in *The Times*). At the same time, his pithy preface to *Resurrection*, published in the Oxford centenary edition, aroused a furore in literary circles, such that Prince Dmitrii Mirsky, an eminent Russian literary historian and critic, described it as a 'scandal' to the whole profession of letters, against which every self-respecting author must protest.[44] While commending Tolstoy's power of literary portrayal, Wells singled out the trial scene as particularly moving, but did not hesitate to add that 'Mr Galsworthy could certainly have done the same thing quite as completely, and it is the best part of the book [...] The story has been bent to fit a situation and psychology has snapped in the process.'[45] He praised the Russian author's stupendous power of observation, but commented on the 'copious garrulousness' of Tolstoy's novels, which he compared with 'the magic of a busy market-place observed through a window'. He insisted that there was 'no depth of humour' in any of his writings, 'no laughter, and no creative fun, and directly the window is perceived not to be a window but a square of incoherently moving shapes, it matters less than nothing and grips not at all.'[46] Referring to his personal experience in voyaging round the country, he then claimed that the end of the book reminded him of a 'bleak dawn in Petrograd', when

> All night the talk has gone on, very very clever talk going on and on and never getting anywhere [...] and a great weariness has come upon us all. We have related anecdotes interminably, and talked of sex and love and God and truth and sex and cruelty and politics and nationality and science and cruelty and sex, and every one is weary and chilly. Then some one with a good voice says 'Listen to this', and takes a New Testament and reads a few irrelevant texts. 'Good', says a fervent voice, 'A new

44 'H.G. Wells berates Russian Writers in Preface to Tolstoi', *Chicago Daily Tribune*, 14 August 1929, p. 29.

45 H. G. Wells, Introduction to Leo Tolstoy, *Resurrection* (London: Humphrey Milford, Oxford University Press, 1928), pp. vii–x (pp. viii–ix).

46 Ibid. pp. ix–x.

> life has dawned for me. I see the truth. I see everything'. And the gathering with a sigh of intellectual and moral satiety rises to disperse.[47]

Wells was quite sceptical with regard to Tolstoy's religious doctrine (hence his comments on the weakness of the second and third books of *Resurrection* where Tolstoy's art as a writer was eclipsed by his preaching[48]), neither would he relate to the ethics and aesthetics of the Russian author. The connection between the two can be most likely found in their understanding of the social objectives of art and culture, their anti-militarist and anti-imperialist perspective, as well as the pacifist ideas noticeable in Wells' later novels, which in some ways echo the motifs of Tolstoy's works.

The second point regarding Wells' literary pursuits, which is less direct but, perhaps, more important in terms of getting to the first sparks of his interest in the Russian question, concerns his relationship with Edward and Constance Garnett. In the late 1890s, the contacts with Edward Garnett brought Wells to their home in Surrey, to which frequent visitors were the exiled Russian anarchists, including Prince Peter Kropotkin, Sergei Stepniak and Felix Volkhovsky. They were all introduced to the Garnetts through Edward's sister Olive Garnett, who attended various Russian anarchists parties in London, and also hosted them in her Museum Street flat: 'Went out to buy cake, lemons etc. for tea', reads her diary entry of 24 February 1892, when the nihilist Volkhovsky was expected.[49] Volkhovsky became Constance Garnett's Russian tutor, when she took up translation work in the early 1890s (he provided considerable assistance in her first project of translating Ivan Goncharov's *A Common Story*). Later on Garnett learnt more Russian with his fellow revolutionary-nihilist Stepnyak-Kravchinsky, by whom she was encouraged to tackle Turgenev's writings. Ford Madox Ford, who lived nearby and was also a frequent guest at the Garnetts, provided vivid recollections of their vibrant cosmopolitan evenings: 'The

47 Ibid. p. x.

48 'Book II and Book III are as complete a failure to achieve any artistic resurrection from this descent as any one can well imagine' (Wells, Introduction to Lev Tolstoy's *Resurrection*, p. ix).

49 Rosemary Ashton, *Victorian Bloomsbury* (New Haven, CT: Yale University Press, 2012) p. 154.

troglodytic cottage on Limpsfield Chart where I lived severely browbeaten by Garnetts and the Good generally, though usually of a Fabian or Advanced Russian variety.'[50]

Similar in this respect to other members of the Fabian group (Mr and Mrs Pease and Shaw), Wells was keenly aware of the activities of the Society of Friends of Russian Freedom (formed in 1892). In 1908 he even signed a petition to ensure justice for Nikolai Chaikovsky, who had been arrested upon his return to Tsarist Russia earlier in the year. The vast campaign was led by Stepniak: the petition was presented to the Tsar's Ambassador in London, endorsed by numerous signatures including those of Edward Elgar, Thomas Hardy, Henry James and H. G. Wells.[51] These growing contacts with the so-called 'advanced Russian variety' came at the time when Wells' relationship with his own circle of the Fabians was on the rocks. These two aspects are not entirely unconnected, and it is worth looking into this in more detail.

Wells joined the Fabian Society in 1903, proposed for the membership by Shaw and Graham Wallas. His books, *The Discovery of the Future*, *Anticipations* and *Mankind in the Making* were favourably reviewed in *Fabian News* (consecutively in March, June and December of 1902), and his membership was very much anticipated. However, as soon as he joined the ranks of the Society, he found its work totally unsatisfactory and started campaigning for reforms. In Wells' opinion, the faults of the Society (summarised in his address to the group on 9 February 1906, and entitled unequivocally *Faults of the Fabian*), were comprehensive: 'It is small, it is shabbily poor, and it is collectively inactive. [...] it is remarkably unbusinesslike, inadaptable, and uninventive in its ways.'[52] To give credit to Wells' enthusiasm and pro-active position, it did attract a considerable number of younger people to the Fabian movement, so that the membership

50 Ford Madox Ford, p. 18.

51 *Free Russia*, January–March 1908, Felix Volkhovsky Papers, Box 3:27, Hoover Institution Archives.

52 Margaret Cole, *The Story of Fabian Socialism* (Stanford, CA: Stanford University Press, 1961), p. 119.

grew from 730 in 1904 to 2,462 in 1909.[53] As Margaret Cole, one of the historians of the Fabian group, pointed out, Wells' views represented those of the younger generation of the circle, which was 'more literary in its tastes, more fundamentalist in its discussions, more anxious to *argue* about the philosophy of Socialism and formulation of policy "for the working class."'[54]

His ways of implementing his theories, however, were almost entirely unrealistic (not to say absurd);[55] and his radicalism was certainly unwelcome to the 'old guard'. Beatrice Webb, for instance, always valued Wells as a creative person, but referred to him as an 'ideological speculator'.[56] The battle began that was to last for over a year. Wells' limited capacity for putting his ideas across in public meeting, especially against Shaw's rhetorical virtuosity, often added to the problem. One of the greatest writers of the time, Wells happened to be a rather incompetent debater; when referring back to these years he admitted his own shortcomings: 'speaking haltingly on the verge of the inaudible, addressing my tie through a cascade of moustache that was no help at all.'[57] On a personal level, there were also quite a few in the Society who were actively concerned about Wells' reputation for sexual promiscuity and his alleged advocacy of free love. Having been exhausted by perpetual arguments and confrontation, in 1908 Wells presented his letter of resignation, indicating that he had 'lost any hope of the Fabian Society contributing effectively to the education of the movement'.[58] His relations with the core members were undoubtedly strained, finding a reflection in the pages of *The New Machiavelli* – the novel of 1911, which

53 Edward R. Pease, *The History of the Fabian Society* (New York: E. P. Dutton & Company, 1926), pp. 185–6.

54 Cole, p. 116.

55 Cole, p. 123.

56 Beatrice Webb, *Our Partnership* (London: Longmans, Green & Co, 1948), pp. 289–90.

57 Wells, p. 661.

58 *Fabian News*, October 1908; quoted in Cole, p. 123.

contained a caricatural portrayal of the Webbs as Oscar and Altiora Bailey – 'two active self-centred people excessively devoted to the public service'.[59]

Generally speaking, Wells shared Fabian socialist ideas of gradual reformism, advocating tenets of social justice and a welfare state model. He was also introduced to the Webbs' theory of the enlightened administrative experts, highly competent in government management and political science. This theory then manifested itself in Wells' order of the noble Samurai – an elite governing body, depicted in the novel *A Modern Utopia* (1905), who would take a major role in designing, guiding and operating a 'kinetic and not static' world state,[60] so as to solve 'the problem of combining progress with political stability'.[61] Given their progressive views, high moral standards and the emphasis on mass literacy and education, the Fabian group can certainly be regarded as a possible prototype for Wells' depiction of the Samurai order. At the same time, bearing in mind his controversial relations and perpetual disagreement (on a smaller or larger scale) with the Fabian circle, it is not unlikely that it was the 'advanced Russian variety', who contributed to his vision of the leading intellectual core.[62]

Having said this, it would not be wrong to contend that Wells' 1906 encounter with Gorky made a noticeable contribution to his concept of enlightened governing experts. Translations of Gorky had been available in England since the beginning of the 1900s, exceeding in their popularity the readers' rating of Chekhov's stories.[63] Wells met Gorky on his visit to

59 H. G. Wells, *The New Machiavelli* (London: John Lane, 1911), p. 189.
'Are the Baileys a libellous picture of the Webbs? That is quite right. I made a pretty recognisable picture of them', wrote Wells in his letter to Frederick Macmillan, 26 September 1910 (*The Correspondence of H. G. Wells*, II, p. 286).

60 H. G. Wells, *A Modern Utopia* (London: Chapman & Hall, 1905), p. 5, 75.

61 Ibid. p. 271.

62 In his tract *The New Machiavelli* (after his break with the Fabian Society), Wells completely denied the Webbs' influence on his notion of the ruling intellectual elite (Anne Fremantle, *This Little Band of Prophets. The Story of the Gentle Fabians* (London: George Allen & Unwin Ltd, 1960), p. 147).

63 'By 1910 Gorky was much better known among the English public than Chekhov (the situation has since been reversed), and surveys of British (and French) magazines put him first in their list of Tolstoy's younger successors, followed by Korolenko,

the USA in April 1906 at a dinner reception (11 April) hosted by Gaylord Wilshire, the editor of *Wilshire's Magazine*, which was advertised as 'the greatest socialist magazine in the world' with a circulation of 300,000 copies. Gorky came to the United States to conduct a fund raising effort for arms to equip Russian revolutionaries seeking to overturn the autocracy of the Tsar. In the interview given at the Wilshires' party, he blamed the anarchy in Russia on the policy of the tsarist clique; and when commenting on his reception in the States, remarked that he felt that he had come to a country of friends.[64] Ironically this 'company of friends' rapidly turned against him, when the American press and public discovered that the lady accompanying Gorky on the visit was, in fact, his long-term mistress, a Moscow Art Theatre actress Mariia Andreeva. A militant anti-Gorky campaign was launched by the media forces to the extent that he found himself thrown out of the hotel where he and Andreeva were staying. In American eyes he had now become a man with despicable morals, spreading subversion against America's ethos, respected values and fundamental concerns. One of the few strong statements in support of the Russian author was produced by Wells: 'I do not know what motive actuated a certain section of the American press to initiate the pelting of Maxim Gorky', he wrote,

> A passion for moral purity may have prompted it but certainly no passion for moral purity ever before begot so brazen and abundant a torrent of lies .... In Boston, in Chicago it was the same. At the bare suggestion of Gorky's coming, the same outbreak occurred, the same display of imbecile, gross lying, the same absolute disregard of the tragic cause he had come to plead.[65]

Potapenko and only then, in fourth position, by Chekhov' (*Anton Chekhov's Life and Thought*, p. 334. The same spectrum of interest was displayed by the German audience: according to *Das literarische Echo*, from October 1901 to May 1902 the German Press published twenty-four articles about Gorky; seventeen about Tolstoy; eight about Gogol and only two about Chekhov (S. Dinamov, 'M. Gorky i Zapad', *Krasnaia Nov'* 10–11 (1931), p. 225).

64 Tovah Yedlin, *Maxim Gorky. A Political Biography* (Westport, CT: Praeger, 1999), p. 72.

65 *Times* (Buffalo), 15 April 1906, *Houston Chronicle*, 15 April 1906; quoted in Yedlin, p. 74.

From their first meeting, Wells perceived that Gorky was fulfilling his need for a kindred spirit. Both were devoted to progressive social improvement, both were advocating the idea of free love,[66] and at that time both were strongly affected by the theories of Nietzsche, particularly by those of the salvation of mankind by a superior type of intellectual elite – the Superman (*Ubermensch*). The latter found its representation in Wells' voluntary order of the noble Samurai in *A Modern Utopia*.[67] Concerning Gorky, Nietzsche's views can be unmistakably traced in the character of Mayakin in his early novel *Foma Gordeev* (1899); the character of Luca in his social drama *The Lower Depths* (1902), which affirmed the Russian author's popularity in the West; and in a number of his allegorical fables: the juxtaposition between the stormy petrel and other birds in *The Song of the Stormy Petrel* (1901), or between the falcon and the grass snake in *The Song of a Falcon* (1902). As a young man, Gorky spent quite a lot of time studying Nietzsche, and according to his contemporaries, grew his iconic moustache to enhance his likeness to the German thinker.[68] Speaking of Gorky's theories of social improvement, which he did not cease to promote in the pages of his *New Life* journal, they were remarkably close to those expressed by Wells through his numerous fictional poetic personas. Both men believed in the primacy of the revolution of the human psyche, which would lead to the formation of the new men (in the terminology of Gorky) or the new enlightened intellectual experts (as in Wells). 'The Revolution,

66 Both men ended up sharing the same mistress, Mura Zakrevskaia Budberg, who was Wells' interpreter on his Russian trip in 1920, and who finally came to stay with him in London in 1933 (see, for instance, Nina Berberova, *Moura: The Dangerous Life of the Baroness Budberg* (New York: Review Books, 2005)).

67 The notion of a Samurai order was also suggested to him (as well as to the Webbs) by reading Nitobe Inazo's *Bushido: The Soul of Japan* (1899) (Michael Sherborne, *H.G. Wells: Another Kind of Life* (London: Peter Owen, 2010), p. 165).

68 Pavel Bassinsky, *Strasti po Maksimu: deviat' dnei posle smerti* (Moscow: Astrel', 2011), p. 189.
For the detailed analysis of Nietzsche's motives in Gorky's works see, for instance, M. Gel'rot, 'Nitsshe i Gorky', *Russkoe bogatstvo* 5 (1903), pp. 24–65; Maxim Gorky, 'Besedy o remesle' (1930); Maxim Gorky, *Sobranie sochinenii*, 30 vols (Moscow: Khudozhestvennaia literatura, 1949–55), XXV (1953), pp. 291–359 (p. 309, 322).

the only one which is capable of freeing and ennobling man', wrote Gorky, 'must take place within him, and it will be accomplished only by cleansing him of the mould and dust of obsolete ideas'.[69]

Wells' close connections with Russian revolutionary circles (he and Gorky met again in May 1907, when the latter came to London to attend the fifth Russian Social Democratic Party Congress), and the similarity of their projects, ideas and opinions, especially against the background of his exasperating confrontation with the Fabian group, were important factors in configuring his attraction to all things Russian. He was actively reading Maurice Baring's *Russian Essays and Stories*:

> Russian Essays is an admirable book, it makes me [sic] catch at one's adjectives before they get out of hand. Sympathetic & vast & a sort of depth of underlying & the sense of beauty alive & active, – I would value it if it came from a stranger and I should want to know you if I didn't;[70]

and towards the end of 1913 he was giving some serious consideration to a visit. 'I think that this January I shall take a little journey to Berlin, Warsaw and Moscow',[71] he wrote to Robert Ross in November.

When analysing Wells' account of Russia, communicated on the basis of his first 1914 journey, attention is drawn to at least two noteworthy observations. Firstly, one should argue in support of Swinnerton's claim regarding Wells being prone to seeing things through the prism of his own preconceptions, or, in Swinnerton's words with a definitive *parti pris*.[72] Secondly, the spectrum of these *a priori* formed inferences and opinions can be described as a somewhat peculiar mixture of time-honoured national clichés, the landmarks derived from Maurice Baring's essays, and the writer's

69 Maxim Gorky, *Novaia Zhizn'*, p. 107 (1918). Quoted in Maxim Gorky, *Untimely Thoughts on Revolution, Culture, and the Bolsheviks 1917–18*, trans. Herman Ermolaev (New York: Paul S. Eriksson, 1968), p. 226.

70 Wells, letter to Maurice Baring, 6 November 1908, *The Correspondence of H. G. Wells*, II, p. 229.

71 Wells, letter to Robert Ross, November 1913, *The Correspondence of H. G. Wells*, II, p. 357.

72 Quoted in Zohrab, p. 10.

own socio-political views. A similar representation pattern will be traceable in Wells' account of his second Russian tour (in 1920), which makes it worthwhile to provide a closer consideration of the earlier trip.

On 13 January 1914 Wells arrived in St Petersburg on a private visit at the invitation of Count Alexander Benckendorff, the Russian Ambassador to the United Kingdom. In his preface to the 1909 Russian edition of his works (translated by Kornei Chukovsky), he claimed that he knew very little of the country, conjuring its image mainly from a number of sparse conversations with Gorky and the great volume of literary sources, which flooded British bookstores of the pre-World War I years. Characteristically it featured Russia's vast landscape, gloomy forests, jolly peasants and wooden huts:

> When I think of Russia, I think of the descriptions of Turgenev and Tolstoi and of my friend Maurice Baring, of a country of heavy winters and bright, hot summers, of vast spaces of rather untidy cultivation, of wide and littered village streets with brightly painted houses and buildings of wood, of a peasant population, genial, humorous, patient, pious, and careless, of icons and bearded priests, of rough and lonely highroads running across great level spaces and through dark pine woods. I wonder how true that picture is?[73]

It seems that the trip added fairly little to his earlier, allegedly romanticised and 'bookish' portrait. Written straight after his return back to England, Wells' essay 'Russia and England. A Study in Contrast' (1914) offered a set of colourful snapshots and descriptions, which still did not differ much from those attributed to the Russian fairground *lubok*-art:

> It thawed on Sunday, and the surface of the ice was covered with inch-deep lakes of water and so rotten with snow slush that always we seemed near upsetting, and once we upset altogether. This water rippled a little under a chilly breeze, and except for that, it might have been an under-sky; the sledges that followed us hung low between clear sky and clear water, they were black against the serene levels of sunset

73 Published in English as 'Mr Wells Explains himself', *T.P.'s Magazine* 3 (1911), pp. 339–43 (pp. 339–40).

> colour, pink and gold and mauve and their high arched yokes nodded over the heads of the horses;[74]

or to the so-called 'stage' Russia, as the author himself called it in his letter:

> Russia is most amoosing. Exactly like the stage Russia – guard in huge furry cap and top boots [...] Outside are unfenced wilderness with deep snow, stunted firs & silver birch & (rarely) stunted hovels. Nobody speaks French or German, & the man who called up my passport called me Vowless.[75]

In the same vein, this largely clichéd and exotified portrayal, which indeed calls to mind the backdrop for a Russian-theme stage set, was reiterated four years later in the Russian chapters of the novel *Joan and Peter* (1918) – a *roman-à-clef*-type narrative, which followed Oswald Sydenham's and his godson Peter's three-week trip to Russia at New Year 1914:

> a sledge drive of ten miles along the ice of a frozen river, a wooden country house behind a great stone portico, and a merry house party that went scampering out after supper to lie on the crisp snow and see the stars between the tree boughs; the chanting service in a little green-cupolaed church and a pretty village schoolmistress in peasant costume; the great red walls of the Kremlin rising above the Moskva and the first glimpse of that barbaric caricature, the cathedral of St. Basil ; the painted magnificence of the Troitzkaya monastery [...] the picturesqueness of Russia had a great effect upon him [*Oswald Sydenham*].[76]

The characters' itinerary ('St. Petersburg – it was not yet Petrograd – visited a friendly house near the Valdai Hills, spent a busy week in and about Moscow, and returned by way of Warsaw'[77]) and impressions provide a

74 H. G. Wells, 'Russia and England: A Study in Contrast', *Daily News*, 21 February 1914.

75 Wells, letter to Catherine Wells, [24] January 1914, *The Correspondence of H.G. Wells*, II, p. 362.

76 H. G. Wells, *Joan and Peter. The Story of an Education* (York, The Macmillan Company, 1918), p. 380.

77 Ibid. p. 379; 'a friendly house near the Valdai Hills' is a reference to Ariadna Tyrkova-Williams' family estate in the Novgorod region (in the village of Vergezha), discussed later in this chapter.

close match for those of the author, whose features are carefully disguised in Oswald and Peter (two different aspects of Wells' personality), while Mr Bailey is portrayed as a Maurice Baring-like figure.[78]

Maurice Baring was Wells' devoted guide and mentor during the Russian trip of 1914. A well-rounded specialist in Russian history and culture, he pursued his interest in the country through a whole spectrum of extensive publications, including such titles as *Landmarks in Russian Literature* (1910), *Russian Essays and Stories* (1908, 1909), *A Year in Russia: 1905–1906* (1907), *The Russian People* (1911), as well as his earlier memorable work on the Russo–Japanese War – *With the Russians in Manchuria* (1906). According to one of his reviewers, Baring's lifetime intention was to reshape British perception of Russia as that of 'fiction and imagination [...] the knout and the half-shaved convict train dragging bloody chains across the snowy steppe'.[79] When it came to reshaping Wells' perception, Baring's undertaking was, perhaps, not entirely successful, but he was certainly instrumental in configuring Wells' interests and pursuits.

Baring's prime concern was the Russian people, their national character, and the reality of life. And it is not coincidental that straight upon his arrival in St Petersburg, Wells also declared that, apart from staying in the capital, he would be interested in observing a Russian village and that he was much more moved by people and their customs than by the monuments and historical relics (this interview for the journal *Rech'* was conducted by Vladimir Nabokov, the father of the famous writer).[80] The same was affirmed by the *Morning of Russia* correspondent. The newspaper reported that he 'categorically rejected an invitation to visit the monuments of antiquity, provided by his acquaintances', and after spending the first day

78 Harrison, p. 53.

79 William Churchill, 'Maurice Baring, *The Russian People* (1911)', *Bulletin of the American Geographical Society* 44.3 (1912), p. 218.

80 V. Nabokov, 'Uells', *Rech'* 14 (15 January 1914), p. 2.
Wells insisted on the same point three days later in another interview to Zinaida Vengerova, a journalist and a writer who had followed Wells' career over the years (Zinaida Vengerova, 'Dzhordzh Uells ego prebyvanie v Peterburge', *Den'* 17 (18 January 1914), p. 3).

in the streets of Moscow, dedicated the second one to following the daily routine of the Trinity Monastery in the small town of Sergiev Posad.[81]

The influence of Maurice Baring on Wells' account of Russia was analysed closely by Militsa Krivokapich, who argued that it was Baring's far more intricate and insightful descriptions that found their match in Wells' self-admittedly 'primitive and as yet half-baked views'.[82] To give but a couple of examples: Baring persistently drew attention to the importance of Christianity in understanding Russia and its people ('Christian charity, their sympathy [...] is by far their most pleasing and attractive state'[83]). Likewise, Wells insisted that in Russia, 'for the first time' in his life he felt he was 'in a country where Christianity is alive'.[84] Both authors wrote about the physical beauty of the Russian landscape, commenting on some mysterious strength originating from its vastness, as well as on the affinity between the national character and the power of the land. 'In the twilight, continents of dove-coloured clouds float in the east', writes Baring,

> the west is tinged with the dusty afterglow of the sunset; and the half-reaped corn and the spaces of stubble are burnished and grow in the heat; and smouldering fires of weed burn here and there; and as you reach a homestead, you will perhaps see [...] a crowd of dark men and women still at their work; and in the glow from the Dame of a wooden fire, in the shadow of the dusk, the smoke of the engine and the dust of the chaff, they have a Rembrandt-like power, the feeling of space, breadth, and air and immensity grows upon one; the earth seems to grow larger, the sky to grow deeper, and the spirit is lifted, stretched, and magnified.[85]

This is paralleled in Wells' novel, when he dwells upon

> The wild wintry landscape of the land with its swamps and wild unkempt thickets of silver birch, the crouching timber villages with their cupolaed churches, the unmade

81 Quoted in Inna Levidova, 'Pervyi priezd G. D. Uellsa v Rossiyu', in I. M. Levidova and B. M. Parchevskaia, eds, *G. D. Uells* (Moscow: Kniga, 1966), pp. 125–9 (pp. 127–8).

82 Krivokapich, pp. 25–7.

83 Maurice Baring, *Maurice Baring's Restored Selections from His Work*, ed. Paul Horgan (London: William Heinemann, 1970), p. 237.

84 Wells, 'Russia and England'.

85 Baring, *Maurice Baring's Restored Selections from His Work*, p. 267.

> roads, the unfamiliar lettering of the stations, contributed to his impression of barbaric greatness [...] In Petrograd, he [Oswald Sydenham] said, 'away from here to the North Pole is Russia and the Outside, the famine-stricken north, the frozen fen and wilderness, the limits of mankind.'[86]

Wells was clearly overwhelmed by the sheer scale and volume of his Russian impressions, maintaining that after spending two weeks in Russia, he found his 'mental arms full of such a jumble of impressions as no other country has ever thrust into them', and that it would take him 'months of reflection before [he] could begin to sort out this indiscriminate loot, this magnificent confusion of gifts'.[87] Krivokapich, however, insightfully points out that despite being dazzled with the immense flow of new thoughts, feelings and observations, Wells displayed a noticeable tendency to highlight those that were specifically akin to or illustrative of his own social schemes.

As a steadfast 'evolutionary collectivist' (believing that 'through a vast sustained educational campaign the existing Capitalist system can be civilised into a Collectivist world system'[88]), Wells was naturally inclined to see mankind's affinity with the surrounding landscape as a necessary prelude to apprehending the world as a community of nations,[89] a cosmic utopian brotherhood, which was one of the cornerstones of his social views. As he pointed out in his introduction to Denis Garstin's *Friendly Russia*, published in 1915, the author was 'engaged here upon one of the most necessary and beneficial tasks of our time, the explanation of a people much maligned, the increase of sympathy and understanding across spaces and ignorances that have separated men from men'.[90]

86 Wells, *Joan and Peter*, p. 381. It seems that Wells was truly moved by the magnetic power of this darkness, reporting to Rebecca West: 'St Petersburg is more like Rebecca than any capital I have seen, alive and dark and untidy (but trying to be better) and mysteriously beautiful' (Wells, letter to Rebecca West, late January 1914, *The Correspondence of H. G. Wells*, II. p. 363).

87 Wells, 'Russia and England'.

88 Wells, *Russia in the Shadows*, pp. 138–9.

89 Further discussed in Krivokapich, p. 27.

90 H. G. Wells, Introduction to Denis N. Garstin, *Friendly Russia* (London: T. F. Unwin, 1915), p. 9.

Along similar lines, Wells' remark on the high level of culture and education in Russia was not entirely coincidental. This aspect was crucial for the formation of the social layer constituted by the enlightened intellectual elite – the backbone of his theories of reforming the human condition. Not unlike Baring, who maintained that 'an all-round development of faculties' was much more common in Russia than in other countries',[91] Wells specifically commented on the intellectual curiosity of the younger part of the Russians' cultural circles:

> far more interesting than the play to him was the audience. They were mostly young people, and some of them were very young people; students in uniform, bright-faced girls, clerks, young officers and soldiers, a sprinkling of intelligent-looking older people of the commercial and professional classes; each evening showed a similar gathering, a very full house, intensely critical and appreciative. It was rather like the sort of gathering one might see in the London Fabian Society, but there were scarcely any earnest spinsters and many more young men [...] This, then, must be a sample of the Intelligentsia. These were the youth who figured in so large a proportion of recent Russian literature. How many bright keen faces were there![92]

It would be, perhaps, unwarranted speculation to assert that during his first visit to Russia Wells started seeing the country's intelligentsia as a potential embodiment of his enlightened class of noble Samurai, who, if roused to action by some external forces, would bring about the new progressive social order. Wells had no illusions regarding the backwardness of Russia: he was acutely aware that in the country, which he portrayed as 'the vast barbaric medley',[93] 'eighty and ninety per cent' of the population were illiterate, 'superstitious in a primitive way, conservative and religious in a primitive way'.[94] However, it is worth bearing in mind that in a series of articles written as early as 1914, he did make reference to the exceptional qualities of the Russian intellectual experts, comparing them to 'the younger and brighter half of the London Fabian'[95] group ('Above these peasants come

91 Baring, *Maurice Baring's Restored Selections from His Work*, p. 236.

92 Wells, *Joan and Peter*, p. 389.

93 Ibid. p. 389.

94 H. G. Wells, 'The Liberal Fear of Russia', *The Nation*, 22 August 1914.

95 Wells, 'Russia and England'.

a few millions of fairly well educated and actively intelligent people. They are all that corresponds in any way to a Western community such as ours').[96]

And he did draw attention to the potential of the country's young cultural vanguard, whose intellectual vitality and critical thinking were pitted against the obtuse doom and repressiveness of the Tsarist order (in the Duma episode of *Joan and Peter*):

> There the figure of the autocrat stood, with its sidelong, unintelligent visage, four times as large as life, dressed up in military guise and with its big cavalry boots right over the head of the president of the Duma. That portrait was as obvious an insult, as outrageous a challenge to the self-respect of Russian men, as a gross noise or a foul gesture would have been.
> 'You and all the empire exist for ME', said that foolish-faced portrait, with its busby a little on one side and its weak hand on its sword hilt ...
> It was to that figure they asked young Russia to be loyal.[97]

Wells was not the only Westerner who was impressed by the Russians and felt an attraction which was difficult to characterise in any specific or meaningful terms without slipping into some sort of vague statement concerning the innate goodness of the Russian people. He saw Russia through the prism of the mystic national idea, the Holy Land of spirituality, nesting in the depth of the mysterious Russian soul: 'Asia advancing on Europe – with a new idea', he wrote,

> One understands Dostoevsky better when one sees this. One begins to realize this Holy Russia, as a sort of epileptic genius among nations – like his Idiot, insisting on moral truth, holding up the cross to mankind [...] They seem to have the Christian idea. In a way we Westerns don't. Dostoevsky, Tolstoy, and their endless schools of dissent have a character in common. Christianity to a Russian means Brotherhood.[98]

Like many others (and despite his scientifically structured thinking), Wells was also falling into the trap of emotive generalisations, and his image of Russia, projected at the time, evidently did not go beyond the cliché-type

96 Wells, 'The Liberal Fear of Russia'.

97 Wells, *Joan and Peter*, p. 388.

98 Ibid. p. 389.

appeal of the mystical and the exotic. This fascination, however, was refracted through his own set of schemes and social models, the clear focal point of which was that of the well-educated cultural vanguard. One may even argue that during his stay in Russia, Wells, in fact, did have a chance to witness a micro-model of his Samurai leadership put into practice (though it was never mentioned in this way in his accounts). He spent some time in the close company of the members of the Russian revolutionary intelligentsia, while staying at the family estate of Ariadna Tyrkova-Williams in the Novgorod region (in the village of Vergezha). Tyrkova's brother, Arkadii Vladimirovich Tyrkov, was a member of the populist-revolutionary movement from the early 1870s. Having spent twenty years in exile in Siberia, he returned back to Vergezha still maintaining a proactive social position, advocating an indigenous version of populist socialism, based upon the massive Russian peasantry layer. Arkadii Tyrkov was very close to the Vergezha peasant community groups, in which Wells was warmly received during his stay with the Tyrkovs.[99]

In this context it is also worth noting that in Russia there existed a bigger gap (in comparison to the West) between the country's intelligentsia and peasant masses,[100] which by way of sheer juxtaposition underscored the cultural affluence of its well-educated revolutionary circles. Upon returning to England Wells therefore expressed even more intense interest in Russia in all its forms. He became a convinced promoter of the Russian language, urging it to become part of the curriculum in secondary education. From a personal perspective, he suggested to the headmaster of his son's (Gip's) school that Russian should be taught there throughout the year – the headmaster dutifully obliged.[101] It was, arguably, at that time

99 Zohrab, p. 4.

100 Wells, perhaps, had a chance to appreciate this gap when staying with the Tyrkovs in the Vergezha village; but the picture of the pervasive drinking and backwardness of the peasant masses could also have been drawn from his reading of Baring's essays (Maurice Baring, *Russian Essays and Stories* (London: Methuen & Co, 1908), pp. 178–9).

101 David C. Smith, *H. G. Wells: Desperately Mortal* (New Haven, CT: Yale University Press, 1986), p. 246.

that Wells started seeing Russia as a prospective social project, and thus became keen on accentuating positive notes in the image of its people, its realities and its cause. 'My own experience of Russia has been of the briefest', he maintained, but

> I went into one or two villages of the Government of Novgorod and into several peasants' houses. They are roomier than English labourers' cottages; they look more prosperous; the people seem more free and friendly in their manners, less suspicious of interference, and in all the essential things of life better off.[102]

The February Revolution was a solid testimony of Wells' predictions (configured back in 1914). 'This great change in Russia, this banner of fiery hope that has been raised over Europe was no farce or spectacle', he wrote,

> It comes, indeed, as the call of God, too, to every liberal thinking man throughout the world. We had not dared to hope it. Even men who, like myself, have been most energetic in pleading the cause of Russia in Western Europe and America, who have been saying ever since the war began: 'You are wrong in your fear of Russia: Russians are by nature a liberal-spirited people, and their autocracy is a weakness that they will overcome' – even we who said that counted on nothing so swift and splendidly complete as this revolution.[103]

His statement was quoted in the open message to the Provisional Government, 'Assure New Russia of British Regard', and, strictly speaking, was nothing more than an affirmation of the author's hopes and sympathies for the new regime. More useful for the purposes of our examination is to look at the issues of Wells' reaction to the Bolshevik uprising, which was formative for shaping the image of Russia projected after the end of his 1920 visit.

A number of articles were published in the *Daily Chronicle*: 'Looking Ahead: World Language' (13 May 1916), 'Tidying up the Language question: With Particular Reference to Russia' (6 June 1916); see also his letter to the editor of the *Daily Chronicle* (16 May 1916) (*The Correspondence of H. G. Wells*, II, pp. 458–60).

102 Wells, Introduction to Denis N. Garstin, *Friendly Russia*, p. 12.

103 Bernard Shaw et al., 'Assure New Russia of British Regard', *New York Times*, 1 April 1917, p. 3.

Unlike many of those in his close social circle, the Bolshevik Revolution did not take Wells by surprise.[104] It was as late as the1920s that the Fabian 'fathers' (Shaw or Sidney and Beatrice Webb) started to display definite signs of interest in the country where their socialist theories were being realised and put into practice. This was due to the introduction of Lenin's New Economic Policy in March 1921, which was seen as creating an effective bridge-passage to the gradualism of Fabian reforms. The first contacts with the leaders of the newly established state also prompted the Fabian idea of intellectual administrative experts. British democratic socialists were pleased to realise that the front-runners of the so-called proletarian revolution were, in fact, not proletarians at all, but rather a group of highly educated political activists. Georgii Chicherin, People's Commissar of Foreign Affairs, was an aristocrat by birth, a distant relative of Aleksandr Pushkin. Chicherin had a degree in history and languages, and could have made a career as a trained competent musician. Anatolii Lunacharsky, the People's Commissar of Enlightenment, was brought up in the family of a statesman. He received his education at the University of Zurich, where he entered the circles of the European Socialists (together with Rosa Luxemburg and Leo Jogiches). He was a playwright and an art critic, and produced a number of essays on the works of Western authors, including Shaw and Marcel Proust.[105] In one of her letters to Wells, Beatrice Webb remarked that Kamenev (Lenin's Deputy Chairman of the Council of People's Commissars) and Krassin (the People's Commissar of Foreign

104 The October events appear to have knocked Shaw into fairly uncharacteristic silence: only once in two years' time, at a meeting of the Fabian Society in 1917, where the Bolsheviks were anathematised and vilified (while the Civil War was being waged), did Shaw raise his voice, saying 'We are socialists. The Russian side is our side' – his words were greeted with silence (quoted in Allan Chappelow, *Shaw – 'The Chucker-out'* (London: George Allen and Unwin Ltd, 1969), p. 231). His first public pronouncements of his support for the Bolsheviks did not appear until April 1919 in an article in *The Labour Leader* (24 April) which asked 'Are we Bolshevists?'. Shaw definitively answered in the affirmative.

105 Anatolii Lunacharsky, 'Bernard Shaw', in A. V. Lunacharsky, ed., *Collected Works* (Moscow: Khudozhestvennaia literatura, 1965), VI, pp. 150–3; first published in *Proletarskii avangard* 8 (1931).

Trade), who arrived in London to conduct negotiations on the Anglo-Soviet trade and commercial agreement, pleasantly surprised her with their extensive knowledge of economic science, political professionalism and managerial skills:

> We had an hour's oration from each of them – one in French, the other in German – at a little private meeting of Fabians and Krassin struck me as a remarkable personality – quite the most remarkable Russian I have ever met. His account of Soviet industrial organisation as it was and as he wished it to be, is that of the most rigid form of state socialism, the dominant note being 'Working to a Plan', conceived by scientific men and applied without any regard to personal freedom or group autonomy.[106]

For Wells all of this was hardly a revelation. During war-time he had a chance to enhance his links with the Russian revolutionaries in exile. He was a regular at the so-called Elders' evenings. In addition to David Elder, his wife Edith, Shaw and many other Freudians and Fabians, the frequent guests at these meetings included Ivan Maisky, who was to return to London as the Soviet Ambassador in 1932; Georgii Chicherin and Ivan Litvinov, appointed in 1917 as the Soviet government representative in Britain, whom Edith Elder's niece, Ivy Low, had married in February 1916.[107] Wells found this circle intellectually stimulating and impressive. In an article published just a couple of months after the October Revolution (15 January 1918), he drew public attention to the fact that the greatest misconception about the Bolsheviks was to see them as an ignorant and illiterate clique of no account: 'when a Bolshevik leader meets a Junker, one might imagine Bottom was meeting Theseus', he wrote.[108] Basing his assertions on his personal contacts and the correspondence with Gorky, he affirmed that the Bolsheviks, contrary to what the British press writes, are

106 Beatrice Webb, letter to H. G. Wells, 8 September 1920, in Sidney and Beatrice Webb, *The Letters of Sidney and Beatrice Webb*, ed. Norman Mackenzie, 3 vols (Cambridge: Cambridge University Press, 2008), III, 141.

107 Ivan Mikhaĭlovich Maĭskiĭ, *The Maisky Diaries: Red Ambassador to the Court of St James's, 1932–1943*, ed. Gabriel Gorodetsky, trans. Tatiana Sorokina and Oliver Ready (New Haven, CT and London: Yale University Press 2015), p. xxxiii.

108 H. G. Wells, 'Mr Wells and the Bolsheviks. Some Disregarded Aspects', *Daily Mail*, 15 January 1918.

> much better educated than our diplomatists. Our public has to realize this fact. These Bolshevik leaders are men who have been about the world; almost all of them know English and German as well as they do Russian, and are intimately acquainted with the Labour movement, with social and economic questions, and indeed with almost everything that really matters in real politics. But our late Ambassador, I learn, never mastered Russian. Just think what that means. Hardly any of our Foreign Office people know anything of Russian, of the Russian Press, or Russian thought or literature. It is they who are ignorant and limited men, and not these Bolshevik people.[109]

Wells himself had no doubts regarding the knowledge and efficiency of these 'Bolshevik people'. Moreover, in many senses they did fall exactly into the category of his enlightened governing elite – the order of the noble Samurai (*A Modern Utopia*), who would lead the uneducated masses in shaping and running the ideal socialist system. The parallels between the two are unambiguously striking; and this, arguably, was one of the most important factors explaining Wells' attraction to Russia and its new regime. Having a distinct penchant for social planning, he did come to regard the Bolshevik government as the real life incarnation of his own fictional intellectual experts. As Henry Arthur Jones argued in his discerning analysis of *Russia in the Shadows* (straight after it was serialised in *The Sunday Express*), there were two main reasons for Wells' positive views of and favourable predictions for the country: his love for the Bolsheviks and his social models, namely a simple consideration that in Russia 'his international theories were being translated into fact'.[110]

Concerning the second point, Wells' projection of the role and activities of the Bolshevik leaders did offer a fairly close fit for the model function of his Samurai order. *Russia in the Shadows* presented a far from prosperous portrait of the country – a society devastated by the consequences of the Civil War, lying in ruins, chaos and economic degradation: broken trams, roads in disarray, a massive fuel crisis,

> every one is shabby; every one seems to be carrying bundles in both Petersburg and Moscow. To walk into some side street in the twilight and see nothing but ill-clad

109 Ibid.

110 Quoted in Brome, p. 58; Krivokapich, p. 57.

> figures, all hurrying, all carrying loads, gives one an impression as though the entire population was setting out in flight.[111]

Wells remarked that the whirl of the Bolshevik revolution was overwhelming and all-embracing, smashing everything and devouring everything by the power of its pull.

Against this grim and ominous setting, the exclusive status of the cultural elite was singled out and highlighted. Cultural institutions, according to Wells, were the only ones to resist the forces of decrepitude and economic chaos; the theatre buildings remained intact and untouched by the traces of robbery and devastation:

> Art, literature, science, all the refinements and elaboration of life, all that we mean by 'civilisation', were involved in this torrential catastrophe. For a time the stablest thing in Russian culture was the theatre. There stood the theatres, and nobody wanted to loot them or destroy them.[112]

The artists and opera singers continued to perform with remarkable devotion, despite hunger, cold and economic deprivation:

> the artists were accustomed to meet and work in them and went on meeting and working; the tradition of official subsidies held good. So quite amazingly the Russian dramatic and operatic life kept on through the extremist storm of violence, and keeps on to this day. In Petersburg we found there were more than forty shows going on every night; in Moscow we found very much the same state of affairs. We heard Shalyapin, greatest of actors and singers, in The Barber of Seville and in Chovanchina; the admirable orchestra was variously attired, but the conductor still held out valiantly in swallow tails and a white tie; we saw a performance of Sadko; we saw Monachof in The Tsarevitch Alexei and as Iago in Othello (with Madame Gorky – Madame Andreievna – as Desdemona).[113]

Special attention was also drawn to the government's persistent support of arts, literature and science, as something not to be neglected even at the time of recession, life-threatening famine, and political unrest. Wells remarked

111 Wells, *Russia in the Shadows*, p. 17.

112 Ibid. p. 35.

113 Ibid. pp. 35–6.

on Gorky's catalytic role in this venture, his efforts in publication of the volumes of world literature in translation and his broad-minded view of the importance of intercultural dialogue and exchange:

> He is possessed by a passionate sense of the value of Western science and culture, and by the necessity of preserving the intellectual continuity of Russian life through these dark years of famine and war and social stress, with the general intellectual life of the world. He has found a steady supporter in Lenin. His work illuminates the situation to an extraordinary degree because it collects together a number of significant factors and makes the essentially catastrophic nature of the Russian situation plain.[114]

Wells was clearly wedded to the idea of a monolithic unity of the intelligentsia and the new socialist order, seeing the former as the vanguard, the executives and the keepers of the latter. In a brief note to Middleton Murry he commented on the prosperous position of cultural luminaries, including Gorky, whom he found 'in pretty good health' and Chaliapin – 'in splendid form'. 'Things are hard – for everyone in Russia', he wrote, 'but all the stuff about a persecution of the intelligentsia is sheer lying'.[115] This also partly explains why in the course of all the polemics concerning his Russian essays, Wells was quick to defend his position against Jones and Churchill, but chose not to respond publicly to the critical remarks of Bunin and Merezhkovsky.[116] Confronting the latter would have cast a shadow on the integrity of the model, adding an element of unnecessary controversy and fracturing the generic image of the Russian enlightened vanguard he was trying to shape. The Bolsheviks' scandalous expulsion of the most eminent representatives of the country's cultural elite – the

114 Ibid. pp. 32–3.
Wells was appalled by the fact that Russian scientists had been deprived of contacts with the world's science since World War I, and upon his return to England he formed a committee to send up-to-date papers and articles to Gorky, who then distributed them to the libraries (David C. Smith, note to *The Correspondence of H. G. Wells*, III, 56).

115 Wells, letter to Middleton Murry, end of October 1920, *The Correspondence of H. G. Wells*, III, p. 49.

116 At least to the best knowledge of the authors (also confirmed in Krivokapich, p. 71), though Wells may have responded in a private letter.

so-called Philosophers' boats – took place only in two years' time (1922). Meanwhile Wells preferred not to focus on the hostility between the intellectuals and the leaders of the new system. The fact that he was well aware of the strain can hardly be questioned, for according to the testimonials of those present at his rally with the Petrograd *men of letters* (carefully staged by Gorky and his devotees), there were very few who supported Wells' optimism with regard to the new leadership and the country's prospects (the general reaction of the audience was overtly hostile).[117] This was also evident from the writer's own note, which he felt obliged to issue in response to the discussion, and which consisted of a tensely dry affirmation of the necessity to disagree on some general philosophical matters:

> We all understand the importance and greatness of Russia and we do not doubt that she is on the eve of a noble future. But the Russian and the British characters are very different, and two peoples cannot go quite the same way.[118]

The example of Chaliapin, whom Wells knew well, and whom he mentioned thriving under the Bolshevik system, would provide another illustration of the growing sense of tension and frustration. By 1921 the artist was already living permanently in the West, though still remaining on perfectly good terms with the English author, whose letter to Koteliansky of 26 September 1921 reads: 'Chaliapin will be dining with us on Tuesday [...] Will you come and dine too?'[119]

As regards Wells' positive appraisal of Lenin and the Bolsheviks, attributed to him by a number of his critics (including Jones' remark on his 'love

117 A. Damanskaia, 'G. Uells v Petrograde', *Narodnoe delo: Organ Komiteta gruppy sotsialistov-revolutsionerov Severo-Zapadnoi oblasti Rossii* 55 (8 October 1920), p. 2; A. V. Amfiteatrov supported Damanskaia's report by publishing his upsetting recollections of the meeting – 'Bitter Notes' (Aleksandr V. Amfiteatrov, 'Gorestnye zamety', *Novaia russkaia zhizn'* (Gel'singfors) 221 (27 September 1921); 222 (28 September 1921).

118 'Mr Wells in Petrograd', *The Times*, 4 October 1920, p. 10; also in *The Correspondence of H. G. Wells*, III, p. 48.

119 Wells, letter to Samuel Koteliansky, 26 September 1921, *The Correspondence of H. G. Wells*, III, p. 87.

of Bolsheviks'), this was somewhat more complicated than a simple series of wrong-headed misconceptions. When raising his voice in support of the Bolsheviks, Wells was hardly talking from the standpoint of an outspoken communist or an assured Marxist, rather the reverse. He repeatedly disengaged himself from the Bolshevik platform ('I have always regarded Marx as a Bore of the extremist sort' or 'I do not agree with either their views or their methods'[120]); and his distinctly anti-Marxist position was conspicuously (and more than once) affirmed in *Russia in the Shadows*:

> I disbelieve in their faith, I ridicule Marx, their prophet, but I understand and respect their spirit. They are – with all their faults, and they have abundant faults – the only possible backbone now to a renascent Russia.[121]

When calling the Bolsheviks 'the only possible backbone now to a renascent Russia',[122] Wells was interested in individuals rather than the system, for it was in these individuals that he saw the agents and the future of his theoretical views. In this respect, Wells' personal encounter with Lenin suggests an illuminating contribution to the point. Prior to his journey, Wells was known to have a fairly negative opinion of the Russian leader. 'Lenin, I assure you is a little beast', he wrote in a letter to Upton Sinclair in early 1919:

> Like this
> [see to the right, Figure 4. H. G. Wells' drawing of Lenin, letter to Upton Sinclair, early 1919.]
>
> He just wants power and when he gets it he has no use for it. He doesn't eat well, or live prettily, or get children, or care for beautiful things ... Lenin is just a Russian Sidney Webb, a rotten little incessant intriguer ... He (Lenin not Sidney Webb) ought to be killed by solid moral sanitary authority.[123]

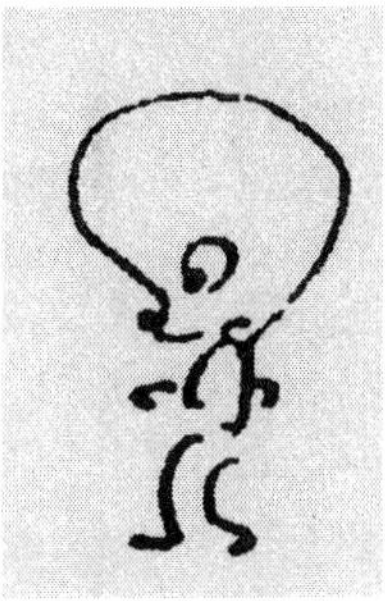

120 Wells, *Russia in the Shadows*, p. 66, 69.

121 Ibid. p. 88.

122 Ibid. p. 88.

123 Wells, letter to Upton Sinclair, early 1919, *The Correspondence of H. G. Wells*, III, p. 3.

Russia in the Shadows, on the other hand, suggested an uncompromising re-shaping of this, strictly speaking, pejorative and denigrating portrait (to that of 'the dreamer in the Kremlin', 'who almost persuaded me to share his vision'[124]), which involves a reasonable question regarding the grounds and the incentive for such an abrupt transformation in the English writer's point of view.

It would not be inappropriate to suggest that it was Wells' personal conversation with his host in the Kremlin that had a crucial impact on the change in his opinion.[125] More specifically, the key element which made all the difference to the outcome of the encounter seemed to lie in the angle taken by Lenin in the course of their exchange. The discussion was focused on the aspects relevant to Wells' social models – education and scientific progress – rather than on ideology, methods and the general issues of the doctrine. Wells remarked that he had come to the meeting expecting to confront the committed Marxist and to struggle with the obscure tenets of the communist thesis; but 'found nothing of the sort'.[126] The two men, instead (led by Lenin's intuition or some sort of thorough preparation), engaged in an extensive discussion on the future of Russia and the course of action required to save the country from the detrimental chaos. For Lenin, as well as for Wells, this was first and foremost the defeat of all reactionary forces, rooted in mass illiteracy, drinking, passivity and social stagnation. Neither man had much care for the inept and materialistically selfish peasant masses;[127] and both believed in the critical necessity of their enlightenment and education. The conversation also turned onto the prospects of electrification of Russia; and although Wells was initially sceptical of its success (softened by the pleasure of encountering a fellow 'Utopian'[128]), the very emphasis on the progressive use of technology and science made him focus on the positive side of the venture:

124 Wells, *Russia in the Shadows*, p. 136.

125 First pointed out in Krivokapich p. 73.

126 Wells, *Russia in the Shadows*, pp. 129–30.

127 Ibid. p. 136.

128 Ibid. p. 135.

> In him I realised that Communism could after all, in spite of Marx, be enormously creative. After the tiresome class-war fanatics I had been encountering among the Communists, men of formulae as sterile as flints, after numerous experiences of the trained and empty conceit of the common Marxist devotee, this amazing little Man, with his frank admission of the immensity and complication of the project of Communism and his simple concentration upon its realisation was very refreshing. He at least has a vision of a world changed over and planned and built afresh.[129]

Judging from Wells' own subsequent reflections, it was Lenin's command of English, his candour and his belief in technology as a cornerstone of socialist construction that made a critical contribution to Wells' perception of and attraction to the Bolshevik cause. Considering himself 'neither Marxist nor Communist, but a collectivist',[130] he believed in his own model of reforming the human condition, based on a broad programme of mass enlightenment and the leadership of the educated cultural elite (given his scientific mind-set, he was more a social modeller than a socialist in its proper ideological sense). This was a scientific kind of socialism, rooted in the orderly, knowable and controllable system of which Russia, led by such impressive leaders as Lenin, was a forerunner to a certain degree. When communicating his account of the 1920 visit, he aimed at assembling an objective image of the country, but his conclusions were clearly refracted through the prism of his own attitudes and political concepts. Later on, in 1932, in an address entitled 'Liberalism and the Revolutionary Spirit', Wells affirmed that the use of the term 'samurai' in his theories of an utopian state was rather absurd, but referred to 'a very remarkable parallelism between those Samurai and Lenin's reorganisation of the Communist world'.[131]

Generally speaking, one can say that Wells' representation of Russia was based on what in cultural theories is termed an 'attitude – not knowledge' approach, which, arguably, speaks more about the perceiver than the culture which one chooses to perceive. At the same time, one has to admit that the very notion of a 'news without views' representation hardly

129 Ibid. pp. 137–8.

130 Ibid. p. 117.

131 H. G. Wells, 'Liberalism and the Revolutionary Spirit', in H. G. Wells, *After Democracy* (London: Watts and Co, 1932), pp. 1–28 (p. 11).

constitutes a reasonable assumption in the domain of intercultural communication: everybody tends to form their views within a certain mind-set of preconceptions, and an attempt to break the stereotypes essentially means replacing them by the new ones. Given that, it would be largely pointless to discuss whether a sensible degree of an unbiased representation of Russia could have ever been achieved in Wells' projection. Instead, it would be, perhaps, more fulfilling to look at the direction in which he wanted to shift an existing commonly established image, and to reflect on the ways in which his approach was put to use.

It is worth bearing in mind that *Russia in the Shadows* was written at a time when Russia was regarded with a high degree of hostility by its Western neighbours; and Wells' intention to project a more appealing image of the country should not be overlooked. To begin with, what he attempted to achieve was to break the stereotypical framework of mental connotations, within which one would readily come up with the notion of the Russian bear, if asked to continue the line of stock collocations including Spanish Jesuits, German officers and French maids. 'Some years ago I became interested in Russia', he wrote back in 1914,

> I took some pains to inform myself about Russia, and finally I went to the country [...] If a large mass of Western people remain saturated with the idea that the mass of Russian people are savagely brutal [...] and the daily life in Russia a profound misery occasionally enlivened by horrible cruelty, I see no hope [...] People had to clear their heads about Russia. That critical indolence of ours which has left it to foolish sensational novels and ignorant melodramas to build up our conception of this great people, is fraught with disastrous consequences for the whole world.[132]

Further to the point, from the perspective of social psychology and the theories of identity construction, people are more willing to form an alliance with other cultures when, firstly, there are some positive common characteristics and attributes to share; and, secondly, when the 'other'

132 H. G. Wells, To the Editor, *North Mail*, December 1914, *The Correspondence of H. G. Wells*, II, pp. 406–12 (p. 409, 412).

culture appears different on a positively valued scale.[133] Both aspects were manifest in Wells' account of the country, as well as in his projection of the Russian viewpoint. By trying to associate Russia with its intelligentsia rather than the exotically barbaric peasant masses, he was striving to place an appealing hallmark on its identity and the image it enjoyed as a social group. For the same reason, he played down the role of state politics and ideological doctrines in the framework of his affiliations, stressing the absence of any political threat from Russia to Britain (i.e. the socialist revolution spreading to other countries[134]), and conjuring the notion of an intellectual stronghold, capable of preserving and advancing the best aspects of the European tradition in the East.

Wells' expectations of Russia did not come into being, and the prospects of a prosperous liberal utopia he hoped to be realised in this country were not fulfilled. However, he was one of the first Western thinkers to project his vision of its people as key players among those defining the destiny of human civilisation. Focused on the long-term broader perspective and combined with an ability to capture and analyse the dialectics of the events, this vision proved to be instrumental for shaping British attitudes to Russia then and now, and for taking yet another step towards what Wells once lucidly defined as interpreting the 'writing on the Eastern wall of Europe'.[135]

133 John C. Turner, 'Towards A Cognitive Redefinition of the Social Group', in Henri Tajfel, ed., *Social Identity and Intergroup Relations* (Cambridge: Cambridge University Press, 1982), pp. 15–40 (p. 26).

134 See, for instance, his views on the impact of Moscow on the miners' strike in Britain in H. G. Wells, *Meanwhile: the Picture of a Lady* (London: George Doran, 1927), p. 45.

135 Wells, *Russia in the Shadows*, p. 153.

CHAPTER 4

J. M. Barrie and *The Truth about the Russian Dancers*

On 21 February 1920, Hayden Church, a special London correspondent for *The Desert News* of Salt Lake City, reported to his newspaper that

> Sir James Barrie, renowned as he is for springing surprises on readers and playgoers, seldom has got his admirers more excited than they are at present over the news that he has broken what for him is new and strange ground by writing a one-act play for Mlle. Karsavina, the famous Russian ballet dancer. It is probable that Karsavina herself will present Sir James's little piece, and appear in the leading part, which is a non-speaking one, at a London theatre early in the spring. Barrie was not particularly attracted by the dancing of the Russian ballet. But during the memorable season at the Alhambra last summer he paid occasional visits and grew more and more enthusiastic. Eventually he decided to write a play about the dancers which should be a tribute and a mark of his appreciation. When it was completed some weeks ago, he presented it to Mlle. Karsavina.[1]

Barrie was absolutely furious when he learned that a garbled account of his play had appeared in the papers. According to Karsavina, the dedicatee of this new theatrical piece, the playwright could not stand his projects being given away in advance. He blamed everything on the prima ballerina's alleged indiscretion and sent her a telegram to the effect that he wanted to have nothing more to do with the play. 'His telegram', Karsavina maintains,

> exploded at me like a bomb. On Benjie's [Karsavina's husband[2]] advice I wrote to Barrie that if there had been an indiscretion it was not mine and that even if he

1 Hayden Church, 'Barrie Writes Play for Russian Ballet Dancer', *The Desert News*, 20 February 1920.

2 Henry James Bruce was a British diplomat, who married Karsavina in 1915.

> withdrew his play I would still feel proud that he had written it for me. This pacified him. Since this one incident nothing ever ruffled our friendship.[3]

Barrie's concern was indeed hardly justified on this occasion: throughout her career as a prima ballerina of the Diaghilev Ballets, Karsavina had never been noted for self-publicity, unscrupulousness, or any kind of indiscretion. Even after the premiere of *The Truth about the Russian Dancers*, when all the newspapers were full of accolades and laudatory reviews, she tried to refrain from any specific comments on the performance, stressing her inability to give an impartial account of a play that according to many was 'one of the season's most important theatrical events.'[4] Regarding the comments, far more puzzling in this respect seems to be the almost unanimous 'discretion' of Barrie's scholars, who scarcely mention *The Truth about the Russian Dancers* in their biographies and critical works.[5] The notable exceptions to the generality of these studies are Janet Dunbar's *J. M. Barrie*, which quotes some of Karsavina's recollections on the production;[6] Denis Mackail's *The Story of J. M. B.*, which presents the sketch as aesthetically 'delicious' and sees in it nothing but a parody of 'the consistent, preposterous and unearthly' world of ballet dancers;[7] and the memoirs of Cynthia Asquith, who observes that this charming 'trifle [...] was written in a day or two, then worked on, altered and polished with infinite care', so that years later she 'found ten different typescript versions of this one little play.'[8]

The Truth about the Russian Dancers, the number of existing draft manuscripts of which had now augmented to fourteen, remained unpublished

3 Tamara Karsavina, Introduction to 'The Truth about the Russian Dancers', *Dance Perspectives* 14 (1962), pp. 4–10 (p. 5).

4 Ibid. p. 5.

5 See, for instance, most recent studies such as Valentina Bold and Andrew Nash, eds, *Gateway to the Modern: Resituating J. M. Barrie* (Glasgow: Scottish Literature International, 2014); or R. D. C. Jack, *The Road to the Never Land: A Reassessment of J M Barrie's Dramatic Art* (Glasgow: Humming Earth, 2010).

6 Janet Dunbar, *J. M. Barrie: The Man Behind the Image* (London: Collins, 1970), pp. 239–40.

7 Denis Mackail, *The Story of J. M. B.* (London: C. Scribner's Sons, 1941), p. 545.

8 Cynthia Asquith, *Portrait of Barrie* (London: James Barrie, 1955), p. 32.

till 1962, when it appeared in the art magazine *Dance Perspectives* with Karsavina's illuminating introduction and a discerning comparison of textual variants, produced by Selma Jeanne Cohen.[9] In this context, Cynthia Asquith's comment is most telling and revealing, for it draws attention to the fact that Barrie's work was slightly more than a skilful parody of or a tribute to the unrelenting Russian craze, induced by a series of Diaghilev seasons in Paris and London. The thoroughness and infinite care with which Barrie worked on the playlet (the idea of which could have been easily nipped in the bud) lends it significance as an artistic statement – a perceptive reflection on cultural dialogism and a searching piece of dramatic criticism, which, it will be shown, suggests a modernist rather than Edwardian outlook on the interaction of the traditional and the exotic and thus puts into new perspective certain aspects of the British perception of what was notoriously categorised as the Russian myth.

The Truth about the Russian Dancers (with an intriguing subtitle 'Showing how they love, how they marry, how they are made, with how they die and live happily ever afterwards') was premiered on 15 March 1920 at the London Coliseum. Set to Arnold Bax's allusively witty music, half

9 J. M. Barrie, 'The Truth of the Russian Dancers', in A. J. Pischl and Selma Jeanne Cohen, eds, *Dance Perspectives* 14 (1962), 12–30. In 1987 the play was reprinted as a paperback by Johnson Reprint Corporation. The published text is based on meticulous analysis and compilation of two holographs and twelve typescripts, produced by Selma Jeanne Cohen, who gives the following description of the source: 'In January 1958, the Henry W. and Albert A. Berg Collection of the New York Public Library acquired from a London dealer two holographs and eleven typescripts of *The Truth about the Russian Dancers*. The catalogues of the Collection classified and described the material as follows: Holograph 1. Incomplete, unsigned and undated; 5 pages, numbered [1] – 6, page 4 missing. Marked "Scene 1," and with the initials E. C. H. [the initials remain unidentified] at the top of the first page. Holograph 2. Signed and dated September 26, 1919, 32 pages. All the typescripts, which fall into five groups – A–E – bear the above date, with the exception of D, which is undated. E 3 is dated also July 1926. No typescript is signed [...] In addition to these, the editors have also examined the script belonging to Madame Karsavina. Typescript K. This is uncorrected and is the copy she actually used' (Selma Jeanne Cohen, 'The Text of "The Truth about the Russian Dancers"', *Dance Perspectives* 14 (1962), pp. 31–4 (pp. 31–2)).

dance-half play, all mockery and all magic – the playlet was framed within the eye-catching 'Anglo-Bakst-ish'[10] designs by Paul Nash, and directed by Gerald du Maurier – a great connoisseur and enthusiast of Barrie's theatre (which brought him to fame), who, according to the reviewer, had a keen 'appreciation of the bizarre in this production.'[11]

The curtain rises at Vere Castle, the peace and quiet of which is queerly disrupted when Karissima – a Russian Ballerina (performed by Karsavina) pays a visit to this ancient stronghold of the conventionally correct. The charming guest can talk with nothing but her toes, and all way through the action Karissima expresses herself exclusively in dance. Naturally, Lady Vere and Bill, her elderly brother-in-law (a passionate golf player and a villain), are utterly dismayed:

> Lady Vere can't get used to being kissed by *Karissima*, who *will* stand upon her lightly with one foot, oddly waving the other meanwhile in the air. Besides it takes too long and *is* rather too demonstrative. And couldn't *Karissima* dear just try to walk with her soles really flat on the ground in the solid English county way? Certainly *Karissima* will try, to please.[12]

Meanwhile, young *Lord Vere* loses his heart and almost immediately marries the irresistible dancer, to the great shock of the dowager duchess – the bride dances 'I will' with a *corps de ballet* of bridesmaids. The child is to be born to a happy couple, but according to the weird and powerful Maestro, who ultimately runs the entire show, Karissima should now sacrifice her life for her little child, for the world of the Russian Dancers is a closed one; and someone must leave this world to make place for a newcomer. Karissima agrees to the horrid condition, and the next moment she is brought out as a corpse on her bier by the maids, who dance their grief. Surprisingly, the corpse rises and dances too. 'But the dead don't dance!', cries in bewilderment the young husband. 'Dead Russian dancers do' answers the Maestro, but his heart is deeply touched. He takes the sacrifice upon himself, lying

10 'Karsavina and Barrie', *The Times*, 16 March 1920, p. 14.
11 'T', 'At the Play', *Punch*, 24 March 1920, p. 236.
12 Ibid. p. 236.

down in Karissima's stead on the bier, and allowing her and her child to live happily ever after in the gloomy luxury of the Vere Castle.

Figure 5. Tamara Karsavina as Karissima and Basil Forster as Lord Vere in *The Truth about the Russian Dancers* (1920). Press Association collection.

The play became a sell-out for the entire stage-run (about a month);[13] and almost every paper had at least half a column dedicated to the production. *Punch* magazine wrote about the ultimate triumph of the author, who had never done anything better – 'more ambitious things, yes, but nothing so free from flaw';[14] *The Tatler* described it as 'the most delightful affair imaginable';[15] while A. B. Walkley from *The Times* thought that words

13 The play was revived on 28 July 1926 at the Savoy Theatre with Karsavina in the leading role (reviewed in 'Savoy Theatre', *The Times*, 29 July 1926, p. 10).

14 'T', p. 236.

15 'Arkay', *The Tatler*, 7 April 1920.

simply could not do justice 'to such a blend of fantasy, irony, and humour'. 'To try to put so light and whimsical a thing as this on paper', he maintained,

> is only to spoil it. Such a blend of fantasy, irony, and humour is, one need hardly say, only to be had from one man. And not for the first time that delightful man has had the happy thought of linking his peculiar charm with another charm not so rare, but equally potent, the charm of the eternal feminine eternally on toe-tip. The appropriate (but fortunately impossible) thing would be to dance one's criticism of Karsavina – who not only dances with the perfection we all know so well, but acts and collaborates in the irony and fun of the thing, with the sympathetic intelligence of the true artist.[16]

Arnold Bax's music ('a separate ecstasy' worth enjoying 'for its own independent sake'[17]) and the directorial mastery of Gerald du Maurier also received a series of fulsome comments; the latter was portrayed as the one who 'brought to triumphant achievement a task, which must have bristled with difficult problems.'[18]

Ironically, the note on 'the problems' (the full spectrum of which was hardly known to the reviewer) turns out to be more telling than a sheer rhetorical trope; and the whole question of Barrie's interest in the Russian dancers deserves closer and more in-depth consideration: firstly, because by the time the play was completed the fame of the Ballets Russes in England had already passed its peak; and secondly, because Barrie had never been a fan of this type of performance.

To give some background on the first point, the peak of the Ballets Russes' fame fell largely in the pre-World War I years, when in 1911 London saw the premiere of the Diaghilev seasons after their unparalleled triumph at the Parisian Théâtre du Châtelet. The audience was completely mesmerised by the performance, for everything in these productions was scandalous, innovative and ambivalently subversive: the ambiguous sexuality of Nijinsky, wearing pearls around his long and muscular neck; the swivelling and stomping of the *Polovtsian Dances*; the gaudy colours of Bakst's

16 'Karsavina and Barrie', p. 14.
17 'Karsavina and Barrie', p. 14.
18 A. E. Johnson, 'The Truth about Karsavina', *Eve*, 1 April 1920, pp. 112–13 (p. 113).

costumes, which dazzled the Western eye like a glimpse of an Oriental market at noon. It was a bittersweet success from scandal, which burst open the confines of the nineteenth-century theatre and embraced both artistic and social spheres. As Green and Swan describe it in their study, upholstery, furnishings, and dress patterns all were affected within the season:

> Fashionable ladies began to wear jupe-culottes, turbans and bandeaux with single peacock feathers affixed – anything that could be called 'Persian' Designers in all sorts of materials matted blue with green and red with orange for the first time. Rooms were furnished with divans, alcoves, censers and gaudy striped cushions on black or purple floor [...] Strong exotic perfumes, like sandalwood and patchouli, which had been the mark of the cocotte, were now bought by women of fashion.[19]

'Announce unparalleled triumph', Diaghilev cabled from London to Astruc, the impresario of the Ballets Russes in Paris, 'Audience indescribably smart.'[20]

The atmosphere became different in less than ten years' time. In 1918 Russia was deserting her former allies on World War I's Eastern Fronts. The Bolshevik government negotiated a separate peace with the Germans under the Brest-Litovsk treaty; as a result, the latter were able to move forces away from Eastern battlefields to the French borders, thus strengthening their hand. This placed additional pressure on the allied troops fighting on the Western frontiers. The common opinion was expressed by *The Times*, which stated that the new Russian government 'has set the seal to their ignominy.'[21]

Russia was now turned into some kind of a public bogy, casting a spell on everything remotely associated with its name. Sergei Lifar, the successor to Nijinsky's primacy in the Russian Ballets, commented on the aura of hostility and tension that surrounded his compatriots in Europe during these post-revolutionary war years. 'All sufferings endured by the Russian troops at the time of their advance to Eastern Prussia', he wrote,

19 Green and Swan, p. 65.

20 Alexandre Astruc, telegram from Diaghilev to Astruc, 23 June 1911, Astruc Papers, Lincoln Centre; quoted in Buckle, p. 205.

21 'Our New War', *The Times*, 21 February 1918, p. 7.

'were instantaneously forgotten, and even the Russian officers, who had been selflessly fighting on the French battlefields, were not spared from the risk of being spit in the face.'[22]

Things were equally difficult for the Russian dancers. In spring 1918 the company found itself stuck in Lisbon and then subsequently in Spain, being completely bankrupted by the political unrest of the Portugal revolution. Coming back to Paris was no longer an option; for even Diaghilev, a firm favourite of the French stage in the pre-War years, 'felt moral qualms about rendering himself to the city' that suddenly had become so ostentatiously anti-Russian.[23] The London Coliseum did offer Diaghilev a contract for the autumn season of 1918, but the terms were abusively poor and restrictive, something that in earlier years would have been rejected on the spot; as Diaghilev wrote in his recollections,

> The War terminated these wonderful seasons, and after the separate Brest-Litovsk treaty, we – the Russians – became so unwelcome that we found ourselves locked in Spain for almost a year. The King of Spain – a godfather of the Russian ballet, as he called himself, made a special effort for us to get permission for travelling to England. One had to secure contacts in London [...] I, then, accepted an invitation from Sir Edward Stoll [*should read Sir Oswald Stoll*]; and although no theatres other than Music Halls have ever favoured our productions, I am grateful to Sir Edward [*Oswald*] for his kind assistance in these difficult times, when politics has erected hard-hitting obstacles in the way of such an apolitical venture as a troupe of ballet artists.[24]

As regards Barrie's sketch on the *Russian Dancers*, it was conceived precisely at this stage when the eminence of all things Russian was largely in decline. Diaghilev's company stayed in England for a major part of 1919; the troupe performed in Manchester and in London; it received a fair degree of enthusiasm and public acclaim, but it was a moderate, lukewarm reception, not remotely comparable to the triumph and accolade of the first seasons. Did the playwright make an attempt to capture the glittering twilight of the fading fashion – to portray something that he felt was

22 Sergei Lifar, *Diaghilev i s Diaghilevym* (Moscow: Vargius, 2005), p. 356.

23 Ibid. p. 357.

24 Ibid. p 360.

disappearing and that was so dear to his memories or to his heart? This, arguably, was hardly in line with the author's initial intentions, for Barrie had never been a great enthusiast of the Russian ballet; moreover, on the whole, he was not particularly fond of the art of music and dance. Peter Davies, one of the Llewelyn Davies brothers, befriended and then informally adopted by Barrie, mentions in his diaries how frustrated he was with Barrie's caustic references to his 'callow enthusiasm for opera' and 'a calf-love for the Russian ballet, then an exciting novelty [...] that was still more emphatically frowned on and ridiculed.'[25] Barrie's own interview (early 1920) on the background of *The Truth about the Russian Dancers* project displays a minimal, on the border of perfunctory politeness, degree of interest in the ballet performance, mentioning an 'occasional visit' to the show for which he 'grew more and more enthusiastic.'[26] These 'occasional visits', however, happened to be not so 'memorable' after all, because no mention of these occasions can be found in Barrie's personal correspondence of the time, apart from a letter to one of his oldest friends Mrs Lucas, dated 19 May 1920 (already after the premiere of *The Truth about the Russian Dancers*),[27] in which he cursorily notes the fact of his attendance at the production: 'Audrey, as I daresay you know, I see sometimes, and tomorrow I'm taking her to the Russian ballet with my sister.'[28]

Barrie was certainly aware of the new run of Diaghilev's seasons in London, but its appeal for him stemmed from the perspective of a professional writer rather than that of a ballet aficionado – a fresh source of plots for story-telling, which had always been his interest, his forte, and, according to many, the very essence of his art.[29] Cynthia Asquith refers to this in a diary entry from February 1919:

25 Diaries of Peter Davies, quoted in Dunbar, p. 205.

26 Church, 'Barrie Writes Play for Russian Ballet Dancer'.

27 Mrs Lucas was in charge of Chateau Bettancourt (near Révigny) where Barrie set up a hospital for the war-victim children of Rheims and its neighbourhood (Viola Meynell, comments to J. M. Barrie, *Letters of J. M. Barrie*, ed. Viola Meynell (London: Peter Davies, 1942), p. 87). Audrey, mentioned in the letter below, was her daughter.

28 Barrie, letter to Mrs Lucas, 19 May 1920, *Letters of J. M. Barrie*, p. 94.

29 Bernard Shaw often described Barrie as a 'born storyteller' (G. B. Shaw, *Our Theatre in the Nineties* (London: Constable and Company, 1932), III, p. 244).

> Barrie, encouraged by Whibley's ready laugh, told several stories, two of which have stayed in my sieve. A London hostess wrote to a Russian dancer to ask what her fee would be for dancing at an evening party. The dancer said she would come for a hundred pounds. The hostess, writing back to agree to this figure, added, 'I think, perhaps, I had better tell you now that I don't introduce the *artiste* to my guests.' To this the dancer replied, 'In that case my fee will be only fifty pounds.'[30]

It is noteworthy that this very story was later on transferred directly to Barrie's *The Truth about the Russian Dancers*; and in her recollections of the rehearsals Karsavina comments on her difficulties in miming the specific details of its plot:

> such lines as Karissima's telling the wicked uncle that her fee for a private appearance is three hundred guineas but only one hundred if she is not asked to mix with the guests [...] Three fingers stuck out? No! No! Three pointedly emphasised *ronds de jambe* and an arrogant toss of the head must make my meaning clear. That 'line' never failed to raise a laugh.[31]

Generally speaking, Barrie was not a musical person. Peter Davies drew attention to the fact that 'music and painting and poetry, and the part that they may be supposed to play in making a civilised being, had a curiously small place in J. M. B.'s view of things [...] Being himself totally unmusical', Peter notes, Barrie 'not only did not encourage such leanings, but in one way and another could not help discouraging them.'[32] He found it stressful when, reportedly, he was 'forced' to go to opera evenings, to which a good cricket game would be undoubtedly preferred. In July 1914, for instance, he wrote to George Davies that in the 'stress of going to the opera' with Peter they had forgotten to wire him the results of the Eton and Harrow cricket match. He insisted that Peter had dragged him to the opera two nights running, and as a result 'neither he nor Michael patronised the match.'[33] And despite the fact that music interludes, as well

30 Asquith, p. 15.

31 Karsavina, Introduction to 'The Truth about the Russian Dancers', p. 7.

32 Diaries of Peter Davies, quoted in Dunbar, p. 205.

33 Barrie, letter to George Davies, 13 July 1914, *Letters of J. M. Barrie*, p. 77. 'The operas were Khovantchina and [...] Boris Godunov, with Chaliapin singing' (Diaries of Peter Davies, quoted in Dunbar, p. 205).

as specially designed dances constituted an important part of his 1904 *Peter Pan* production (for which he took meticulous care in the rehearsals[34]), it was the lighter side of life – 'games and fishing, as well as of course being thoroughly good *mens sana in corpore sano* specimens' that, in the words of the Davies brothers, he painstakingly catered for.[35]

One, of course, may surmise that such an aversion arose from his early and profoundly negative experience as a librettist, when he and Arthur Conan Doyle together produced a script for Richard D'Oyly Carte's new Savoy opera, pretentiously entitled *Jane Annie or the Good Conduct Prize*. Premiered in May 1893 with the music of Ernest Ford, it was closed as a complete flop after a small run of approximately fifty evenings. And although the subsequent tour of the production (in Bradford, Newcastle, Manchester, and Birmingham) was more successful than the original London show, the *Academy* still called it 'one of the weakest librettos ever written and the number of weak librettos has been large'; and Bernard Shaw, when reviewing the opera for the *World*, presented it as 'the most unblushing piece of tomfoolery that two respectable citizens could conceivably indulge in publicly.'[36] It is difficult to judge as to the degree of trauma left by this infamous venture on Barrie's aesthetic preferences and future intentions (his second attempt at producing a musical, *Rosy Rapture* (1915) was

34 Lisa Chaney, *Hide-And-Seek with Angels: The Life of J. M. Barrie* (London: Arrow Books 2006), p. 224.

35 Diaries of Peter Davies, quoted in Dunbar, p. 205.

36 G. B. Shaw, 'London Music – Jane Annie', *World*, 24 May 1893 (Bernard Shaw, *Music in London 1890–1894* (London: Constable and Company, 1932), II, p. 315); 'Bibliographical', *The Academy* 58 (1900), p. 178.
It was Barrie who brought his idea for *Jane Annie* to D'Oyly Carte, but having been delayed by a severe illness, he had to resort to his friend, Conan Doyle's assistance in order to complete the commissioned work in time (Barrie's telegram read, 'Come at once if convenient – if not convenient, come all the same'). Although regarding the plotline Doyle did not have much room for manoeuvre, he stepped in and did his best. Afterwards he would say, 'The only literary gift which Barrie has not got is the sense of poetic rhythm, and the instinct for what is permissible in verse' (Chaney, p. 115).

equally disastrous[37]), but throughout his life he always categorised himself as musically unreceptive. With some wonderfully light-hearted irony he commented on this subject in a letter to Cynthia Asquith (1 April 1921): 'Nicolas has arrived, and they have at once purchased gramophone records that roar and hiss louder than they ever roared and hissed before. I don't see how I can help becoming musical in the end.'[38]

As regards the Russian theme in Barrie's artistic worldview, this too had never been the centre of his fundamental interests and literary pursuits. In spring 1917, when many of the British intellectuals (and his close friends such as, for instance, Shaw and H. G. Wells) were signing open telegrams in support of the Russian anti-monarchist revolution,[39] Barrie's name did not appear in these lists. Given that, like many others, he was swayed by the burgeoning patriotism at the start of World War I (conveyed in the pages of *The Times* in a special interview to the American correspondent[40]), he must have been appalled by the Bolsheviks' separate Brest-Litovsk treaty (for that was precisely the time, winter 1918, when Barrie actively chaired a number of Red Cross auctions, collecting money for the war cause[41]), but he never made any public assertion in this regard.

Notwithstanding his later interest in Russian authors, he was far too young to make personal acquaintance with Turgenev, who arrived in

37 Leonee Ormond, *J. M. Barrie* (Edinburgh: Scottish Academic Press, 1987), p. 115.

38 Barrie, letter to Cynthia Asquith, 1 April 1921, *Letters of J. M. Barrie*, p. 188.

39 Shaw, 'Assure New Russia of British Regard'.

40 The interview was given in February 1917, when the US joined the Allied forces; it read: 'The other night he [Isaac F. Marcosson, a United States journalist and a contributor to the *Saturday Evening Post* and *Everybody's Magazine*] was sitting by a fire smoking and discussing the war with a man who by his genius, fancy, imagination, and heart had bound all the English-reading peoples of the world into a common friendship – the man who wrote Peter Pan. (Loud cheers,) "My friend", said J. M. Barrie to him, "I have been stirred and thrilled by these recent events more than I have ever been in my life. Have you stopped to think what it means to have the two great English-speaking communities at last fighting together for a common cause, linked together in a great crusade of humanity against inhumanity? Why, it is greater than the war itself"' ('U. S. and the War. New York Journalist on National Awakening', *The Times*, 10 February 1917, p. 5).

41 Mackail, p. 516.

London for a winter's stay in November 1870. As a widely educated and cultured person, he certainly read the writings of Tolstoy and Dostoevsky: in the first decades of the twentieth century everyone was enthralled by the newly published translations of their works. This was reflected in one of his letters to Mrs Lucas, where Barrie mentions *War and Peace* as his bedtime reading.[42] And although he does not go into any further comments regarding his impressions of the novel, he was known to have joined the group of British intellectuals, who, in an open statement to *The Times*, expressed their gratitude to the Russian men of letters for their contribution to the progress of the world's literary thought. 'It was a strange world that opened before us', they wrote,

> a world full of foreign names which we could neither pronounce nor remember, of foreign customs and articles of daily life which we could not understand. Yet beneath all the strangeness there was a deep sense of having discovered a new home, of meeting our unknown kindred, of finding expressed a great burden of thought which had lain unspoken and half-realised at the depth of our own minds. The books were very different one from another, sometimes they were mutually hostile; yet we found in all some quality which made them one, and made us all one with them. We will not attempt to analyse that quality.[43]

Written in December 1914, and signed by thirty-four illustrious British authors (including Arnold Bennett, Arthur Conan Doyle, Thomas Hardy, John Galsworthy, Henry James, and H. G. Wells), the letter was obviously 'heated' by the allied spirit of World War I; but apart from that instance of congenial fervour, Barrie did not seem to be particularly moved by Russophilia, which captured quite a few among his literary circle. Unlike the Garnetts and Ford Madox Ford's family, he did not become a member of the Free Russian Library in London.[44] Unlike Bernard Shaw, he never

42 'Now I am off to read *War and Peace* in bed' (Barrie, letter to Mrs E. V. Lucas, 3 July 1918, *Letters of J. M. Barrie*, p. 92).

43 'Russia in Literature. Tribute by British Men of Letters', *The Times*, 23 December 1914, p. 10; reprinted in 'Causerie', *New York Times*, 24 January 1915.

44 Rebecca Beasley and Philip Ross Bullock, 'Introduction: Against Influence: On Writing about Russian Influence in Britain', in Beasley and Bullock, *Russia in Britain, 1880–1940: From Melodrama to Modernism*, pp. 1–18 (p. 16).

joined the Friends of Russian Freedom association, at the time when the prominent Russian anarchists – Prince Kropotkin, Volkhovsky and Stepniak-Kravchinsky – started to promote Russian literature as a part of their activities in London at the end of the 1880s and in the 90s. And, unlike Galsworthy, he was never involved in entertaining the Russian authors at the dinners of the newly established P. E. N. Club, attended by the Soviet envoy Boris Pilniak (1923) and by the future Nobel Prize laureate Ivan Bunin (1925).[45] Generally speaking, Barrie was a rare guest at this kind of important social occasion, to the extent that at times people failed to recognise who he was. Marjory Watts, one of the organisers of the club meetings and the daughter of Amy Dawson Scott – a co-founder of P. E. N., notes an embarrassing episode during the First International P. E. N. Congress dinner in May 1923:

> One small incident at that banquet has stayed with me: as I walked among the guests, with my sitting list, a very small man with a moustache smiled at me and asked. 'And where do I sit?' 'Well, who *are* you?' I asked, and he said gently, 'My name is Barrie.'[46]

It is not incidental therefore, that Barrie's idea to write a play about the Russian dancers came from a purely personal perspective. In autumn 1918, after her spectacular success with the London public, Lydia Lopokova, a prima ballerina of Diaghilev's troupe, sent a letter to Barrie suggesting he write a play for her.[47] She had just returned from a tour in the United States, where she had not only been thrilled by Maude Adams (in the Broadway production of *Peter Pan*), but developed a great fascination for Barrie's books. They met and became friends, retaining deep fondness for each other to the end of their lives, when Lopokova, now Lady Keynes (she married the British economist John Maynard Keynes) used to spend her time with Barrie chatting and sitting comfortably on his knee – they were both

45 Marjory Watts, *P. E. N. The Early Years 1921–1926* (London: Archive Press, 1971), p. 26 and 30. Bunin was awarded the Nobel Prize for Literature in 1933, a year after John Galsworthy.

46 Ibid. p. 25.

47 Mackail, p. 536.

comparable in height: both about five feet tall.[48] Lydia must have made quite an impression on Barrie, for almost immediately he thought of a sketch, inspired by the vivacious 'Russianness' of his charming acquaintance (he could not have got to know at the time that this 'vivaciousness' would go far beyond the limits of anything one could possibly imagine).

By 1918, the twenty-seven-year-old Lydia Lopokova (born Lopukhova[49]), had already become an uncontested prima of the Russian Ballet. A pupil of Mikhail Fokine and Karsavina's younger tutee at the Russian Imperial Ballet School, her star chance came when she was invited to join the Diaghilev Ballets on their European tour of 1910 (Fokine, her teacher, was then the leading choreographer of the troupe). Always avid for sensation, and capitalising on Lopokova's miniature figure and striking complexion, Diaghilev knocked a year off her age and promoted her as a teenage prodigy, starring in Fokine's *Carnival*, Stravinsky's *Petrushka* and even in *L'Oiseau de feu* – effectively in all Karsavina's leading roles, although, unlike Karsavina, she was never compared to the iconic type of a flaming princess – only 'to a sparrow, a canary, or at best to a humming bird.'[50] Her appearance was not remotely close to that of a ballerina of the classic formation. At just five feet, she was too short, with round, fairly plump shoulders. Her *ports de bras* were not perfect and neither were her *tours*, but she responded instinctively to Mikhail Fokine's expressive choreography and his rebellion against the stiff academicism of the classical style. Swift, tiny and light as a feather, with a springing leap almost comparable to that of Nijinsky, her running on points, according to her brother, a prominent dancer and choreographer Fedor Lopukhov, was

48 Judith Mackrell, *Bloomsbury Ballerina: Lydia Lopokova* (London: Weidenfeld & Nicolson, 2008), p. 208.

49 She changed (anglicised) the spelling of her name in 1914, during her stay in the US, when she tried to launch herself as an actress (E.Ya. Surits, 'Malen'kaia Lopukhova: Lidiia Lopukhova (1891–1981), ee zhizn' i tvorchestvo za rubezhom', in *Khudozhestvennaia kul'tura russkogo zarubezh'ia 1917–1939* (Moscow: Indrik, 2008), pp. 366–80 (p. 371)); see also Mackrell, p. xv.

50 Mackrell, p. xix.

> infectiously gay and light, as if she were tripping on air [...] Her leg muscles were remarkable and she could achieve an incredibly big leap, almost masculine in its power, yet, at the same time, her flight through the air was as delicate, as was her landing. Whereas [Nijinsky's] leap reminded one of the jump and flight of a grasshopper, Lydia's resembled the [...] descent of dandelion down, like little angels portrayed in the masterpieces of the quattrocento artists.[51]

At nineteen she was the latest sensation of Diaghilev's seasons; praised by Jean Louis Vaudoyer (in the *Variations on the Russian Ballet*) for her 'ingenious virtuosity, tempered', in his words, 'by the imperceptible awkwardness of youth.'[52]

It was indeed this astonishing combination of Lydia's captivating expressiveness, her Imperial grace and childlike enthusiasm[53] that the public invariably took to their hearts. 'Bewitching and piquant' a critic for *The Globe* called her;[54] and the *New York Times* stated that 'Lopokova's dancing was thoroughly charming and of the kind to make the audience hang on every gesture and change of expression.'[55] Being somewhat the wrong shape and size for a ballet-prima, she was, nonetheless, very pretty and was blessed with natural vivacity and a sense of drama and rhythm. Cyril Beaumont, who wrote at length about Lopokova, testifies that being accustomed 'to the sweet sadness of Karsavina's intensely poetic style of dancing', he was struck by Lopokova's personality, as much as by her ballet performance. 'She never put on ballerina's airs', he notes,

> As soon as she had taken leave of those who came to pay her homage, she would wipe off her make-up – she never put on very much – and change into a simple short skirt,

51 F. V. Lopukhov, 'Lydia Vasil'evna Lopukhova: A Choreographic portrait', in *Lydia Lopokova*, ed. Milo Keynes (London: Weidenfeld and Nicolson, 1983), pp. 50–3 (p. 52).

52 Tamara Karsavina, *Theatre Street* (New York: E. P. Dutton & Co, 1961), p. 219.

53 Thus, when listing to the journalists all things she favoured in the US, she was reported to say 'Of all the things which I like here most in America, the very most is the short cake strawberry' (*New York Review*, 12 August 1911, also quoted in Mackrell, p. 63).

54 *The Globe*, 20 January 1916; quoted in Nesta Macdonald, *Diaghilev Observed by Critics in England and the United States, 1911–1929* (London: Dance Horizons, 1975), p. 142.

55 'Diaghileff Ballet Dances "Carneval"', *New York Times*, 20 January 1916, p. 10.

> woolly jumper, and tam-o'-shanter, skipping home, like a schoolgirl let out of school. She had an ingenuous manner of talking, but she was very intelligent and witty, and, unlike some dancers, her conversation was not limited to herself and the Ballet.[56]

Unsurprisingly, Picasso, with whom Lopokova struck up a friendship while she was starring as a female acrobat in *Parade*, for which the artist designed the setting, found her irresistibly expressive (Lydia was also close friends with Olga Khokhlova – Picasso's then wife and a former Diaghilev ballerina). He was very keen on sketching Lydia dancing; there remain several of his drawings of Lopokova, including a number of sketches of her performing the can-can in *La Boutique fantasque*, and the one (in green ink), where she is depicted alongside Diaghilev and Massine, as well as a pencil drawing of the ballerina as a sitter. It is also known that on his later visits to England in the 1950s, Picasso mentioned Lydia, as the first, and perhaps the only one, among his former acquaintances, whom he wished to talk to.[57]

Picasso, of course, was not alone among the men falling for the charms of the fascinating Russian. Lovers were played off against one another, even though Lydia had very little in her presence of what is commonly attributed to the seductively glossy type of *femme fatale*. In the words of Lydia Sokolova, one of Diaghilev's ballet dancers: 'She was sweet to everybody, never jealous and never coveting another dancer's roles; but she always seems to be hopping off somewhere, and obviously valued her private life more than her life in a ballet troupe.'[58] She left her fiancé, the American journalist Heywood Broun, and instead married Randolfo Barocci (in 1916), the current business manager of the Ballets Russes – a smooth-talking cosmopolitan, who one day stole all her jewellery, and whom she eventually (1925) managed to divorce on the grounds of his bigamy, which he had difficulties to conceal. In the midst of the wartime European tour, she had an on-off fling with Stravinsky, who was still married to Ekaterina

56 Annabel Farjeon, 'Lydia Lopokova and Serge Diaghilev', in *Lydia Lopokova*, ed. Milo Keynes (London: Weidenfeld and Nicolson, 1983) pp. 71–83 (p. 74).

57 Surits, p. 374.

58 Lidiia Sokolova, *Dancing for Diaghilev* (London: John Murray, 1960), p. 73.

Nosenko at the time, but already attracted to the Parisian actress Vera Sudeikina (who eventually became his second wife).[59]

When the Ballets Russes arrived in London in 1918, all men were quickly at her feet. Lopokova took part in practically every ballet performed during the season, and had a stunning success with both the public and the critics. She danced witty and coquettish Mariuccia in *The Good-Humoured Ladies* (based on Goldoni's *Le Donne di buon umore*, music by Domenico Scarlatti), a Snowmaiden in Rimsky-Korsakov's *Le Soleil de nuit*, a bacchante in *Cleopatra* (with new stage designs by Robert Delauney), and a doll in Rossini's *La Boutique fantasque* (premiered on 5 June 1919) – the story of two mischievous dolls, who elope from a Victorian toyshop. This ballet, produced by Leonide Massine, Diaghilev's latest choreographer – far more daring than all his predecessors,[60] was a highlight of the 1919 London season. It provided a satirical outlook on nineteenth-century mores: with its caricatural human characters, and its dancing toys (Lopokova and Massine) strangely incongruous, as well as oddly touching. Roger Fry claimed that André Derain's post-impressionist recreation of the ballet's Victorian setting had refracted 'the artistic impression of the past' into a strikingly contemporary aesthetics.[61]

Everyone loved it, including the most sceptical and the most demanding. The crowd filled every seat and every inch of the standing space in the Alhambra Theatre; and when Massine and Lydia danced their frenzied

59 Mackrell, p. 155.

60 In 1917 Massine collaborated with Satie, Picasso and Cocteau on *Parade* – the most overtly avant-garde, and outrightly 'cubist' creation of the Ballets Russes (premiered on 18 May 1917 at the Théâtre du Châtelet in Paris). As regards his *Boutique fantasque*, Ezra Pound, writing under a pseudonym for the *New Age*, commented: 'The costumes and staging give more of the spirit and "message" (or whatever they call it) of modern (very modern) art than all the dozen shows of greenery-yallery that a contemporary art-critic is called upon to see in a year [...] Rossini fitted in perfectly, but was given new life, and the dancing exposed a new emotional violence [...] The Boutique seems to me worthy of a permanent place in the art of the ballet' (William Atheling [Ezra Pound], 'At the Ballet', *New Age*, 16 October 1919, p. 412).

61 Roger Fry, 'The Scenery of La Boutique Fantasque', *Athenaeum*, 13 June 1919, p. 466; see also Adrian Stokes, *Russian Ballets* (London: Faber and Faber, 1934), pp. 17–54.

can-can, which transformed her from an indolent porcelain doll into a bacchante, 'the audience began screaming and chanting their names.'[62] Cyril Beaumont leaves the following recollection of his impressions:

> Her body bends and sways as though fashioned of India rubber, her foot leaps above her head, wrists twist, turns revolve amidst a sea of foaming lace and ribbons [...] it is a thing of delirious joy leaving not a trace of the vulgarity that it might obtain were it performed by a lesser artist.[63]

Barrie must have been aware of the stunning success of the performance: in March 1919 the revival of his one-act play *Half an Hour* at the London Coliseum was placed in a double bill with the Diaghilev Ballets. The run lasted for a couple of weeks, and the playwright, who had always been sceptical regarding the worthiness of the art of ballet, had an opportunity to get to know it at closer quarters. He, perhaps, became slightly more persuaded by *The Boutique* production, as a reference to it can be found in his sketch on the Russian dancers, the stage directions to which read: 'The procession should be impressive – something like the carrying in the Boutique ballet.'[64]

He started working on *The Truth about the Russian Dancers* in spring 1919. The new project was a full length fantasy play, featuring a Russian ballerina called Uvula – a 'little grape' (from Latin), which, as it seemed, was a telling emblem of Barrie's petite, but extremely lively new friend. Uvula's 'bird-like motions' and 'hesitant English'[65] suggested further allusions to Lopokova, who was meant to take the lead in the play at the Haymarket in the autumn.[66]

62 Mackrell, p. 146.

63 Cyril W. Beaumont, *The Art of Lydia Lopokova* (London: Beaumont Press, 1920), p. 5; Cyril Beaumont, 'Lydia Lopokova, an appreciation, 1920', in *Lydia Lopokova*, ed. Milo Keynes (London: Weidenfeld and Nicolson, 1983), pp. 224–8 (p. 227).

64 Barrie, 'The Truth about the Russian Dancers', p. 30.

65 Lopokova's idiosyncratic use of English was notoriously termed 'Lydian English' by Maynard Keynes (Mackrell, p. 198).

66 Mackail, p. 537.

The existing holograph contains only the opening scene of the original project, but the framework of the love story between Uvula and the English aristocrat Lord Vere becomes evident from the start. The scene is laid at the Veres' private golf links with a distant view of the ancient house on a sunny summer morning. The Countess of Vere and her unmarried brother Bill (described as a 'dark, designing villain') are going to play against young Lord Vere and Mlle Uvula:

> Lord Vere appears with Uvula, who makes 'bird-like motions.' Her English is somewhat hesitant, and when she is offered a putter, she stretches out her arms to Lord Vere, intimating that he should explain for her, and he interprets, saying that she wants to play her own games. The little golf dance follows [...] Uvula then goes off proudly on her toes – with Lord Vere, leaving Bill to tell Lady Vere that this is cheating. The latter protests the dancer's innocence, but adds: 'All the same one never knows.'[67]

Two things are particularly notable about Barrie's fantasy playlet. Its plotline turned out to be surprisingly prophetic: Lopokova did become the wife of an English aristocrat. In 1925 she married an illustrious economist John Maynard Keynes (to the utter dismay of his Bloomsbury circle, who were very disdainful of Lydia's origin and manners[68]), and duly acquired the title of Lady Keynes, when her husband was ennobled (1942) as Lord Keynes, Baron of Tilton.

67 Cohen, pp. 31–2.

68 On 4 November 1923, Virginia Woolf wrote to Jacques Reverat: 'On Sep 7th we went to stay with them at Studland – a ducal home, in which they fared rather uneasily, I thought, because the duke's servants were in the pantry; and Lydia's habits, of course, are not ducal [...] I assure you it's tragic to see her sitting down to King Lear. Nobody can take her seriously: every nice young man kisses her. Then she flies into a rage and says she is like Vanessa, like Virginia [...] – a serious woman.' And on 8 June of the same year: 'Maynard is passionately and pathetically in love, because he sees very well that he's dished if he marries her, and she has him by the snout. You can't argue solidly when Lydia's there, and as we set now to the decline, and prefer reason to any amount of high spirits, Lydia's pranks put us all on edge' (Milo Keynes, 'Lydia Lopokova', in *Lydia Lopokova*, ed. Milo Keynes (London: Weidenfeld and Nicolson, 1983), pp. 1–38 (pp. 19–20)).

As regards the staging, ironically, the project has never been put into being (at least in its original version), for in July 1919, when *The Truth about the Russian Dancers* was nearly half-written, Lopokova suddenly vanished, giving nobody any warning and abruptly breaking all her obligations to Diaghilev's troupe. 'There is some stir tonight about the absence of Mlle. Lydia Lopokova from the Russian Ballet at the Alhambra',[69] wrote *The Manchester Guardian*, 'Everyone was more or less mystified concerning her non-appearance, and no one seemed to know where she was. The stage manager wore a harassed, anxious look, and Mlle. Nempchinova, her understudy, wandered restlessly about the stage in nervous excitement.'[70] In a note left to the company manager Sergei Grigoriev, she pleaded ill health, exhaustion and a nervous breakdown and for a couple of months nobody had any idea of what had become of her.[71] She broke her absence in February 1921 in New York, where she performed in Mikhail Fokine's production (rather poor) of *The Rose Girl*, and in spring despite all odds, she was dancing again with the Diaghilev Ballets, first in Madrid, then in Paris and finally in London. Diaghilev, known for his intolerance of any kind of disciplinary matters, seemed to have a soft spot for his little prima: 'Will you have Lopokova back?', Lopokova's manager cabled to him in Paris, 'Yes, if it is the same Lopokova I knew' – followed the reply.[72]

Meanwhile, Barrie had difficulties in proceeding with the play. He was distinctly annoyed by the ballerina, on whom he counted for the entire venture; hence a menacing subtitle that he added to the subsequent draft of *The Truth about the Russian Dancers* (dated September 1920), which was

69 'Our London Correspondence', *The Manchester Guardian*, 12 July 1919.

70 'The Russian Ballet. From behind the Scenes', *Manchester Guardian*, 29 July 1919.

71 Surits, p. 375. An attempt to account for these months of Lopokova's life can be found in Mackrell, pp. 158–60).

72 Quoted in Keynes, p. 6. According to the other members of the troupe, Lopokova had a unique ability to stand up to the anger of the 'Big Serge': 'When she stood looking up at Big Serge (which was what she called Diaghilev) with her screwed-up little bun of hair, the tip of her nose quivering, and an expression between laughter and tears, I defy anybody to say she wasn't worth her weight in gold' (Sokolova, p. 74).

now to be called 'A Warning in One Act'.[73] And although this 'warning' was eventually effaced from the final version of the playlet, it shows how deeply Barrie was affected by the events. Moreover, one can say that *Mary Rose*, one of Barrie's major plays completed precisely during these summer months of 1919, also bears some features of the disturbing Lopokova affair. The female protagonist of *Mary Rose* keeps vanishing without any trace each time she sets foot on a particularly remote Scottish Island: firstly for weeks and then for decades, turning eventually into a ghost. When she is found again, she is not a single day older and has no awareness of the passage of time. While completing *Mary Rose*, Barrie of course could not have known of Lopokova's miraculous reappearance in Diaghilev's ballets, but the parallel between her desertion and an odd habit of evaporation of the main character in *Mary Rose* should not be overlooked.

Given the difficulty of the situation, it is not clear why the story of the Russian dancers had not been dropped altogether and forgotten. In a few months, however, it was successfully reconfigured into a one-act extravaganza and targeted at another uncontested prima of the Diaghilev Ballets. Tamara Karsavina was living in London at the time. Barrie happened to know her through the family of his godson Peter Scott, the son of Captain Robert Scott, who led two expeditions to the Antarctic regions.[74] This is how Karsavina describes it in her recollections:

> At the end of 1919 [20 October[75]] Kathleen Scott [widow of the Antarctic explorer] had told me that Sir James Barrie had been working on a play for me. I could not however bring myself to believe my luck until one day Kathleen took me to see Barrie

73 Cohen, p. 32.

74 The widow of the explorer, Kathleen Scott, née Edith Agnes Kathleen Bruce, was related to Karsavina's husband Henry James Bruce ('Benjie') – an English diplomat who married the ballerina in 1915 in St Petersburg (Benjie's father, Sir Hervey Juckes Lloyd Bruce, was Kathleen's first cousin).

75 The date is given in the diaries of Kathleen Scott, who presents a very similar description of this episode: 'I took Karsavina to see Barrie. When she said "How do you do?", he said "Oh, you can talk! I didn't know you could talk," She faltered something about her accent. He replied, "No, but it's so disappointing. I thought you couldn't talk, except with your feet." Poor Tamara was beginning to think I had brought her

> 'I have written a play for you,' he (Barrie) said in his peculiar rasping voice, and had a fit of coughing.
> 'I speak English with a Russian accent,' I replied.
> 'Oh, can you speak at all? I didn't know.'
> He then read the play. His strong Scotch accent, his cough, and to tell the truth, the play itself, rather overwhelmed me. I even thought at times that he was pulling my leg. After the reading he told me that he first intended the name Uvula for me, but it occurred to him that it might be taken as an allusion to the part of the palate so-called, and he changed it into Karissima, which should be spelt with a K so as to resemble my own name.[76]

One of the most obvious themes of Barrie's sketch on the Russian dancers is that of cultural dialogue and communication, which can be read as a playful double-edged parody directed evenly and neutrally at both sides. On the one hand, the Russian dancers clearly stand out from everything associated with the acceptable norm. They are called into being by a mysterious master-spirit – something of a Diaghilev or, perhaps of the magician in *Petrushka* – and can only express themselves through their own medium ('they find it so much jollier to talk with their toes'[77]), which remains incomprehensible to the respectable traditionalists, like the elderly Veres:

> LADY VERE Whatever I say to Karissima she dances the reply, and I must admit that keeping up a conversation with her is rather a strain. Roger tells me that the clever London audiences understand at once what she is saying to them with her toes, but I am too stupid.[78]

In brief, their origin is hazy – an inauspicious sign for respectable society, and their language is improper – the parallel with Shaw's *Pygmalion* (1914)

---

to see a madman, but presently discovered what he meant, and all went well. He read an entertaining play, in which everyone else talks and she dances. She is made love to, gets married, has a baby, and dies, all dancing – very beautiful and Barrie' (Kathleen Scott [Lady], *Self-Portrait of an Artist* (London: John Murray, 1949), p. 178).

76 Karsavina, Introduction to 'The Truth about the Russian Dancers', p. 4.

77 Barrie, p. 14.

78 Ibid. p. 14.

springs to mind. Nonetheless, within the medium of their communicative habits, the Russian Dancers seem to be inherently more creative and possess a greater degree of freedom of expression than that allocated to their English counterpart by the prescriptiveness of their lines. Karissima's unspoken part (as well as those of her maids) is presented exclusively by way of stage directions; and it is effectively for the performer to translate this outline into her own version of dramatic gestures and dance. Here are but a few examples: 'KARISSIMA *makes some steps [...] of an excited, endearing character*'; 'KARISSIMA *is eager*'; 'KARISSIMA *makes movements which mean all this is Greek to her*'; 'KARISSIMA *approaches her in movements that are an appeal for love*'; 'KARISSIMA *droops pathetically*.'[79] Such a distinct difference in the mode of communication has a clear symbolic meaning on the compositional level of Barrie's playlet: the element of fantasy and beauty associated with the 'Russianness' of the Dancers is pitted against the unimaginative rigidity and conventionality of the English life ('there is no feeling for art in this country'[80]).

In this context, it is worth pointing out that the figure of the Maestro is liminal with regard to this symbolic separation. Strictly speaking the Maestro should also express himself through the language of mime; for who is more a member of the world of the Russian dancers than their master himself? This apparent inconsistency was noted by certain critics, who pointed out that 'the author commits the mistake of giving him [the Maestro] a speaking part.'[81] And indeed, the division between two worlds, 'the conventional' and 'the exotically Russian', would have been more pronounced, given that the ballet master had also expressed himself by way of gestures and dance (though the directions assert that 'he should probably be a dancer and have ballet movements of a restrained order'[82]). Some revisions in this regard were tried out in the 1926 revival of the performance,

79 Ibid. pp. 18–19.

80 Ibid. p. 29.

81 Johnson, p. 113.

82 Barrie, p. 22.

in which according to *The Times*, the Maestro was 'blessed neither with speech nor dancing', and yet expressed 'himself to every one's satisfaction.'[83]

Judging from the number of amendments in the earlier versions of the playlet, Barrie had certain difficulties (or hesitations) in conveying the 'Russianness' of his Maestro. Initially (in the draft) the latter was associated with Diaghilev in a much clearer and more straightforward manner (thus being perceived as unequivocally Russian); and two names of the well-known patrons of the Diaghilev Ballets, Edward Marsh and Lady Edwards, were conspicuously mentioned in relation to Maestro's identity and his past:

LORD VERE Uncle, in confidence, what do they say about him in London?
BILL Wonderful – colossal!
LORD VERE But what do those in the know say about him? What does Eddie Marsh say – or Lady Edwards?[84]

Sir Edward Marsh or Eddie, as he is called in the draft, was private secretary to Winston Churchill and a great patron of avant-garde art. He famously called Diaghilev's *Jeux* a 'Post-Impressionist picture put in motion', and made a lot of positive comments on the Ballets Russes in his correspondence, as well as in contemporary publications such as *The English Review*, *The New Statesman*, *The Nation*, and *Rhythm*.[85] As regards Lady Edwards, although Selma Jeanne Cohen describes her as a fictitious character in her notes to Barrie's playlet,[86] one can argue that the name suggests a clear reference to Misia Sert (Edwards), who was known for her long-lasting association with Diaghilev, her involvement in all creative aspects of the Ballets Russes,

83 'Savoy Theatre', *The Times*, 29 July 1926, p. 10.

84 Cohen, p. 32.

85 Garafola, p. 475; see also Susan Jones, 'Knowing the Dancer: Modernism, Choreography, and the Question of Authority', in *Authority Matters: Rethinking the Theory and Practice of Authorship*, ed. Stephen Donovan, Danuta Zadworna-Fjellestad and Rolf Lundén (Amsterdam and New York: Rodopi, 2008), pp. 193–222 (p. 198). It is in his letter to Edward Marsh that Rupert Brooke expressed his wish to become a ballet-designer, like Diaghilev: 'They, if anything, can redeem our civilisation, I'll give everything to be a ballet-designer' (Marsh, p. lxxvii, also quoted in Buckle, p. 236).

86 Cohen, p. 34.

and for her friendship with its major dancers. Throughout the years Misia was the monetary ballast for the often financially ruined Maestro. It was she who rescued the opening night of *Petrushka*, when it was delayed twenty minutes because the creditors refused to release the costumes without a payment: 'pale and agitated he [Diaghilev] asked if she could give him four thousand francs to pay for the costumes. "In those happy days," Misia said, "one's chauffeur was always waiting". In ten minutes she was back with money.'[87] Misia became the wife of José Maria Sert in August 1920,[88] and was still known as Misia Edwards when Barrie was working on *The Truth about the Russian Dancers*. At that time she was married (unhappily) to Alfred Edwards, the newspaper magnate and the founder of *Le Matin*, a French adaptation of the British daily newspaper *The Morning News*.

These associations were effaced from the later versions of the script, and instead, the Russianness of the Maestro was affirmed by giving him a miming part – the same mode of expression as the Russian ballerinas. The stage directions of this draft manuscript say that 'he can only express himself in dancing and dramatic look and actions'. For instance, when Lord Vere comments on his wife's beauty, 'Maestro indicates how glorious he thinks her. Indicates her figure better made'; and when Karissima dies, Maestro's actions are interpreted by Lord Vere in words his mother can understand; in this case, Barrie remarks, Maestro is to 'say his lines, not with dramatic gestures, but with movements of his feet'.[89]

Maestro's speech is retained in the final version of the text, and he is not given any more specific features relating him to the celebrated Russian ballet-master (Diaghilev). For reasons unknown, Barrie decided to play down the Russian overtones of his whimsical lot, associating it more with the notion of 'the bizarre' (the scene 'must have a look of the bizarre, as in the Russian ballet'[90]) rather than with the specific markers of the Russian tradition. Towards the end, he even began to have certain doubts about

87 Arthur Gold and Robert Fizdale, *Misia: The Life of Misia Sert* (New York: Morrow Quill Paperbacks, 1981), p. 141.

88 Mackrell, p. 160.

89 Cohen, p. 33.

90 Barrie, p. 13.

the Russian affiliation in the title, for in one of the later versions of the manuscript 'he crossed out "The Truth about the Russian Dancers", calling it simply a "Ballet-Play"'.[91]

It would be sheer speculation to discuss why Barrie came up with such a decision. Most of the time he was driven by intuition rather than by any kind of rational concerns: 'Don't ask me what I mean, I don't know myself', he used to respond to Karsavina's questions.[92] His play unreservedly charmed everyone who came to see it; even the ballet connoisseurs fell under its spell, for, as Denis Mackail put it in his biography of Barrie,

> his words and story were in entire and flattering sympathy with the most mysterious of the arts.[…] and no one had a keener eye for absurdity, but he had seen and made others see the Russian Ballet […] leading a consistent, preposterous, and unearthly life of their own.[93]

It is difficult to disagree with Mackail's perceptive comment, which leads to some further inferences to be discussed. With his keen sense of irony and his feel for the unreal, Barrie managed to see through the icon that for years was associated with the notion of *echt*-Russian, and conventionally taken as an embodiment of what was then characterised as the Russian myth. As it happens, there was not much 'Russianness' in Barrie's *Dancers* (concerning the text, as well as the production), which effectively put under question the emblematic authenticity of the reference source.

As regards the decorative aspect of the performance, although Paul Nash's costumes and designs were labelled by the papers as being appropriately 'Anglo-Bakst-ish',[94] put together in such an imaginative way that they received 'the Diaghileff blessing',[95] the play's scenery and decorations

91 Cohen, p. 33.

92 Karsavina, Introduction to 'The Truth about the Russian Dances', p. 6.

93 Mackail, p. 545.

94 'Karsavina and Barrie', p. 14. The colours of the original were: walls, a wide range of gray; balcony, doors and staircase, pink; stair carpet and candles, Indian red; window curtains, dark blue (illustration in *Theatre Arts Magazine* 6 (1920), p. 188).

95 Huntley Carter, 'About the Theatre in London', *Theatre Arts Magazine* 6 (1920), 217–19 (p. 218).

bore hardly any resemblance to Bakst's characteristically brazen, exuberant and gaudy settings (not to mention any specific Russian references and overtones).

Figure 6. Original design: *The Truth about the Russian Dancers* by Paul Nash. Victoria and Albert Museum.

In the early post-World War I years, Paul Nash was working in a semi-abstract Cubist-influenced style – hence his fascination with theatre as a particular form of abstraction of the real. Early in 1919 Nash was engaged on paintings commissioned by the Department of Information for the newly established Imperial War Museum. 'His poetic imagination', writes Myfanwy Piper, 'instead of being crushed by the terrible circumstances of war, had expanded to produce terrible images – terrible because of their combination of detached, almost abstract, appreciation and their truth to appearance.'[96] His paintings of the time, for instance *The Menin Road* (1919),

96 Myfanwy Piper, rev. Andrew Causey, 'Nash, Paul (1889–1946)', *Oxford Dictionary of National Biography* (Oxford: Oxford University Press, 2004), online edn, May 2009 <http://www.oxforddnb.com/view/article/35186> [accessed 2 September 2016].

look almost like deserted theatre sets with side screens and backdrops, revealing his interest in this stage-like style of interpretative generalisation.[97] It was at the time of Nash's experimentation with abstract techniques that he created the settings for *The Truth of about the Russian Dancers*, which certainly bore witness to this type of formal explorations, and which, as Henry James Bruce (Karsavina's husband) pointed out, came as a bit of a shock for the unsuspecting author:

> [Paul Nash] had designed a set for the stately Scottish home where the action of the play was to take place which gave Barrie, when he saw it, a gasping shock. He had no doubt, bless his heart, visualized a nice 'straight' set with lots of old oak and antlers. What he got was something very different. He could only hastily write a line into somebody's speech about the stately home having 'gone a little queer' owing to the presence of a Russian dancer and let it go at that.[98]

Barrie's added line ('the scene [...] must have a touch of the bizarre as in the Russian ballet'[99]) has never been written into the characters' speeches. The phrase occurs only in the author's stage directions, but what is more important in this context is the promptness with which a link was created between the Russianness and 'the bizarre', and the readiness to read the former as an emblem of 'the weird' rather than in line with its proper cultural connotation.

97 His paintings of this period, for instance *The Menin Road* (1919), are almost like deserted stage sets with side screens and backdrops, revealing his interest in the theatre (see David Boyd Haycock, *Paul Nash* (New York: Harry N. Abrams, 2002), p. 45).

98 Henry James Bruce, *Thirty Dozen Moons* (London: Constable, 1949), p. 45.

99 Barrie, p. 13.

Figure 7. Costume design by Paul Nash (for Tamara Karsavina).
Victoria and Albert Museum.

Figure 7. Continued.

The allegedly Russian tone of the show (if one has to find any) floated up exclusively through Arnold Bax's 'allusively witty'[100] music. Out of

100 'T', p. 236.

the three main 'authors' of the production, which was at once decorative, musical and dramatic, he was the only one familiar with Russian culture, to which he did make some impressionistic allusions in the incidental score he composed for the play. In 1910 Bax spent almost a year travelling around Russia and Ukraine in vain pursuit of a faithless Ukrainian beauty, Natalia Skarginska. His travels brought him to St Petersburg, Moscow and Lubny (near Kiev), and provoked a life-long fascination with the Russian theme. And although his relationship with Skarginska resulted in an emotional agony, from which he never recovered, the Russian theme inspired his first and second piano sonatas (composed respectively in 1910 and 1919 they were notably influenced by Liadov and Glazunov[101]), as well as a series of shorter piano pieces such as *Nocturne–May Night in the Ukraine* and *Gopak (Russian dance)* of 1912, and *In a Vodka Shop* of 1915.

Like many lovers of theatre and performance arts, he was infatuated by the first series of Diaghilev's seasons, to the extent that in 1911 he produced *Tamara* – a little Russian fairy tale in action and dance, dedicated to Tamara Karsavina. Unfortunately, by the time he had completed the composition, the title happened to have been used in another Karsavina-related ballet, *Thamar*, set to the music of Mily Balakirev and premiered on 20 May 1912. To avoid confusion, Bax changed the title to *King Kojata* (after a relatively minor character) before abandoning it altogether. Karsavina knew nothing about the ballet until after Bax's death and despite her friendship with the composer in connection with Barrie's playlet. Bax also wrote few pieces for Diaghilev Ballets. In 1919–20 he was one of the four British composers to be commissioned to write an orchestral interlude for the Ballets Russes London season (for the commission, he incorporated the three above-mentioned piano works into the *Russian Suite* for orchestra); and subsequently Diaghilev asked him to orchestrate two short movements by Liadov (*Prelude* and *Lament*) for the 1919 revival of *Les Contes Russes*. It would certainly appear that Bax and Harriet Cohen, a famous pianist and Bax's mistress, became well known among Diaghilev's circle. Cohen wrote how

101 Lewis Foreman, *Bax: A Composer and His Time* (Woodbridge: Boydell Press, 2007), p. 169.

> at the Savoy grill after rehearsals or performance, we would all sup gaily enough and sit later in Diaghilev's suite until all hours making plans and discussing decors. It was through these discussions that I was fired with love of impressionistic and contemporary art. It was here that incredible drolleries about music were said, especially when Prokovieff was around. I shall ever remember the two Sergeis on the one hand, vying with Evans and Bax in their iconoclasms, on the other. 'Sewing-machine music', said Arnold of Bach's Suites (he did not object to the later Preludes and Fugues, it seemed); but Diaghilev rather shocked the others in his denunciation of Beethoven, whom he described as a 'mummy, a corpse', dismissing the whole of the Violin Concerto, which he said was 'music from the morgue', whereas they said it was only the 'Rondo' they could not stand – 'turning and spinning like some horrible top.' Stravinsky of course, was frequently at hand with wonderful ideas.[102]

Initially, Bax was introduced to Diaghilev by Edwin Evans, a well known contemporary music critic and a great champion of the Russian composers associated with the Russian Ballets. Later on, Evans became Karsavina's music adviser,[103] and it is not coincidental therefore that it was he who suggested Bax should write the music for Barrie's playlet.[104] Bax wrote the score very quickly, using parts of his earlier (1911–12) unpublished *Tamara* ballet, which belonged to the time when his compositional ideas were considerably influenced by the Russian theme. The Russian references are conspicuously enhanced in the finale, through a direct quotation from Balakirev's *Thamar*, which always remained one of Bax's favourite pieces.[105] In the words of Bax's biographer (Lewis Foreman), however, the music he composed for *The Truth about the Russian Dancers* gained its Russian overtones not through the direct citations *per se*, but through 'rather clever suggestions of the characteristics of the music played for the Russian Ballet'.[106]

102 Harriet Cohen, *A Bundle of Time* (London: Faber and Faber, 1969), p. 46.

103 As a result, Bax was commissioned to write a solo piece for the ballerina (the *Slave-Girl* for piano), which she performed during a fortnight's season at the Coliseum with Harriet Cohen at the piano (Cohen, p. 48).

104 Foreman, p. 173. The movements from the ballet were all broadcast during the late 1960s and early 1970s, as a part of a suite from the whole work, though in no case were more than five movements (out of eight) done at any one time (Foreman, pp. 174–5).

105 Ibid. p. 175.

106 Ibid. p. 175.

Being deeply interested in Diaghilev's style, Bax developed a keen sense of the theatrical and the parodic, and it was these essentially modernist overtones that he highlighted in his work.

The same can be said about Barrie's own projection of the Russian dancers. Within the framework of the playlet, they were presented as different, innovative, aesthetically pleasing, mesmerising and exotic, but hardly representative of their own country, of its native idiom, of its tradition and its cause. Their world constituted an expressive medium of its own; and their Russianness was employed not for highlighting the folkloric, but in a typically modernist way of challenging and defamiliarising the norm. Furthermore, it is acutely uncanny how in this insightful observation Barrie managed to encapsulate the very essence of Diaghilev's project, with regard to both its aesthetic platform and its social status in the early 20s, when the dramatist was working on his play.

Concerning its aesthetic features, according to the majority of scholars, it was largely this modernist, and essentially cosmopolitan, idea of 'the evocative' and 'the expressive', to which Diaghilev responded in his ballets. Simon Karlinsky, for instance pointed out that

> In Petrouchka Stravinsky turned his back on both the ethnographic approach and the Western-style sugarcoating of folklore that were implicit in the nineteenth-century Russian musical aesthetic, this process was deepened in *The Rite*, where [...] Stravinsky deformed both Lithuanian and Slavic materials with a sovereign freedom in a manner that may be termed cubistic.[107]

Similarly, Ramsay Burt argued that it was not the authenticity of the folk material *per se* that was important for Nijinsky and Stravinsky, 'but the meaning that, in its fragmented form, it evoked in a dislocated, modern

107 Simon Karlinsky, 'Igor Stravinsky and Russian Preliterate Theatre', in *Confronting Stravinsky: Man, Musician, and Modernist*, ed. Jann Pasler (Berkley: University of California Press, 1986) pp. 3–15 (p. 6).
See also Gareth Thomas, 'Modernism, Diaghilev and the Ballets Russes in London, 1911–1929', in *British Music and Modernism, 1895–1960*, ed. Mathew Riley (Farnham: Ashgate Publishing, 2010), pp. 67–92 (p. 68).

context, and the affective impact they could achieve through its use.'[108] Diaghilev believed that the artist's role was not to reflect or interpret the idiom of the native culture, but to create a new one of its own; and in this reality of imagination, art should be the means of unlocking experience. Moreover, although in the West the innovative qualities of the Russian Ballets were linked, at least at the beginning, to the 'otherness' of the Russian cultural tradition, Prince Lieven (one of the first historians of the Ballets Russes) maintained that it all seemed as provocative and new to the Russians, as to anyone else.[109] In this context, it is also worth quoting Alexander Benois' revealing comment. As one of Diaghilev's most influential stage designers and an instrumental figure in the formation of his aesthetic imagination and taste, he drew attention to the fact that the very idea behind the project could not be further removed from that of a 'Russian export campaign': 'the point was that we showed to Europe *the European*, though miraculously preserved, invigorated and transformed; this lent special significance to our performance and facilitated our noteworthy success.'[110]

In the same vein, concerning its social and cultural affiliation, there was fairly little Russianness left in the company by the early 20s. Could Diaghilev and his dancers be regarded as the representatives of the Imperial Russian tradition? This was hardly the case, for the great Maestro was known for his low opinion of the latter. His company was founded as a rebellion against the Russian Imperial Ballet, which Diaghilev persistently dismissed as monotonously obsolete and devoid of perspective. (The Imperial Court, in its turn, affirmed separation by instructing the Embassies not to lend countenance to the Ballets Russes[111]). Even less, however, could Diaghilev be equated with the notion of the contemporary Russian socialist agenda. By 1918 Diaghilev, his choreographers and his dancers were stateless exiles

108 Ramsay Burt, *The Male Dancer: Bodies, Spectacle, Sexualities* (London and New York: Routledge, 2003), p. 74.

109 Peter Lieven, *The Birth of the Ballet Russes*, trans. L. Zarine (New York: Dover Publications, 1973), p. 21.

110 Alexander Benois, *Vospominaniia* (Moscow: Nauka, 1980), II, p. 536.

111 Green and Swan, p. 63.

from a Bolshevik country wracked by the rampages of the Civil War. In the past Diaghilev had regarded Russia's aristocrats with a mixture of diffidence and disdain. Now he had no choice other than to rally the troupe's prestige in the eyes of London highborn émigré circles, by organising charity galas in aid of the Russian Relief Fund and others, and conspicuously identifying himself with their cause.[112] Thus, for instance, when declining an invitation to attend a public banquet honouring the Russian ballet, he asserted,

> While our country is in its present tragic condition, we Russians naturally feel [...] unable to accept the offer of a public festivity, even on artistic grounds. Especially now, when the Dowager Empress has arrived in England a fugitive, and when we hear daily that people are dying of hunger in Petrograd, we feel it behoves us to abstain from public functions of this kind.[113]

As a person with a considerable social and artistic sensibility Diaghilev could not but feel that the belle époque that had seen the birth of the Ballets Russes had been shattered forever. All references that supported the notable strand of the so-called Russian style, which he forged, nourished and developed, were irrevocably effaced; it was time to move on. Subsequently, Diaghilev's great themes – Russia, the classical world and the Orient – became treated in the contemporary context, acquiring some distinctly international tones and reflecting such topical interests as beach culture, cinema and sport. By 1920 the company underwent a considerable revision of its repertoire, to which new ballets were added each year. French avant-garde artists such as Matisse, Derain and Braque designed productions, which were no longer dominated by Russian music, and Leonide Massine emerged as a talented new choreographer, drawing on influences from the countries of his travels, notably Italy (*The Good-Humoured Ladies*, 1917, music by Scarlatti; *La Boutique fantasque*, 1919, music by Rossini) and Spain (*Le Tricorne* or *El sombrero de tres picos*, 1919, music by Manuel de Falla).

112 Garafola, p. 333.

113 'The Russian Ballet. No Public Festivity', *The Times*, 14 May 1919, p. 14; also quoted in Garafola, p. 333.

Both socially and artistically the Ballets Russes were no longer representative of all things Russian: the company became an artificially maintained artistic project, which relied largely on Diaghilev's personal charisma and led a fairly detached life of its own.

All these overtones were keenly conveyed in Barrie's *The Truth about the Russian Dancers*, though in his characteristically subtle, symbolist metatheatrical way. Moreover, in Barrie's playlet one can also pick up the reference concerning the end of the Russian Ballets. Regardless of the play's joyful gaiety and happy resolution, the closing scene suggests that the world of the Russian dancers is doomed to perish; and in this respect, it is not coincidental that the motif of dying was highlighted in the playbill, announcing that *The Truth about the Russian Dancers* would be 'showing how they love [...] how they are made with how they die.'[114] According to the script, Karissima's life is miraculously spared. However, it is the death of Maestro ('LORD VERE (*examines him and indicates that life is extinct*)'[115]) that signifies the ultimate end of the world of the Russian dancers, for there will be no one 'to mend' and 'fix' his precious ballerinas or produce a replacement for those who are 'broken' beyond repair. Remarkable as it may seem, Barrie's flow of fantasy, or maybe a premonition, does bring to mind the real end of the Russian Ballets (for which Diaghilev had always been a pivotal driving force and *raison d'être*). Not unlike the death of the almighty Maestro in Barrie's playlet, Diaghilev's death in Venice almost a decade later in 1929, resulted in the definitive end of the Ballets Russes project, and the company was virtually instantaneously dispersed.

It is highly ironic, in this context, that it may well be Diaghilev himself who should be credited for the play's ending. The first version of the manuscript did not end on a positive note; and a happy resolution turned out to be a relatively late addition to the script. Lady Kathleen Scott mentions in her diaries that on 1 November 1919 (in three months' time after Barrie introduced the play to Karsavina) she went to the ballet. 'Diaghilev came and talked to me', she maintains, 'and said he liked Barrie's play for

114 'Casts of *The Truth about the Russian Dancers*', *Dance Perspectives* 14 (1962), p. 37.

115 Barrie, p. 30.

Karsavina, but disliked the end. She ought at least to come to life again.'[116] It would be sheer speculation to assume that Lady Scott passed Diaghilev's idea to Barrie, but as it happens, the playwright did change the ending along his lines.

Barrie has rarely been regarded as an overt social commentator. He did not belong to the so-called contemporary New Drama movement searching to revise both the Edwardian theatrical conventions and the conservative consumerist ideology promoted by the bourgeois Society drama. Unlike some of his fellow playwrights (Shaw, Galsworthy and to a certain extent Granville-Barker), he was firmly associated with the West End commercial stage. His plays were frequently revived and produced by the most successful administrators (such as, for instance, Charles Frohman); and 'in a time in which revolt had become something of a convention, Barrie had been distinguished by standing apart from the protestants.'[117]

Nonetheless, this should not be taken as meaning that Barrie used to remain deaf to the artistic polemics and theatrical controversies of his time. Critics often saw his works as pamphlets or an 'ironical treatise';[118] and William Archer 'solemnly expressed his doubts whether the dramatist had the smallest idea of the immensity of his attack upon the constituted social order of the country.'[119] As Jean Chothia pointed out, Barrie somehow 'stands between the Society dramatists and the writers of minority drama, whose themes he often absorbed into lighter, less testing, plotting and characterisation'.[120] And indeed, Barrie frequently resorted to theatrical form itself to expose the limitations of the conventional drama and theatre practice. *Alice-Sit-By-The-Fire* (1905), for instance, underscores the contrived nature of the 'well-made play'. William Archer called it 'an effective

116 Scott, p. 178.

117 Thomas H. Dickinson, *Contemporary Drama of England* (Boston, MA: Little Brown, 1931), p. 230.

118 H. M. Walbrook, *J. M. Barrie and the Theatre* (London: F. V. White & Co, 1922), p. 69.

119 Ibid. p. 73.

120 Jean Chothia, *English Drama of the Early Modern Period (1890–1914)* (London: Longman, 1996), pp. 83–4.

piece of dramatic criticism', which, he maintained, is 'like a commentary-in-action upon [his] article of last week; but it will do more [...] to render impossible the play of artificial situation and mendacious self-sacrifice.'[121] *A Slice of Life* (1910), Barrie's pointed satire of the 'discussion play', was read by the *Times* reviewer as 'a picture of the absurdities and self-conscious tricks of the modern play, which is a masterpiece of most delicate and searching dramatic criticism.'[122] The same can be said about his *Rosy Rapture* (1915) – a lighthearted parody of a musical with 'its incompetent chorus [and] the grotesqueness of melodrama';[123] and his *Punch: A Toy Tragedy* (1906), which places 'conventional theatre' next to the 'new drama' in the same way as the dated and worn out puppets are juxtaposed to the cheerful and energetic 'Superpunch' (a witty reference to Shaw's *Man and Superman*[124]).

One can see that Barrie never stopped participating in the debates on contemporary theatre and its problems, although employing to this effect his own critical methods and representation techniques. His mode and his language were more akin to those of Symbolist drama. It is not coincidental that Maurice Maeterlinck once declared that *Peter Pan* was the father

121 William Archer, 'The Theatre', *World*, 11 April 1905, p. 622.

122 'St James's Theatre', *The Times*, 2 July 1910, p. 8.

123 *Graphic*, 27 March 1915, p. 412.

124 The reference is conspicuously highlighted in the stage directions, when Barrie mentions that his character should look 'not like Mr Shaw, but like the man who played Superman'. Barrie's precision in this comment was bluntly teasing and ironic, for Mr Granville-Barker, who played John Tanner in *Man and Superman* at the Court Theatre in 1905, was made up so that he had a distinctly Shavian look. (See Leon H. Hugo, 'Punch: J. M. Barrie's Gentle Swipe at "Supershaw"', *Shaw: Annual of Bernard Shaw Studies* 10 (1990), pp. 60–72 (p. 62); Jan McDonald, 'Barrie and the New Dramatists', *Gateway to the Modern: Resituating J. M. Barrie*, ed. Valentine Bold and Andrew Nash (Glasgow: Scottish Literature International, 2014), pp. 1–16 (p. 6).) Shaw did not miss the joke, and when his own play, *Press Cuttings* (1909), was refused a licence because living characters (allegedly Lord Roberts) were presented on stage, he protested claiming that he himself had been thus '"represented on the stage" [...] in a little fantasy by no less well-known an author than [his] friend Mr J. M. Barrie' (G. B. Shaw, 'The Censor's Revenge', *The Times*, 26 June 1909, p. 10).

of the *Blue Bird*;[125] and it is within the framework of this notion that one has to look for interpretation in Barrie's works.

In *The Truth about the Russian Dancers*, the idea of the alienated, self-contained and self-referential world of Diaghilev's Ballets finds its symbolic manifestation in the claustrophobic group of Russian ballerinas, which, similar to an exclusive club, has a strictly fixed number of lifetime members, and someone has to drop out (die) in order to make a space for the newcomers. As the Maestro put it, 'a dancer, past her best, can always be found to give her life for a newcomer'[126] to enable the eminence of Russian ballet to live on. Curious as it may seem, by highlighting these notions of auto-referentiality and exclusive focus on the medium Barrie touched upon something (albeit inadvertently) that in several decades would be foregrounded by modern theorists of culture as the major characteristic traits of modernist works. In his *Politics of Modernism*, for instance, Raymond Williams maintains that it was the experience of exile, of uprooting and migrating to a foreign metropolis that was central to the creation of the formal innovation made by the early modernists in their art:

> Liberated or breaking from their national or provincial cultures, placed in quite new relations to those other native languages or visual traditions, encountering meanwhile a novel and dynamic common environment from which many of the older forms were obviously distant, the artists and writers and thinkers of this phase found the only community available to them: a community of the medium; of their own practices.[127]

Similarly, when analysing the sense of 'the new' in Diaghilev's ballets, Ramsay Burt sees it in their exclusive focus on and exploration of the medium, as well as in the fact that they effectively 'purged the ballet vocabulary of outmoded representational forms and conventions'.[128]

In this sense, Barrie's imaginary world of the Russian dancers can be regarded as an interpretative abstraction. On a mythopoetic level, the notion of its auto-referentiality, or using Burt's wording 'the exclusive focus

125 Ormond, p. 151.

126 Barrie, p. 29.

127 Raymond Williams, *Politics of Modernism* (New York: Verso, 1989), p. 45.

128 Burt, p. 75.

on the medium', is inferred by the fact that all these ballerinas are 'crafted' out of nowhere with a chisel and putty.

BILL	Hold my hand, Jane, something awful is coming. It is said that he [Maestro] makes them.
LADY VERE	Made Karissima?
BILL	Made all of the Russian Dancers!
LADY VERE	Are you going crazy! How can he make them?
BILL	I don't know yet. That is what I have to find out – But he makes them somehow – with chisels and putty, I daresay.
LADY VERE	That sweet girl! I have always found her so truthful, Bill. I am sure if she was made with chisel and putty she would have told me so.
BILL	I don't suppose she knows – I daresay none of them know. That man keeps a lot of things up his sleeve.[129]

This idea is persistently reiterated in various forms throughout the playlet, including, for instance, the episode when Maestro practically manufactures Lord Vere and Karissima's child in the likeness of his father's portrait:

> MAESTRO *returns carrying a bag and an easel* [...] *The canvas is an incomplete picture of a baby which must be very like* LORD VERE. *He compares the two pictures thoughtfully, then out of bag takes a wax arm of a child and puts it against child picture. Evidently he is making a child to pass off as Lord Vere's. He produces a chisel and putty*;[130]

or the midnight conversation between Lord Vere and Maestro:

LORD VERE	She is exquisite, Maestro! [...] All women are so inferior.
MAESTRO	She is so much better made.[131]

One can say that at times the text effectively lends itself to the notion of ekphrasis, praising Karissima as an exquisite object of art:

129 Barrie, p. 15.

130 Ibid. p. 25.

131 For instance, in the midnight conversation between Maestro and Lord Vere: 'LORD VERE: She is exquisite, Maestro! [...] All women are so inferior. MAESTRO: She is so much better made' (Ibid. p. 24).

MAESTRO	It was I who made her – fashioned her so exquisitely.
LORD VERE	Made her? That strange tale is true?
MAESTRO	Just as I made the child – just as I made them all. But there was none so wonderful as Karissima.[132]

In connection to this, the reference to Pygmalion (this time to the myth) is brought to mind by these lines. Akin to Galatea, the world of the Russian dancers is an admirable icon of perfection – an Apollonian source of creativity, which dazzles and enchants everyone who happens to step into its light.

The marriage of the young couple, Karissima and Lord Vere, is shown, symbolically, as a positive way forward; hence the child – a symbol of the future, who in no time acquires the language 'spoken' by his Russian side, and chases butterflies specifically on his toes:

MAESTRO	She is glad that he is chasing butterflies. Does he chase them on his toes?
LORD VERE	Yes.
MAESTRO	Then all is well.[133]

Not unlike the marriage of Pygmalion and Galatea, blessed with their son Paphos, the future is bestowed upon the offspring of 'the traditional' and 'the exotic', who, according to the Maestro, is 'by far more beautiful than those who come in the common English way'.[134] Even the most conservative seemed to be persuaded by the union, expressing their readiness to start the conversation *à-la-Russe* with their toes: 'They all join in the dance on their toes. Even LORD VERE, LADY VERE and BILL are on their toes. It should be wildly gay.'[135]

Further to the point, it is worth looking deeper into Barrie's interpretation of this dialogue with the 'other', for at the beginning of the 1920s a simple reference to 'the wonderfully exotic' was hardly seen as an original stance. Since the years of the industrial revolution, the arts of the East have

132 Ibid. p. 29.
133 Ibid. p. 29.
134 Ibid. p. 29.
135 Ibid. p. 30.

been regarded as an antidote to the rationalism of European civilisation; and it is along these lines that the emotionally charged Russian tradition (Karissima) is juxtaposed to the rigid conservatism of English life. Moreover, not only were non-Western societies thought of as being untainted by the perilous effects of industrialisation, they were also perceived as morally superior in terms of being sincerer and in a certain sense more devout than their metropolitan counterparts. Owen Jones draws attention to this interesting connection between ethics and aesthetics describing objects from India that were considered exemplars of good design as in

> the works of a people who are still faithful to their art as to their religion, habits and modes of thought which inspired it. [...] we find no struggle after an effect; every ornament arises quietly and naturally from the object decorated, inspired by some true feeling, or embellishing some real want.[136]

The trend drew further upon elements of Japanese art ('japonisme'), which flooded Western markets, mainly in the form of prints, after trading rights were established with Japan in the 1860s, becoming one of the key elements of the avant-garde style that may be loosely defined as Art Nouveau. By the end of the century, however, the myth of the exotic had already been fully appropriated, not to say commodified, by Western culture. Oriental images were used to sell everything from cigarettes to candy, and the exoticism in interior design became associated with fantasies of glamour, opulence and barbaric splendour.

In the generation that came of age after 1918, this notion extended its authority but became more complex. Western civilisation failed to prevent the horrors of World War I. As Green and Swan put it: 'The material aesthetic grandeur glowed more richly, but its justifying moral righteousness faded. The crown jewels looked like loot.'[137] To be affiliated with such loot induced a sense of moral unease, for which the aesthetical 'otherness' provided the natural mode of representation. The examples are manifold and can be found in the characters of Aldous Huxley's novels, and in the

136 Quoted in Michael Snodin and Maurice Howard, *Ornament: A Social History Since 1450* (New Haven, CT: Yale University Press, 1996), p. 200.

137 Green and Swan, p. xv.

theatricality of the Bloomsbury group's lifestyle, as well as in the gaudy gatherings at the salons of Ottoline Morrell. As regards Barrie's playlet, a similar comment on moral credibility is provided by Karissima's effort to 'dance' or to mime the highbrow rhetoric of her wedding vows. The effect is comparable to that achieved through post-modernist deconstruction, when a conventional idiom (or a so-called frozen metaphor) is turned into parody by way of underscoring its 'other' (literal), non-canonical sense:

> CLERGYMAN And keep him in sickness and in health?
> *She shows this by giving him medicine.*
> And forsaking all others keep thou only unto him as long as ye both shall live?
> *She kisses* LORD VERE *and* BILL, *then runs to* LORD VERE *to indicate she's done with all but him forever.*[138]

The 'otherness', in this context, represented not only a recoil from dominant and respected values, but also an attack on them by aesthetic and ethical means. And it is exactly in this sense that the Russianness was employed in Barrie's humorous playlet.

Through a straightforward juxtaposition of the 'the conventional' and 'the other' one's sense of decorum was considerably disturbed; one's self-respect as an aesthete fell into question, undermining the entire notion of traditionalism and the norm. True, the Russianness in his sketch was largely taken as 'otherness' rather than in its specific cultural context, but it worked as a lens for casting light on the idea of 'authenticity' and 'the real'. It did indeed have the effect of alienating the audience from the object of its humour, challenging the conservative forms and conventions, and producing this unique type of cultural critique, which was at once original and witty, thought-provoking and playfully engaging.

138 Barrie, p. 21.

CHAPTER 5

D. H. Lawrence: 'Russia Will Certainly Inherit the Future'

D. H. Lawrence has always provoked strong and divisive reactions among his critics, his censors and his readers, being often dismissed for celebrating sexuality and rejoicing in the lubricious moments abundantly present in his works. Boldly innovative, deeply sensual and radically experimental, he was surprisingly prone to the whims of literary fashion; but, in distinction to the majority of the modernist oeuvre associated primarily with the high-brow aestheticism of the elite, his works did have a broader cultural impact on the readership of the time, being listed among the top literary bestsellers and the best examples of fiction written during the inter-war decades.[1]

Lawrence never went to Russia, though his intention to make a trip to the country was persistently mentioned in his personal correspondence.[2] Just like almost the entire artistic world of the pre-World War I era, he was greatly affected by the vogue of Russomania: by the spellbinding otherness of the Russian novels and the glamour of Diaghilev's Paris and London seasons. These memorable shows found their most vivid representation in the pages of *Women in Love* (1920):

> A servant came, and soon reappeared with armfuls of silk robes and shawls and scarves, mostly Oriental, things that Hermione, with her love for beautiful extravagant dress, had collected gradually [...] It was finally decided to do Naomi and Ruth and

1 Jane Bingham, *Popular Culture: 1920–1939* (London: Raintree, 2013), p. 36, 56.

2 See, for instance, letters to Samuel Koteliansky (1 May 1917, 6 December, 18 December 1925, 11 January 1926); to Catherine Carswell (17 December 1922); and to Carl Seelig (7 January 1926); D. H. Lawrence, *The Letters of D. H. Lawrence* (respectively) III, p. 121; V, p. 365, p. 374; IV, p. 352; V, p. 271.

> Orpah. Ursula was Naomi, Gudrun was Ruth, the Contessa was Orpah. The idea was to make a little ballet, in the style of the Russian Ballet of Pavlova and Nijinsky.[3]

Nijinsky entered Lawrence's artistic world through the connection fostered between the Ballets Russes and Ottoline Morrell, who was greatly impressed by the Russian seasons and in 1912 started inviting both Diaghilev and Nijinsky to her bohemian gatherings at Bedford Square. And although Lawrence would become friendly with Morrell only in two years' time (in spring of 1914), he himself took great pleasure in participating in the improvised amateurish *à la Russe* dancing shows arranged by David Garnett (the son of Edward and Constance Garnett, and an active member of Ottoline Morrell's circle), who in the summer of 1912 paid a visit to Lawrence and his wife-to-be Frieda in Icking. 'We are awfully fond of him', Lawrence wrote about Garnett,

> He imitates Mordkin, Pavlova's partner in Diaghilev Russian Ballet [sic], dancing with great orange and yellow and red and dark green scarves of F's, and his legs and arms bare, while I sit on the sofa and do the music, and burst with laughter, and F. stands out on the balcony in the dark, scared.[4]

Lawrence must have had warm recollections of these evenings, which later on were fictionalised in *Mr Noon*,[5] his autobiographical novel drafted

3 D. H. Lawrence, *Women in Love* (New York: The Viking Press, 1920), pp. 83–4.

4 Lawrence, letter to Edward Garnett, 4 August 1912, *The Letters of D. H. Lawrence*, I, p. 429.

5 The story tells of Gilbert and Johanna staying in a small Bavarian village; they are visited by 'a botanising youth of twenty-one [...] called Terry' (David Garnett), who in the course of long summer evenings enthusiastically coaches them in an uproarious Diaghilev scene of Judith and Holofernes:

> The Russian Ballet with Anna Pavlova and Nijinsky had just come to London. Neither Gilbert nor Johanna knew it. But Terry drilled them. He was a brawny fellow. He stripped himself naked save for a pair of drawers and a great scarlet turban and sat in a corner intensely playing knuckle-stones. Gilbert, feeling rather a fool, sat on the bed in Johanna's dressing-gown, turned the scarlet side outwards, and with a great orange and lemon scarf round his head, and being Holofernes. Johanna, handsomely rigged in shawls, was to be Judith charming the captain. So Terry, as a slave, squatted in his corner and buried himself

between 1920 and 1921 (the year of publication of *Women in Love*). The novel remained unfinished and unpublished during the author's lifetime, but this connection between the Russianness and the new expressive physical language, which gives voice to the deepest layers of the subconscious, became a key point in the configuring and projecting of his Russian point of view.

One of the key figures of the British modernist tradition, Lawrence belonged to the generation who had to face the so-called existential crisis of consciousness prevailing in the inter-war years: the demotion of the idea of man as an intellectual centre of the world, governed by the impersonal laws of reason. Against the downfall of rationalism and Western logo-centric modes of thinking, Nietzsche's reading of the human self as a dialectical unity of mind and the mysterious world of instincts – the true life force – came increasingly under the spotlight. For Lawrence, this type of complex ambivalence and polarisation – this naturally embedded desire for physical liberation, forever striving with the debilitating tendency towards intellectualisation, found its 'objective correlative' in the notion of the Russian, shaped and projected as a new model of the self and its ways of engagement with the 'otherness' of human civilisation.

Judging from his personal correspondence, his criticism and literary translations, Lawrence had a long-standing interest in the work of Russian authors: not only writers, but also philosophers such as Lev Shestov, Dmitrii Merezhkovsky and Vladimir Solov'ev. In September 1911 he was introduced to Edward Garnett (and later on, in June 1913, to his wife Constance Garnett),[6] who was pivotal in promoting the works of

---

in his knuckle-stone business. Gilbert and Johanna were deeply impressed. Johanna began to swim forward like a houri or a Wagner heroine, to Gilbert, who was perched cross-legged, in the scarlet-silk wadded dressing-gown, upon the large bed. But Gilbert looked so uneasy and Johanna herself felt such a fool she fell to laughing, and laughed till her shawl arrangements fell away. Then the slave in the corner grew really angry, and it was all a fiasco (D. H. Lawrence, *Mr Noon*, ed. Lindeth Vasey (Cambridge: Cambridge University Press, 1984), pp. 255–6).

6 Richard David Garnett, *Constance Garnett: A Heroic Life* (London: Sinclair-Stevenson, 1991), p. 273.

Russian literature in Britain, and whom Joseph Conrad even nicknamed the 'Russian Embassador [sic] to the Republic of Letters'.[7] Garnett was a valued friend and a crucial figure in launching Lawrence's career as a writer. When Lawrence fell in love with Frieda Weekley, a married woman at the time, Garnett became a confidant, and the couple even stayed at his house before eloping to Germany in 1912. As the young writer's literary mentor, Garnett secured a publishing contract for *The Trespasser* (1912), Lawrence's second novel, and then provided considerable assistance in editing the manuscript of his *Sons and Lovers* (1913). Whether Lawrence's work implies an intentional allusion to Turgenev's *Fathers and Sons* is not definitively proven, but a certain homonymy in the title is difficult to disregard.[8] Lawrence was intimately familiar with the writings of Turgenev, which had been available in several English translations since 1894.[9] As a student, long before his acquaintance with the Garnetts he became enthusiastically engaged in reading the works of the Russian authors. Jessie Chambers (Wood), Lawrence's partner in his early twenties, maintains in her memoirs that 'He liked Turgenev immensely, and gave me his copy of *Fathers and Sons*, and impressed upon me that I must read *Rudin*.' She also recollects that

---

In the words of David Garnett, it was, in fact, long before 1911 that Lawrence knew about their family's literary tradition:

> In the miner's cottage where he was brought up they 'regarded with a reverence amounting to awe' (E. T. (Jessie Chambers Wood), *D. H. Lawrence: A Personal Record* (London: Jonathan Cape, 1935), p. 92) a set of Richard Garnett's most imposing legacy to posterity, the twenty-volume *International Library of Famous Literature* (1899). Lawrence read widely in it and gained a good knowledge of the world's literature, though it was curiously weak in translations from the Russian, and when he first heard of Edward in September 1911 he mistook him for its editor (Richard Garnett, p. 268).

7 Kaye, p. 32.

8 The reference seemed transparent enough to John Galsworthy, one of the major proponents of Turgenev's writings in Britain (see Chapter 2 in this book), who did not hesitate to condemn Lawrence's novel (John Galsworthy, letter to Edward Garnett, 13 April 1914, *Letters from John Galsworthy 1900–1932*, p. 219).

9 *The Novels and Tales of Ivan Turgenev*, trans. Constance Garnett, 17 vols (London: Heinemann, 1894–1906); *The Novels and Stories by Ivan Turgénieff*, trans. Isabel Hapgood, 13 vols (New York: Scribner, 1903–05).

Lawrence brought her 'his own copy of Tolstoy's *Anna Karenina*', saying that it was 'the greatest novel in the world'.[10] The reference to Gorky appears in Lawrence's first novel *The White Peacock* (1911), started as early as 1906;[11] and Lettie Beardsall, one of the main characters of the novel, uses an endearing Russian word for 'mother' – *matouchka* – in her conversation.[12]

At the time Lawrence must have been deeply moved by the Russians, for his letters of 1910 are also coloured by occasional insertions of emotionally charged Russian words: 'My affairs, like those of my friend [Ezra Pound], go a bit criss-crossy. It is very probable I shall have to return in September to home, to a little mining village in the midlands. *Bóhze moï* [my God]' (to Grace Crawford, 24 June 1910); 'I'm so miserable about my '*matouchka*' (to Louie Burrows, 14 December 1910); 'Well *golubchick* (pretty word!) – little pigeon – oh black swan' (to Louie Burrows, 28 December 1910).[13] The word 'matouchka' is given in French, rather than English transliteration ('matushka'), which, perhaps, gives an indication of the language in which Lawrence read some of his first Russian novels. According to Natalya Reinhold, however, who was the first to draw attention to these Russian insertions in Lawrence's letters,[14] he might have learned these words directly from Jessie Chambers, whose interest in Russian culture was deep enough for her to embark subsequently on literary translations.

10 E. T. (Jessie Chambers), p. 114, 121.

11 'I've been reading Maxim Gorky'; 'People must be ill when they write like Maxim Gorky' (D. H. Lawrence, *The White Peacock* (London: Heinemann, 1911), p. 165, 166).

12 'It's really my fault, in the end. Don't be piggling and mean and Grundyish, Matouchka' (Lawrence, *The White Peacock*, p. 265). Although the novel was rewritten several times and published only in 1911, it is likely that the Russian word was retained from the earlier drafts, as it was also used in Lawrence's play *A Collier's Friday Night*, written between 1906 and 1909: 'Is it a fact though, Matoushka? Why didn't you tell us before?' (D. H. Lawrence, *A Collier's Friday Night* (London: M. Secker, 1934), p. 20).

13 Lawrence to Grace Crawford, 24 June 1910; to Louie Burrows, 14 December 1910; to Louie Burrows, 28 December 1910, *The Letters of D. H. Lawrence*, I, p. 166, 202, 217.

14 Natalya Reinhold, 'The Russian Pigeons in the Groves of Eastwood', *Études Lawrenciennes* 44 (2013), pp. 97–110.

Generally speaking, Russia-centred discussions were fairly prominent in Lawrence's close circle of friends and personal connections. Firstly, one should mention the Hueffer (Ford Madox Ford) circle, with which Lawrence got in touch in 1908, following the publication of his poems in *The English Review*.[15] Ford Madox Ford's sister, Juliet Hueffer, was married to David Soskice, a Russian revolutionary and exile, head of a Russian Law Bureau in Lincoln's Inn Fields. Through Soskice, as well as through his own friendship with the Garnetts, Lawrence started off numerous and almost uniformly cordial relationships with a number of prominent members of the Russian anarchist groups. Among others, he spoke very highly of Fanny Stepniak (Sergei Stepniak-Kravchinsky's widow), portraying her as 'a beauty infinitely lovelier than the beauty of the young women I know. [...] She *knows* what life consists in, and she never fails her knowledge.'[16] In January 1914, when staying in the small village of Albergo delle Palme, Lawrence and Frieda spent a month in the company of Felix Volkhovsky's wife Vera, who accompanied Constance Garnett on her Italian visit. Vera's arrival attracted a series of new encounters at some highly cosmopolitan social soirées, among which there was a memorable gathering, hosted by a popular and prolific Russian writer Alexander Amphiteatrov – 'a motley of tutors and music teachers for the children – an adopted son of Maxim Gorky [Zinovii Peshkov], little dark, agile, full of life and a great wild Cossack wife whom he had married for passion and come to hate.'[17] And although the odd assortment of this 'rum show' made Lawrence suddenly feel 'English and stable and solid in comparison', he seemed to love these people 'for their absolute carelessness about everything but just what interested them.'[18] Lawrence was very fond of Maxim Litvinov, the husband of his close friend Ivy Litvinov *nee* Low (married to Litvinov in 1916), who had been living in exile in London since 1908, and after the revolution was

15 Ford Madox Ford was the founder (1908) and the first editor of the journal.

16 Lawrence, letter to Sallie Hopkin, 22 April 1917, *The Letters of D. H. Lawrence*, III, p. 116.

17 Lawrence, letter to Arthur McLeod, 14 March 1914, *The Letters of D. H. Lawrence*, II, p. 155.

18 Ibid. p. 155.

appointed Foreign Representative of the Bolshevik State (to be People's Commissar for Foreign Affairs from 1930 to 1939). 'As for Russia, I still think I should like to go, in spite of all these "rulers"', he wrote to Samuel Koteliansky in 1925, 'Don't I remember Litvinov in a steam of washing and boiled cabbage?'[19]

Samuel Koteliansky, or 'Kot', as he was affectionately known among the Bloomsbury circle, was the person who in many ways was pivotal regarding shaping Lawrence's view of Russia and its culture. As a Ukrainian emigrant, Kot arrived in England in 1911 to escape Tsarist anti-Semitic repression and started working as a translator for the Russian Law Bureau in London (and later for Leonard and Virginia Woolf's Hogarth Press). In July 1914 Lawrence and Kot found themselves in the company of two other friends on a walking tour in the Lake District. Koteliansky would later tell Catherine Carswell that Lawrence was described to him as 'a writer chap with ideas about love' and that on the second night of the walk,

> they had to be put in a cottage where there was only one bed [...] Lawrence, as the delicate one, was made to sleep in the bed and Koteliansky as the visitor was urged to share it. He was very unwilling. Never in his life had such a thing befallen him. But Lawrence was so gay and easy that all shyness vanished.[20]

Lawrence also had some vivid recollections of the occasion, depicting it in full detail to Cynthia Asquith:

> I had been walking in Westmorland, rather happy with water-lilies twisted round my hat – big, white and gold water-lilies that we found in a pool high up – and girls who had come on a spree and who were having tea in the upper room of an inn, shrieked

19 Lawrence, letter to Samuel Koteliansky, 18 December 1925, *The Letters of D. H. Lawrence*, V, p. 355.

20 Quoted in Galya Diment, *A Russian Jew of Bloomsbury: The Life and Times of Samuel Koteliansky* (Montreal: McGill-Queen's University Press 2011), p. 52. Lawrence's relationship with Koteliansky is discussed in great detail in Diment's study; see also George J. Zytaruk, Introduction to George J. Zytaruk, *The Quest for Rananim: D. H. Lawrence's Letters to S. S. Koteliansky* (Montreal: McGill-Queen's University Press, 1970); and Harry T. Moore, *The Priest of Love: A Life of D. H. Lawrence* (New York: Farrar, Straus and Giroux, 1974), p. 111.

> with laughter. And I remember also we crouched under the loose wall on the moors and the rain flew by in streams, and the wind came rushing through the chinks in the wall behind one's head, and we shouted songs and I imitated music-hall turns, whilst the other men crouched under the wall and I pranked in the rain on the turf in the gorse, and Koteliansky groaned Hebrew music – Ranani Sadekim Badanoi.[21]

Almost instantly they became friends and collaborated on various projects. Koteliansky assisted in arranging the translation of Lawrence's works into Russian, and even suggested 'Rananim', a Hebrew word for 'rejoice', as the name for Lawrence's idea of a utopian commune. Lawrence, on the other hand, took part in a number of Koteliansky's English translations, including Lev Shestov's *All Things Are Possible*, Ivan Bunin's *The Gentleman from San Francisco*, Dostoevsky's notebooks, and Maxim Gorky's *Reminiscences of Leonid Andreyev*. In 1930 Koteliansky translated *The Grand Inquisitor* as a free-standing work and asked Lawrence to write a preface. According to George Zytaruk's pioneering study of Lawrence's response to Russian literature, Lawrence, generally speaking, read and often acted as an unacknowledged editor for almost everything that Koteliansky attempted to translate.[22]

This, of course, fell on the fertile ground of the writer's own fascination with the subject, and during his lifetime Lawrence acquired an extensive knowledge of the Russian literary oeuvre: from Russian classics to the less known contemporary authors such as Rozanov, Artsybashev, Kuprin and Bunin. His perception of these writings, however, differed considerably throughout the years. In the introduction to Koteliansky's translation of *The Grand Inquisitor* he wrote,

> It is a strange experience, to examine one's reaction to a book over a period of years. I remember when I first read *The Brothers Karamazov*, in 1913, how fascinated yet unconvinced it left me [...] Since then I have read *The Brothers Karamazov* twice, and each time found it more depressing because, alas, more drearily true to life. At

21 Lawrence, letter to Cynthia Asquith, 31 January 1915, *The Letters of D. H. Lawrence*, II, p. 268.

22 Zytaruk. *Lawrence's Response to Russian Literature*, pp. 13–36.

> first it had been lurid romance. Now I read *The Grand Inquisitor* once more, and my heart sinks right through my shoes.[23]

Being known for his ruthless attacks on Dostoevsky,[24] whom he did not cease to criticise in his essays, letters and fiction, Lawrence nonetheless claimed to have a 'subterranean love' and 'the greatest admiration'[25] for the Russian author, pitched in this type of a love–hate duality mode straight after his first reading of *Crime and Punishment* in 1909 (the French translation): 'I remember how he frowned in a puzzled way and said', he wrote in the memoirs of Jessie Chambers, 'It's very great, but I don't like it, I don't quite understand it. I must read it again.'[26] A somewhat more judgemental response to the novel can be found in Lawrence's letter to Blanche Jennings (May 1909), where he deplored the work as a 'tract, a treatise, a pamphlet compared to Tolstoy's *Anna Karenina* or *War and Peace*.'[27] Lawrence read Tolstoy as a university student, acclaiming *Anna Karenina* as the greatest novel of frank sexuality;[28] later on he recommended it to May Holbrook, Jessie Chambers' elder sister, as a remedy for the provincial isolation and narrowness of Eastwood, praising the author as a 'great man' of the same calibre as Balzac and Ibsen.[29] Not unlike his further reflections on Dostoevsky, Lawrence subsequently dismissed Tolstoy's futile moral objectives and social

23 D. H. Lawrence, Introduction to *The Grand Inquisitor*, in D. H. Lawrence, *Introductions and Reviews*, ed. N. H. Reeve and John Worthen (Cambridge: Cambridge University Press, 2005), pp. 127–36 (p. 127).

24 Lawrence's response to Dostoevsky was analysed in detail by Peter Kaye (Kaye, pp. 29–65).

25 Lawrence, letter to Samuel Koteliansky, 8 April 1915, *The Letters of D. H. Lawrence*, II, p. 314.

26 E. T. (Jessie Chambers), p. 123.

27 Lawrence, letter to Blanche Jennings, 8 May 1909, *The Letters of D. H. Lawrence*, I, p. 126.

28 E. T. (Jessie Chambers), p. 114.

29 Lawrence, letter to May Holbrook, 2 December 1908, *The Letters of D. H. Lawrence*, I, p. 96.

preaching: 'His *Resurrection* is the step into the tomb', he wrote, 'And the stone was rolled upon him.'[30]

Around 1912 (at the time he was writing his own plays) his attention was drawn to Chekhov, whose plays he characterised as 'exceedingly interesting [...] – a new thing in drama'.[31] He even drew a parallel between his own works and those of the Russian author: 'Just as an audience was found in Russia for Tchekhov, so an audience might be found in England for some of my stuff.'[32] Yet again, he changed his opinion later, describing Chekhov as 'a second-rate writer.'[33]

By 1914, Lawrence seemed to be less convinced by the writing of the entire cohort of the Russian authors:

> The certain moral scheme is what I object to. In Turgenev, and in Tolstoi, and in Dostoevsky, the moral scheme into which all the characters fit – and it is nearly the same scheme – is, whatever the extraordinariness of the characters themselves, dull, old, dead.[34]

30 D. H. Lawrence, 'Resurrection', in *Phoenix*, ed. Edward D. McDonald (London: Heinemann, 1936), pp. 737–39 (p. 737). For Lawrence's response to Tolstoy, see George J. Zytaruk, *Lawrence's Response to Russian Literature*, pp. 59–60.

31 Lawrence, letter to Philip Smith, 22 April 1912, *The Letters of D. H. Lawrence*, I, p. 385.

32 Lawrence, letter to Edward Garnett, 1 February 1913, *The Letters of D. H. Lawrence*, I, p. 509.

33 Lawrence, letter to Rhys Davis, 25 December 1928, *The Letters of D. H. Lawrence*, VII, p. 94.

34 Lawrence, letter to Edward Garnett, 5 June 1914, *The Letters of D. H. Lawrence*, II, pp. 182–3.
Jessie Chambers points out that Lawrence never cared much for Gorky (E. T. (Jessie Chambers), p. 121); while Lawrence himself states the opposite in his letter to Edward Garnett: 'I've read all the 4i[d] Maxim Gorky's, I believe – I love short stories' (Lawrence, letter to Edward Garnett, 2 March 1913, *The Letters of D. H. Lawrence*, I, p. 524). As regards other contemporary authors, as he put it in his letter to Katherine Mansfield: 'Kot gave me a Kuprin. It reads awfully well. But I don't think much of these lesser Russians' (Lawrence, letter to Katherine Mansfield, 11 March 1916, *The Letters of D. H. Lawrence*, II, p. 577).

It was a certain degree of insincerity that he sensed in the Russian literary endeavour, finding it exceedingly didactic, intellectually overblown and emotionally contrived. On 2 December 1916 he wrote to Catherine Carswell,

> Oh, don't think I would belittle the Russians. They have meant an enormous amount to me; Turgenev, Tolstoi, Dostoevsky – mattered almost more than anything, and I thought them the greatest writers of all time. And now, with something of a shock, I realise a certain crudity and thick, uncivilised, insensitive stupidity about them, I realise how much finer and purer and more ultimate our own stuff is.[35]

Lawrence, of course, was not the first who saw reflective intellectualism as a 'tragic flaw' of the Russian literary oeuvre. Since the first half of the nineteenth century the Russian cultural elite had been divided into so-called Westernisers (including such figures as Peter Chaadaev, Alexander Herzen and Vissarion Belinsky) and Slavophiles (represented by Aleksei Khomiakov and Konstantin Aksakov, and then followed by the poet Fedor Tiutchev, the lexicographer Vladimir Dahl and the composers of the 'Mighty Five' group). The latter were convinced that the Western drive to discover and explain grated against the Russians' inherited instinct for the preservation of mystery and distrust of analytical dissection. It is not that understanding was irrelevant to Russians, but certain things demanded a different kind of understanding than that offered by the enlightened Western approach. To someone with a traditional Russian sensibility, the Western methods of analysis seemed to trample on the sacred and destroy beauty through meticulous analysis and systematisation: the essential holistic quality of the being, or truth, seemed to be given up in the very process of inquiry and cognition.

Although it is unlikely that Lawrence was aware of this long-term socio-philosophical division, his doubts concerning the excessive analytical didacticism of the Russian classics appears to be surprisingly in tune with the tenets of the Slavophiles' doctrine. At first glance, his reasoning was fairly schematic: as a paragon of Western civilisation ('Since Peter the Great

35 Lawrence, letter to Catherine Carswell, 2 December 1916, *The Letters of D. H. Lawrence*, III, p. 45.

Russia has been accepting Europe [...] What she has actually uttered is her own unwilling, fantastic reproduction of European truths'[36]), Russia was drowned in intellectual reflexivity, completely alien to the natural sensuality of the Russian soul, as one reads in his 1925 essay *The Novel*:

> how boring, in a great nation like Russia, to let its old-Adam manhood be so improved upon by these reformers, who all feel themselves short of something, and therefore live by spite, that at last there's nothing left but a lot of shells of men, improving themselves steadily emptier and emptier, till they rattle with words and formulae.[37]

Lawrence's conception of the Russian theme and the Russian spirit, however, turns out to be more nuanced and more complex. Essentially it had deep parallels in the theories of Lev Shestov, a contemporary Russian philosopher, whose essays he was editing in Koteliansky's translation (published under the title *All Things Are Possible* in 1920[38]). Lawrence was clearly captivated by Shestov's punchy style and the broad spectrum of his vision, which had a crucial impact on substantiating and configuring his own socio-cultural thoughts:

> I have been editing, for a Russian friend of mine, a rather amusing, not very long translation of a book of philosophy by one of the last of the Russians, called *Shestov*. It is by no means a heavy work – nice and ironical and in snappy paragraphs. Would it be in your line?[39]

One of the key points of Shestov's philosophical stance consisted in the uniqueness of the Russian socio-historical path, which, according to the thinker, stemmed from the nation's relatively short-term exposure to

36 D. H. Lawrence, Foreword to Lev Shestov, *All Things Are Possible*, trans. S. S. Koteliansky (London: M. Secker, 1920), pp. 7–12 (pp. 7–8).

37 D. H. Lawrence, 'The Novel', in D. H. Lawrence, *Selected Critical Writings*, ed. Michael Herbert (Oxford: Oxford University Press, 1998), pp. 179–90 (p. 187).

38 The book was positively reviewed by Benjamin de Casseres ('Shestov's Challenge to Civilisation', *New York Times Book Review and Magazine*, 3 October 1920, p. 19), highlighting Lawrence's 'brilliantly written foreword'.

39 Lawrence, letter to Martin Secker, 2 September 1919, *The Letters of D. H. Lawrence*, III, 481–2.

the 'civilising' influence of the European tradition ('our simplicity and truthfulness are due to our relatively scanty culture'[40]):

> Scratch a Russian and you will find a Tartar. Culture is an age-long development, and sudden grafting of it upon a race rarely succeeds. To us in Russia, civilisation came suddenly, whilst we were still savages. At once she took upon herself the responsibilities of a tamer of wild animals, first working with decoys and baits, and later, when she felt her power, with threats. We quickly submitted. In a short time we were swallowing in enormous doses those poisons which Europe had been gradually accustoming herself to, gradually assimilating through centuries. Thanks to which, the transplanting of civilisation into Russia turns out to be no mild affair.[41]

This is not to say that Shestov tended to align himself with the classic framework of Slavophile ideas. His vision could be reduced to neither a simple rejection of the external Western impact, nor mechanical acceptance of the European cultural scheme. The essence of his understanding of the Russian cultural hybridity lay in the notion of creative dynamism and transformation – in forging a national identity that exists in between the two, capitalising on both polarities of the spectrum (without merging them), and raising this encounter onto a new level of dialectical interaction, to the effect that the whole is greater than the elemental sum of its parts. 'That is why', he argues, 'we have always taken over European ideas in such fantastic forms. Take the sixties, for example' – the era of such influential thinkers as Turgenev, Tolstoy and Dostoevsky: 'with its loud ideas of sobriety and modest outlook, it was a most drunken period. Those who awaited the New Messiah and the Second Advent read Darwin and dissected frogs.'[42]

Lawrence's Foreword to the collection of Shestov's essays (as well as his later writing on the subject[43]) displays his keen understanding of the philosopher's concept of the synergy of elements in the Russian identity hybrid, the dangers of any distortive excess, and the advantages of the

40 Lev Shestov, *All Things Are Possible*, trans. S. S. Koteliansky (London: M. Secker, 1920), p. 233.

41 Shestov, *All Things Are Possible*, p. 39.

42 Ibid. p. 238.

43 *The Novel* (1925), *On Being in Love* (1925), *The Crown* (written in 1915, revised for publication in 1925); The Review of 'Solitaria' by V. V. Rozanov (1927).

dialectical balance: 'Our speech and feeling are organically inevitable to us', he argued,

> With the Russians it is different. They have only been inoculated with the virus of European culture and ethic [...] What she has really to utter the coming centuries will hear. For Russia will certainly inherit the future. What we already call the greatness of Russia is only her prenatal struggling.[44]

Formally speaking, the text of the foreword hardly gives any specific indication of what exactly Lawrence understood by the indigenous Russian paradigm and the genuine Russian spirit. His fiction, his critical essays and translations suggest a clearer and a wider projection of his viewpoint, which, as will be shown, is closely affiliated with Shestov's concept of Russia's liminality (the inseparability and distinctness of its Slavic and Western sides) and the implications of its 'otherness' in the European social context.

In this regard, the area of Lawrence-Koteliansky translational collaboration requires further, more in-depth consideration, for Lawrence's contribution to this work should be seen as much more complex than that of a native-speaker editor and proof-reader. Like many other modernists, who revolutionised translation methods and strategies in ways that questioned the notion of accuracy and blurred the boundaries between the target and the source texts, Lawrence saw translation as a unique avenue of intercultural communication.[45] Apart from his general interest in languages and cultures, each with its own peculiar way of rendering the idea of the real, he was preoccupied with projecting the distinct spirit and distinct quality of the foreign culture, which he termed as 'the spirit of the place' (in the essay that opens *Studies in Classic American Literature*, 1923):

> Every continent has its own great spirit of place. Every people is polarised in some particular locality, which is home, the homeland. Different places on the face of the earth have different vital effluence, different vibration, different chemical exhalation,

44 Lawrence, Foreword to Lev Shestov, *All Things Are Possible*, pp. 7–8.

45 G. M. Hyde, *D. H. Lawrence and the Art of Translation* (London: Palgrave Macmillan, 1981), pp. 11–35.

> different polarity with different stars: call it what you like. But the spirit of place is a great reality.[46]

The above words imply that any cultural product, including a work of literature and art, is meant to reflect this intrinsic synergy between the place, its inhabitants and their language; as Lawrence further specified in his essay 'Morality and the Novel' (1914): 'The business of art is to reveal the relation between man and his circumambient universe, at the living moment. [...] And this perfected relation between man and his circumambient universe is life itself, for mankind.'[47] It is in the exploration of this specific synergy and this intimate relation that Lawrence saw the purpose of any aesthetic endeavour; and it is in accordance with this notion of rendering 'the spirit of the place' that one should look at his editor's touch when he worked on Koteliansky's translations.[48]

According to George Zytaruk there were three instances of their active collaboration: the first time was in 1919 when they worked on *All Things Are Possible* by Shestov; the second was Ivan Bunin's *The Gentleman from San Francisco* in 1922, followed by Maxim Gorky's *Reminiscences of Leonid*

46 D. H. Lawrence, *Studies in Classic American Literature* (London: Heinemann, 1964), pp. 5–6.
The same concept is mentioned earlier in his *Sea and Sardinia* collection (1921): 'The spirit of place is a strange thing. Our mechanical age tries to override it. But it does not succeed. In the end the strange, sinister spirit of place, so diverse and adverse in differing places, will smash our mechanical oneness into smithereens, and all that we think the real thing will go off with a pop, and we shall be left staring' (D. H. Lawrence, *Sea and Sardinia*, ed. Mara Kalnins (Cambridge: University Press, 2002), p. 57).

47 D. H. Lawrence, 'Morality and the Novel', *Phoenix*, pp. 527–32 (p. 527).

48 As Koteliansky put it, Lawrence was not keen on positioning himself as a translator, feeling that it would be damaging for his reputation with publishers as a creative writer (Moore, p. 347): 'I don't want my names printed as a translator. It won't do for me to appear to dabble in too many things. If you don't want to appear alone – but why shouldn't you? – put me a nom de plume like Richard Haw or Thomas Ball' (Lawrence, letter to Samuel Koteliansky, 10 August 1919, *The Letters of D. H. Lawrence*, III, p. 381).

Andreev in 1924.[49] In many ways, Bunin's *The Gentleman from San Francisco* (published in Russian in 1915) was, arguably, the highlight of this trio, for here Koteliansky managed to bring together two real literary giants with similar sensibilities and artistic talents.

In early June 1921, Koteliansky wrote to Lawrence asking whether he would '"English" a translation he had made of a Russian story'.[50] Two months later the translation was complete. Lawrence liked the story so much that he wrote to Koteliansky, expressing his wish to proceed with other stories from Bunin's collection, but by then Koteliansky had already began working on *Gentle Breathing, Kazimir Stanislavovich and Son* with Leonard Woolf. The translation first appeared in the *Dial* and then was included in the 1922 Hogarth Press volume. Woolf was full of praising comments for Lawrence's version, calling it 'a masterpiece or near-masterpiece.'[51] Lawrence, on the other hand, was not that flattering about Woolf's work: 'Some of Wolf's [sic] sentences', he noted, 'take a bit of reading.'[52] In this opinion he was joined by *The Times* reviewer: 'The other three stories in the book are in comparison, slight', he claimed, commenting on the positive synergy of the Lawrence-Bunin association:

> In the Russian it is written as a kind of prose-poem, a style of writing well adapted to express the heated yet sombre imaginative glow with which the story is suffused. But the present translation, by D. H. Lawrence and S. S. Koteliansky, although it cannot reproduce precisely the style of the original, is a remarkably able piece of

49 George J. Zytaruk, 'D. H. Lawrence's Hand in Translation of Maxim Gorki's "Reminiscences of Leonid Andreev"', *The Yale University Library Gazette* 46.1 (1971), pp. 29–34. Zytaruk maintains that in the first two cases it has not been possible to identify Lawrence's specific contributions, despite the fact that the entire manuscript of *All Things Are Possible* has been preserved in Lawrence's handwriting; the *Reminiscences of Leonid Andreev* is different in this regard: there is a typescript with Lawrence's handwritten revisions.

50 Lawrence, letter to Samuel Koteliansky, *The Letters of D. H. Lawrence*, IV, p. 23.

51 Leonard Woolf, *Beginning Again: An Autobiography of years from 1811 to 1918* (New York: Harcourt, Brace & World, 1964), III, p. 248.

52 Lawrence, letter to Samuel Koteliansky, 9 July 1921, *The Letters of D. H. Lawrence*, IV, p. 275.

> work. A better translation is hardly possible [...] The other three stories in the book are in comparison, slight[53]

In his restrained and dignified way, Bunin, who excelled not only as a prose writer, but also as a musician and a first-rate poet, was one of the greatest stylists in the Russian language. His prose unmistakably reflects the poet's sensitivity in his cool verbal precision and his keen eye for accurate detail. All short-story writers rely on significant detail, but Bunin's images are particularly sharp; and his fluent economy of diction was rarely matched by any of the Russian authors. This type of writing found a very particular resonance in Lawrence's own mode of expression. Both linguistically and poetically, his English text represented Bunin's style with a remarkable exactness of tonal gradations. Compare for instance, Lawrence's artistically nuanced translation with a somewhat plainer version produced by Yarmolinsky in 1918:

> The rest of the tourists hardly deserved any attention. There were a few Russians, who had settled on Capri, untidy, absent-minded people, absorbed in their bookish thoughts, spectacled, bearded, with the collars of their cloth overcoats raised.[54]

And in Lawrence we read:

> There were other arrivals too, but none worthy of notice: a few Russians who had settled in Capri, untidy and absent-minded owing to their bookish thoughts, spectacled, bearded, half-buried in the upturned collars of their thick woollen overcoats.[55]

Lawrence, himself a painter and a poet, obviously responded to the graphic aestheticism of the Russian author. Moreover, in Bunin's story, Lawrence's

53 'Ivan Bunin', *The Times*, 17 May 1922, p. 16.

54 Ivan Bunin, 'The Gentlemen from San Francisco', in *Lazarus* by Leonid Andreev and *The Gentlemen from San Francisco* by Bunin, trans. Abraham Yarmolinsky (Boston: The Stratford Company Publishers 1918), pp. 32–58 (pp. 43–44).

55 Ivan Bunin, *The Gentleman from San Francisco and Other Stories*, trans. S. S. Koteliansky and Leonard Woolf (Richmond: Hogarth Press, 1922), pp. 1–40 (p. 19); the book contains a note saying: 'Owing to a mistake Mr Lawrence's name has been omitted from the title page'.

sensibility and mastery in projecting 'the spirit of the place' came across with an almost uncanny degree of insight and perception. Not without an implicit reference to the overwhelming vastness of the Russian land and the iconic wildness of the Russian spirit, the uncontrollable realm of the gale-swept sea was juxtaposed to the man-made power of the ship (on which the gentleman travels across the Atlantic) – an embodiment of the eternal war waged between the elemental forces of nature and the artificial mind-constructs of modern civilisation. In the narrative, this opposition takes on a spiritual or even metaphysical dimension, for the ship is ruled by a mysterious captain, akin to a pagan idol; while the devil himself watches the struggle of the ship against the sea from the shoreline. It is, on the other hand, made very clear that modern civilisation has now created its own gods and its own man-made devils, next to which the elemental Old World's notion of Hell seems almost irrelevant and powerlessly unimportant:

> still they danced, amid a storm that swept over the ocean, booming like a funeral service, rolling up mountains of mourning darkness silvered with foam. Through the snow the numerous fiery eyes of the ship were hardly visible to the Devil who watched from the rocks of Gibraltar, from the stony gateway of two worlds, peering after the vessel as she disappeared into the night and storm. The Devil was huge as a cliff. But huger still was the liner, many storeyed, many funnelled, created by the presumption of the New Man with the old heart. The blizzard smote the rigging and the funnels, and whitened the ship with snow, but she was enduring, firm, majestic and horrible. On the topmost deck rose lonely amongst the snowy whirlwind, the cosy and dim quarters where lay the heavy master of the ship, he who was like a pagan idol, sunk now in a light, uneasy slumber.[56]

56 Bunin, *The Gentleman from San Francisco and Other Stories*, pp. 37–38. Compare with Yarmolinsky's version:

> On the second and the third night there was again a ball – this time in mid-ocean, during a furious storm sweeping over the ocean, which roared like a funeral mass and rolled up mountainous seas fringed with mourning silvery foam. The Devil, who from the rocks of Gibraltar, the stony gateway of two worlds, watched the ship vanish into night and storm, could hardly distinguish from behind the snow the innumerable fiery eyes of the ship. The Devil was as huge as a cliff, but the ship was even bigger, a many-storied, many-stacked giant, created by the arrogance of the New Man with the old heart. The blizzard battered the ship's rigging and its broad-necked stacks, whitened with snow, but it

Through Lawrence's encounter with Bunin, his understanding of the Russian theme acquired yet another degree of reflective assertion. It appeared as if, quite suddenly, he glimpsed exactly what for years he had been trying to capture and conceive. Firstly, one of the most fundamental aspects of Bunin's world-view was an acute sense of the precariousness of existence, an omnipresent awareness of the impermanence of all human constructions and achievements, and a constant recognition that everything one values can be snatched away at any moment (like the fully accidental and inconsequential death of the gentleman from San Francisco). Yet this sense of volatility and doom does not lead to apathy and despair, but draws attention to the most vivid appreciation of the sensual experience, the physicality of life and the spontaneity of human emotions. In this respect, Lawrence's first reaction to Bunin's story was quite telling and revealing: 'In spite of its lugubriousness', he maintained, 'it is screamingly good of Naples and Capri: so comically like reality;'[57] and it was this very type of sensation that several years later would acquire a definitive shape in his reflective comments on Rozanov's *Solitaria*:

> He is the first Russian, as far as I am concerned, who has ever said anything to me. And his vision is full of passion, vivid, valid. He is the first to see that immortality is in the vividness of life, not in the loss of life. The butterfly becomes a whole revelation to him: and to us. When Rozanov is wholly awake, and a new man, a risen man, the living and resurrected pagan, then he is a great man and a great seer, and perhaps, as he says himself, the first Russian to emerge.[58]

---

remained firm, majestic – and terrible. On its uppermost deck, amidst a snowy whirlwind there loomed up in loneliness the cosy, dimly lighted cabin, where, only half awake, the vessel's ponderous pilot reigned over its entire mass, bearing the semblance of a pagan idol. He heard the wailing moans and the furious screeching of the siren, choked by the storm, but the nearness of that which was behind the wall and which in the last account was incomprehensible to him, removed his fears (Bunin, in *Lazarus* by Leonid Andreev and *The Gentleman from San Francisco* by Bunin, pp. 56–7).

57 Lawrence, letter to Samuel Koteliansky, 16 June 1921, *The Letters of D. H. Lawrence*, IV, p. 37.

58 D. H. Lawrence, 'Solitaria, by V. V. Rozanov', in *D. H. Lawrence: Selected Criticism*, ed. Anthony Beal (New York: Viking Press, 1956). pp. 247–9 (p. 248); the review was

Secondly (though very much connected with the previous point), it was the spirit of pagan Russianness incarnated in the uncorrupted power of natural physicality (as in Bunin's portrayal of the sea), which for Lawrence was missing in the works of the Russian literary classics: 'Instinctive animal Russia, with its miseries and splendours', had been replaced by 'a thinking, or pseudo-thinking Russia, enacting a few old thoughts, the best spontaneity destroyed.'[59] In Dostoevsky, for instance, Lawrence saw a writer, who was torn between 'the complete selflessness of Christian love' and the 'complete self-assertion of sensuality', and, instead of forging a productive unity of the two, took both principles to destructive extremes:

> Dmitri Karamazov and Rogozhin will each of them [...] obtain the sensation and the reduction within the flesh, add to the sensual experience, and progress towards utter dark disintegration, to nullity. Myshkin on the other hand will react upon the achieved consciousness or personality or ego of everyone he meets [...] obtaining the knowledge of the factors that made up the complexity of the consciousness [...] [then] reduce further and further back, till himself is a babbling idiot, a vessel full of disintegrated parts[60]

This division, leading to the perilous dissolution of one's personal self, was regarded by Lawrence as a purely mental construct:

> If there were no ascetics, there'd be no lewd people. If you divide the human psyche into two halves, one half will be white, the other black. It's the division itself which is pernicious. The swing to one extreme causes the swing to the other [...] But you can't blame the soul for this. All you have to blame is the craven, cretin human intelligence, which is always seeking to get away from its own centre;[61]

---

first published in *Calendar of Modern Letters* (July 1927). For a more detailed analysis see George J. Zytaruk, 'The Phallic Vision: D. H. Lawrence and V. V. Rozanov', *Comparative Literature Studies* 4.3 (1967), pp. 283–97.

59 D. H. Lawrence, 'On Being in Love', in D. H. Lawrence, *Reflections on the Death of a Porcupine and Other Essays*, ed. Michael Herbert (Cambridge: Cambridge University Press, 1988), p. 386.

60 D. H. Lawrence, 'The Crown', in D. H. Lawrence, *Reflections on the Death of a Porcupine*, pp. 251–307 (p. 282).

61 Lawrence, 'Solitaria', p. 249.

and was seen as characteristic of almost all Russian nineteenth-century authors. He referred to this as a peculiar 'Russianitis' disease – a spiritual and psychological affliction, which manifests itself as a love of one's own split-personality, a love 'to be dual, and divided against themselves.'[62] To give but a few examples: according to Lawrence, this triumph of reflexive consciousness revealed itself most evidently in the failure of free love in Tolstoy's writings, when the tragic love of Anna and Vronsky turns out to be pointlessly destroyed by 'the judgement of men', as opposed to the 'judgement of their own souls or the judgement of God.'[63] Consequently, he was very critical of Tolstoy's 'poetic' support of those, in his view, pathetic figures like Prince Nekhlyudov (*Resurrection*), who having engaged himself in a calculated routine of moral penance, eradicated the authentic sensual part of his identity and his soul. 'All that is quick, and all that is said and done by the quick, is, in some way, godly', Lawrence argued in the *Novel*,

> So that Vronsky's taking Anna Karenina we must count godly, since it is quick. And Prince in Resurrection, following the convict girl, we must count dead. The convict train is quick and alive. But that would-be-expiatory Prince is as dead as lumber.[64]

In Tolstoy, as in Dostoevsky, Lawrence saw a writer whose unbalanced duality manifested itself through the celebration of an overly rational and moralistic concept of the human – a perverse denial of desires and an excessive exaltation of the mind without appropriate 'grounding' in the physicality of carnal instincts. It is symptomatic in this sense that the original title of Shestov's essay – 'The Apotheosis of Groundlessness', rejected by

62 Ibid. pp. 247–8.
The reason for Lawrence's attraction to such a writer as Rozanov lies largely in the fact that he was drawing not from the reflective framework of mental postulations, but from the vast old sensual background of pagan Russia: 'Rozanov has more or less recovered the genuine pagan vision, the phallic vision, and with those eyes he looks, in amazement and consternation, on the mess of Christianity' (Lawrence, 'Solitaria', p. 248).

63 Zyatruk, *Lawrence's Response to Russian Literature*, p. 83.

64 Lawrence, *The Novel*, p. 183.

Lawrence as unsuitable for the English reader[65] – is echoed almost directly in *Women in Love*'s narrative (published in 1920, the same year as the translation of Shestov), when Gudrun comments, rather insightfully, on the 'rootless life of the Russians.'[66]

An insightful attempt to reflect upon this innate duality within the notion of the Russian (as an essentialist model, which can be expanded into the area of any intercultural, ethnic and sexual interaction) is projected in Lawrence's own fiction.[67] In *Women in Love* it comes across in its most direct way in the figure of Maxim Libidnikov – a 'prim young Russian',[68] whose name in itself suggests an interesting interplay of the body-soul ambivalent associations, referring to 'libido' as a physical connotation on the one hand, and to Dostoevsky's Lebezyatnikov – on the other. The latter is a relatively minor character in *Crime and Punishment*, who serves as a mouthpiece for certain allegedly 'superfluous' Western ideas (such as for instance, Nihilism and Utilitarianism), received with a degree of criticism by the Russian author.[69]

Maxim's first appearance in the gathering of the middle-class London intellectuals asserts the ambivalence of the division. His features are described in unambiguously sensual terms: 'He was dark, and smooth-skinned, and full of a stealthy vigour' with 'smooth, warm-coloured face and

65 'His [Shestov's] attitude amuses me – also his irony, which I think is difficult for the English readers […] "Apotheosis of Groundlessness" will never do. What can one find instead, for a title?' (Lawrence, letter to Samuel Koteliansky, 9 August 1919, *The Letters of D. H. Lawrence*, III, p. 380).

66 Lawrence, *Women in Love*, p. 203.

67 Ben Richardson's unpublished MA Thesis 'Unwrapping the Enigma: Russia in the Works of Wyndham Lewis, T. S. Eliot, and D. H. Lawrence, 1912–1939' (University of Canterbury, New Zealand, 2012) presents an interesting and detailed account of Lawrence's engagement with the Russian theme, albeit he takes a different line from that taken in this study.

68 Ibid. p. 62.

69 The meaning of the name was explained by Dostoevsky in the drafts of the novel: 'Lebeziatnikov – fawning, being obsequious or servile'; followed by an important clarification: 'Nihilism is a servitude of thought' (E. A. Shklovsky, Notes to Fedor Dostoevsky, *Crime and Punishment* (Moscow: Olma-Press, 2005), pp. 744–62 (p. 744)).

black, oiled hair.'[70] At the same time he is shown to be self-controlled and socially restrained, for, in the company where almost everyone appears to be drunk, he strikes Gerald Crich as 'the only one who seemed to be perfectly calm and sober.'[71] Similarly, his voice 'sounded in the blood rather than in the air',[72] but his speech suggested a high level of carefully cultivated intellectual sophistication, expressed in a 'precise', 'refined', 'quick', 'hushed' and 'elegant manner.'[73] There is a clear allusion to Maxim's homoerotic relationship with Julius Halliday, as Gerald discovers 'the young men by the fire stark naked.'[74] However, the Russian's tendency to struggle with, and ultimately suppress the inherent physicality of his nature becomes evident in the episode where Maxim takes an affrontingly cynical stance against Birkin's idea of the divinity of sexual desire (denigrating it as a form of 'religious mania'[75]); and his spontaneous interest in the subject ('"Go on – go on," said Maxim. "What comes next? It's really very interesting"'[76]) is shown to be concurrently suppressed and kindred ('go on reading'[77]) through the conflicting mental and instinctive pulses: '"Yes, yes, so do I", said the Russian. "He is a megalomaniac, of course, it is a form of religious mania. He thinks he is the Saviour of man – go on reading."'[78]

This inherent duality characteristic of the Russian psyche is maintained throughout the novel and is linked to a more general, culturally significant discourse of the East (primeval) – West (rational) juxtaposition.[79] Maxim's cultural liminality, in this respect, comes across by the way in which he fulfils the role of a symbolic meta-textual mediator (in Gerald's

70 Lawrence, *Women in Love*, p. 62.
71 Ibid. p. 62.
72 Ibid. p. 62.
73 Ibid. p. 374, 69, 63.
74 Ibid. p. 70.
75 Ibid. p. 375.
76 Ibid. p. 375.
77 Ibid. p. 375.
78 Ibid. p. 375.
79 In the novel Maxim's appearance often acquires a connotational quality of the natural world: 'with the black hair growing fine and freely, like tendrils, and his limbs like smooth plant-stems'; 'the Russian golden and like a water-plant' (Ibid. p. 71).

mind) between the European and the pagan pre-Christian (African) civilisation. Thus, for instance, Gerald finds the physicality of Maxim's naked body humiliating and prohibitively repulsive ('Gerald looked at him, and with a slight revulsion saw the human animal, golden skinned and bare, somehow humiliating'[80]) in the same way as he is repelled by the sight of the wooden statue of an African woman 'abstracted' in utter physical stress ('It was a terrible face, peaked, abstracted almost into meaninglessness by the weight of sensation beneath'[81]). What is significantly striking in this context is that the description of the sculpture – 'a statuette about two feet high, a tall slim, elegant figure from West Africa, in dark wood, glossy and suave'[82] – is cast by reference to a set of epithets almost identical to those used for the portrait of the Russian: 'his suave, golden coloured body'; 'in his quick, hushed, elegant manner'.[83]

To Lawrence, African art expresses the history of an ancient race older than Christianity, which has sensual rather than spiritual values to offer – something 'of the extreme of physical sensation, beyond the limits of mental consciousness'[84] (or as he remarks later in the novel: the statue 'had thousands of years of purely sensual, purely unspiritual knowledge behind her. It must have been thousands of years since her race had died, mystically'[85]). When stylistically associated with the statue, Maxim is, metaphorically speaking, bridging the gap between the civilised and the savage; and the fact that in the novel he is more often called 'the Russian', or 'the young Russian', rather than by his proper name, signifies that his liminal identity is seen as ethnically archetypal and paradigmatic, rather than singular and person-specific.

One can say that the effect of Lawrence's exploration of the Russian cultural hybridity is at least two-fold. On the one hand, it certainly sheds light on his vision of the complexity of the Russian psyche, with its innate

80 Ibid. p. 70.
81 Ibid. p. 71.
82 Ibid. p. 245.
83 Ibid. p. 71, 63.
84 Ibid. p. 67.
85 Ibid. p. 245.

sensuality tarnished by the dominance of consciousness and intellectual pursuits. On the other, attention is drawn to the fact that Lawrence's projection of this interethnic or intercultural mixing is implicit within a tendency to keep all their elements separate from each other, or to use effects of hybridity to emphasise the intransitiveness of the division. Thus, for instance, Gerald Crich finds the presence of the young Russian profoundly disturbing ('He was so healthy and well-made [...] why did one feel repelled?'[86]), especially in distinction to his English homoerotic partner, Julius Holliday, who, in contrast to the Russian's human–animal hybridity, is perceived in terms of the comforting aestheticism of the Western tradition: 'heavy, slack, broken beauty, white and firm. He was like a Christ in a Pieta.'[87] The encounter with foreign hybridity here becomes an imperative catalyst for self-assertion – for reaffirmation of Englishness and the implicit purity of one's own line. In this regard, a parallel comes to mind with Lawrence's own experience in such a cosmopolitan, Anglo–Russo–Italian, context. As he described it in a letter, the motley assortment of this 'rum show' made him suddenly feel very 'English and stable and solid in comparison.'[88]

Lawrence's specific perspective on the concept of intercultural hybridity is, of course, ideologically motivated: it reflects a clear tendency towards ethnic and cultural essentialism, which, according to many critics, was a distinct and noticeable feature of his work. Fiona Becket, for instance, argues that such essentialism is in keeping with Lawrence's more general preoccupation with polarisation of the opposites, seen in the context of the Heideggerian notion of

> Intimacy, whereby the relationship [...] between any two factors [...] is not to be understood as synthesis. Focused on opposition, Lawrence's concentration is typically on separateness, nearness, and distance that 'nearness' paradoxically implies, between the two elements or bodies that figure at any point in his thought.[89]

86 Ibid. p. 71.

87 Ibid. p. 70.

88 Lawrence, letter to Arthur McLeod, 14 March 1914, *The Letters of D. H. Lawrence*, II, p. 155.

89 Fiona Becket, *D. H. Lawrence: The Thinker as Poet* (Basingstoke: Macmillan, 1997), p. 156.

This conjunction of 'inseparability' and 'distinctness' in Lawrence is requisite to the productive interaction of difference – to a dynamic tension rather than equalising synthesis or syncretic merge. To illustrate, one finds this conceptual structure in Birkin's idealisation of love as 'pure duality of polarisation' – as a union of 'two strong beings', man and woman, who are 'constellated like two stars.'[90] Moreover, Howard J. Booth argues that for Lawrence, the notion of this dynamic union goes far beyond the framework of gender relations. He draws attention to the fact that, in 1917 (the year when *Women in Love* was being substantially revised), Lawrence's thought manifested a shift away from viewing the heterosexual relationship as the source of transformational encounter. Instead, he moved towards exploring 'racial differences and cultural otherness' as a potential trigger of the transformative change.[91]

The Rainbow and *Women in Love* represent, arguably, the most comprehensive and sustained reflection of Lawrence's perspective on the potency of such a transformative intercultural mixing (as a dynamic tension of the elements), in which the notion of Russian 'otherness' is employed as a 'buoying up' of the author's philosophical views. The Brangwen sisters' personal drama, their difficulties in finding equilibrium between their convoluted inner selves and the surrounding social milieu, stems directly from their original ethnic liminality – their intercultural hybridity formed of Slavic emotional physicality and the rationalism of the English mind. The formation, as well as the detailed examination of the interaction of elements in such a mixture is explored in *The Rainbow* – the 1915 'prequel' to *Women in Love*, which follows the social and spiritual evolution of three generations of the Lensky women – the 'well born' descendants of Polish 'landowners',[92] integrated through their marital relations into the English family of Brangwen men.

90 Lawrence, *Women in Love*, p. 201.

91 Howard J. Booth, 'Lawrence in Doubt: A Theory of the "Other" and its Collapse', in *Modernism and Empire*, ed. Howard J. Booth and Nigel Rigby (Manchester: Manchester University Press, 2000), pp. 197–223 (p. 203).

92 D. H. Lawrence, *The Rainbow* (New York: Modern Library, 1915), p. 34.

The fact that the Lenskys – Lydia, Anna and then Ursula and Gudrun – happen to be of Polish rather than Russian extraction is, perhaps, of low importance in this context, as there are several factors suggesting that Lawrence's portrayal of them should be largely considered on a paradigmatic level – as an archetypal projection of his Russian or, generally speaking, pan-Slavic point of view. Firstly, to anyone familiar with the Russian literary oeuvre, the family name Lensky will sound intimately Russian, through its reference to Vladimir Lensky, the main character in Pushkin's *Eugene Onegin*. Secondly, at the time when Lawrence was working on the novel Poland was still an assimilated part of the Russian Empire. And finally, and perhaps more importantly, it is worth bearing in mind that for Lawrence the concept of nationality was inherently connected to ethnicity; as his characters affirm in *Women in Love*, at least in Europe 'nationality roughly corresponds to race.'[93] Similarly, in *Movements in European History* he claims that in the development of mankind it is 'a different spirit and idea' of the race that configures its evolution (or in Lawrence's terms, 'its own growing tip') as a nation: 'Every branch has its own direction and its growing tip [...] for each branch is, as it were, differently grafted by a different spirit and idea, which becomes it own spirit and idea.'[94]

In Lawrence's fiction, this specific 'spirit and idea' of the Slavs is often highlighted through the 'otherness' of their mode of self-expression. When they need to find a voice for their inner selves they move away from the European logo-centric tradition and express the inexpressible through the gestural language of dance, akin to the irrational world of their pagan forebears.[95] In this regard one can mention Anna Brangwen's outburst of

93 Lawrence, *Women in Love*, p. 22.

94 D. H. Lawrence, *Movements in European History*, ed. Philip Crumpton (Cambridge: Cambridge University Press, 2002), p. 256.

95 During these years Lawrence was galvanised by the studies of primitive cultures and more specifically by Edward B. Tylor's anthropological study, *Primitive Culture*: (London: John Murray, 1903), which traces the emergence of language systems back to the expression of states of mind through shared gestures. On 7 April 1916 he wrote to Ottoline Morrell: 'It is a very sound substantial book, I had far rather read it than The Golden Bough or Gilbert Murray' (Lawrence, letter to Ottoline Morrell, 7 April 1916, *The Letters of D. H. Lawrence*, II, p. 593). The laudatory comment is repeated

frustration with her marriage when, pregnant and naked, she dances all by herself in front of the mirror in an intensely charged private moment of self-determination: 'She would not have had anyone know. She danced in secret, and her soul rose in bliss. She danced in secret before the Creator. She took off her clothes and danced in the pride of her bigness;'[96] or Gudrun's dance before the bull, where her feminine power is fused with some kind of bestial potency and the elemental irrationality of the sun and the moon:

> quicker, fiercer went Gudrun in the dance, stamping as if she were trying to throw off some bond, flinging her hands suddenly and stamping again, then rushing with face uplifted and throat full and beautiful, and eyes half closed, sightless. The sun was low and yellow, sinking down, and in the sky floated a thin, ineffectual moon.[97]

It is not certain whether Lawrence ever attended a performance of *The Rite of Spring*, based on the Russian pagan sacrificial ritual. He started working on *The Rainbow* in 1913, in the year after the ballet's riotous premiere in Paris. According to certain scholars, however, his imaginative depiction of the dancing scenes certainly brings to mind the writer's fascination with the physicality of the Diaghilev dancers; and his heroines' language of inner expression 'uncannily suggests (even unconsciously) the performance strategies' of the Russian *Rite*.[98] As Hugh Stevens argued in his study, 'Ursula at times is like a dancer in the *ballets russes*, dancing madly to the powerful wild colours and smells of nature.'[99] The conflicting relationship between the Lenskys' natural sensuality and the Brangwens'

---

in a letter to Thomas Dunlop, written over three months later (Lawrence, letter to Thomas Dunlop, *The Letters of D. H. Lawrence*, II, p. 630).

96 Lawrence, *The Rainbow*, p. 171.

97 Lawrence, *Women in Love*, p. 158.

98 Jones, p. 113. In her study Susan Jones draws a strong connection between Lawrence's fiction and the work of Diaghilev's company (pp. 109–27).

99 Hugh Stevens bases his claim on the following quote from *The Rainbow*: 'the scents of autumn were like a summer madness to her. She fled away from the little, purple-red button-chrysanthemums like a frightened dryad, the bright yellow little chrysanthemums smelled so strong, her feet seemed to dither in a drunken dance' (Lawrence, *The Rainbow*, p. 289). The extravagant colour scheme (the purple-red and bright yellow), he argues, serves to 'suggest the influence of the visual aesthetics of Bakst

'rule of mind' displayed in *The Rainbow* is crucial for understanding the way in which Lawrence conceives the prospects of interaction between Western civilisation and the 'otherness' of the Slavs. As he once explained it to his close friend Dorothy Brett, the rainbow is 'the meeting half way of two elements. The meeting of the sun and of the water produce [sic] at exactly the right place and moment, the rainbow. So it is in everything, and that is eternal.'[100]

The first two generations of the Brangwens and the Lenskys quintessentially embody the principle of opposites that attract, but cannot master their co-existence in a balanced and self-preserving mode. The passionate and emotionally charged 'otherness' of the Lenskys' women is mesmerising and almost mystically enticing to the Brangwens, but any interaction between them turns out to be disastrously destructive for both sides. Both couples (Tom and Lydia, as well as Lydia's daughter Anna and Will) live their lives in a permanent psychological battle. While trying, subconsciously, to reclaim their autonomy from the 'other', they happen to be unable to reject the urge towards self-sacrificial effacement imposed by the very concept of the bond. Thus, most of the time Tom and Lydia's relationship is characterised by antagonism, unrelieved hostility and strain. Tom is haunted by the feeling that he is incapable of penetrating the true essence of Lydia's being, and consequently cannot 'bear to be near her, and know the utter foreignness between them, know how entirely they were strangers to each other.'[101] Lydia, in turn, is psychologically afflicted in her husband's presence:

> and almost savagely she turned again to life, demanding her life back again, demanding that it should be as it had been when she was a girl, on the land at home, under the sky. Snow lay in great expanses, the telegraph posts strode over the white earth,

---

and the Ballets Russes' (Hugh Stevens, 'From Genesis to the Ring: Richard Wagner and D. H. Lawrence's Rainbow', *Textual Practice* 28.4 (2014), pp. 611–30 (p. 621)).

100 Norman Page, *D. H. Lawrence: Interviews and Recollections* (London: MacMillan, 1981), II, p. 241.

101 Lawrence, *The Rainbow*, p. 42.

> away under the gloom of the sky. And savagely her desire rose in her again, demanding that this was Poland, her youth, that all was her own again.[102]

Being desperate for her own emotional freedom and self-realisation, she nonetheless negates the very idea of granting the same to her other half: 'it irritated her to be made aware of him as a separate power.'[103] Anna's irrational conflict with Will also goes off into obscure accusations, power games and mutual hatred ('Every moment of your life you are doing something to me, something horrible, that destroys me'[104]), which, paradoxically, leads to a striking thought of non-existence or even self-annihilation in the absence of the 'other': 'He hated her for what she said [...] And the shame was a bitter fire in him, that she was everything to him, that he had nothing but her.'[105]

According to Lawrence this type of interaction, in which both parts have to surrender their personalities in a self-annihilating act of syncretic merging, is suffocating and destructive. As he maintains in *Aaron's Rod* (1922), such a relationship fosters 'abysses and maudlin self-abandon and self-sacrifice, the degeneration into a sort of slime and merge [...] wherein the soul and body ultimately perish.'[106] This type of union is essentially corrupt. And although in *The Rainbow* there is a clear emotional attraction within the families, which transcends their ethnic differences and the lack of cultural affinity (Lydia feels that 'there was an inner reality, a logic of the soul, which connected her with' Tom; and Anna senses a 'fragile flame of love came out of the ashes of this last' quarrel with Will[107]), such mode of intercultural synthesis can hardly be interpreted (within the symbolic framework of the novel) as a viable way forward.

The ability to transcend the tension and to capitalise on the inseparability and distinctness of the opposites, surpassing the damaging self-sacrificial aspect of the coming together, manifests itself in the character of Ursula

102 Ibid. p. 46.
103 Ibid. p. 54.
104 Ibid. p. 174.
105 Ibid. p. 174.
106 D. H. Lawrence, *Aaron's Rod* (New York: Penguin, 1976), p. 201.
107 Lawrence, *The Rainbow*, p. 34, 163.

– the first born of the third generation of the Anglo–Slavic intercultural hybrid of the Lenskys and the Brangwens.

> She was the naked, clear kernel thrusting forth the clear, powerful shoot, and the world was a bygone winter, discarded, her mother and father and Anton, and college and all her friends, all cast off like a year that has gone by, whilst the kernel was free and naked and striving to take new root, to create a new knowledge of Eternity in the flux of Time. And the kernel was the only reality; the rest was cast off into oblivion.[108]

Not unlike her ancestors, Ursula is clearly aware of her essential ethnic 'otherness', as she overtly identifies 'herself with her Polish' line.[109] From a broader perspective, however, she is portrayed as manifesting all traits of her cultural forebears accumulated equally from both sides (mind/flesh, consciousness/sensuality): being endowed with a 'quick, intelligent' and 'instinctive' mind,[110] her 'blazing heart was fierce and unyielding'[111] and it 'burnt in isolation, like a watchfire lighted.'[112] In the course of her personal journey she is enabled to trace a median line in between the paradoxically related opposites, making the most of the competing principles of English rationalism and passionate sensuality of the Slavs. The examples are manifold: towards the end of her schooling, for instance, she manages to configure her worldview as a form of metaphysical dualism, applying the form of rational reasoning to the need of human aspiration for the divine: 'They [Ursula together with her school teacher] took religion and rid it of its dogmas, its falsehoods [...] Gradually it dawned upon Ursula that all the religion she knew was but a particular clothing to a human aspiration.'[113] Similarly, in her decision to engage in the study of botany she essentially combines the rigour of taxonomy with the inexplicable variety of natural manifestation:

108 Ibid. p. 464.
109 Ibid. p. 240.
110 Ibid. p. 253.
111 Ibid. p. 451.
112 Ibid. p. 451.
113 Ibid. p. 322.

> She would take honours in botany. This was the one study that lived for her. She had entered into the lives of the plants. She was fascinated by the strange laws of the vegetable world. She had here a glimpse of something working entirely apart from the purpose of the human world.[114]

Moreover, Ursula's increasing sense of balance within the duality of her personal self, allows her, unlike her mother and her grandmother, to reject the prospect of a marital union with Anton Skrebensky, 'who was attractive, but whose soul could not contain her in its waves of strength, nor his breast compel her in burning, salty passion.'[115] This union, she feels, does not offer enough capacity, enough space for the wholeness of her multi-dimensional nature. It would be suffocating for her identity and her individual self-expression, leading to a reductive self-abandonment in affiliation with a man, whose personality is uniformly more simplistic and more plain, lacking, as Ursula claims, 'a sort of strong understanding [...] a dignity, a directness [...] a jolly reckless passionateness.'[116]

Capitalising on her ethnic liminality, rather than attempting to blur the distinction between the parts, Ursula is shown to become psychologically more self-contained and more complete, rising above the metaphysical necessity to be attracted to 'the other' in order to attain a sense of wholeness and fulfilment. The potency of such a complex dialectical identity, forged out of the dynamic tension of the opposites, is symbolised by the rainbow, which she sees shining above the town of Beldover in the concluding lines of the novel:

> The arc bended and strengthened itself till it arched indomitable, making great architecture of light and colour and the space of heaven, its pedestals luminous in the corruption of new houses on the low hill, its arch the top of heaven.[117]

The array of colours in the rainbow comes out as a symbol of the ideal unity based on inseparability and distinctness of the elements; which according

114 Ibid. p. 411.
115 Ibid. p. 451.
116 Ibid. p. 449.
117 Ibid. p. 467.

to R. S. Sharma, can be seen as Lawrence's 'vision of immediate salvation' of the West,[118] achieved through its productive encounter with the 'otherness' of Slavic culture.

Lawrence's defence, as well as the desire to reanimate and cultivate this Russian 'otherness' for the purposes of the prolific dialogical interaction with the West, was one of the reasons for his initial support of the Bolshevik October Revolution. He saw Bolshevism as a visceral populist force, drawing Russia away from the corrupt materialism of European civilisation, and towards the primeval naturalism of the pagan Slavs, as he put it in one of his 1918 letters:

> As for Russia, it must go through as it is going. Nothing but a real smelting down is any good for her: no matter how horrible it seems [...] chaos is necessary for Russia. Russia will be all right – righter, in the end, than these old stiff senile nations of the West. I do not think chaos is any good for England. England is too old.[119]

In the same vein, his Foreword to Shestov's *All Things Are Possible*, published in 1920, was instilled with enthusiasm for the new system, which, it seemed at the time, could not be anything but auspicious for the indigenous Russian spirit:

> It seems as if she had at last absorbed and overcome the virus of old Europe. Soon her new, healthy body will begin to act in its own reality, imitative no more, protesting no more, crying no more, but full and sound and lusty in itself. Real Russia is bom. She will laugh at us before long. Meanwhile she goes through the last stages of reaction against us, kicking away from the old womb of Europe.[120]

Generally speaking, given Lawrence's working-class background, his predominantly left-wing social milieu and some serious problems with conservative state censorship (his novels were suppressed for immorality), his overall opposition, ethical as well as political, to the Western bourgeois

118 Radhe S. Sharma, *The Rainbow: A Study of Symbolic Mode in D. H. Lawrence's Primitivism* (Hyderabad: Trust Publishers, 1981), p. 107.

119 Lawrence, letter to Samuel Koteliansky, 16 September 1918, *The Letters of D. H. Lawrence*, III, p. 284.

120 Lawrence, Foreword to Lev Shestov, *All Things Are Possible*, p. 8.

system was scarcely surprising. He was a long-term champion of a broadly socialist-orientated position, critical of the exploitative capitalist classes and supportive of a certain form of communism with regard to a planned economy and the abolition of money (though against the intellectualised form of what might be termed the 'champagne socialism' of the Fabians[121]). These views were conveyed, for instance, in his letter to Bertrand Russell in 1915:

> There must be a revolution in the state. It shall begin by the nationalising of all … industries and means of communication, and of the land – in one fell blow. Then a man shall have his wages whether he is sick or well or old … no man amongst us, and no woman, shall have any fear of the wolf at the door, for all wolves are dead;[122]

and to Catherine Carswell in 1922: 'I belong to Europe, though not to England. I think I should like to go to Russia in the summer. After America, it appeals to me. No money there (they say).'[123]

In 1918 Lawrence was seriously thinking of providing active assistance to the leading figures of the Independent Labour Party ('I want to know Robert Smillie, Philip Snowden, Mary Macarthers and Margaret Bondfield', he wrote to Koteliansky, 'I must find somebody to bring me to them. It is no good. One cannot wait for things to happen'[124]); and to the Bolsheviks in Russia: 'I am so glad that Litvinov has got this office […] It pleases me immensely. I sit here and say bravo', he wrote to Catherine Carswell, 'I almost feel like asking Litvinov if I can't help – but I don't suppose I'm of much use at this point.'[125] In mid-1919 he also kindled a long-term friendship with Douglas Goldring – an international leftist radical, who at the time was

121 Lawrence, letter to Cynthia Asquith, 11 December 1916, *The Letters of D. H. Lawrence*, III, p. 49.

122 Lawrence, letter to Bertrand Russell, February 1915, *The Letters of D. H. Lawrence*, II, p. 282.

123 Lawrence, letter to Catherine Carswell, 17 December 1922, *The Letters of D. H. Lawrence*, IV, p. 362.

124 Lawrence, letter to Samuel Koteliansky, 18 September 1918, *The Letters of D. H. Lawrence*, III, p. 284.

125 Lawrence, letter to Catherine Carswell, 16 February 1918, *The Letters of D. H. Lawrence*, III, p. 210.

describing himself as 'an uncompromising anti-war propagandist, rapidly turning into a Socialist revolutionary.'[126] Not unlike Goldring, who was an active member of the '1917 Club', created (December 1917) in support of the Russian Revolution by Leonard Woolf and Oliver Strachey,[127] Lawrence welcomed the downfall of Tsarism in February (March) 1917, placing on Russia his 'chiefest hope for the future' and calling it the 'young country', which he loved 'inordinately'.[128] At that time he started contemplating a visit to this country and was even attempting to learn the language: 'We will go to Russia. Send me a Berlitz grammar book, I will begin to learn the language – religiously.'[129]

It is not unlikely (judging from the subsequent changes in his position) that out of all the possible reasons for his optimism and hopes, the main one was that related to the prospects of revival of the primeval sensuality of the Slavic spirit. For Lawrence, the Bolshevik uprising represented a wild outpouring of the natural, previously repressed energy always bubbling within popular masses – the revolt against the imposed framework of social conventions, forged by the rational consciousness of the bourgeois: 'It is, finally, a passionate, mindless vengeance taken by the collective' he wrote in *Kangaroo* (1923), 'vertebral psyche upon the authority of orthodox MIND. In the Russian revolution it was the EDUCATED classes that were the enemy really: the deepest inspiration the hatred of the conscious classes.'[130] This belief went as far as hailing (in 1921) the country's political and economic isolation, imposed on Bolshevik Russia by the European powers, which he saw as a kind of incubational environment and a considerable asset in terms of fostering the inward-looking regeneration of the primeval. 'Russia with her Third International', he claimed,

126 Quoted in James T. Boulton and Andrew Robertson, Introduction to *The Letters of D. H. Lawrence*, III, pp. 1–12 (p. 5).

127 Victoria Glendinning, *Leonard Woolf: A Biography* (New York and London: Free Press, 2006), p. 192.

128 Lawrence, letter to Samuel Koteliansky, 1 May 1917, *The Letters of D. H. Lawrence*, III, p. 121.

129 Ibid. p. 121.

130 D. H. Lawrence, *Kangaroo* (London: Martin Secker, 1923), pp. 337–8.

> is at the same time reacting most violently from all other contact, back, recoiling on herself, into a fierce, unapproachable Russianism [...] I am glad that the era of love and oneness is over: hateful homogeneous world-oneness. I am glad that Russia flies back into savage Russianism, Scythism, savagely self-pivoting.[131]

Quite soon, however, Lawrence came to realise that Bolshevism could not be further removed from a liberating and a naturally driven social movement; and the period of the early 1920s displayed a gradual change in his hopes and views. As early as 1921, he mentioned in a letter that apparently 'only some sort of Bolshevism is inevitable' for Europe, which 'is having a slight reactionary swing, back to conservatism.'[132] A distinctly critical vision was projected in his *Movements in European History* (written in 1918 and 1919 and first published in 1921), which suggested that the Bolsheviks' policies and actions were in contradiction with the very notion of socialism *per se*, designed as a system based on:

1. A desire for the welfare of all people.
2. A hatred of all masters and of all authority, a hatred of all superior.[133]

The Bolsheviks, in Lawrence's opinion, displayed a remarkable ineptitude in both of the above aspects. 'I believe', he maintains regarding the latter, 'that a good form of socialism, if it could be brought about, would be the best form of government. But let us come down to experience.'[134] Concerning the egalitarian society, when 'the communists succeeded in forcing *their* will' on other people, Bolshevism deteriorated 'into a mere worship of Force.'[135] At the same time (referring to the first aspect), they had arrived at a fairly dammed down welfare system based on strictly utilitarian considerations, whereby: 'Every family is rationed, for food, clothing, and even house-room. That is what commonsense works out to. For rationing

131 Lawrence, *Sea and Sardinia*, p. 89.

132 Lawrence, letter to Samuel Koteliansky, 27 May 1921, *The Letters of D. H. Lawrence*, III, p. 728.

133 Lawrence, *Movements in European History*, p. 262.

134 Ibid. p. 262.

135 Ibid. p. 263.

is commonsense. But do we like it? Did we like it during the war? – We didn't. We hated it.'[136]

It is difficult to say what exactly constituted the turning point in Lawrence's vision, but his correspondence of 1923 to 1926 shows that Bolshevism was no longer regarded as a way forward, but as a dogmatic, mechanical and essentially rationalistic social doctrine, hardly different from that prevailing in the West, apart from its denial of the free market economy practice.[137] 'My desire to go to Russia has died again', he conveyed bitterly to Carl Seelig in May 1925, 'I hear such dreary accounts of it. Moscow so Americanised, the proletariat are becoming Yankee and mechanical. That bores me.'[138] The same thoughts were affirmed in January 1926: 'I wonder if Russia has had all her troubles and her revolutions, just to bring about a state of complete materialism and cheapness. That would be sad. But I suppose it's on the cards;'[139] and later the same year: 'My desire to go to Russia disappeared again. I feel that Bolshevists are loutish and common – I don't believe in them, except as disruptive and nihilistic agents. Boring!'[140]

It is within the framework of this critical viewpoint that the image of the new Soviet Russia was projected in Lawrence's writings of the time. 'Each man a machine-part, and the driving power of the machine, hate ... hate of the bourgeois. That, to me, is Bolshevism', he remarks in *Lady*

136 Ibid. p. 260.

137 James T. Boulton and Andrew Robertson remark that it was a period when Lawrence started developing his 'distinctly anti-collective viewpoint. He was making a beginning on some of the essays on Classic American Literature, in which he deplored American democracy for its encouraging a mass identity and its opposition to individualism.' His 'Reality of Peace' articles (published in the *English Review* May–August 1917) were also significant in terms of articulating his contempt for the 'egoism of the flock' (Boulton and Robertson, p. 4).

138 Lawrence, letter to Carl Seelig, 21 May 1925, *The Letters of D. H. Lawrence*, V, p. 461.

139 Lawrence, letter to Samuel Koteliansky, 4 Jan 1926, *The Letters of D. H. Lawrence*, V, p. 367.

140 Lawrence, letter to Samuel Koteliansky, 17 May 1926, *The Letters of D. H. Lawrence*, V, p. 455.

Chatterley's Lover (1928).[141] His attitude comes across strongly in a long narrative poem *Hibiscus and Salvia Flowers*, written as early as 31 January 1921.[142] The author's praising of the Bolsheviks' ascent to power is underscored by the rhetorical question casting doubts on the genuineness of the cause ('How do we know then, that they are they?'):

> Hark! Hark!
> The dogs do bark!
> It's the socialists in the town.
>
> Sans rags, sans tags,
> Sans beards, sans bags,
> Sans any distinction at all except loutish commonness.
>
> How do we know then, that they are they?
> Bolshevists.
> Leninists.
> Communists.
> Socialists.
> –Ists!–Ists![143]

The ironic gap between the experience and the idea is gradually intensified throughout the poem, culminating in the conspicuous rejection of the doctrine:

> But not a trace of foul equality,
> Nor sound of still more foul human perfection.
> You need not clear the world like a cabbage patch for me;
> Leave me my nettles,
> Let me fight the wicked, obstreperous weeds myself, and put
> them in their place,[144]

141 D. H. Lawrence, *Lady Chatterley's Lover* (London: Collector's Library, 2005), p. 61.

142 James T. Boulton, Comments to *The Letters of D. H. Lawrence*, III, p. 659.

143 D. H. Lawrence, 'Hibiscus and Salvia Flowers', in D. H. Lawrence, *The Complete Poems of D. H. Lawrence*, ed. Vivian de Sola Pinto and Warren Roberts, 2 vols (New York: Viking Press, 1971), I, p. 313.

144 Lawrence, 'Hibiscus and Salvia Flowers', p. 316.

and a personal appeal to stay away from such a system:

> Never
> To be a bolshevist
> With a hibiscus flower behind my ear.[145]

This poem ties in well with Lawrence's, to a certain degree auto-referential, irony regarding naïve enthusiasm for the Soviet regime, expressed through the character of Jim Bricknell in *Aaron's Rod* (1922). Bricknell's self-confessed advocacy of the Bolshevik 'revolution and the triumph of Labour' is perceived as nothing but a sheer mockery in the context of his other political absurdities, such as, for instance, the rising hegemony of Ireland and Japan as 'the two poles of the world', which would 'settle' everything for other nations.[146] It would be a bit of a speculation to see Lawrence's own letter as a source-text of this statement, but a parallel with the writer's credulous assertion concerning the prospects of Russia's dominance is difficult to overlook: 'Russia seems to me now the positive pole of the world's spiritual energy, and America the negative pole. But we shall see how things work out.'[147]

Speaking of Lawrence's projection of the image of Russia at that time, attention should be drawn to a series of his later poems, put together in the collection *Pansies* of 1929. The title of this collection is in many ways revealing. Lawrence generally saw poems as an expression of personal sentiments and emotional moments; and the sense of spontaneity, emblematised by the flower, was in this regard particularly vital. More importantly, the title was simultaneously a pun on the French word 'panser' (meaning 'to dress' or 'to bandage a wound') and a reference to Blaise Pascal's *Pensées* (as Lawrence made explicit in the introduction to *New Poems*):

> These poems are called *Pansies*, because they are rather *Pensées* than anything else. Pascal or La Bruyère wrote their Pensées in prose, but it has always seemed to me

145 Ibid. p. 317.

146 Lawrence, *Aaron's Rod*, p. 87.

147 Lawrence, letter to Samuel Koteliansky, 3 July 1917, *The Letters of D. H. Lawrence*, III, p. 136.

> that a real thought, a single thought, not an argument, can only exist in verse, or in some poetic form.[148]

The author's thoughts on the Russian theme, presented in the collection, were indeed charged with the sense of disillusionment and incessant pain, as if coming from an unhealing wound. Yet again the image of Russia was cast along the lines of traumatic 'in-betweenness': Russia was portrayed as being torn apart by the opposing forces of its intrinsic Slavic humanity and the Bolsheviks' Utilitarianism, which, in Lawrence's perception, came into being due to the *laissez-faire* attitude of the Russian cultural elite.

One of the central poems of the collection *Now It's Happened* refers to the October upheaval directly as 'her crisis', as a result of which the best qualities of this inherently passionate and vibrant nation – 'The big, flamboyant bewildered Russia'[149] – have been effaced. The society is indoctrinated by Marxism – a profoundly mechanistic and pragmatic doctrine, which renders human beings 'cold and devilish hard like machines'.[150] In Lawrence's poem, the responsibility for such an impoverishing transformation is placed on the Bolshevik governing regime, on the one hand ('spy-government everywhere'[151]), and on the leading Russian intellectuals, on the other; the latter should have

> stood up for themselves, and
> seen
> Russia across her crisis,
> instead of leaving it to Lenin.[152]

The Russian intelligentsia (especially the literary figures) were seen by Lawrence as an influential class of opinion makers. Consequently, it is the intelligentsia whom he finds guilty of not stopping the Bolsheviks' rise

148 D. H. Lawrence, Introduction to *Pansies*, in D. H. Lawrence, *The Complete poems of D. H. Lawrence*, I, pp. 417–24 (p. 423).
149 Lawrence, 'Now It's Happened', in *The Complete Poems*, p. 536.
150 Ibid. p. 537.
151 Ibid. p. 536.
152 Ibid. p. 536.

to power and allowing Marxist theories to 'leak' into the group mentality of the nation. In this series of poems Lawrence evidently returns to his old criticism of the Russian intellectuals as prone to being superfluous, remote from real life and, in other words, infected by the virus of 'Russianitis', as he termed it in his essays of the late 1920s. Those to blame include the major creators of the literary gallery of superfluous people (which 'ruined a nation's fibre'):[153] Tolstoy, who was toying with the populist theories:

> But Tolstoi was a traitor
> to the Russia that needed him most,
> the clumsy, bewildered Russia
> so worried by the Holy Ghost.
> He shifted his job on to the peasants
> and landed them all on toast;[154]

Dostoevsky – with his false over-reflective version of Christianity ('sham christianity' written specifically with a small letter):

> Dostoevsky, the Judas,
> with his sham christianity
> epileptically ruined
> the last bit of sanity
> left in the hefty bodies
> of the Russian nobility.[155]

153 The concept acquired its official literary designation in 1850, with the publication of Turgenev's *Diary of a Superfluous Man* and its protagonist Chulkaturin. The term became widespread in literature through the articles of Alexander Herzen 'Ochen' opasno' ('Very Dangerous', 1859) and 'Lishnye lyudi i zhelcheviki' ('Superfluous People and the Venomous Men' 1860), where he introduces the paradigmatic series of the superfluous men that formed the literary canon – Onegin, Pechorin, and Oblomov. The notion was developed by N. A. Dobroliubov and D. I. Pisarev who, though without using the term, extended the series by incorporating into it Alexander Herzen's Bel'tov and Turgenev's Rudin. Considering Lawrence's critical reception of Dostoevsky and Tolstoy, Stepan Trofimovich Verkhovensky (*Demons*), Andrei Bolkonsky (*War and Peace*) and Dmitrii Nekhliudov (*Resurrection*) may fit into the set.

154 Lawrence, 'Now It's Happened', p. 536.

155 Ibid. p. 537.

Both authors are accused of being drowned in unnecessary philosophising, instead of offering a stronger forward-looking model to follow:

> Too much of the humble Willy wet-leg
> and the holy can't-help-it touch,
> till you've ruined a nation's fibre
> and they loathe all feeling as such.[156]

The image of the Russian intelligentsia as largely outdated and inept – an effigy of the past rather than a vanguard of the future – is persistently highlighted in Lawrence's verse and prose of the time. Thus, for instance, in *Kangaroo* (1923) he claims that 'in the Russian revolution it was the educated classes that were the enemy really.'[157] The same idea comes across in the poem 'Fate and the Younger Generation': a list of canonical icons drawn from the Russian classics is presented as a sequence of meaningless nonentities, 'wiped out' from the pages of the nation's history and its future:

> It is strange to think of the Annas, the Vronskys, the Pierres,
> all the Tolstoyan lot wiped out.
> And the Aloyshas and Dmitris and Myshkins and Stavrogins,
> the Dostoevsky lot all wiped out.
> And the Tchekov wimbly-wombly wet-legs all wiped out.
> Gone! Dead, or wandering in exile with their feathers
> plucked.[158]

This is not to say that Lawrence calls for the dismissal of the entirety of the Russian cultural oeuvre, belittling its artistic value and its contribution to the development of European literary thought. The idea of effacing, or being 'wiped out', concerns not the oeuvre *per se*, but the superfluous archetypes configured within the framework of this oeuvre, which are in no way comparable with the new realities of the day:

156 Ibid. p. 537.
157 Lawrence, *Kangaroo*, p. 338.
158 D. H. Lawrence, 'Fate and the Younger Generation', in *The Complete Poems*, pp. 533–4 (p. 533).

> Anyhow the Tolstoyan lot simply asked for extinction:
> 'Eat me up, dear peasant!' – so the peasant ate him.
> And the Dostoevsky lot wallowed in the thought:
> 'Let me sin my way to Jesus!' – So they sinned
> themselves off the face of the earth.
> And the Tchekov lot: 'I'm too weak and lovable to live!'[159]

Having shaped its self-identity along the lines of these archetypal literary models, the Russian intelligentsia, in Lawrence's view, was turned into nothing but a self-parody – a self-gratifying figment of their own mind, totally insubstantial and detached from the flesh and blood people. He therefore puts under the spotlight the absurdity of the widespread Western fascination with Russia as an icon of pagan splendour, which, arguably, lacks a real life referent and, consequently, is fundamentally contrived. This fascination, in the first place, was launched into fashion by the English middle-class circles, often shallow, poorly informed and undiscriminating in their perception. More importantly, it was largely solicited by the vogue of the Russian literary oeuvre, centred on the figures of weak and impotent intellectuals, who could not be further removed from the idealised image of the 'blessedly exotic'. The generation of these intellectuals was doomed, in Lawrence's opinion, and any attempt to imitate them would be fatal for the Europeans (the poem mentions the French – 'the Proustian lot' and the English – 'our little lot'):

> Now the Proustian lot: Dear darling death, let me
> wriggle my way towards you
> like the worm I am! – So he wriggled and got there.
> Finally our little lot: 'I don't want to die
> but by Jingo if I do!'
> – Well, it won't matter so very much either.'[160]

It seems that when reflecting on the role played by Russia in the world-wide social and cultural arena, Lawrence, in distinction from H. G. Wells, was more concerned with the limitations rather than the progressive potential

159 Ibid. p. 534.
160 Ibid. p. 534.

of the Russian intellectual vanguard. As regards his image of the Russian revolutionary leaders (a specific branch of the intelligentsia) this offers yet another degree of complexity to the writer's point of view.

Since the early twenties Lawrence had been developing his hierarchical theory of leadership, largely akin to Raskolnikov's ideas in *Crime and Punishment* and to Nietzsche's concept of the *Übermensch*. Richard Somers, a semi-autobiographical character in *Kangaroo* (broadly based on Lawrence's own experience of travelling in Australia), claims, for instance, that society ought to be fundamentally based on the idea of the 'mystic recognition of difference and innate priority, the joy of obedience and the sacred responsibility of authority'.[161] These ideas surfaced in a number of Lawrence's writings of the time, including such novels as *Fanny and Annie* (written in 1919, published in 1921), *Kangaroo* (1923), *The Plumed Serpent* (1926), and his collection *The Woman Who Rode Away and Other Stories*, published in 1928. They found their most ardent defence in Lawrence's Introduction to Dostoevsky's chapter *The Grand Inquisitor* (from *The Brothers Karamazov*), translated by Koteliansky and published as a self-standing work in 1930.

In his penetrating analysis of Lawrence's response to the writings of Dostoevsky, Peter Kaye[162] claims that Lawrence defends the arguments put forward by the Grand Inquisitor as 'the final and unanswerable criticism of Christ',[163] reflecting a fairly correct judgment of human limitation. Lawrence, who shares the Inquisitor's stance, recognises that the masses lack the strength to live 'free and limitless'.[164] He has ascertained their essential and unalterable need for mystery, miracle and authority antithetical to freedom best served by bread and a heroic authority to worship. According to Lawrence, the vision of the universal state led by a select superior few is born of compassionate realism. The Inquisitor seeks to provide for the popular majority, in contrast to Christ, who overestimates human abilities. His 'inadequacy [...] lies in the fact that Christianity is too difficult for men,

161 Lawrence, *Kangaroo*, p. 115.

162 Kaye, pp. 54–5.

163 Lawrence, Introduction to *The Grand Inquisitor*, p. 127.

164 Ibid. p. 129.

the vast mass of men.'[165] It offers a strictly speaking unattainable ideal, for 'it makes demands greater than the nature of men can bear'.[166] The man who would be saviour offered a freedom nearly impossible to achieve, unlike The Inquisitor, who loved humanity 'more tolerantly and more contemptuously than Jesus loved [...] for itself, for what it is and not for what it ought to be.'[167] Christ's idealism imposes too heavy a burden on the masses, thus entailing destructive consequences: 'Most men cannot choose between good and evil because it is extremely difficult to know which is which.'[168] Lawrence argues that Christ undermines the very notion of the so-called visionary leaders, who alone can give meaning to the life of the masses. His insistence on free choice does not 'let the specially gifted few make the decision between good and evil, and establish the life-values against the money-values'[169] (which the majority would be naturally inclined to prioritise). 'The many', as Lawrence put it, would 'accept the decision with gratitude, and bow down to the few in the hierarchy.'[170] The question now comes down to the ability to recognise these naturally superior authoritarian figures and to distinguish them from a long line of imposters.

It is within the framework of these ideas that one should look at Lawrence's poem 'When Wilt Thou Teach the People'?, which conveys the author's reflections on Soviet Russia, and Lenin's leadership in particular, as a further example of salvation on offer. The preceding instances included Napoleon and the republicans, who while getting rid of the power of the nobility, put people under the new, dehumanising power of industrial capitalism and material possessions:

165 Ibid. p. 128.
166 Ibid. p. 128.
167 Ibid. p. 129.
168 Ibid. p. 134.
169 Ibid. p. 134.
170 Ibid. p. 134.

> You are saved,
> therefore you are our savings, our capital
> with which we shall do big business.[171]

On the one hand, the author seems to be gripped by the idea of socialism as an alternative to bourgeois modernity; and at the same time he is acutely aware that such an alternative mirrors the modernity it would aspire to replace. Lenin's regime, therefore, is regarded as nothing but yet another link in the historical sequence:

> Or Lenin says: You are saved, but you are saved wholesale.
> You are no longer men, that is bourgeois;
> you are items in the soviet state,
> and each item will get its ration,
> but it is the soviet state alone which counts
> the items are of small importance.[172]

While drawing people out of the capitalist system, he hands them over to another, equally dehumanised, 'Soviet state' of dead materialism, which turns them into the nuts and bolts – the 'items' – of the socialist machine:

> The items are all of small importance,
> The state having saved them all.[173]

The series of political fiascos depicted here does not imply that Lawrence calls his theories of leadership into question. The issue, yet again, inheres in the discrepancy between the concept *per se* and its practical realisation. Within the context of Lawrence's authoritarian theory, Lenin features as a fairly accurate impersonation of the gap between to 'be' and 'to appear'. In his reflections Lawrence rarely goes in for analysing the Bolshevik tenets, but the reasons for Lenin's failure as a naturally superior leader are most frequently and unambiguously discussed in his critical essays. In contrast to

171 D. H. Lawrence, 'When Wilt Thou Teach the People?', in *The Complete Poems*, pp. 442–3 (p. 442).
172 Ibid. p. 443.
173 Ibid. p. 443.

Attila the Hun, Napoleon and George Washington, who, as Lawrence put it, possess 'the old divine power' and who, even if they were a scourge, were at least a 'scourge of God', Lenin is regarded as lacking all the credentials of a leader, having 'never had the right smell, [...] never even roused real fear', nor 'real passion'.[174] Lawrence was clearly drawn to the controversial nature of Lenin's power; and some more elaborate considerations on this subject are presented in *Apocalypse and the Writings on Revelation* – Lawrence's very last book, written between 1929 and 1930. 'Lenin', Lawrence argues,

> sincerely wanted the well-being of every individual in the State. He was, in a sense, the god of the common people of Russia, and they are quite right, in the modern sense, to worship him. 'Give us this day our daily bread.' And Lenin wanted above all things to give them their daily bread. And he could not do even that. What was love in theory became hate in practice. He loved the people because he saw them powerless – and he was determined that power should not exist on earth. He himself was the final power which should destroy power. It was the Church of Christ in practical politics. And it was anomaly, it was horrible. Because it was unnatural.[175]

Among others, two points are of particular importance in this statement. The first one concerns Lawrence's framework of analysis, which is clearly derived from *The Grand Inquisitor*'s model, namely from the distinction between 'earthly' and 'heavenly' bread and temptation by power. This in itself is a noteworthy implication, casting light on the deep impact which Dostoevsky produced on Lawrence's track of thinking and ideas, despite all the controversy in his response to the writings of the Russian author. As regards the authenticity of Lenin's power, according to Lawrence, the leader of the Russian Revolution fails both aspects emphasised in *The Grand Inquisitor*'s model: 'It was the Church of Christ in practical politics. And it was anomaly', he claims.[176] The question, yet again, is considered from the essentialist perspective: Lenin is shown to be unable to master the dialectical

174 D. H. Lawrence, 'Blessed Are the Powerful', in *Reflections on the Death of a Porcupine*, pp. 319–38 (p. 328).

175 D. H. Lawrence, *Apocalypse and the Writings on Revelation*, ed. Mara Kalnins (Cambridge: Cambridge University Press, 2002), p. 165.

176 Ibid. p. 165.

polarity of the body and the spirit. Firstly, this applies to the 'earthly' and 'heavenly bread' opposition ('And Lenin wanted above all things to give them their daily bread. And he could not do even that'[177]), which effectively refers back to what Lawrence specified earlier in the Introduction to *The Grand Inquisitor*: 'Lenin, surely, rose to great power simply to give men – what? The earthly bread. And what was the result? Not only did they lose the heavenly bread, but even the earthly bread disappeared out of wheat-producing Russia.'[178] Secondly (but intimately connected to the first issue), Lenin's authority was not supported by authentic popular recognition, but reduced to sheer coercion and the exaltation of force – 'what was love in theory became hate in practice.'[179] The latter is different from the notion of real power, which, in Lawrence's view, is a deeply humanistic concept, rooted in apostolic trust, devotion and love – akin to the 'heavenly bread', which Lenin fails to deliver to the masses. 'We only know dead power, which is force,' he wrote. 'Mere force does not commend our respect. But power is not mere force. It is divine like love. Love and power are two divine things in life.'[180]

To sum up, one can see that Lawrence did not have much time for the specific content of the Bolshevik doctrine as such, but it nonetheless provided him with a useful paradigm of political intervention and thereby made a significant contribution to the development of his socio-philosophical thoughts. 'Most men are wage-slaves', he maintained in a letter in 1928,

> Under Bolshevism, it is pretty much the same: they are still slaves, machine-slaves, party-slaves. The real activity of life is the great activity of *developing consciousness*, physical, mental, intuitional, religious – all-round consciousness. This is the real business of life, and is the great game of grown men. All that other affair, of work and money, should be settled and subordinated to this, the great game of real living,

177 Ibid. p. 165.

178 Lawrence, Introduction to *The Grand Inquisitor*, p. 131.

179 Lawrence, *Apocalypse and the Writings on Revelation*, p. 165. As he argued earlier in *Movements of European History*, Bolshevism 'has denigrated into a mere worship of Force' when 'the communists succeeded in forcing *their* will' (Lawrence, *Movements in European History*, p. 263).

180 Lawrence, *Apocalypse and the Writings on Revelation*, pp. 164–5.

> of developing ourselves physically, in subtlety of movement, and grace and beauty of bodily awareness, and of deepening and widening our whole consciousness, so that we really become men, instead of remaining the poor, cramped, limited slaves we are.[181]

Up to the very end, Russia for Lawrence was to remain the country of unrealised potential, the country still to overcome its adolescent fascination with the sophistication of reason and its exaltation over natural, down to earth human feelings. But it was this potential that mattered the most: he was convinced that 'Russia will certainly inherit the future', as soon as it learns to break away from 'her own unwilling, fantastic reproduction of European truths'.[182]

None of the great twentieth-century writers were at all kindly disposed towards Western industrialism and its inevitable social corollaries, which included urbanism, liberalism, egalitarianism, the spread of religious scepticism and dehumanisation. Of all haters of the modern world, Lawrence was, perhaps, one of the most intense and unremitting. In the context of his radical criticism of Western civilisation, shaped by man's unbalanced commitment to the rule of reason, which resulted in society's alienation from the natural world, Russia was seen as a potent bearer of energy, capable of rejuvenating the decadent and corrupt culture. The concept was not new, but in Lawrence's frame of thinking, this revitalising power of the 'other' was no longer linked to the country's iconic exoticism and its personification of the 'savage', but rather to its liminality and cultural hybridity – to its inherent potential to forge a more complex and powerful whole that can be raised to a higher level than the simple sum of its parts. Lawrence was convinced that one day this powerful whole would find its practical realisation. 'But wait! There is life in the Russians. Something new and strange will emerge out of their weird transmogrification into Bolshevists', he claimed.[183] In Lawrence's essentialist vision of society and human nature, consistently argued out from book

181 Lawrence, letter to Charles Wilson, 28 December 1928, *The Letters of D. H. Lawrence*, VII, pp. 103–04.

182 Lawrence, Foreword to Lev Shestov, *All Things Are Possible*, p. 9.

183 Lawrence, 'The Novel', p. 187.

to book and essay to essay, Russia featured prominently as a model or an 'objective correlative' of his evolving theories, views and convictions. And what is, perhaps, most significant in relation to this model is that in place of viewing Russia as a pathogenic threat to the purity of European tradition, he offered a remarkably advanced vision of Anglo–Russian and, generally speaking, multi-cultural interactions, based on the self-preservation and autonomy of the components devoid of any hierarchical connections – the dialogue of truly liberated men, 'who are distinct and easy in themselves like stars.'[184]

184 D. H. Lawrence, 'The Reality of Peace', in *Phoenix*, pp. 669–94 (p. 687).

CHAPTER 6

'Lappin and Lapinova': Woolf's Beleaguered Russian Monarchs

'Lappin and Lapinova' is outwardly a modest piece, one of Woolf's least extended short stories, running to fewer than 4,000 words. The story it tells, of a quintessentially upper-middle-class London couple who anticipate in a number of ways Clarissa and Richard Dalloway in *Mrs Dalloway* of 1925,[1] has most often been interpreted in terms of the troubled relationship between the sexes in a conventional British marriage from this period and in Woolf's own social class. With the exception of Meredith Wattison's highly perceptive and imaginative recent article,[2] most critics make little if anything of the fact that a Russian name 'Lapinova' is given to the heroine. It will be argued in this chapter that the choice of a Russian frame of reference is very far from accidental or inconsequential. Indeed the tale provides an opportunity to consider and compare the early and later stages of Woolf's engagement with Russian literature and Russian culture more generally.

The history of the tale's production in the form in which it was eventually published covers some twenty years. The tale is an example of what Leonard Woolf describes as Woolf's customary method, when it came to the composition of short fiction:

1 Indeed Clarissa, if not Richard Dalloway, had already made an appearance in Woolf's first published novel, *The Voyage Out* of 1915.

2 Meredith Wattison, 'This Furred Place – the Woolfs anthropomorphism, bunnies in people suits and the zoomorphic other', *Plumwood Mountain* 2.1 (2015). <https://plumwoodmountain.com/articles-and-essays/> [accessed 8 September 2016].

> All through her life, Virginia Woolf used at intervals to write short stories. It was her custom, whenever an idea for one occurred to her, to sketch it out in a very rough form and then put it away in a drawer. Later, if an editor asked her for a short story, and she felt in the mood to write one (which was not frequent), she would take a sketch out of her drawer and rewrite it, sometimes many times. Or if she felt, as she often did, while writing a novel that she required to rest her mind by working at something else for a time, she would either write a critical essay or work upon one of her sketches for short stories.[3]

Although this tale may very likely be the earliest example of a character with a Russian name in Woolf's fiction, even when Woolf first drafted the tale she had in fact been engaging intensively with Russian literature as a reader for some six or seven years. Indeed, it could be argued that her engagement with the idea of Russia went still further back, to her adolescence, before the death of her father, Sir Leslie Stephen, in 1904:

> It was the Elizabethan prose writers I loved first & most wildly, stirred by Hakluyt, which father lugged home for me … He must have been 65; I 15 or 16, then … I became enraptured … the sight of the large yellow page entranced me. I used to read it & dream of those obscure adventurers & no doubt practised their style in my copy books.[4]

And the interest in Hakluyt, and his accounts of Richard Chancellor, the sixteenth-century English adventurer who visited the court of Ivan the Terrible, was still there when she reached twenty.[5] Moreover, during the 1920s Woolf was to review an edition of Hakluyt which appeared in the period.

Woolf's sustained exposure to Russian literature seems to have begun in 1910 with Tolstoy, then proceeded two years later to take in Dostoevsky. 'Lappin and Lapinova', whose first draft is from six years later, is most commonly seen as inspired in some measure by Woolf's own marriage to Leonard, but even here a Russian component is also involved. For the tale

3 Leonard Woolf, Foreword to Virginia Woolf, *A Haunted House and Other Stories* (New York: Harcourt Inc., 1944), pp. v–vi (p. v).

4 Woolf, *The Diary of Virginia Woolf*, III, p. 271 (8 December 1929), quoted in Hermione Lee, *Virginia Woolf* (London: Vintage Books, 1997), p. 142.

5 Woolf, *The Diary*, II, p. 310 (15 August 1924), quoted in Lee, p. 142.

'Lappin and Lapinova' opens with the young newly married couple, Ernest and Rosalind Thorburn, after their London wedding, five days into a honeymoon spent at what sounds like (but is not spelled out as such) the Swiss lakes. If Woolf in this tale is recalling her own honeymoon in 1912, that included an important Russian element, for her reading during her travels with Leonard (to Spain and Italy rather than what seems to be Switzerland in the tale) was dominated by her first experience of Dostoevsky's *Crime and Punishment*, a love story of a certain kind, it might be said, if not normally regarded as a romantic novel. In Woolf's 'Lappin and Lapinova' the bride: 'sat in the bow window of the hotel looking over the lake to the mountains, and waited for her husband to come down to breakfast'.[6]

Rosalind is still adjusting to her acquisition on marriage of her husband's name as 'Mrs Ernest Thorburn'.[7] 'Perhaps she would never get used to the fact that that she was Mrs Ernest Anybody, she thought'[8] the bride reflects on her dissatisfaction with her husband's forename: 'Ernest was a difficult name to get used to. It was not the name she would have chosen. She would have preferred Timothy, Antony, or Peter. He did not look like Ernest either.'[9] And, prompted by the sight of her husband eating, and perhaps by French (the lingua franca of a Swiss hotel?), Rosalind, the wife, comes up with a soubriquet for him:

> But here he was. Thank goodness he did not look like Ernest – no. But what did he look like? She glanced at him sideways. Well, when he was eating toast he looked like a rabbit. Not that anyone else would have seen a likeness to a creature so timid

6 Virginia Woolf, *A Haunted House and Other Stories* (New York: Harcourt Inc., 1944), p. 68.

7 Wattison points out that a pictorial volume by an artist called Archibald Thorburn, and including a prominent illustration of a white female hare, was published three years after the first drafting of 'Lappin and Lapinova' in 1921. Wattison mentions that the volume observes that 'the Hare and Rabbit have never been known to interbreed'. There is no record of Woolf having actually possessed or read any of Thorburn's work, but he was already a widely published author in 1918, having exhibited work since the 1880s.

8 Woolf, *Haunted House*, p. 68.

9 Ibid. p. 68.

> and diminutive in this spruce, muscular young man with the straight nose, the blue eyes, and the very firm mouth.[10]

The young wife's mind makes a number of imaginative leaps:

> His nose twitched very slightly when he ate. So did her pet rabbit's. She kept watching his nose twitch; and when she had to explain, when he caught her looking at, why she laughed.
> 'It's because you're like a rabbit, Ernest', she said. 'Like a wild rabbit', she added, looking at him. 'A hunting rabbit; a King Rabbit; a rabbit that makes laws for all the other rabbits.'[11]

Initially the husband plays along with the fantasy of being 'that kind of rabbit',[12] though he has not noticed any such characteristic hitherto:

> since it amused her to see him twitch his nose – he had never known that his nose twitched – he twitched it on purpose. And she laughed and laughed; and he laughed too, so that the maiden ladies and the fishing man and the waiter in his greasy black jacket all guessed right; they were happy.[13]

When they are taking a picnic, 'seated on a clump of heather beside the lake', the wife develops the fantasy:

> 'Lettuce, rabbit?' said Rosalind, holding out the lettuce that had been provided to eat with the hard-boiled eggs. 'Come and take it out of my hand', she added, and he stretched out and nibbled the lettuce and twitched his nose.[14]

Perhaps most readers, and just briefly the heroine herself, whose consciousness is at the heart of the tale, perceive Ernest as a domesticated rabbit. However the heroine then makes another sudden imaginative leap:

10 Ibid. pp. 68–9.
11 Ibid. p. 69.
12 Ibid. p. 69.
13 Ibid. p. 69.
14 Ibid. p. 69.

> 'Good rabbit, nice rabbit', she said, patting him, as she used to pat her tame rabbit at home. But that was absurd. He was not a tame rabbit, whatever he was. She turned it into French. 'Lapin', she called him. But whatever he was, he was not a French rabbit.[15]

And this leads to a further train of thought:

> He was simply and solely English-born at Porchester Terrace, educated at Rugby; now a clerk in His Majesty's Civil Service. So she tried 'Bunny' next; but that was worse. 'Bunny' was someone plump and soft and comic; he was thin and hard and serious.[16]

Prompted by this sense of hardness and seriousness, Rosalind triumphantly dubs him: '"Lappin, Lappin, King Lappin," she repeated. It seemed to suit him exactly; he was not Ernest, he was King Lappin. Why? She did not know.'[17] Woolf at this point allows the wife, Rosalind's fantasy to expand from the individual to the collective: 'When there was nothing new to talk about on their long solitary walks … she let her fancy play with the story of the Lappin tribe.'[18]

The animal identities for the couple are developed further when Ernest reciprocates and enters into the imaginative game: 'Ernest put down the paper and helped her. There were the black rabbits and the red; there were the enemy rabbits and the friendly.'[19] Ernest (Lappin), by now identified by Rosalind as 'a great hunter'[20] also hits upon a cognate identity for his wife:

> 'And what', said Rosalind, on the last day of the honeymoon, 'did the King do today?' In fact they had been climbing all day; and she had worn a blister on her heel; but she did not mean that.
> 'Today', said Ernest, twitching his nose as he bit the end off his cigar, 'he chased a hare'. He paused; struck a match, and twitched again.
> 'A woman hare', he added.
> 'A white hare!' Rosalind exclaimed, as if she had been expecting this. 'Rather a small hare; silver grey with bright eyes?'

15 Ibid. p. 69.
16 Ibid. p. 70.
17 Ibid. p. 70.
18 Ibid. p 70.
19 Ibid. p 70.
20 Ibid. p 70.

> 'Yes', said Ernest, looking at her as she had looked at him, 'a smallish animal; with eyes popping out of her head and two little front paws dangling'. It was exactly how she sat, with her sewing dangling in her hands; and her eyes, that were so big and bright, were certainly a little prominent.
> 'Ah, Lapinova', Rosalind murmured.
> 'Is that what she's called?' said Ernest – 'the real Rosalind?' He looked at her. He felt very much in love with her.
> 'Yes; that's what she's called', said Rosalind. 'Lapinova.' And before they went to bed it was all settled. He was King Lappin; she was Queen Lapinova.[21]

Four pages into the tale the Russian associations become explicit. However, there are many curious anomalies in the nomenclature which Woolf chooses. It might well be argued that giving an animal identity to one's lover is not associated with any particular national culture. Indeed, as if to prove this point, Rebecca West was actively referring to her lover H. G. Wells as 'panther' in their correspondence from much the same period. In real life Leonard Woolf was the marmoset and Virginia the mandrill.[22] However there is also evidence of a specifically Russian dimension to the adoption of animal nicknames within the Bloomsbury group in the years when 'Lappin and Lapinova' was being drafted. David Garnett (who had independently been dubbed 'bunny' ever since infancy) makes the following remarks in his memoirs:

> Adrian [Bell] had nicknamed Duncan the Bear and I and some other friends of his called him by the name. Adrian himself was the Corbie and Virginia was the Goat. Vanessa was called the Dolphin because of her undulating walk, but the name was rarely used. Later on I called Duncan [Grant] Misha, which is the Russian peasant name for all bears.[23]

Although both animal rather than human, the alternative identities assumed by the pair in Woolf's story actually call into question their status as a viable, authentic couple. There is a strong sense of mismatch or even misalliance about Lappin and Lapinova, for this is a union not between two

21 Ibid. p 71.
22 Lee, p. 309.
23 David Garnett, *Flowers of the Forest* (London: Chatto and Windus, 1955), p. 130.

fellow rabbits, but between two separate species, a rabbit and a hare.[24] Paradoxically the feminine form which Rosalind chooses is spelled with a single 'p' whereas her husband's name has two, to distinguish it from the French name for rabbit. The choice of 'Lapinova' clearly suggests the Russian language, but if it is intended to indicate 'wife of Lappin' it should surely have two 'p's, and more importantly Rosalind should strictly take the name 'Lapina', making the title, to be strictly logical 'Lappin and Lappina', just as Tolstoy's novel about a couple (where the wife, like Rosalind Thorburn, is marginalised within marriage) is called 'Anna Karenina', not 'Anna Kareninova'. The form 'Lappin and Lapinova' may indicate Woolf's relative ignorance of the Russian language, at this comparatively early date, and therefore argue for the choice of Russian name being exercised when the initial draft was made in 1918, rather than this exotic name being added in 1938.[25] Woolf does make a point about Western readers' virtual ignorance of the Russian language in her essay 'The Russian Point of View', where she first says that an American lately turned Briton, Henry James must nevertheless remain in some key degree culturally alienated from those who have been born and brought up in Britain, for all his near forty years' residence in England. But this, says Woolf, is nothing compared to the degree of alienation non-Russians must experience when reading Tolstoy, or any of the other famous Russian writers – Dostoevsky and Chekhov are the names she gives – and this is on account of their virtually total ignorance of the Russian language. Anglophone enthusiasts of and experts on Tolstoy are always kept at some distance by the language barrier:

24 Wattison points out that the hare and the rabbit cannot be successfully cross-bred. This is common knowledge among those who farm livestock, but it is not clear whether Woolf would have been aware of this.

25 There are, however, instances where Woolf changed the name of a major character in her fiction only a long way into the drafting process – the names of characters in her first novel *The Voyage Out* were certainly revised, and at the other end of her career, in *The Years* the character of Nicholas was initially Russian before being subsequently made Polish in the published version. The name of Richard for the husband in *Mrs Dalloway* is a case in point, and it cannot be ruled out that the names 'Lappin' and 'Lapinova' might have been added at the later date, when the tale was being revised for *Harper's Magazine*.

> Not only have we all this to separate us from Russian literature, but a much more serious barrier – the difference of language. Of all those who feasted upon Tolstoi, Dostoevsky, and Tchekov during the past twenty years, not more than one or two perhaps have been able to read them in Russian. Our estimate of their qualities has been formed by critics who have never read a word of Russian, or seen Russia, or even heard the language spoken by natives; who have had to depend, blindly and implicitly, upon the work of translators.
>
> What we are saying amounts to this, then, that we have judged a whole literature stripped of its style. When you have changed every word in a sentence from Russian to English, have thereby altered the sense a little, the sound, weight, and accent of the words in relation to each other completely, nothing remains except a crude and coarsened version of the sense. Thus treated, the great Russian writers are like men deprived by an earthquake or a railway accident not only of all their clothes, but also of something subtler and more important – their manners, the idiosyncrasies of their characters. What remains is, as the English have proved by the fanaticism of their admiration, something very powerful and very impressive, but it is difficult to feel sure, in view of these mutilations, how far we can trust ourselves not to impute, to distort, to read into them an emphasis which is false.[26]

Woolf's own curious, strictly illogical system of nomenclature which leads to 'Lapinova', if the name was chosen in 1918, appears to bear out her own point concerning the language barrier, and would probably reflect her own relative lack of knowledge of the Russian language at this point. That could have been expected to change, at least to some degree, once Woolf started studying the Russian language with Samuel Koteliansky, the Russian-speaking émigré, who had come to Britain before World War I, fleeing the pogroms in the Ukraine. Woolf had in fact met Koteliansky, together with another of Russian–Jewish extraction, the artist Mark Gertler, in 1918, shortly before the drafting of 'Lappin and Lapinova', but it was only in 1921 that she and Leonard started their extended series of Russian language lessons with Koteliansky.

If this point seems to confirm that Woolf was still essentially a beginner in the Russian language yet in another sense the very choice of the rabbit as the animal emblem for Ernest proves uncannily authentic in a Russian context, and suggests considerably greater familiarity with the Russian

26 Woolf, 'The Russian Point of View', pp. 173–4.

language and Russian culture. For the word 'krolik' ('rabbit') is used by Russian wives as a standard term of endearment for their husbands. And the etymology of the word 'krolik' can be traced back through Polish to Old High German, where 'kunig', is related to 'koenig', the word for 'king'. The word is also related to the Italian 'conegliano', the archaic English 'coney' and the Latin 'cuniculus'. And Woolf's Lappin is not merely a rabbit, a tame, domesticated rabbit, but 'King Lappin', a king rabbit roaming in the wild. Incidentally the Latin word for hare is 'lepus', which is certainly heading in the direction of 'Lapinova'. The 'ova' ending (which misleadingly suggests 'daughter of') tends to imply that the Russian names were given by Woolf to the characters in the story as early as 1918 or 1919, when her knowledge of the Russian language was still embryonic, whereas the very fact of hitting upon 'rabbit' as a term of endearment for a husband seems perhaps to indicate the greater knowledge of Russian she probably did not have in 1918 and which she and Leonard should however have acquired by the late 1930s. That said, by November 1920 Woolf was able to translate Chekhov,[27] so she might certainly be expected to have acquired this degree of knowledge of idiomatic Russian by the 1930s and the revising of 'Lappin and Lapinova'.

The English names chosen by Woolf in this story are themselves also far from innocent or devoid of intertextual significance. Ernest, as Semino has suggested,[28] brings in the question of assumed names, when Wilde's *The Importance of Being Earnest* is recalled, but of greater interest as regards Woolf's output as novelist, though also relating to drama, is the heroine's name. 'Rosalind' brings to mind Shakespeare's comedy *As You Like It*. This play involves two marriages (Celia's with Oliver and Rosalind's with Orlando.) Again, depending on the names given to the characters in the original draft, there is considerable significance as regards the name Rosalind. For this would make 'Lappin and Lapinova' the first instance of an association between Russia and Shakespeare in Woolf's fiction. Woolf

27 Edward Bishop, *A Virginia Woolf Chronology* (London: Palgrave Macmillan, 1989), p. 59.

28 Elena Semino, 'Blending and characters' mental functioning in Virginia Woolf's Lappin and Lapinova', *Language and Literature* 15 (2006), pp. 55–72 (p. 71).

says of Dostoevsky in 'The Russian Point of View' 'out of Shakespeare there is no more exciting reading',[29] and later in the 1920s Woolf was to go on to produce a novel named after the hero of *As You Like It*, *Orlando* (1928). This novel involves an encounter between an English and a Russian lover, which ultimately ends in betrayal and separation. Moreover the Shakespeare comedy entails cross-dressing between genders, just as Woolf's novel's hero returns from Turkey as a woman. More specifically, the motif of the tree is shared by *As You Like It* and *Orlando*. And, as Guiguet remarks, a woodland setting is common to both Shakespeare's play and this short story 'Lappin and Lapinova':

> The protagonists of 'Lappin and Lapinova' triumph for a while, thanks to the artifice of a personal and secret world in which they take refuge. Their escapades into the new Forest of Arden into which Rosalind has led her solemn sensible Ernest, where he becomes King Lappin and she, the little silver-grey hare with big protruberant eyes, a little crazy but none the less a Queen, bring them together while separating and protecting them from everyday life – their own and that of others.[30]

In both play and short story the woodland represents an area where fiction can prevail over unimaginative quotidian reality, and where everyday roles are transformed. As her husband Ernest, at least initially, remarks 'Is that what she's called – the real Rosalind?' At this early stage, fresh from honeymoon, not yet backsliding into the imaginative death which it is suggested or implied that marriage is prone to become, the husband is the spouse who refers to the exotic, outlandish Russian Lapinova identity as 'the real Rosalind', presumably to distinguish her from the quiet and retiring urban human ensconced in middle-class marriage in London. The admittedly fragile fictional fantasy world shared by the eponymous couple in 'Lappin and Lapinova' is also Russian by distinction from the very English world either of Porchester Terrace and Bayswater, or 'a saddler's shop in South Kensington, not far from the Tube station.'[31] where the young couple

29 Woolf, 'The Russian Point of View', p. 178.

30 Jean Guiguet, *Virginia Woolf and her Works* (London: Hogarth Press, 1965), p. 339.

31 Woolf, *Haunted House*, p. 75.

take up residence after marriage. Yet Woolf (through Lapinova's eyes) subverts Rosalind's in-laws' superficial English respectability:

> Rosalind (Lapinova) 'looked at her father-in-law, a furtive little man with dyed moustaches. His foible was collecting things – seals, enamel boxes, trifles from eighteenth-century dressing tables which he hid in the drawers of his study from his wife. Now she saw him as he was – a poacher.'[32]

And Woolf, besides giving animal identities to the newlywed couple also extends the principle to cover the bride's superficially very conventional in-laws, the Thorburns:

> And Celia, the unmarried daughter, who always nosed out other people's secrets, the little things they worked to hide – she was a white ferret with pink eyes, and a nose clotted with earth from her horrid underground nosings and pokings. Slung round men's shoulders, in a net, and thrust down a hole – it was a pitiable life – Celia's; it was none of her fault. So she saw Celia.[33]

The Celia in the Woolf short story shares some of the retiring and passive qualities of Duke Frederick's daughter in the Shakespeare comedy, as well as the same name, though she is also given a more sinister dimension thanks to the animal imagery. The rural aspects (bear in mind that the action of Woolf's story takes place in Bayswater and South Kensington) are also nurtured by the characterisation of Ernest's mother (with a bit of gender transposition to add to the sense of disorientation and challenge to convention) as a squire:

> And then she looked at her mother-in-law – whom they dubbed The Squire. Flushed, coarse, a bully – she was all that, as she stood returning thanks, but now that Rosalind – that is Lapinova – saw her, she saw behind her the decayed family mansion.[34]

And Lapinova perceives herself as saved from being overwhelmed by her in-laws only by her new husband's twitching nose, and his animal and

32 Ibid. p. 74.
33 Ibid. p. 74.
34 Ibid. p. 74.

regal identity as Lappin: '"Oh, King Lappin!" she cried as they went home together in the fog, "if your nose hadn't twitched just at that moment, I should have been trapped!"'.[35]

Much depends upon when exactly the heroine in the short story was given her Russian forename, and Ernest described as 'King Lappin'. The absence of any 1918 manuscript makes it ultimately impossible to say whether these were in the tale from the outset or only added when the tale was revised for publication in *Harper's Magazine* in the late 1930s. If the earlier date is assumed this would make the short story a reflection of the great wave of Russophilia which inundated British cultural life in the first three decades of the twentieth century. In 1918 Woolf may have been giving a character a Russian name for the first time, but this was by no means the beginning of Woolf's obsession with Russia and Russian literature. After reading *Crime and Punishment* on her own honeymoon in 1912, Woolf proceeded to read Dostoevsky's *The Idiot* in January 1915 and *The Insulted and the Injured* in October of the same year, while in February 1917 she read and reviewed for the TLS *The Eternal Husband and Other Stories*, followed by *The Gambler* in October 1917. Dostoevsky at this date was rated very favourably by Woolf and his qualities were identified as those which were most sorely missing in canonical Western novelists. Reviewing *The Idiot* in January 1915, Woolf said: 'Scott merely makes superb ordinary people, & Dostoevsky creates wonders, with very subtle brains, & fearful sufferings',[36] and Woolf prefaced her enthusiastic description of Dostoevsky's *The Insulted and the Injured* to Lytton Strachey, on 22 October 1915, by censuring Henry James, an old and close friend of her father's, and at this date still alive:

> I should think I had read 600 books since we met. Please tell me what merit you find in Henry James. I have disabused Leonard of him; but we have his works here, and I read, and can't find anything but faintly tinged rose water, urbane and sleek, but vulgar, and pale as Walter Lamb. Is there really any sense in it? I admit I can't be

35 Ibid. p. 75.

36 Woolf, *The Diary*, I, p. 22 (19 January 1915).

> bothered to snuff out his meaning when it's very obscure. I am beginning the *Insulted and Injured*; which sweeps me away.[37]

Woolf's immersion in Russian literature was by no means narrowly confined to Dostoevsky. As far back as 1910 she had read Tolstoy in the summer of that year 'in bed at Twickenham', and pronounced the experience 'a revelation', and in February 1917 Woolf reviewed for the TLS Louise and Aylmer Maude's translation of *The Cossacks and Other Tales of the Caucasus*, by Tolstoy, followed in November 1917 by the Slavophile Sergei Aksakov's autobiographical *A Russian Schoolboy*, and in May 1918 Chekhov's collections *The Good Wife and Other Stories* and *The Witch and other Stories*, both translated by Constance Garnett. In October 1918 she reviewed the Silver Age Symbolist Valerii Briusov's *The Republic of the Southern Cross and Other Stories*.

This engagement with Russian literature was complemented by an abiding interest in Russian current affairs. The Shakespeare play *As You Like It* is ultimately a comedy of love, but this comedy takes place in its mysterious woodland setting only because Frederick has organised a political uprising and forced his older brother Duke Senior into exile. It is worth observing that the notion of the hero and heroine as a Russian king and queen in exile may not have been entirely an act of imaginative fantasy on Woolf's part. Since the early years of the twentieth century the Russian Grand Duke Michael Mihailovich, a cousin of Tsar Nicholas II, had been resident in London. In an act worthy of any Shakespeare comedy, he had been banished by the Tsar for contracting a morganatic marriage with a bride who, though descended from Pushkin, no less, was considered of too low aristocratic rank to serve as consort for one so close to the imperial succession as Grand Duke Michael. The couple took up residence at Kenwood in 1909. Their movements were announced in the Court Circular and the couple played a prominent role in fashionable London society, hosting a grand ball at Kenwood in the summer of 1914, just months before the declaration of war. They also performed charitable functions and attended

37 Woolf, letter to Lytton Strachey, 22 October 1915, in *The Letters of Virginia Woolf*, II, p. 67.

theatrical events, such as the premiere of what became a very successful run of an adaptation of Tolstoy's *Anna Karenina* at the Ambassadors Theatre, starring the Russian émigrée actress Lydia Javorska, herself married to Prince Baryatinsky until her divorce. That production closed only owing to the outbreak of war in 1914. Thus there were manifold examples of political parallels with the Shakespeare play, with a Russian and regal dimension in the London society in which Woolf and the Bloomsbury group were active. Moreover, by the time Woolf came to write 'Lappin and Lapinova' the Grand Duke had found his circumstances seriously reduced, following the abdication of the tsar who had formerly banished him, and been forced to move out of Kenwood House. Furthermore, 'Lappin and Lapinova' ends with the death of one who has formerly been styled 'Queen Lapinova', and in precisely the same time Woolf would have been aware of the fate of the Russian imperial family at Ekaterinburg, their titles removed by the Bolsheviks prior to the mass execution. The degree to which Woolf and the rest of the Bloomsbury group were following political events in Russia is demonstrated nowhere more clearly than in the founding of the 1917 Club. Woolf's husband Leonard was instrumental in setting this institution up together with the Labour MP and future prime minister Ramsay MacDonald. The 1917 Club was not just an association of like-minded people united by a wish to celebrate the end of absolute monarchy in Russia and the setting up of a provisional government which was supposed to blossom as a Western-style democracy, but was a real social club with permanent premises in Gerrard Street (in the part of Soho which is today London's Chinatown).[38] Virginia Woolf found the club very much to her liking and called in frequently, while other members included E. M. Forster, Middleton Murry, and H. G. Wells. Some of the membership were communists and Bolshevik-supporters, but the club was set up to support the idea of democratic socialism, although ironically by the time it opened its doors towards the end of 1917 Kerensky was already being outflanked and forced into exile by the Bolsheviks under Lenin and Trotsky.

38 Interestingly, the eighteenth-century prostitute's lodgings in *Orlando* are also located in Gerrard Street (Virginia Woolf, *Orlando: A Biography* (London: Wordsworth Classics, 1995), p. 106).

The drafting of Woolf's first novel *The Voyage Out*, eventually published in 1915, began as early as the first months of 1908, and in the novel Russia crops up periodically in the speculative conversation of the well-to-do English with whom its plot is concerned. In Chapter XV Russians are singled out together with the Chinese, as the true hope for the survival of the human race. The idea that out-and-out Orientals (the Chinese) are to be bracketed along with the liminal, questionable fellow Europeans (the Russians), as the true hope for the future of the human race, is striking indeed, albeit also satirised here:

> 'And the future?' she reflected, vaguely envisaging a race of men becoming more and more like Hirst, and a race of women becoming more and more like Rachel. 'Oh no', she concluded, glancing at him, 'one wouldn't marry you. Well, then, the future of the race is in the hands of Susan and Arthur; no – that's dreadful. Of farm labourers; no – not of the English at all, but of Russians and Chinese.' This train of thought did not satisfy her, and was interrupted by St. John, who began again:
> 'I wish you knew Bennett. He's the greatest man in the world.'[39]

Later in the novel a subsidiary character, the gauche and outspoken Evelyn Murgatroyd, voices views which reflect the atmosphere surrounding the failed uprising against the Tsarist government in 1905, prompted by Russia's ignominious defeat at the hands of the Japanese the previous year:

> 'The bother is', she went on, 'that I mayn't be able to start work seriously till October. I've just had a letter from a friend of mine whose brother is in business in Moscow. They want me to stay with them, and as they're in the thick of all the conspiracies and anarchists, I've a good mind to stop on my way home. It sounds too thrilling.' She wanted to make Rachel see how thrilling it was. 'My friend knows a girl of fifteen who's been sent to Siberia for life merely because they caught her addressing a letter to an anarchist. And the letter wasn't from her, either. I'd give all I have in the world to help on a revolution against the Russian government, and it's bound to come.'[40]

In this extended extract evidence emerges of the view of Tsarist Russia, widely espoused among liberal and left-leaning artistic circles in London

39 Virginia Woolf, *The Voyage Out* (London: Vintage, 2004), p. 213.
40 Ibid. p. 213.

since the pogroms in the last decades of the nineteenth century, as a paranoid police state where the innocent and dissidents are sent off to prison camps in Siberia on the flimsiest of pretexts. The character who delivers these lines, Evelyn Murgatroyd, has been introduced as resembling a 'gallant lady of the time of Charles the First leading royalist troops into action'[41] but later shows herself to be fixated with the idea of revolution, albeit the romance of Garibaldi and the Risorgimento is what first and foremost appeals to her, when she makes her entrance, rather than the Russia of 1905. Evelyn instils an initial attitude of panic and fear in the thoroughly English, and thoroughly repressed, St John Hirst:

> 'Do you think Garibaldi was ever up here?' she asked Mr Hirst. Oh, if she had been his bride! If, instead of a picnic party, this was a party of patriots, and she, red-shirted like the rest, had lain among grim men, flat on the turf, aiming her gun at the white turrets beneath them, screening her eyes to pierce through the smoke! So thinking, her foot stirred restlessly, and she exclaimed:
> 'I don't call this life, do you?'
> 'What do you call life?' said St. John.
> 'Fighting – revolution', she said, still gazing at the doomed city. 'You only care for books, I know.'
> 'You're quite wrong', said St. John.
> 'Explain', she urged, for there were no guns to be aimed at bodies, and she turned to another kind of warfare.
> 'What do I care for? People', she said.
> 'Well, I am surprised!' she exclaimed. 'You look so awfully serious. Do let's be friends and tell each other what we're like. I hate being cautious, don't you?
> But St. John was decidedly cautious, as she could see by the sudden constriction of his lips, and had no intention of revealing his soul to a young lady.[42]

Moreover St John snubs Evelyn's too forward advances in favour of bestowing his attentions on an inanimate object and a dumb animal: '"The ass is eating my hat," he remarked, and stretched out for it instead of answering her.'[43]

41 Ibid. p. 131.
42 Ibid. p. 133.
43 Ibid. p. 133.

The discourse here, with the references to St John's 'soul' and Evelyn's exclamation 'I don't call this life, do you?' fits very much within the terms of the discourse among British readers during the era of Russophilia, with the frequent references to 'soul' remarked upon by Woolf in relation to Dostoevsky's work.[44] In Woolf's other early novel *Night And Day*, reflecting the intensity of the Russophilia of the second decade of the twentieth century, further references to Russia are also to be found, although these are relatively 'ornamental' rather than being central or conveying deeply held views about Russia. Mary Datchet, the feminist suffragist is described as having 'a ruffled appearance, as if she had been running her fingers through her hair in the course of her conversation; she was dressed more or less like a Russian peasant girl.'[45] Earlier in the same chapter, William Rodney, a poet of sorts, and Cassandra Otway, a cousin of the heroine Katharine Hilbery, spar in terms of their knowledge of Russian literature:

> Cassandra's voice rose high in its excitement.
> 'You've not read "The Idiot"!' she exclaimed.
> 'I've read "War and Peace"', William replied, a little testily.
> '"WAR AND PEACE"!' she echoed, in a tone of derision.
> 'I confess I don't understand the Russians.'
> 'Shake hands! Shake hands!' boomed Uncle Aubrey from across the table. 'Neither do I. And I hazard the opinion that they don't themselves.'
> The old gentleman had ruled a large part of the Indian Empire, but he was in the habit of saying that he had rather have written the works of Dickens.[46]

The exchange, though only in passing, the prelude to a discussion of Shakespeare, is nonetheless telling. It is the young woman who seems to have great enthusiasm for Dostoevsky, and to defend his own cultural capital the scion of the English upper classes, educated at Winchester and Cambridge, asserts that while he may not have read Dostoevsky's *The Idiot* he can still claim to have read *War and Peace*. At this date (published in 1919, *Night And Day* was composed between November 1917 and the Armistice in

44 Woolf, 'The Russian Point of View', p 173.
45 Woolf, *Night And Day*, p. 302.
46 Ibid. p. 295

November 1918) Dostoevsky, translated into English by Constance Garnett in the past two decades, may also have enjoyed primacy with Virginia Woolf. However William Rodney's claims to be taken seriously on the strength of having read *War and Peace* are then humorously qualified by his admission 'I confess I don't understand the Russians'; and the irony is completed when Uncle Aubrey, retired stalwart of the British Raj, says that he would rather have been Charles Dickens – perhaps perceived by him as the quintessentially English polar opposite of Tolstoy and Dostoevsky – than enjoy the status he attained as ruler in India. Uncle Aubrey seems to be venerating English literature, even to the detriment of British geopolitical prowess, and he continues in this superficially self-deprecating manner by saying that he, like William Rodney, fails to understand the Russians as a race. Finally, he ventures the opinion that the Russians are doomed to act irrationally, not even able to understand themselves. This seems to perpetuate the stereotype of the Russians as an impulsive, irrational, even mystical people.

While these exchanges in *The Voyage Out* and *Night And Day* are of interest as indicators of the views of Russia held among the British metropolitan intelligentsia in the first two decades of the twentieth century, it should be stressed that neither novel resembles the works for which Woolf went on to become celebrated in the 1920s, which represent radical and self-conscious departures in the craft of the novel. In her work in these first two decades and on into the 1920s as critic, reviewing Russian literature, and the work of Dostoevsky especially, Woolf repeatedly admires the quality of 'soul' which is to be found in this author's novels, and their sheer power and emotional force. She says in 'The Russian Point of View', where she describes his novels as 'seething whirlpools' and readers are 'filled with a giddy rapture' that 'They are composed purely and wholly of the stuff of the soul.'[47] She welcomes the way in which their power of feeling makes formal concerns secondary and on occasion capable of being put aside altogether. By contrast she expresses frustration with the form of the traditional Victorian and Edwardian English novel, with its predictable

47 Woolf, 'The Russian Point of View', p. 178.

and measured formula of thirty-two chapters.[48] Here 'Lappin and Lapinova', first drafted in 1918, may be seen, for all its brevity, as presaging the experiments with narrative method which were to come with *Jacob's Room*, on which she began the next year, *Mrs Dalloway* of 1925, *To The Lighthouse* of 1927, *Orlando* of 1928 and *The Waves* of 1931, arguably her most avant-garde and experimental novel. 'Lappin and Lapinova' includes parallel narratives (the couple's lives as humans and their lives as hare and rabbit, indoors and outdoors, by day and by night). Moreover the border between the two modes of existence is subtle and permeable. The kind of rapid, audacious shifts found in this story are to become central to her next, and first experimental novel.

The Russian contribution to *Jacob's Room* should not be overstated, but again there are some remarks of consequence in terms of the discourse presenting Russia as non-European and non-civilised. Part of the scheme of the novel is to show the importance for patriarchy at this date of the idea of classical Greek as part of the educated Englishman's upbringing and Woolf presents Jacob Flanders and his fellow public school and Cambridge educated contemporary Timmy Durrant as products of this system:

> The Greeks – yes, that was what they talked about– how when all's said and done, when one's rinsed one's mouth with every literature in the world, including Chinese and Russian (but these Slavs aren't civilized), it's the flavour of Greek that remains. Durrant quoted Aeschylus – Jacob Sophocles. It is true that no Greek could have understood or professor refrained from pointing out – Never mind; what is Greek for if not to be shouted on Haverstock Hill in the dawn? Moreover, Durrant never listened to Sophocles, nor Jacob to Aeschylus. They were boastful, triumphant; it seemed to both that they had read every book in the world; known every sin, passion, and joy. Civilizations stood round them like flowers ready for picking. Ages lapped at their feet like waves fit for sailing. And surveying all this, looming through the fog, the lamplight, the shades of London, the two young men decided in favour of Greece.[49]

And the novel's hero gives the opinion: '"Probably," said Jacob "We are the only people in the world who know what the Greeks meant."'[50]

48 Woolf, 'Modern Fiction', p. 149.

49 Virginia Woolf, *Jacob's Room* (London: Hogarth Press, 1990), p. 70.

50 Ibid. p. 70.

Before the novel is over Woolf alludes both positively and negatively to Russia. Overall she is determined to suggest that the veneration of classical culture has played a malign and disastrous role in the British war machine leading to the slaughter of World War I – while in this instance the Russians may be dismissed as once again able to be bracketed with out-and-out Orientals such as the Chinese. The statement is indeed made by Jacob that 'these Slavs aren't civilized', and elsewhere reference is made to the widespread enthusiasm then sweeping Britain for the Ballets Russes 'have you heard the news? life in the capital is gay; the Russian dancers ....'[51]

In another exchange Woolf satirises the British intelligentsia's fixation with literature in other languages (which, as she points out in the 'The Russian Point of View' essay, remains largely unknown to them in terms of any nuance, owing to the language barrier):

> But at dinner that night Mr. Williams asked him whether he would like to see the paper; then Mrs. Williams asked him (as they strolled on the terrace smoking – and how could he refuse that man's cigar?) whether he'd seen the theatre by moonlight; whether he knew Everard Sherborn; whether he read Greek and whether (Evan rose silently and went in) if he had to sacrifice one it would be the French literature or the Russian?[52]

And finally Woolf suggests the tyranny of taste wrought by the Russophilia of the age: '"And now," wrote Jacob in his letter to Bonamy, "I shall have to read her cursed book" – her Tchekov, he meant, for she had lent it him.'[53]

Woolf's character Jacob Flanders may rail against having to read and come up with an opinion on Chekhov's short stories, purely as a matter of social form, but for Jacob's creator, Woolf herself, Chekhov was arguably a key Russian author in the development of the aesthetics which dominate her characteristic style in the fiction of the 1920s. Woolf rebelled against the formulaic nature of the English novel at this date, still very much under the influence of the Victorians, and it was Dostoevsky with his immediacy who perhaps first represented an alternative set of creative and expressive

51 Ibid. p. 87.
52 Ibid. p. 139.
53 Ibid. p. 139.

aesthetics. Dostoevsky's work is characterised for Woolf by intensity of passionate feeling, and by spiritual drama. She associates Dostoevsky most of all the Russians with 'soul'. From Chekhov she took a greater emphasis upon wistfulness – the doomed sense of a passing social order, highly articulate, but to little practical purpose, great talkers, but powerless to withstand social change following the emancipation of the serfs and the social unrest which was eventually to manifest in the 1905 attempted revolution, just a year after Chekhov's death. And Chekhov also influenced Woolf's approach to form. No writer could be further than Chekhov from the idealistic zeal and certainty of Dostoevsky, with his Slavophile rejection of modern liberalising Russia, and Tolstoy, with his anarchistic challenge to the state. The others court didacticism, while Chekhov eschews easy messages or even conclusions, whether as short story writer (Woolf focuses on 'Gusev' in 'Modern Fiction') or as playwright. The eschewal of messages or conclusions has technical implications.

These are clearly demonstrated in what is possibly the shortest of all Woolf's short stories, if it can be regarded as such rather than as a sketch. 'Uncle Vanya' is a piece of prose by Woolf which, like 'Lappin and Lapinova', has no certain date of composition, though it most likely comes from the late 1930s. It amounts to less than a page in length and is the interior monologue of an English woman who has just attended a performance of *Uncle Vanya*. For all that, its method is nonetheless complex and polyphonic. Within twenty-five lines we are presented with the woman's thoughts, the words being delivered as text on stage, the gunshot near the end of the play, and then the non-theatrical reality of the early twentieth century in a British theatre intrudes, with the playing of the National Anthem, a practice at that date still *de rigueur*, and neatly reminding the audience that the Russian spell, and suspension of disbelief are over. The woman in the audience describes the stage sound effects: 'Now we hear the bells of the horses tinkling away in the distance.'[54] The woman remarks to herself silently and continues,

54 Woolf, *A Haunted House*, p. 241.

> 'And is that also true of us?' she said, leaning her chin on her hand and looking at the girl on stage. 'Do we hear bells tinkling away down the road?' she asked, and thought of the taxis and omnibuses in Sloane Street, for they lived in one of the big houses in Cadogan Square.'[55]

The piece, for all its extreme brevity, is formally and technically remarkable. There is a fluidity of movement from words which are actually heard but are a text (Chekhov's from *Uncle Vanya*, albeit in an English translation) to unuttered words, which are the woman in the audience's thoughts, at times unsignposted as such. The play ends anti-climatically, and the woman reflects whether the truth of the play extends to the reality of that particular moment, and, perhaps, of the British rather than Russian setting. Then the woman in the audience reveals that she has completely misunderstood the religious connotations of Sonya's line in the play 'we shall rest', which in a Russian context would immediately be understood as a statement about death and the afterlife. By contrast the woman in the audience seems to feel that she and her husband have been insufficiently stretched by their evening in the theatre 'we're not even tired'. Most irrationally of all the woman announces 'As for us', as her husband helped her on with her cloak, 'we've not even loaded the pistol. We're not even tired.'[56]

Having begun thinking 'Don't they see through everything – the Russians?' by the end of the sketch the woman in the audience at least, if not her husband, and, conceivably the majority of the English audience also, have failed completely to see the point of the piece. It as if British obtusity is the other side of Russian disillusioned pessimism.

The exact date of this short story has not been established, although Woolf saw a performance of Chekhov's *Uncle Vanya* on 16 February 1937 and wrote it up in her Diary. It represents a stage where Chekhov has become part of the Russian theatrical repertory in Britain but his plays are deprived of their true impact. But that is also Woolf's ironic point. The significance of Chekhov for her career as novelist could not have been more far-reaching. Chekhov's inconclusiveness, his refusal to end with an

55 Ibid. p. 241.
56 Ibid. p. 241.

obvious or melodramatic conclusion is seminal for Woolf. In May 1922 Woolf wrote to Janet Case, 'There's not a single living writer (English) I respect: so you see, I have to read the Russians' and in August 1923 she wrote to Gerald Brenan 'do not start with a snap like the stories of Maupassant and Mérimée' and in precisely this period, to which 'Lappin and Lapinova' may be seen as a prelude on a modest scale, Woolf starts work on *Jacob's Room*, with its elided confusions of narrative voice, its celebrated initial allusion to the opening of one of the most canonical of Victorian novels, George Eliot's *Adam Bede*:

> With a single drop of ink for a mirror, the Egyptian sorcerer undertakes to reveal to any chance comer far-reaching visions of the past. This is what I undertake to do for you, reader. With this drop of ink at the end of my pen, I will show you the roomy workshop of Mr. Jonathan Burge, carpenter and builder, in the village of Hayslope, as it appeared on the eighteenth of June, in the year of our Lord 1799.
> The afternoon sun was warm on the five workmen there, busy upon doors and window-frames and wainscoting.[57]

becomes in Woolf's hands in 1922, the momentous year of modernism for writers in English, when Joyce published *Ulysses* (the Woolfs' Hogarth Press declined the honour) and Eliot published *The Waste Land* (which the Hogarth Press did publish), a sly exercise in subversion of nineteenth-century intrusive narration:

> 'So of course', wrote Betty Flanders, pressing her heels rather deeper in the sand, 'there was nothing for it but to leave.'
> Slowly welling from the point of her gold nib, pale blue ink dissolved the full stop; for there her pen stuck; her eyes fixed, and tears slowly filled them. The entire bay quivered; the lighthouse wobbled; and she had the illusion that the mast of Mr. Connor's little yacht was like a wax candle in the sun. She winked quickly. Accidents were awful things. She winked again. The mast was straight; the waves were regular; the lighthouse was upright; but the blot had spread.
> '... nothing for it but to leave', she read.
> 'Well, if Jacob doesn't want to play' (the shadow of Archer, her eldest son, fell across the notepaper and looked blue on the sand, and she felt chilly – it was the third of

57 George Eliot, *Adam Bede* (Oxford: Oxford University Press, 2001), p. 5.

September already), 'if Jacob doesn't want to play' – what a horrid blot! It must be getting late.[58]

Chekhov's inconclusiveness as regards form – the end of the scene may precede it and then prove not in fact to be the end at all – a whimper usually follows a bang – was a vital ingredient in allowing Woolf to move on from the essentially late Victorian and Edwardian version of the novel which she had been confined to in *The Voyage Out* and *Night And Day*. While discussion of Russia and ideas of Russian culture had permeated those novels to some considerable degree it was only in the works of the 1920s that a Russian approach to form may be said to have predominated in her fiction. In *Jacob's Room*, Woolf, also operating under the influence of cubism (a major factor since Fry's post-impressionist exhibitions just before World War I), exploited the kind of freedom of structure she found in Chekhov to provide a template for her own experiments:

I have been reading Tchekov this afternoon, and feeling Good Lord, why does he mention this? There is a perpetual unexpectedness in his mind which is, I think, the interest of him. Perhaps all the Russians have it. It is only in France and England that events seem threaded like beads on a string – for which our best stories are so dull. How dull Mérimée is![59]

(Woolf does not seem to have remembered that Mérimée was fluent in the Russian language and a key figure in the translation of Russian literature into French.)

The simile 'like beads on a string' echoes the famous formula decrying the formulaic in 'Modern Fiction':

Life is not a series of gig lamps symmetrically arranged; life is a luminous halo, a semi-transparent envelope surrounding us from the beginning of consciousness to the end. Is it not the task of the novelist to convey this varying, this unknown and

58 Woolf, *Jacob's Room*, p. 1.

59 Woolf, Letter to Gerald Brenan, 10 August 1923, in *The Letters of Virginia Woolf*, III, p. 63.

> uncircumscribed spirit, whatever aberration or complexity it may display, with as little mixture of the alien and external as possible?[60]

And further on in the same essay Woolf sets up Chekhov as the model of what modern literary style should aspire to:

> It is the saint in them which confounds us with a feeling of our own irreligious triviality, and turns so many of our famous novels to tinsel and trickery. The conclusions of the Russian mind, thus comprehensive and compassionate, are inevitably, perhaps, of the utmost sadness. More accurately indeed we might speak of the inconclusiveness of the Russian mind. It is the sense that there is no answer, that if honestly examined life presents question after question which must be left to sound on and on after the story is over in hopeless interrogation that fills us with a deep, and finally it may be with a resentful, despair. They are right perhaps; unquestionably they see further than we do and without our gross impediments of vision.[61]

The last sentence above is very close to that allocated to the woman in the audience in the short story 'Uncle Vanya':

> Don't they see through everything – the Russians? All the little disguises we've put up? Flowers against decay; gold and velvet against poverty; the cherry trees, the apple trees – they see through them too', she was thinking at the play. Then a shot rang out.[62]

But ultimately in the 'Modern Fiction' essay Woolf shies away from embracing the Russian approach completely. She perceives an element of the comic to be a fundamental strength of English literature and to be signally missing from Russian writers:

> But perhaps we see something that escapes them, or why should this voice of protest mix itself with our gloom? The voice of protest is the voice of another and an ancient civilisation which seems to have bred in us the instinct to enjoy and fight rather than to suffer and understand. English fiction from Sterne to Meredith bears witness to our natural delight in humour and comedy, in the beauty of earth, in the activities of the intellect, and in the splendour of the body. But any deductions that we may

60 Woolf, 'Modern Fiction', p. 150.

61 Ibid. p. 153.

62 Virginia Woolf, 'Uncle Vanya', in *A Haunted House*, ed. Susan Dick (London: Vintage, 1985), p. 241.

> draw from the comparison of two fictions so immeasurably far apart are futile save indeed as they flood us with a view of the infinite possibilities of the art and remind us that there is no limit to the horizon, and that nothing – no 'method', no experiment, even of the wildest – is forbidden, but only falsity and pretence.[63]

This too is of interest. The woman in the audience in the 'Uncle Vanya' short story may show an ignorance of Russian literature which Woolf portrays in satirical comedy, entirely mistaking the religious implications of 'we shall rest', but Woolf herself seems here to be regarding Chekhov in the same breath as Dostoevsky and Tolstoy, neither of whom is known primarily for comedy. Yet Chekhov himself declared that another of his plays *The Cherry Orchard* was a comedy in four acts and an English contemporary of Woolf's, Dorothy Sayers, said of *The Cherry Orchard* 'in its blackest moments it is inevitably doomed to the comic gesture':[64]

> That we are more advanced, less advanced, or have advanced in an entirely different direction. At any rate, the English person who finds himself at dawn in the nursery of Madame Ranevskaia feels out of place, like a foreigner brought up with entirely different traditions. But these traditions are not (this, of course, is a transcript of individual experience) so ingrained in one as to prevent one from shedding them only without pain but with actual relief and abandonment.[65]

In fact the Russian cultural influence may also in some respects have peaked before the end of the 1920s. Arguably, it was the inconclusiveness of Chekhov, and his refusal to share either Dostoevsky's slavophile and religious engagement or Tolstoy's fundamental anarchistic challenge to the state, which most enabled Woolf to pursue a radical openness of literary form which is above all seen in *Jacob's Room*, *Mrs Dalloway* and *To The Lighthouse*, as well as *The Waves* from the first year of the following decade. *Mrs Dalloway*, with its twenty-four hour compression of time and confinement to a single geographical setting, and its interior monologue (thought by many critics to owe more to Proust than to James Joyce),

63 Woolf, 'Modern Fiction', p. 154.

64 Dorothy Sayers, letter to *New Statesman*, February 17 1937, *Letters of Dorothy Sayers*, 2 vols (Cambridge: Dorothy L. Sayers Society, 1997), II, p. 11.

65 Virginia Woolf, review of *The Cherry Orchard* (1920), quoted in Rubenstein, p 77.

certainly represents a departure from *The Voyage Out* and *Night And Day*. In reality, however, the Russian influence upon it is, as Rubenstein and Liza Knapp have shown, considerably indebted to Tolstoy's *Anna Karenina*. Mrs Dalloway's party is modelled in some ways on the dinner hosted in *Anna Karenina*; and Clarissa's unfulfilling marriage to Richard Dalloway follows in the tradition of Anna and Karenin, and with the device of the double plot borrowed in the English novel. Moreover both novels involve suicide, albeit it is only contemplated by the heroine in Woolf's novel, whereas it is actually carried out by Anna.

Formally *To The Lighthouse* is yet further from the conventional novel, with its distinct approaches to the passage of time in each of its three sections. Although not extending to matters of form, nevertheless the predominant Russian influence here is surely that of Tolstoy rather than Dostoevsky or Chekhov. The parallels between the dinner which Stepan Obolonsky very much takes over from his wife Dolly in Tolstoy's novel, with its potage Marie Louise, and in Woolf's novel, the dinner offered by Mrs Ramsay, reaching its climax with 'boeuf en daube' are notable. Moreover the young lovers Dolly and Levin are paralleled in *To The Lighthouse* by Paul Rayley and Minta. Woolf makes the link to *Anna Karenina* explicit (in comic vein) when she has Paul Rayley name the novel:

> Anyhow, she was free now to listen to what Paul Rayley was trying to say about books one had read as a boy. They lasted, he said. He had read some of Tolstoi at school. There was one he always remembered, but he had forgotten the name. Russian names were impossible, said Mrs. Ramsay. 'Vronsky', said Paul. He remembered that because he always thought it such a good name for a villain. 'Vronsky', said Mrs. Ramsay; 'Oh, ANNA KARENINA!' but that did not take them very far; books were not in their line. No, Charles Tansley would put them both right in a second about books, but it was all so mixed up with, Am I saying the right thing? Am I making a good impression? that, after all, one knew more about him than about Tolstoi, whereas, what Paul said was about the thing, simply, not himself, nothing else. Like all stupid people, he had a kind of modesty too, a consideration for what you were feeling, which, once in a way at least, she found attractive. Now he was thinking, not about

> himself, or about Tolstoi, but whether she was cold, whether she felt a draught, whether she would like a pear.[66]

In isolation this might be no more remarkable than the name-checking of *War and Peace* and Dostoevsky's *The Idiot* the previous decade in *The Voyage Out*, but here, at least for the reader with a more retentive memory than Paul Rayley's, the proliferation of other parallels points to a far more in-depth relationship between the English and Russian novels. Even so, it is hard to argue that it is the Tolstoy influence which produces the radically experimental narrative form and techniques of *To The Lighthouse*.

On the face of it, at least in one regard, Woolf's last novel of the 1920s, *Orlando* can be seen as, on a much grander scale, following the example set by 'Lappin and Lapinova', when that story was first drafted at the end of the previous decade. 'Lappin and Lapinova' might perhaps today be described as an example of magic realism, a literary genre which has chiefly flourished since the 1960s, its most famous exponents being Vargas Llosa and Salman Rushdie, although Franz Kafka can also be seen as an important precursor. There is no record of whether Virginia Woolf knew of any of the work of the Czech writer, let alone had read it. If she did it would certainly have occurred after the initial 1918 drafting of 'Lappin and Lapinova' and around the time of its publication in revised form for *Harper's Magazine* at the end of the 1930s. English language translations by Edwin and Willa Muir of 'The Burrow' and 'Investigations of a Dog', both of which involve and element of anthropomorphism appeared in 1933 and onwards, continuing after Woolf's death. A. L. Lloyd produced an English language version of 'The Metamorphosis' in 1937, which Woolf could conceivably have read. If she was among the relatively small numbers of English readers of Kafka at that point there is no record. Any parallel between Kafka's anthropomorphism in the short stories 'The Burrow' or 'A Report To Academy', where the animal comes close to the human, and 'Lappin and Lapinova' is therefore more likely coincidental rather than conscious. It is also of interest that the animal identities assumed by Ernest and Rosalind in 'Lappin and Lapinova' are put on through the exercise of imaginative willpower,

66 Virginia Woolf, *To The Lighthouse* (Harmondsworth: Penguin, 1992), p. 117.

and the shared fantasy ends when the husband refuses to continue playing along with the game. Of course Kafka's single most celebrated short story, 'The Metamorphosis' involves transformation from the human to the animal, in fact to the insect form. Unlike the hero and heroine in 'Lappin and Lapinova' Gregor Samsa undergoes a strictly one way process. He is released from his ordeal as a giant bug only through death. The nearest equivalent to this notion of metamorphosis in Woolf's fiction comes not in a short story, but in a novel, indeed the novel whose plot has by far the longest and least realistic timespan among all of Woolf's works. *Orlando*, of 1928, involves a central eponymous character who lives to an age of over 300 years. Perhaps closer to home, David Garnett's 1922 novella *Lady Into Fox*, which was admired by Woolf, might be cited as a possible influence upon both the finished 1938 version of 'Lappin and Lapinova' and, on account of its unbridled fantasy, *Orlando* in 1928. Like Gregor Samsa, and like the wife in Garnett's tale, Orlando undergoes a transformation from which he never reverts. Orlando wakes up one morning (from a trance slumber of several days' duration while on a diplomatic mission to Turkey) and discovers that a profound, irreversible change has taken place involving him, although in Woolf's novel, unlike Kafka's short story, this moment occurs mid way through rather than at the outset of the narrative. It must be added, of course, that in Woolf's novel the profound transformation is not of species but of sex, from male to female. Yet there are also important references to the animal in *Orlando*, and at least one of these turns out to be linked to questions of national stereotypes involving Russia.

When Orlando first encounters Sasha, the daughter of the Muscovite Ambassador, in 1683 during the Great Frost which renders the Thames a temporary skating rink (and perhaps too by the same token makes normally temperate England seem as close as it can get to Russia), Sasha is presented as figure of gender ambiguity:

> Orlando, it is true, was none of those who tread lightly the corantoe and lavolta; he was clumsy and a little absentminded. He much preferred the plain dances of his own country, which he danced as a child to these fantastic foreign measures. He had indeed just brought his feet together about six in the evening of the seventh of January at the finish of some such quadrille or minuet when he beheld, coming from the pavilion of the Muscovite Embassy, a figure, which, whether boy's or woman's,

> for the loose tunic and trousers of the Russian fashion served to disguise the sex, filled him with the highest curiosity.[67]

When Orlando begins the affair with Sasha he gives her this name because it belonged to a specifically Russian fox he had owned as a boy:

> Hence, Orlando and Sasha, as he called her for short, and because it was the name of a white Russian fox he had had as a boy – a creature soft as snow, but with teeth of steel, which bit him so savagely that his father had it killed – hence, they had the river to themselves.[68]

Just as the human characters devised alternative names in 'Lappin and Lapinova' and associated them with animal identities, as rabbit and hare, so here Orlando chooses the Russian abbreviation of Alexandra partly because it is not gender specific, being used equally for males and females in Russian, and partly because it is in his personal history associated with a pet animal he once owned: a specifically Russian fox. Before Sasha's arrival in person with the Muscovite delegation, Orlando already had an association with Russia, albeit in the form of a Russian animal, which, despite being 'soft as snow' had 'teeth of steel' and 'bit him so savagely that his father had it killed.'

Orlando's prior experience of the Russian character was something simultaneously 'soft' yet savage. The premonition of a tragic end to the relationship here is also charged with ironies. For Sasha is destined to remain female but to die like any ordinary mortal (as the fox has earlier died), whereas Orlando will 'die' as a male but live on to a superhuman age only after changing sex to female:

> 'All ends in death', Orlando would say, sitting upright on the ice. But Sasha who after all had no English blood in her but was from Russia where the sunsets are longer, the dawns less sudden, and sentences often left unfinished from doubt as to how best to end them – Sasha stared at him, perhaps sneered at him, for he must have seemed a child to her, and said nothing. Ransack the language as he might, words failed him. He wanted another landscape, and another tongue. English was too frank, too candid,

67 Woolf, *Orlando*, p. 35.

68 Ibid. p. 20.

> too honeyed a speech for Sasha. For in all she said, however open she seemed and voluptuous, there was something hidden; in all she did, however daring, there was something concealed. So the green flame seems hidden in the emerald, or the sun prisoned in a hill. The clearness was only outward; within was a wandering flame. It came; it went; she never shone with the steady beam of an Englishwoman – here, however, remembering the Lady Margaret and her petticoats, Orlando ran wild in his transports and swept her over the ice, faster, faster, vowing that he would chase the flame, dive for the gem, and so on and so on, the words coming on the pants of his breath with the passion of a poet whose poetry is half pressed out of him by pain.[69]

Further anecdotes which the lovers Orlando and Sasha tell each other include one of another wild animal questionably domesticated:

> And then, wrapped in their sables, they would talk of everything under the sun; of sights and travels; of Moor and Pagan; of this man's beard and that woman's skin; of a rat that fed from her hand at table; of the arras that moved always in the hall at home; of a face; of a feather. Nothing was too small for such converse, nothing was too great.[70]

Arguably the influence of Russian culture for Woolf changed towards the end of the 1920s. Although the events of its plot – a protagonist whose life lasts for over 300 years, and the change of gender from the third chapter onwards qualify the label 'magic realist' – in terms of its narrative technique *Orlando* is far less experimental than *Jacob's Room*, *Mrs Dalloway* or especially its immediate precursor *To The Lighthouse*. In this novel, which is a parody of history and of biography, chronology is rather more straightforward than the limitation to twenty-four hours from which there are Proustian flashbacks, moments of being, in *Mrs Dalloway*. Orlando's memory is uninterrupted by the change of sex. Nor is there the contrapuntal double plot of that novel, nor the second-by-second crawling through time found in the first part of *To The Lighthouse* or the racing through ten years and the biggest conflict in world history represented by the mere eighteen pages of 'Time Passes', the middle section from the same novel. If it is compared with the central 'Oxen of the Sun' section of Joyce's *Ulysses*,

69 Ibid. p. 22.
70 Ibid. p. 21.

where the author shifts in rapid order through one historical form of the English language from the Anglo-Saxon of *Beowulf* by way of Middle English, Elizabethan English and the English of the eighteenth-century Enlightenment and nineteenth century Victorianism,[71] it can be seen that, for all its outrageous plot, *Orlando* is not an excessively demanding experience for the reader.

Orlando is also written at what may be a key juncture in Woolf's engagement with Russia and Russian culture. This hard to classify novel, part *jeu d'esprit*, part parody of traditional biography and history, turns out to have been started at a time when the friend with whom Woolf had become besotted, Vita Sackville West, had recently visited Russia. While West was in Teheran for the coronation of the Shah, she was informed by Woolf that she and Leonard had an official invitation to travel to Russia:

> I am writing at great speed. For the third time I begin a sentence, The truth is I'm so engulfed in Orlando I can think of nothing else. It has ousted romance, psychology and the rest of that odious novel completely. Tomorrow I begin the chapter which describes Violet and you meeting on the ice … It will be a little book, about 30,000 words at most, and at my present rate which is feverish (I think of nothing but you all day long, in different guises, and Violet and me and Elizabeth and George the 3rd) I shall have done it by Christmas. That's to say, if we don't go to Russia; Do you want me to go to Russia? We've been asked to go there, free, by the Government, to celebrate the anniversary of the Revolution for one month. Don't you think one should take the chance, my love, and risk the cold? Tell me what you think. I must settle by Tuesday.[72]

In a fine instance of what was never more than a possibility in real life being turned into fiction, the counterfactual or 'magic realist' novel *Orlando* was called into being in precisely the same period as a very real invitation from the Bolshevik regime in what was now termed the USSR. Neither Leonard Woolf nor Virginia accepted the invitation, and it is not recorded

71 James Joyce, *Ulysses*, ed. Jeri Johnson (Oxford: Oxford University Press, 1993), pp. 366–407.

72 Woolf, letter to Vita Sackville-West, 19 October 1927, in *The Letters of Virginia Woolf*, III, p. 439.

whether the invitation was made by the regime to husband or wife primarily, and on the grounds of Leonard's political achievements or Virginia's literary accomplishments. Certainly the Woolfs sit rather oddly among the succession of Fabian figures like H. G. Wells, the Webbs and George Bernard Shaw who were feted by the communist regime. Perhaps some Kremlin apparatchik misinterpreted the revolutionary credentials of the 1917 Club, still in existence at this date. Woolf went on reviewing Russian literature in the next decade, and there are important Russian influences upon, and references to the idea of Russia and Russian culture in *The Years* and *Between the Acts*.

Russia continued to afford Woolf cultural capital into the next decade, but in a rather different form, with the English author drawing upon Turgenev and Chekhov predominantly. Her opinion of Turgenev was fundamentally revised when she reread his novels for the purposes of writing criticism after 1930, and it is perhaps not coincidental that the last novel published in Woolf's lifetime, *The Years* (1937) is widely regarded as an example of more traditional narrative than the majority of the works she had produced in the 1920s, with their strong emphasis upon technical experimentation. In many ways this tantalising declined invitation in the late 1920s serves as an end point for Woolf's most intense and forward-looking involvement with the myth of Russia.

Figure 8. Photo of Angelica Bell, daughter of Vanessa Bell and niece of Virginia Woolf, in costume as the Russian Princess from Woolf's novel *Orlando*. Tate Archive.

CHAPTER 7

'Not a Story of Detection, of Crime and Punishment, but of Sin and Expiation': T. S. Eliot's Debt to Russia, Dostoevsky and Turgenev

T. S. Eliot's case, as an example of engagement with Russian culture, differs in a number of respects from some of the other writers covered in this book. Eliot is the only writer considered here who came from outside Europe. He is the only writer who, strictly speaking, lived in Britain as an émigré. Like his great predecessor in American literature Henry James, Eliot made a definitive move to Europe near the outset of his literary career. Indeed, Eliot took the step of becoming a British subject considerably earlier in his life than James did. Eliot is also the only writer of the six discussed who underwent a significant religious conversion, and this reconversion to Christianity took place during the period when he was perhaps most intensely under the influence of Russian literature.

There is nothing particularly novel about pointing out that T. S. Eliot's work owes a debt to Russian literature.[1] Yet, on the face of it, the Russian influence upon Eliot's work is largely confined to the earliest part of his output, and appears at first glance, in many respects, to diminish as his career progressed. Such a trend would be very much in line with the pattern observable with other writers covered in this study. However, it is vital to differentiate between overt, explicit references to and quotations from Russian literature (and evocations of Russian culture more generally) found

1 See especially Olga Ushakova, 'Russia and Russian Culture in *The Criterion* 1922–1939', in *A People Passing Rude*, ed. Anthony Cross (Cambridge: Open Book, 2012) pp. 231–40; and Ben Richardson, unpublished MA Thesis 'Unwrapping the Enigma: Russia in the Works of Wyndham Lewis, T. S. Eliot, and D. H. Lawrence, 1912–1939' (University of Canterbury, New Zealand, 2012).

in his creative work, and allusions which are far less obvious and, as it were, encrypted, yet frequently more significant in their implications for Eliot's literary standing, and as such constitute examples of the use of Russian literature as a form of cultural capital. It is also necessary to distinguish between the published texts of Eliot's poetic canon and the very different picture which emerges when the drafts of his work are examined in close detail. Furthermore, a distinction must be drawn between Eliot as poet and Eliot as playwright (a role he embraced increasingly in the inter-war years), and in addition between both of these creative aspects and Eliot in his capacity as editor, critic and essayist. When this wider field is considered the story of Eliot's engagement with Russian literature and culture is shown to be significantly more nuanced, and by no means a sequence which necessarily ends by the beginning of the 1930s, as is perhaps more commonly the case among the other writers reviewed here.

Eliot does not quote directly from anything in Russian in the published text of his most celebrated poem *The Waste Land* (1922), and this has arguably had the effect of focussing attention elsewhere in his work, and ample evidence has indeed been adduced of considerable influence from Dostoevsky on the work with which Eliot established himself, *The Love Song of J. Alfred Prufrock*, published in 1917. Scholarly assertions of the links between *Crime and Punishment* and the poem go back to 1945, although the value of the first such article, by John Pope, was subsequently qualified, because it misattributed the English translation of Dostoevsky involved. In fact Eliot himself said that he had begun the drafting of the poem at a date some four years earlier than Pope supposed. Eliot did nonetheless unequivocally confirm the importance of Dostoevsky's novels, including *Crime and Punishment* for his first major poem:

> During the period of my stay in Paris, Dostoevsky was very much a subject of interest amongst literary people and it was my friend and tutor, Alain-Fournier, who introduced me to this author. Under his instigation, I read *Crime and Punishment*, *The Idiot*, and *The Brothers Karamazov* in the French translation during the course

> of that winter. These three novels made a very profound impression on me and I had read them all before *Prufrock* was completed.[2]

Both the central idea of the fundamentally divided psyche of the hero of a poem which begins 'Let us go then you and I'[3] and Prufrock's more general failure to fit into contemporary urban society, almost a *locus classicus* of 'anomie' à la Emile Durkheim, and more specifically the importance of encountering female others on staircases, follow on from those moments which feature especially towards the beginning of *Crime and Punishment*. Eliot's actual, geographical setting for the poem – if it is anywhere specific – is most likely Paris or Boston – just possibly London – almost certainly *not* St Petersburg. But in literary terms the Russian, Dostoevskian parallel is hard to ignore. Compare the following passages from the novel:

> Raskolnikov went out in complete confusion. This confusion became more and more intense. As he went down the stairs, he even stopped short, two or three times, as though suddenly struck by some thought. When he was in the street he cried out, 'Oh, God, how loathsome it all is! and can I, can I possibly ... No, it's nonsense, it's rubbish!' he added resolutely. 'And how could such an atrocious thing come into my head? What filthy things my heart is capable of. Yes, filthy above all, disgusting, loathsome, loathsome! – and for a whole month I've been ...[4]

while in Chapter II:

> Raskolnikov was not used to crowds, and, as we said before, he avoided society of every sort, more especially of late. But now all at once he felt a desire to be with other people. Something new seemed to be taking place within him, and with it he felt a sort of thirst for company.[5]

2 John Pope, 'Prufrock and Raskolnikov Again', *American Literature* 18.4 (1947), pp. 319–21. (p. 319).

3 T. S. Eliot, *The Poems of T. S. Eliot*, ed. Christopher Ricks and Jim McCue, 2 vols (London: Faber & Faber, 2015), I, p. 5.

4 Fyodor Dostoevsky, *Crime and Punishment*, trans. Constance Garnett (New York: P. F. Collier & Son Corp., 1917), p. 8.

5 Ibid. p. 10.

Again, in Chapter VI: 'He rushed to the door, listened, caught up his hat and began to descend his thirteen steps cautiously, noiselessly, like a cat.'[6] And Prufrock's Hamlet-like indecisiveness tallies closely with Raskolnikov's disturbed state of mind:

> We may note in passing, one peculiarity in regard to all the final resolutions taken by him in the matter; they had one strange characteristic: the more final they were, the more hideous and the more absurd they at once became in his eyes. In spite of all his agonising inward struggle, he never for a single instant all that time could believe in the carrying out of his plans.[7]

Similarly, in Eliot's poem:

> There will be time, there will be time
> To prepare a face to meet the faces that you meet
> There will be time to murder and create,
> And time for all the works and days of hands
> That lift and drop a question on your plate;
> Time for you and time for me,
> And time yet for a hundred indecisions,
> And for a hundred visions and revisions,
> Before the taking of a toast and tea.[8]

Moreover, in Dostoevsky's novel the prominent theme of indecisiveness is arguably a clear and close precursor of Prufrock's procrastination:

> The question whether the disease gives rise to the crime, or whether the crime from its own peculiar nature is always accompanied by something of the nature of disease, he did not yet feel able to decide.
>
> When he reached these conclusions, he decided that in his own case there could not be such a morbid reaction, that his reason and will would remain unimpaired at the time of carrying out his design, for the simple reason that his design was 'not a crime …' We will omit all the process by means of which he arrived at this last conclusion; we have run too far ahead already […] We may add only that the practical, purely material difficulties of the affair occupied a secondary position in his mind.

6 Ibid. p. 70.

7 Ibid. p. 70

8 Eliot, *The Love Song of J. Alfred Prufrock*, p. 6.

> 'One has but to keep all one's will-power and reason to deal with them, and they will all be overcome at the time when once one has familiarised oneself with the minutest details of the business' [...] But this preparation had never been begun. His final decisions were what he came to trust least, and when the hour struck, it all came to pass quite differently, as it were accidentally and unexpectedly. One trifling circumstance upset his calculations, before he had even left the staircase.[9]

Having established the sources of Eliot's poem in *Crime and Punishment*, crucial distinctions must also be made. Although Prufrock talks of having 'time to murder and create', as Peter Lowe observes,[10] it is only Raskolnikov who in reality dares to take this action, whereas Prufrock asks 'do I dare disturb the universe?', and although the biblical allusion to the raising of Lazarus as an example of spiritual rebirth is found in both the earlier[11] and later works, it is only in Dostoevsky's novel, through the agency of Sonia Marmeladov, the erstwhile prostitute, that this can be achieved. It is almost as if Prufrock, having never dared to sin in the first place, is denied Raskolnikov's prospect of redemption and rebirth. Emphasising the contrasting sense of incompletion in Eliot, by comparison with the Russian novel, the female figures in Eliot's poem are characterised by fragmentation, dismembered, as it were, into their arms in isolation (and certainly not their legs):

> And I have known the arms already, known them all, –
> Arms that are braceleted and white and bare [...]
> Arms that lie along a table, or wrap about a shawl[12]

By contrast with Dostoevsky's prostitute, Eliot's female figures – if more than isolated arms – are mermaids, devoid of legs and as such of full female sexual identity: 'I have heard the mermaids singing, each to each.'[13]

9 Dostoevsky, *Crime and Punishment*, pp. 71–2.

10 Peter Lowe, 'Prufrock in St Petersburg', *Journal of Modern Literature* 28.3 (2005), pp. 1–24 (p. 10).

11 Dostoevsky, *Crime and Punishment*, p. 265.

12 Eliot, *The Love Song of J. Alfred Prufrock*, p. 7.

13 Ibid. p. 9.

Stylistically, it can be said that Eliot is strongly influenced by a key expressive device in Dostoevsky (as indeed in Russian fiction more generally), the ellipse. While critics have argued about which geographical real life city may have inspired Eliot's poems, and while it is granted that Eliot had not visited Russia at this date (nor was indeed ever to do so), the observation that the street layout, wherever it may be geographically, is first and foremost simply a representation of Prufrock's mind should nonetheless take into account the fact that the street plan peters out into an ellipsis:

> Streets that follow like a tedious argument
> Of insidious intent
> To lead you to an overwhelming question ...

And here it is surely relevant to quote from Eliot's fellow modernist, future publisher, and fellow Russophile Virginia Woolf, writing a decade later in *Orlando*,

> 'All ends in death', Orlando would say, sitting upright on the ice. But Sasha who after all had no English blood in her but was from Russia where the sunsets are longer, the dawns less sudden, and sentences often left unfinished from doubt as to how best to end them – Sasha stared at him, perhaps sneered at him, for he must have seemed a child to her, and said nothing.[14]

Dostoevsky is surely the most obvious candidate for Russian influence exerted upon Eliot and this has been discussed in the critical literature for almost seventy years, since the American critic John C. Pope produced his article *Prufrock and Raskolnikov* (1945). Yet Eliot himself was able to demonstrate that assumed references in the text to 1914 were in fact coincidental, since his poem had actually been written in France as early as 1911. And the supposed verbal allusions to the text of Garnett's English translation were also shown to be chance coincidences, Eliot having originally read *Crime*

14 Woolf, *Orlando*, p. 22; although, ironically, here Woolf employs the hyphen or dash rather than three dots of the ellipse so characteristic of Dostoevsky and Turgenev. (It is worth noting, also, that *Le Grand Meaulnes* (1913), by Eliot's tutor Alain-Fournier, whom Eliot credits for introducing him to Dostoevsky, is another novel famed for this stylistic device.)

and Punishment not in English but in French. In 1910 to 1911, in Paris, Eliot had met both Alain-Fournier, soon to be the author of *Le Grand Meaulnes*, and Jean Verdenal, later the posthumous dedicatee, 'mort aux Dardanelles', of *Prufrock and Other Observations*, and he was introduced to Dostoevsky's work by them.[15] This factor is of interest because it put Eliot to some extent in a different position from many other writers in England in the period, who were dependent to a greater extent upon the Constance Garnett translations, which were later criticised by Russian native speakers such as Vladimir Nabokov as 'dry and flat and always unbearably demure'[16] In the context of the present study, in the period leading up to and through the 1920s, Eliot may thus be distinguished from many literary acquaintances in London with whom he was on close terms, who do appear to have been more heavily reliant on the Garnett translation into English.

Eliot's correspondence certainly confirms the deep effect exerted upon him by his reading of Dostoevsky, which would have been reinforced by a dramatised version of *The Brothers Karamazov* then playing on the Paris stage, at the Théâtre des Arts in April 1911, directed by Copeau, which he is known to have witnessed. In the period around the end of World War I, after his removal to Britain, when he was working in a bank in London and had been married for more than a year to Vivien Haigh Wood, Dostoevsky is again mentioned by Eliot in his letters. His marriage was already beginning to unravel, at least in part thanks to Vivien's mental instability. Eliot himself was far from stable during this period, a little later undergoing a nervous breakdown from which he famously sought relief on Lake Geneva: 'By the waters of Leman I sat down and wept'[17] and then at a resort on the Kent coast:

> on Margate Sands.
> I can connect
> Nothing with nothing.[18]

15 David Chinitz, ed., *A Companion to T. S. Eliot* (London: Blackwell, 2009), p. 5.

16 Quoted in May, p. 38.

17 Eliot, *The Collected Poems of T. S. Eliot*, I, p. 62.

18 Ibid. p. 66.

Against such a backdrop Eliot wrote to his cousin Eleanor Hinkley on 21 July 1917:

> Life runs so rapidly over here that we never hear twice of the same person as being in the same place or doing quite the same thing. It is either killed or wounded, or fever, or going to gaol, or being let out of gaol, or being tried, or summoned before a tribunal of some kind. I have been living in one of Dostoevsky's novels, you see, not in one of Jane Austen's. If I have not seen the battle field, I have seen other strange things, and I have signed a cheque for two hundred thousand pounds while bombs fell about me. I have dined with a princess and with a man who expected two years hard labour, and it all seems like a dream. The most real thing was a little dance we went to a few days ago, something like yours used to be in a studio with a gramophone; I am sure you would have liked it and the people there.[19]

At this early point in his career Eliot sets up a binary opposition between the quintessentially English Austen (presumably deemed placid and domestic) and, as a Russian, Dostoevsky, visionary, but also possessed by visions. This same opposition occurred just two years later to Virginia Woolf. She produced her review of Dostoevsky's *An Uncle's Dream* entitled 'Dostoevsky in Cranford' published in the TLS in 1919. Focussing on Dostoevsky's violence and lack of restraint, Woolf quotes a speech from Constance Garnett's translation of Dostoevsky's novella 'The Uncle's Dream', originally published in Russia in 1859, which she cites as an example of the author in comic vein:

> But Dostoevsky cannot keep to that tripping measure for long. The language becomes abusive and the temper violent. This comedy has far more in common with the comedy of Wycherly than with the comedy of Jane Austen. It rapidly runs to seed, and becomes a helter-skelter, extravagant farce. The restraint and aloofness of the great comic writers are impossible to him [...] Because of his sympathy his laughter passes beyond merriment into a strange violent amusement which is not merry at all [...] Still we need not underrate the value of comedy because Dostoevsky makes the perfection of the English product appear to be the result of leaving out all the most important things. It is the old, unnecessary quarrel between the inch of smooth ivory and the six feet of canvas with its strong coarse grains.[20]

19 T. S. Eliot, *Letters of T. S. Eliot*, ed. Valerie Eliot and Hugh Haughton, 5 vols (New Haven, CT: Yale University Press, 2009–2014), I (2009), p. 189.

20 Virginia Woolf, *Books and Portraits* (London: Hogarth, 1977), pp. 121–2.

Beyond the 'strange violent amusement which is not merriment at all' Woolf identifies Dostoevsky's tendency to be insufficiently selective in his approach to narrative technique. That distinction between being selective and attempting to describe every detail, is what Woolf identifies as Dostoevsky's weakness, although also, she argues, his essential quality and therefore what makes him the figure he has become. Woolf says Dostoevsky 'because of his sympathy [...] is incapable, even when his story is hampered by the digression, of passing by anything so important and lovable as a man or a woman without stopping to consider their case and explain it'.[21]

This idea of the unselective is signally relevant to Eliot's most extended poem after *Prufrock*, *The Waste Land* of 1922. For here, thanks to the intervention as editor of a second poet, Eliot's fellow American émigré in Europe Ezra Pound, the question of selection comes very much to the fore. On the strength of the published text of the poem, which appeared in pamphlet form by way of the Hogarth Press in London that year, there appears to be far less of a Russian character to Eliot's work here than had been the case five years earlier.

In the trajectory of Eliot's early poetic career, a poem written between *Prufrock* and *The Waste Land*, the short, metrically regular and highly focussed 32 line *Whispers of Immortality* might initially be interpreted as the last petering out of an initial interest in Russian culture (representing a 'falling off' indeed from a Russian classic, Dostoevsky's most famous work *Crime and Punishment*, which had permeated *Prufrock*.) The bulk of Eliot's poem of May/June 1918 appears at first reading to be exclusively associated with English literature. (Though fresh from studying philosophy at Harvard, Eliot here limits himself to 'our metaphysics', by contrast with the near contemporary *Sweeney Erect*, where he mentions the philosopher Emerson by name.) The title *Whispers of Immortality* is an ironic allusion to Wordsworth's *Ode. Intimations of Immortality* (1815), and this almost seems to go against the grain of Eliot's pronouncements as critic in *The Sacred Wood* collection of essays of 1919, which amount to a rejection of romanticism and its cult of personality and feeling. By contrast, in 'Tradition

21 Ibid. p. 121.

and the Individual Talent' Eliot proclaims the primacy of 'impersonality'. Beyond the expectations set up by the title, the opening half of *Intimations of Immortality* – the first four quatrains – appears to assert Englishness, admittedly of an older vintage than that of the Romantics. Eliot alludes first to the Jacobean playwright Webster, author of *The Duchess of Malfi* and *The White Devil*, and brings in images of death and decay – 'the skull beneath the skin', and even subverts Wordsworth's romanticism by comparing dead eyeballs to 'daffodils', evoking Wordsworth's 'I Wandered Lonely As a Cloud' lyric of 1807. From Webster Eliot proceeds to John Donne, preeminent among the metaphysical poets, who is also associated with death and decay:

> He knew the anguish of the marrow
> The ague of the skeleton.[22]

However, from the middle of the poem, the fifth quatrain, there is a significant change of gear. From classic figures of the tradition of English literature (as chosen by an American), – a full century old in Wordsworth's case, over 300 years in the case of Donne and Webster – the poem comes emphatically into the London of the early twentieth century. Yet the London Eliot offers the reader is (appropriately, given that the author is himself an American émigré, still the best part of eight years away from taking British citizenship) distinctly cosmopolitan. For the figure from contemporary London is a Russian woman 'Grishkin' who is not primarily a literary but a real life personality. Moreover, Eliot compares her to a 'sleek Brazilian jaguar'.[23] Grishkin is in fact depicted as being more 'feline' than the Brazilian tiger, and sexually alluring, 'uncorseted', 'friendly', with her 'bust' giving 'promise' of 'pneumatic bliss', although it may be observed that Grishkin promises but may perhaps not deliver 'pneumatic bliss'. Of interest is that the representative of Russia here, Grishkin is not first and foremost taken from Russian literature but very much from real life. Grishkin is merely an invented

22 Eliot, *The Poems of T.S. Eliot*, I, p. 78.

23 Ibid. p. 48.

pseudonym,[24] and the real life figure who inspired her was identified in Ezra Pound's memoirs *Pavannes and Divagations* as the Russian prima ballerina, trained at the Mariinsky Theatre and subsequently a star of the Ballets Russes, Serafima Astafieva (1876–1934), who had danced in the west with the Ballets Russes and then settled there, founding a ballet school in London in 1914. She was a friend of Ezra Pound, and he calculatedly (by his own admission) took Eliot to meet her in 1918, in the hope that a poem would result from the encounter between the sensual prima ballerina and poet: 'I took Parson Elyot to see the Prima Ballerina and it evoked "Grushkin"'.[25] It duly did, although the poem seems perversely to have been born of the intense repulsion which Eliot evidently experienced towards the dancer. His reaction does not really tally with that of others who met Astafieva. Pound himself felt that Eliot had dealt harshly with her, when he recalled this meeting (long after Eliot's reconversion to Christianity, and indeed after the publication of the explicitly Christian *Four Quartets*.) What is of interest here is that the Russian figure is equated with the animal. Just as the first half of the poem balances Webster and Donne, so here a Russian female human figure is partnered, as it were, with a Brazilian panther, a supremely predatory creature. Henry James's metaphor for fear of sexual intimacy 'The Beast in the Jungle' in his 1903 short story of that name is called to mind. The character is introduced beguilingly into the poem: 'Grishkin is nice'. However, even that word may be undercut. Eliot has already put the reader in mind of the Jacobean tragedian Webster and the metaphysical poet *par excellence* John Donne, and in the English of that period 'nice' can carry the connotation 'wanton'.[26] The Russian is in one sense equated with the subhuman and the bestial, yet at the same time

24 Jeffrey Perl says that the name of the heroine, a 'louche cosmopolitan' is 'griskin with a Russian accent' and 'means the lean part of the loin of a bacon pig' (Jeffrey Perl, *A Dictatorship of Relativism* (Durham, NC: Duke University Press, 2007), p. 353).

25 Ezra Pound, *Pavannes and Divagations* (New York: New Directions, 1958), p. 161.

26 William Shakespeare, *Love's Labour's Lost*, in *The Plays of Shakespeare*, 9 vols (London: William Pickering, 1825), II, p. 166. 'These are complements, these are humours, these betray nice wenches that would be betrayed without these' (Shakespeare, *Love's Labour's Lost*, II, p. 162).

denied even the authenticity of the animal. For Grishkin's bust only promises 'pneumatic bliss' and her appearance is a masterpiece of artifice 'her Russian eye ... underlined for emphasis'. The London setting is invaded by creatures from the tropical jungle – the 'marmoset' and 'Brazilian jaguar' and the equally exotic but also equally 'rank' smelling and feline Russian femme fatale. Russia may be said to feature prominently in the poem, but scarcely to its credit.

Where *The Love Song of J. Alfred Prufrock* had taken its setting (the staircase) and the idea of the split personality and the indecisions from a classic narrative of Russian literature much admired by Eliot, here the Russian element appears to be much slighter, albeit sinister, and the animus experienced by the poet towards the female Russian figure is hard to account for. Where *Prufrock* had alluded to *Crime and Punishment*, a novel in which a prostitute (Sonia Marmeladova) is a redemptive figure and associated with religious conversion, here the Russian element seems to be confined to a single real life Russian, a friend of his closest literary associate, whose character Eliot is bent upon assassinating. Astafieva [Grishkin] is all but labelled a prostitute, and associated with 'effluence of cat'.[27] Ezra Pound himself later had regrets, though responsible for the encounter in the first place, for having deliberately pitted the intellectual and diffident Eliot against a star of the ballet who, now ageing, appears to depend upon artifice for the impression she creates, and perhaps can only promise and allure rather than actually satisfy lusts. By the date of this poem Astafieva would already have been reaching retirement as a dancer and moving into a career as a teacher. (Born in 1876, she was a full dozen years Eliot's senior.)

Perhaps Pound cannot be blamed for having entertained greater hopes of the meeting between the American and Russian. Eliot certainly did not react negatively to the ballet and ballet dancers in general. He first developed an enthusiasm specifically for Russian ballet during his stay in Paris between 1909 and 1911 – when the writer Jacques Rivière, Verdenal and Alain-Fournier shared his enthusiasm. But in Paris he was viewing the dancers at a distance, on stage, whereas the encounter in real life and in

27 Eliot, *The Poems of T. S. Eliot*, I, p. 47.

London provokes a quite different response, half a dozen years later, characterised by distrust and a charge of artifice. It is ambiguous whether Eliot is accusing Grishkin of in some way passing herself off as Russian by means of make-up, when in reality she is something else; or whether he is saying that Russia is synonymous with artifice and seduction achieved by means of cosmetics. There might even be at least some likelihood that the former is the case, if Eliot thought that Astafieva was of Russian–Jewish descent. This is not clear from the poem, but Eliot suggests Russian Jewish descent in another poem from the same period 'Sweeney Among the Nightingales', where the prostitute is called 'Rachel *née* Rabinovitch'[28] and in similarly animal fashion 'Tears at the grapes with murderous paws'. Alternatively, the implication is that all Russians, whether gentile or Jewish, are inclined to create a false persona by artificial means such as the use of make-up. The further irony here is that, according to Virginia Woolf (and others), Eliot was himself not averse to wearing make-up.[29] Not only is Eliot's personal animus towards Astafieva surprising – her celebrated pupils Anton Dolin and Anna Markova spoke warmly and admiringly of her – but the suggestion of artifice conveyed by 'Whispers of Immortality', when her biography is considered, appears perverse in the extreme. For Astafieva in fact came from a distinguished aristocratic family[30] and was related to Leo Tolstoy, who was her great uncle. Indeed one of her forebears is mentioned in *Anna Karenina*:

> As is invariably the case, after they had been asked at what price they wanted rooms, it appeared that there was not one decent room for them; one decent room had been taken by the inspector of railroads, another by a lawyer from Moscow, a third by Princess Astafieva from the country.[31]

28 Ibid. p. 51.

29 12 March 1922, Woolf reports that Mary [Hutchison] says Eliot 'uses violet powder to make him look cadaverous' (Woolf, *Diary*, II, p. 171); and again 27 September 1922: 'I am not sure that he does not paint his lips' (Woolf, *Diary*, II, p. 204); quoted in Lee, p. 443.

30 At her death, in London in 1934, she was styled Princess Astafieva.

31 Leo Tolstoy, *Anna Karenina*, trans. Nathan Dole (New York: Thomas Crowell, 1899), p. 329.

On this occasion at least, it appears that Eliot, normally so keenly aware of literary allusions, was obstinately blind to Astafieva's true social status. In terms of the overall development of Eliot's career, viewed after *Prufrock*, *Whispers of Immortality* definitely appears to suggest a decline in the importance of Russia and Russian culture for the American poet. While *Prufrock* depends crucially upon a knowledge of a classic novel, one of the cornerstones of Russian culture for which Eliot himself expressed great reverence, here the immortal literary works of Wordsworth, Webster and Donne are contrasted with a Russian figure who, as a dancer, was not strictly creative in the first place, and whose art form, ballet, as a performance art is highly ephemeral. The ageing prima ballerina is now libelled as a high class (but also highly artificial) prostitute. This represents a marked progression from *Crime and Punishment* , the Russian influence upon *The Love Song of J. Alfred Prufrock*, whose heroine Sonia is both prostitute and a figure of redemption for Raskolnikov.

On the strength of this seeming decline in the prominence of Russian culture in Eliot's poetry it should come as no surprise to discover that his most celebrated, and at that date most extended poem *The Waste Land*, of 1922, makes no obvious and inescapable references to Russia, Russians or Russian culture. Although it slips at will into French, German and the Italian of Dante, has an epigraph in Latin and Ancient Greek, and ends in the Sanskrit of the Upanishads, the poem does not quote anything in Russian, a language which, unlike his contemporaries Lawrence, Mansfield, and Woolf, Eliot does not appear to have known at all. Near the beginning of the poem's first section 'The Burial of the Dead' the voice of Marie Laritsch, the fin-de-siècle Bavarian courtier and sometime intermediary in the Mayerling scandal, says

> 'Bin gar keine Russin., stamm' aus Litauen, echt deutsch'[32]
> ['I am no Russian but a Lithuanian, a true German']

And this seems to be as close as Eliot comes to evoking Russia directly in his lament for the decline of Western civilisation catalysed by World War

32 Eliot, *The Poems of T. S. Eliot.*, I, p. 55.

I. Annexed to Russia since 1795, in the era of Catherine the Great (ironically herself of German descent), Lithuania enjoyed de facto independence from Tsarist Russia from 1915, when it was occupied by Germany's forces under Kaiser Wilhelm III, and declared its independence at the end of World War I, but was invaded by the fledgling Bolshevik regime in 1919, then reoccupied by the Poles in 1920. At the time when Eliot was composing *The Waste Land*, in Switzerland, Lithuania was joining the League of Nations, whose headquarters were adjacent at Geneva. Eliot's poem reflects European political events which were unfolding even as he drafted it, but the speaker overheard at this point is at pains to deny Russian nationality and to assert that she is a Lithuanian of pure German, and not Slav pedigree.

Yet though on the surface the published version of *The Waste Land* may make little obvious reference to Russia, perusal of the poet's widow's 1971 facsimile edition of the preliminary drafts of the poem, so drastically edited by Pound, reveals a quite different picture. On p. 127, for example, in her notes for 'The Fire Sermon' Valerie Eliot mentions that Eliot drafted 'the two paragraphs that follow, ending with a parody of *Prufrock*:

> If one had said, yawning and settling a shawl
> Oh no, I did not like the *Sacre* at all, not at all.'[33]

And Pound's marginalia at this point spell out the name of Grishkin (he uses the spelling 'Grushkin') once again. In fact, recently published research by Christopher Ricks and Jim McCue reveals that these lines were actually a 'part-reconstruction and "part-reimagining" of the opening of Part III' and were published in an article in *The Criterion* for April 1924. In *Letters of the Moment* by 'F. M.' in *The Criterion,* April 1924, the couplets were 'flung' as 'obsequies' for the 'Caroline renovations' by the Phoenix Society, such as the production of Wycherly's *The Country Wife* in February that year.[34] Thus, far from Eliot's interest in Russia having faded since 1918, with *Prufrock* and *Whispers of Immortality* lying definitely in the past, the Russian

33 T. S. Eliot, *The Waste Land: a facsimile & transcript*, ed. Valerie Eliot (London: Faber & Faber, 1971), p. 127.

34 Eliot, *The Poems of T. S. Eliot*, I, p. 648.

frame of reference still meant enough to the poet in 1924 for him to rewrite a part of *The Waste Land* emphasising the Slav dimension, restoring aspects which had been toned down by Pound's editing in 1922. And elsewhere in the original drafts of the poem Eliot had also said (in the deleted 'Fresca' stanzas which initially formed the first seventy-two lines, all in rhyming couplets à la Pope,) that the female figure here is an example, along with Scandinavian literature (presumably Ibsen, possibly Strindberg) and the nineteenth-century aesthetes, of the Russian craze:

> Women grown intellectual grow dull,
> [who] ... lose the mother wit of natural trull.
> Fresca was baptized in a soapy sea
> Of Symonds – Walter Pater – Vernon Lee.
> The Scandinavians bemused her wits,
> The Russians thrilled her to hysteric fits.[35]

Furthermore, Pound's manuscript marginalia annotating 'The Fire Sermon' lines 138–9 reveal that Pound at least thought Grishkin was still being evoked here, when Eliot presents the figure of the 'typist home at teatime' who is involved in a crude and perfunctory sexual encounter with the 'young man carbuncular':

> A bright kimono wraps her as she sprawls
> In nerveless torpor on the window seat;
> A touch of art is given by the false
> Japanese print, purchased in Oxford Street.[36]

Against these lines in the early draft Pound scribbles 'mix up of the couplet & grishkin not good'.[37]

The spelling of Grishkin's name is, in itself, in some ways akin to Woolf's 'Lapinova' in her short story (see Chapter 6), a contradictory curiosity. For no Russian name for a woman would end in '-in' but rather would normally take the form 'Grishkina'. Pound, both in his marginalia for *The Waste Land*

35 Eliot, *The Waste Land: a facsimile and manuscript*, p. 41.
36 Ibid. p. 45.
37 Ibid. p. 45.

and in his later references to Astafieva in the *Pisan Cantos*, often uses the variant spelling 'Grushkin'. This is certainly a common Russian surname, and Grusha can be an abbreviated form of the male name 'Gavril'. The name may even conceivably be intended to recall 'Grushenka'. If this is the case a possible Russian literary allusion to the femme fatale in Dostoevsky's *The Brothers Karamazov* may be involved. Eliot had certainly read this novel in French translation, as well as *Crime and Punishment* and *The Idiot* on the recommendation of Alain-Fournier in 1910. In Dostoevsky's novel Agrafena Alexandrovna Svetlova (also known as Grushenka, Grusha, or Grushka) is a kept woman and moreover a temptress, who plays off Dmitrii Karamazov against his father Fyodor, both rivals for her affections. If Pound coined the nickname (Astafieva was his friend rather than Eliot's in the first instance) this literary allusion is possible, and, having read *The Brothers Karamazov*, Eliot might equally have come up with this formulation. Whatever the exact spelling and origin of the heroine's name, this poem serves as an interesting marker in the developing story of Eliot's engagement with Russia. Where in *Prufrock* he had been drawing upon literary sources here he was, in the first instance, responding to a real-life Russian whom he was encountering socially. Eliot's poem seems to betray very little of Astafieva's actual history, for as already mentioned in relation to *Whispers of Immortality*, Astafieva came from a well-connected family. This, however, appears to have been lost on Eliot, who simply prefers to suggest that she is morally louche and moreover superficial and almost a fake. But then, it has been observed that Eliot was actually drawn to the Ballets Russes less by the ballerinas than by the male principals. Susan Jones in *Literature, Modernism and Dance* has remarked on how Eliot praised Leonid Massine for achieving in dance the 'impersonality', which he exalted in his critical essay 'Tradition and the Individual Talent' of 1919, and describes him as 'unhuman, impersonal and abstract'.[38] These characteristics are, ironically, closer to the metaphysical forms and pure ideas with which Eliot, in 'Whispers of Immortality' contrasts the sensual and carnal Astafieva (Grishkin) with the 'Abstract Entities'. For once Eliot, the author on whom no literary allusion seems to

38 Jones, p. 234.

have been lost, seems fundamentally to have misjudged a literary allusion as it were brought to life in his own time.

If Eliot failed to respond to Astafieva, in this he was much at odds with at least one of his heroes from the Ballets Russes, Anton Dolin, who, with Alicia Markova, was to organise a fitting tribute to Astafieva, when she died in the mid-1930s, not yet seventy years old. Eliot's enthusiasm for Dolin and Massine, as well as above all for Nijinsky is in marked contrast with the attack on Astafieva. He reports of Leonid Massine 'I quite fell in love' with him' and a whole section 'The Death of Saint Narcissus' (ultimately deleted thanks to Pound) formed part of the early drafts of *The Waste Land*. It seems ironically apt (given his diffidence towards Astafieva) that Eliot should base a whole (subsequently deleted) section of *The Waste Land* on the male figure from Greek mythology who was most oblivious to the charms of the female. This section was inspired by the ballet *Narcisse*, set to music by and choreographed and danced by Vaslav Nijinsky. Eliot had the opportunity to watch it in Paris. According to Nancy Hargrove, 'Eliot's knowledge of the dance, which seems to have begun in Paris in 1911, influenced his poetry, drama, and critical ideas far more heavily than has been generally realised'[39] and the figure of the completely self-absorbed male dancer is at the far end of the spectrum from Astafieva with her 'coquetry'. By contrast St Narcissus is described as 'a dancer to God', forswearing the lusts of the flesh, and dedicating himself to God some years before Eliot's reconversion to Christianity, in 1926.

Thus, thanks to the Diaghilev Ballets Russes, the Russian influence appears to have persisted with Eliot into the mid-1920s, indeed he even went to the lengths in *The Criterion*, the quarterly literary journal which he had been editing since October 1922, of reasserting Russian references in *The Waste Land* which Pound had edited out prior to its first publication. Further evidence of the continuing importance of both Dostoevsky and a view of the Russian sphere in general is to be found, not in either lines deleted or added, but in the notes which Eliot appended to the poem from its first appearance. There may be no point in the poem where it is suggested

39 Nancy Hargrove, 'T. S. Eliot and the Dance', *Journal of Modern Literature* 21.1 (1997), 61–88 (p. 62).

that the 'unreal city' (variously Athens, Jerusalem, Athens, Alexandria,/ Vienna, London) is identified as either Moscow or St Petersburg, yet Eliot's notes to lines 366 of the poem's concluding section 'What the Thunder Said' 'what is that sound high in the air' are the occasion for Eliot to quote, in the original German, from Hermann Hesse's then very recent essay 'Blick ins Chaos' (1920). In the English translation, by Eliot's friend and fellow contributor to *The Criterion*, Stephen Schiff (under the pseudonym Stephen Hudson), this reads:

> Already half Europe, at all events half Eastern Europe, is on the road to Chaos. In a state of drunken illusion she is reeling into the abyss and, as she reels, she sings a drunken hymn such as Dmitri Karamazov sang. The insulted citizen laughs that song to scorn, the saint and seer hear it with tears.[40]

Earlier in the essay Hesse had said:

> The ideal of the Karamazov, primeval, Asiatic, and occult, is already beginning to consume the European soul. That is what I mean by the downfall of Europe. This downfall is a return home to the mother, a turning back to Asia, to the source, to the *Faüstischen Muttern* and will necessarily lead, like every death on earth, to a new birth.[41]

And having identified this essence as coming from a source outside Europe, which is Oriental: 'What is that Asiatic Ideal that I find in Dostoevsky, the effect of which will be, as I see it, to overwhelm Europe?'[42] Hesse says that this 'Asiatic Ideal' will amount to

> 'the rejection of every strongly-held Ethic and Moral in favour of a comprehensive *laissez-faire*.' ... The saintly Alyosha becomes ever more worldly, the worldly brothers more saintly; and similarly the most unprincipled and unbridled of them becomes

40 Hermann Hesse, *In Sight of Chaos*, trans. Sydney Schiff (Zurich-Seldwyla-London: A Zwemmer, 1923), p. 13.

41 Ibid. p. 14.

42 Ibid. p. 14

> the saintliest, the most sensitive, the most spiritual prophet of a new holiness, of a new morality, of a new mankind.[43]

Hesse's is a pessimistic view, albeit the process of the interaction of a decadent Europe and an invasive Russia is dynamic:

> It seems, then, that the 'New Ideal' by which the roots of the European spirit is being sapped, is an entirely amoral concept, a faculty to feel the Godlike, the significant, the fatalistic, in the wickedest and in the ugliest, and even to accord them veneration and worship [...] Dangerous, emotional, irresponsible, yet conscience-haunted; soft, dreamy, cruel, yet fundamentally childish. As such one still likes to regard the 'Russian man' to-day, although, I believe, he has for a long time been on the road to becoming the European man. And this is the Downfall of Europe.[44]

Hesse asserts that the idea of the 'Russian' man archetype was not born with Dostoevsky, but has merely been demonstrated most effectively by this author:

> Let us look at this 'Russian man' a moment. He is far older than Dostoevsky, but Dostoevsky has finally shown him to the world in all his fearful significance. The 'Russian man' is Karamazov, he is Fyodor Pavlovitch, he is Dmitri, he is Ivan, he is Alyosha. These four, different as they may appear, belong inseparably together. Together they are Karamazov, together they are the 'Russian man', together they are the approaching, the proximate man of the European crisis.[45]

Hesse then specifies the dichotomy between 'civilised' and 'European' on the one hand and 'Russian' and 'hysterical' on the other:

> Next notice something very remarkable. Ivan in the course of the story turns from a civilised man into a Karamazov, from a European into a Russian, out of a definitely formed historical type into the unformed raw material of Destiny.[46]

43 Ibid. pp. 14–16.
44 Ibid. pp. 16–17.
45 Ibid. pp. 17–18.
46 Ibid. p. 18.

Hesse also identifies the phantasmagorical or delirious quality in Dostoevsky which is perhaps akin to the qualities in the first half of *Crime and Punishment* which Eliot had exploited in *The Love Song of J. Alfred Prufrock*:

> There is a fairy-like dream-reality about the way in which Ivan slides out of his original psychology: out of his understanding, coolness, knowledge. There is mystical truth in this sliding of the apparently solid brother into the hysterical, into the Russian, into the Karamazov-like. It is just he, the doubter, who at the end holds speech with the devil! We will come to that later on;[47]

but then complicates his analysis by saying that the Russian psyche in fact embraces all the extremes which can never be appreciated from the rational and moral, yet also imaginatively limited European standpoint:

> So the 'Russian man' is drawn neither as the hysterical, the drunkard, the felon, the poet, the Saint, but as one with them all, as possessing all these characteristics simultaneously. The 'Russian man', Karamazov, is assassin and judge, ruffian and tenderest soul, the completest egotist and the most self-sacrificing hero. We shall not get a grasp of him from a European, from a hard and fast moral, ethical, dogmatic standpoint. In this man the outward and the inward, Good and Evil, God and Satan are united.[48]

Hesse goes on to account for the European-Russian (Asiatic) dichotomy in terms which take in World War I:

> The 'Russian man' has long existed, he exists far outside Russia, he rules half Europe, and part of the dreaded explosion has indeed in these last years been audibly evident. It shows itself in that Europe is tired, it shows itself in that Europe wants to turn homeward, in that Europe wants rest, in that Europe wants to be recreated, reborn.[49]

And while highly critical of the limitations of Kaiser Wilhelm III, Hesse thinks that, though neither wise nor profound, the German autocrat nevertheless identified accurately the threat to Europe from Russia and the Orient:

47 Ibid. pp. 18–19.
48 Ibid. pp. 18–19.
49 Ibid. p. 21.

> I allude to the Kaiser Wilhelm [...] he warned the European nations to guard their 'holiest possessions' against the approaching peril from the East [...] The Kaiser knew but partially the import of his words and how uncommonly right he was. He certainly did not know the Karamazovs, he had a horror of profound thought, but he had an uncannily right foreboding. The danger was coming nearer every day. That danger was the Karamazovs, the contagion from the East. What he unconsciously but rightly feared was the staggering back of the tired European spirit to the Asiatic mother.[50]

The quotation by Eliot in the notes to the poem, of merely the last four lines of Hesse's essay, with the image evoked of half of the European continent coming under the sway of Russia, perceived here as the 'staggering back of the tired European spirit to the Asiatic mother' casts Russia as a kind of primordial earth-mother figure, from which sophisticated Europe has distanced itself hitherto, and to which it must now, in its decadence, inevitably return. Detailed scrutiny, as above, of the Hesse essay reveals that the idea of Russia as fundamentally and inevitably Oriental and Asiatic is here expressed with unqualified force.

In 1925, Eliot's next extended poem after *The Waste Land*, *The Hollow Men* begins with the following lines:

> We are the hollow men
> We are the stuffed men
> Leaning together
> Headpiece filled with straw, Alas![51]

This has been interpreted in many different ways: by reference to the English tradition of burning straw effigies of the 1604 Gunpowder Plotter and would-be regicide Guy Fawkes each 5 November; to Ancient Roman rituals; and by reference to Frazer's *The Golden Bough*, which Eliot had already made extensive use of in *The Waste Land*. Perhaps Eliot left the image deliberately unglossed – though the epigraph he gives *The Hollow Men* is borrowed from Conrad's 1899 novella *Heart of Darkness*, which might suggest some kinship with the skulls on poles around Kurtz's hut in that tale. Claiming the authority of Eliot himself, Valerie Eliot says that he told her

50 Ibid. pp. 22–3.
51 Eliot, *Poems of T. S. Eliot*, I, p. 81.

they were inspired by the figure of the puppet of that name in Stravinsky's 1909 ballet *Petrushka*. Certainly Eliot maintained a pronounced enthusiasm over two decades for Diaghilev's company, and perhaps especially for the pioneering works of Stravinsky which they performed, so such an attribution is perfectly reasonable, and on numerous occasions editorial articles in *The Criterion* praised Diaghilev's troupe. It might even be possible that this image in Eliot's poem inspired the image of the straw doll of the Moor with which Woolf, who saw Eliot regularly during this period, opens *Orlando* (although that might equally be associated with Shakespeare's *Othello*):

> He – for there could be no doubt of his sex, though the fashion of the time did something to disguise it – was in the act of slicing at the head of a Moor which swung from the rafters. It was the colour of an old football, and more or less the shape of one, save for the sunken cheeks and a strand or two of coarse, dry hair, like the hair on a cocoanut. Orlando's father, or perhaps his grandfather, had struck it from the shoulders of a vast Pagan who had started up under the moon in the barbarian fields of Africa; and now it swung, gently, perpetually, in the breeze which never ceased blowing through the attic rooms of the gigantic house of the lord who had slain him.[52]

And when Orlando, in the company of Sasha, comes upon a performance of *Othello* it is, aptly, almost mistaken for a Punch and Judy show:

> The main press of people, it appeared, stood opposite a booth or stage something like our Punch and Judy show upon which some kind of theatrical performance was going forward. A black man was waving his arms and vociferating. There was a woman in white laid upon a bed. Rough though the staging was, the actors running up and down a pair of steps and sometimes tripping, and the crowd stamping their feet and whistling, or when they were bored, tossing a piece of orange peel on to the ice which a dog would scramble for, still the astonishing, sinuous melody of the words stirred Orlando like music.[53]

By the mid-1920s the Diaghilev element of Russophilia was arguably on the wane, even before the early death of the impresario, and there appears also to be a move away from the emphasis upon Dostoevsky which had so dominated both Woolf and Eliot in the second and early third decades

52 Woolf, *Orlando*, p. 13.

53 Ibid. p. 54.

of the century. Turning to Eliot in his capacity as editor of *The Criterion*, rather than as poet, in the mid-1920s Turgenev recurs in his relationship with Russian literature. Back in the second decade Eliot had likened his own early married life to a Dostoevsky novel, but now it is Turgenev whom he alludes to in a prose piece about contemporary Britain published in February 1925. For this piece borrowed its title from one of the most canonical of Russian nineteenth-century novels, Turgenev's *On the Eve* of 1860. This novel dealt very much with the concept of creating a 'typical Russian' character in fiction, as observed by Edward Garnett, when Constance Garnett's English translation appeared 35 years later. In the introduction to the English translation of *On the Eve* (1895) Edward Garnett says:

> This creation of an universal national type, out of the flesh and blood of a fat taciturn country gentleman, brings us to see that Turgenev was not merely an artist, but that he was a poet using fiction as his medium. To this end it is instructive to compare Jane Austen, perhaps the greatest English exponent of the domestic novel, with the Russian master, and to note that, while as a novelist she emerges favourably from the comparison, she is absolutely wanting in his poetic insight. How petty and parochial appears her outlook in *Emma*, compared to the wide and unflinching gaze of Turgenev. She painted most admirably the English types she knew, and how well she knew them! but she failed to correlate them with the national life; and yet, while her men and women were acting and thinking, Trafalgar and Waterloo were being fought and won. But each of Turgenev's novels in some subtle way suggests that the people he introduces are playing their little part in a great national drama everywhere around us, invisible, yet audible through the clamour of voices near us.[54]

This is certainly at odds with Hesse's notion of the Russian character, by reference to *The Brothers Karamazov* in 'Blick ins Chaos', or Eliot's description of his own high-pressure, almost dream-like life during wartime, which he likened to 'living in one of Dostoevsky's novels, you see, not in one of Jane Austen's.' Yet clearly, for all his use of Dostoevsky, Eliot also demonstrated the profound and lasting influence upon him of his polar opposite within Russian literature, Ivan Turgenev. Looking at Eliot's correspondence with Eleanor Hinkley on 31 December 1917, we find him recommending

54 Edward Garnett, Introduction to Ivan Turgenev, *On the Eve*, trans. Constance Garnett (London: Macmillan Company, 1920), pp. i–xvi (pp. xiii–xiv).

Turgenev to her, in company with Henry James and Stendhal: 'I have been reading Turgenev with great delight – he is one of the very greatest.'[55] And again on 1 April 1918:

> I think you might like Turgenev. I admire him as much as any novelist, but especially in the *Sportsman's Sketches*. His method looks simple and slight, but he is a consummate master with it. A *House of Gentlefolk* is good. I come more and more to demand that novels should be well written, and perceive more clearly the virtues and defects of the Victorians.[56]

Here Eliot's praise 'I admire him as much as any novelist' is arguably ambiguous, since elsewhere the poet, as editor of *The Criterion*, is known to claim that prose fiction, presumably by contrast with poetry or drama – which for Eliot always had to be poetic drama – was something whose value he could only dimly appreciate, something he considered perhaps irredeemably banal: 'When prose-fiction, after its strange and millennial birth struggles, got itself born at last Dullness saw her chance and took it.'[57]

One of Eliot's abiding ideas, both implicitly in an essay such as 'Tradition and the Individual Talent', and explicitly in his *Criterion* editorials, is the notion of a European culture, and a common European tradition: 'The general idea is found in the continuity of the impulse of Rome to the present day. It suggests Authority and Tradition [...] It is in fact the European idea – the idea of a common culture of Western Europe.'[58]

When assessing the importance for Eliot of Russian culture, and in particular Russian literature, the question which inevitably arises is whether Eliot actually considered Russia to be part of Europe. The answer is ambiguous. Sometimes Eliot appears to conform with the widely held view that Russian culture is under-developed and, overall, insubstantial, at least by

55 T. S. Eliot, letter to Eleanor Hinkley, 31 December 1917, Eliot, *Letters of T. S. Eliot*, I, p. 217.

56 Eliot, letter to Eleanor Hinkley, 1 April 1918, *Letters of T. S. Eliot*, I, p. 227.

57 *The Criterion 1922–1939* (London: Faber, 1967), I.1 (1922), p. 13; quoted in D. Chinitz, *T. S. Eliot and the Cultural Divide* (Chicago: University of Chicago Press, 2005) p. 54.

58 T. S. Eliot, 'Commentary', *The Criterion* 4. 2 (1926), 221–2 (p. 222).

comparison with ('other') European examples, such as presumably France and Germany, perhaps Italy. Here is what Eliot dogmatically asserts in a 'Commentary' (editorial) for the October 1923 edition of *The Criterion*: 'Three or four great novelists do not make a literature, though *War and Peace* is a very great novel indeed.'[59] However, at other points Eliot appears to be more inclined to regard Russians as belonging to the same cultural world as his own. When talking of the genetic and ethnic roots of later European culture, Eliot seems to have no problem about including Russia. For example, in the same Commentary, Eliot repeats the idea that Europeans had their racial origins in Scythia, the suggestion being that the Greek and Latin traditions share a common ancestry with the Slavs. It is possible that Eliot might have been influenced in this assertion by ideas to be found in Garnett's preface to her translation of Turgenev:

> How doubly welcome that art should be which can lead us, the foreigners, thus straight to the heart of the national secrets of a great people, secrets which our own critics and diplomatists must necessarily misrepresent. Each of Turgenev's novels may be said to contain a light-bringing rejoinder to the old-fashioned criticism of the Muscovite, current up to the rise of the Russian novel, and still, unfortunately, lingering among us; but *On the Eve*, of all the novels, contains perhaps the most instructive political lesson England can learn. Europe has always had, and most assuredly England has been over-rich in those alarm-monger critics, watchdogs for ever baying at Slav cupidity, treachery, intrigue, and so on and so on. It is useful to have these well-meaning animals on the political premises, giving noisy tongue whenever the Slav stretches out his long arm and opens his drowsy eyes, but how rare it is to find a man who can teach us to interpret a nation's aspirations, to gauge its inner force, its aim, its inevitability. Turgenev gives us such clues.[60]

and equally in the text itself of Turgenev's novel *On the Eve*, where Shubin declares in Chapter II,

> 'I would have another bathe, said Shubin, 'only I'm afraid of being late. Look at the river; it seems to beckon us. The ancient Greeks would have beheld a nymph in it. But we are not Greeks, O nymph! we are thick-skinned Scythians.'
> 'We have *roussalkas*', observed Bersenyev.

59 T. S. Eliot, 'Notes', *The Criterion* 2. 5 (1923), 104–5 (p. 104).

60 Edward Garnett, Introduction to *On the Eve*, p. xvi.

> 'Get along with your *roussalkas!* What's the use to me – a sculptor – of those children of a cold, terror-stricken fancy, those shapes begotten in the stifling hut, in the dark of winter nights? I want light, space ... Good God, when shall I go to Italy? When –'[61]

All of which raises the question of 'On the Eve', a title referring here not to Turgenev's canonical novel but to an original, although little known, prose work published under T. S. Eliot's name in January 1925. The T. S. Eliot Society website refers to the 1917 piece 'Eeldrop and Appleplex', published in *The Little Review*, as Eliot's only piece of prose fiction.[62] Yet that narrative is not in fact entirely unique in his oeuvre, for in 1925 Eliot published in *The Criterion* a short piece of prose fiction – just five or six pages – which goes under the title 'On the Eve'. Whether the piece can be considered authentic Eliot has been disputed by scholars. Behr says that it was 'written by Vivienne Eliot; Extensively revised by T. S. Eliot'[63] Vivien Eliot's biographer, Carole Seymour-Smith, says the piece 'appeared in the *Criterion* under T. S. Eliot's name ... but has all the marks of his wife's writing, and his editing'[64] Whether or not the text originated with T. S. Eliot or his wife, may be a matter of debate. Vivien made other contributions to *The Criterion* on numerous occasions, using pseudonyms (most commonly as Feiron Morris, Fanny Marlow and Felix Morrison) which surely begs the question of why she did not use a comparable *nom-de-plume* in this particular instance. Seymour-Smith takes the view 'By January 1925 Tom and Viv were writing so closely together that it was sometimes hard to tell who was the author of a piece: the January issue of *The Criterion* carried 'On The Eve: A Dialogue', whose style is characteristically Vivien's but was extensively edited by her husband [and] was published under his name.'[65]

61 Ivan Turgenev, *On the Eve*, trans. Constance Garnett (London: Macmillan Company, 1920), p. 16.

62 'The only piece of fiction by the adult Eliot', *Works by T. S. Eliot* <http://www.eliotsociety.org.uk/works-by-tseliot/> [accessed 20 September 2016].

63 Caroline Behr, *T. S. Eliot: A Chronology of His Life and Works* (London: Macmillan, 1983), p. 102.

64 Carole Seymour-Smith, *Painted Shadow: a Life of Vivienne Eliot* (London: Constable, 2001), p. 652.

65 Seymour-Smith, pp. 391–2.

The sketch's subheading is 'A Dialogue', but it is nonetheless given a setting and some props, which qualify it for categorisation as prose fiction rather than drama. Present are 'Horace' and 'Rose' as well as 'Alexander' and 'Agatha', who seem to be acquaintances – perhaps relatives of some sort. The reader is never told precisely. What is of importance is that they all belong to the echelons of the polite upper middle class, those who make up the guests at country house parties. So they themselves are typically British, or English, as observed by the cosmopolitan American Eliot. Although by this date married for some eight years to Vivien (who was English and may also have had a hand in this piece, as she earlier had a hand in section II 'A Game of Chess' from *The Waste Land*), Eliot had not yet either assumed British nationality or reconverted to Christianity in its Anglo-Catholic form.

But having established that the protagonists are British, there is nevertheless an emphatically Russian frame of reference to this curious little piece. First we are told that the country house guests are eating pancakes, which are of course, in the form of blinis, a traditional Russian dish. And furthermore Russia keeps obtruding into the conversation:

> 'But Alexander', said Agatha, continuing a discussion arising out of her country-house visit, which had begun before the arrival of the pancakes, 'What I want to know is where they keep their money. It can't be in this country or they wouldn't be trying to work up a revolution.' [...] My few bits of stuff which pay me about twopence a year are all *absolutely* unsaleable – and we all know, don't we, Alexander? that we shall be completely and utterly ruined if there is an extreme socialist government. *We* shall be destitute. But *they* won't suffer. That's obvious. They go on spending just as much, living in the lap, and yet their one interest and amusement is to pull down and shatter England.'[66]

And Agatha later continues,

> 'But I must just tell you', interrupted Agatha. 'Tilly said, the other night, "after all the Russia Loan would not have cost so much as a General Election!"' and she imitated Tilly's drawl.
> 'Pooh – bosh', said Horace, 'but talking of Russia, I'll tell you what old Sir Charles Allwell actually did say to me only the other night at the club' he went on eagerly,

66 T. S. Eliot, 'On the Eve', *The Criterion* 3.10 (1925), 278–81 (p. 278).

> 'and this'll show you, because, mind you he is an absolute Whig and they always have been for centuries – well, he said that in *his* opinion the two great menaces to civilisation were *England* and Russia.'[67]

Here we see the idea that conventional (European) civilisation is besieged, perhaps predictably, by Russia, depicted as a strange, wild, exotic, as it were primitive culture complicated by the development of Bolshevism since the end of World War I, but also, more insidiously, Europe is besieged from within. It is the spoiled and detached ruling class of what was still the most extensive political unit in the world at this date, the British Empire, who are also to be feared in equal measure. 'They go on spending just as much, living in the lap, and yet their one interest and amusement is to pull down and shatter England.'[68]

This airs the view that Russia in its present political form constitutes a threat to the European order, presumably implying that it is itself somehow non-European in nature. Through the title he has chosen Eliot is alluding to a Russian literary source, and at the same time reflecting contemporary political anxieties in Britain. This was the period of the Zinoviev Letter, now known to have been a propaganda ploy devised by the British intelligence services with the successful aim of unseating the country's first Labour government. The Letter (purporting to come from the leading Bolshevik politician Grigori Zinoviev), suggested that Labour politicians were in league with a Bolshevik Russia still, at this date, before the expulsion of Trotsky, formally dedicated to world communism and perpetual revolution. The Macdonald government lost a vote of no confidence in Parliament precipitated by its refusal to prosecute the editor of *Workers Weekly* for exhorting British soldiers never to take up arms against British workers. Just a matter of months later the General Strike was to take place. Eliot's prose piece reflects that context. It is often thought that Eliot used *The Criterion* as a mouthpiece for his own reactionary views as a

67 Eliot, 'On the Eve', p. 279.

68 Ibid. 281.

'classicist in literature, Royalist in politics and anglo-catholic in religion',[69] but that is an over-simplification and also unfair to Eliot's record as an editor. During its seventeen years, all of them under Eliot's editorship, *The Criterion* published authors whose work Eliot did not greatly care for, such as Aldous Huxley, E. M. Forster and Edith Sitwell, and he frequently engaged Herbert Read, even though he was a self-proclaimed anarchist (albeit not above accepting a knighthood), who had a scant regard for the term 'culture'. Thus it cannot be said that authors who did not share Eliot's reactionary political opinions were excluded. In fact, while, as Terry Eagleton and others have pointed out, *The Criterion*'s stance over the Spanish Civil War was 'disinterested' and 'extravagantly Olympian'[70] and noncommittal, there are plenty of instances where fascism comes in for criticism to the same degree as communism. Eliot expresses the view that both fascism and communism in practice, whatever their virtues in theory, are failures: 'Both Russian communism and Italian fascism seem to me to have died as political ideas, in becoming political facts.'[71] But the remaining question is whether Eliot regards communism, as a reality in his own time, as flawed in essence or merely vitiated by virtue of having become more Russian than Marxist-internationalist in character, which would lead back to the conclusion that a philosophy born out of the European Enlightenment – Eliot says he does not necessarily disapprove of Marx's materialism – has been as it were de-Europeanised by Leninist Bolshevism as practised beyond what many in Europe regarded as the continent's eastern borders, in suspiciously backward and irrational Russia. Here, within the framework of prose fiction, Eliot, for all his supposedly unbending reactionary political views, attacks both the communist elements in society and the parasitic 'rentier' class represented in the sketch – British society is under attack from both without and within. Gareth Reeves, in *T. S. Eliot: A Virgilian Poet* (1989), sees Eliot here attacking contemporary British political progressives, and

69 T. S. Eliot, *For Lancelot Andrewes*: *Essays on Style and Order* (London: Faber and Gwyer, 1928), p. ix.

70 Terry Eagleton, 'Nudge-Winking', *London Review of Books*, 19 September 2002, p. 7.

71 T. S. Eliot, 'The Literature of Fascism', *The Criterion* 8.31 (1928), 280–90 (p. 290).

suggesting that their progressivism has merely served to undermine them. He quotes 'Alexander' in the sketch:

> 'They have always stood for "progress" – and the progress which they set in motion is on the point of obliterating them for ever' [...] They have stood for the extension of democracy – and now democracy is on the point of deposing them in favour of a new oligarchy stronger and more terrible than their own' [...] 'Constitutional government [...] is no longer possible. It does not matter how this election turns out. No election matters now. The best we can hope for, the only thing that can save us, is a dictator.'[72]

The dictator suggested as saviour is the first of the fascist leaders, of the Italian variety: '"Good old Mussolini!" shouted Agatha.'[73]

It is Italian fascism which is Reeves's primary interest at this date in Eliot's career. Eliot was not alone among intellectuals in Britain in turning enthusiastically to Mussolini. George Bernard Shaw, whose professed politics were as much of the Left as Eliot's were of the Right, was also enthusiastic at this date. And Reeves does not pursue the Russian literary resonances of the title given to the *Criterion* sketch. Yet in Turgenev's novel of the same name Insarov anticipates the idea of revolutionary politics in the context of Russia on the brink of the Crimean War. This in turn provides a model for the domestic turmoil – involving a declining Liberal party, a rising Labour party, and exploitation by the Intelligence Services of paranoia about the latter's alleged links to revolutionary Bolshevik Russia – which Eliot (who was to take British nationality the year after next) observed in his soon-to-be adoptive country.

Finally, to return to the context of the January 1925 number of *The Criterion* in which 'On the Eve' appears, it is worth noting that Russia also appears elsewhere in its pages. Samuel Koteliansky's translations of four letters by Tolstoy feature and the editorial 'Commentary' for that number, among three themes, covers two topics in which Russia and Europe are involved. The first part of the editorial is a positive welcome for Diaghilev's Ballets Russes, and an expression of the wish that London may have the opportunity

72 Eliot, 'On The Eve', p. 279.

73 Ibid. p. 279.

to witness the *Sacre du printemps*; the middle section is a piece on Matthew Arnold, and especially the idea of European culture in *Culture and Anarchy*, while the third is a negative review by Eliot of Trotsky's *Problems of Life*, recently translated into English. After considering Arnold, with his central distinction between culture and anarchy, Eliot proceeds to critique the Bolshevik project, as described in Trotsky's terms:

> Against Arnold and his party has arisen in the east a new prophet of culture. To the point of view of a periodical like THE CRITERION much of what has been said and written in impeachment and in defence of Soviet Russia is of minor interest. Not that it is possible, or even right for any individual to regard such matters from the point of view of pure intelligence alone; but it is well that we should all regard them from that point of view now and then. Any person, therefore, who is aware of 'culture' at all, will be aware that there are and have been various cultures, and that the difference between our own culture and alien culture is different from the difference between culture and anarchy, or culture and pseudo-culture. We may not like the notion of cannibalism or head-hunting, but that it formed part of a distinct and tenable form of culture in Melanesia is indisputable. Consequently, I was prepared to find in Trotsky's book an exposition of a culture repellent to my own disposition; but I hoped that it would be distinct and interesting. A revolution staged on such a vast scale, amongst a picturesque, violent, and romantic people; involving such disorder, rapine, assassination, starvation, and plague should have something to show for the expense: a new culture horrible at the worst, but in any event fascinating. Such a cataclysm is justified if it produces something really *new*: *Un* [sic] *oasis d'horreur dans un désert d'ennui*.[74]

Having conceded that the Russian Revolution might in some degree have been conceivably justified, for all its excesses, if it had represented something culturally new, Eliot goes on to say that it has in practice proved nothing of the sort:

> It is not justified by the dreary picture of Montessori schools, crèches, abstinence from swearing and alcohol, a population warmly clad (or soon to be warmly clad) and with its mind filled (or in process of being filled) with nineteenth century superstitions about Nature and her forces. Yet such phenomena as this are what Mr Trotsky proudly presents as the outcome of his revolution; these form his 'culture'. Here is the

74 T. S. Eliot, 'Light from the East', *The Criterion* 3.10 (1925), 160–4 (p. 163).

> Eastern prophet of the new age speaking in the smuggest tones of the Bourgeoisie: 'The cinema amuses, educates, strikes the imagination with images, and liberates you from the need of crossing the Church door.' It remains only to observe that there is no mention of Mr Trotsky's Enchiridion of Culture or such an institution as the ballet; and that his portrait shows a slight resemblance to the face of Mr Sidney Webb.[75]

Leaving aside Eliot's dismissal of the reality of Bolshevism in practice as being worthy of the 'smuggest … Bourgeoisie', what is telling here are the traditional characteristics still ascribed to the Russian people, 'picturesque, violent, and romantic', which suggests that Eliot conforms to the traditional stereotype favoured in Britain in previous centuries. While he may enthuse about Diaghilev's Ballets Russes as a manifestation of Russian high culture, that is an émigré institution, and Eliot clearly considers that Russians *en masse* in Russia itself remain benighted and backward.

Coming after the youthful interest in Dostoevsky as one of the influences upon *Prufrock* as early as 1911, this brief and obscure piece of prose fiction by Eliot, 'On the Eve', represents an interesting nod in the direction of Turgenev. The allusion intended by the appropriation of Turgenev's title is presumably to suggest a doomed social class on the brink of a cataclysm. Turgenev's flawed characters, the pampered serf-owners whose days are numbered – Elena's egotistical and adulterous father, for example – teeter on the brink of the Crimean War, which would bring about the Emancipation. Eliot in the same vein gives us Agatha and Alexander, living off their dividends, fearing that the reforming Liberals, still at this date given their old label of Whigs, are fatally disabling the established social order, while an additional, external threat comes from Russian Bolshevism. This is quite closely tied to the political and economic circumstances of the first half of the 1920s as regards Russo–British relations. Lloyd George, as leader of a coalition after World War I, had been more conciliatory towards the fledgling Bolshevik regime than was Churchill, very much the instigator of attempts to keep Britain involved in the Russian Civil War on the side of the Whites. It might have been possible to reach some form of rapprochement with the Bolsheviks at the Treaty of Genoa, if the Germans

75 Ibid. p. 163.

and Bolsheviks, repeating their form in 1918 with the Brest-Litovsk treaty, had not agreed the terms of the Treaty of Rapallo on their own independent initiative. In 1924, however, following huge electoral gains the Labour Party, aided by full male and, by the end of the decade, full female suffrage, was in the process of displacing the Liberals as the radical alternative to the Conservatives. It was the socialist Ramsay MacDonald, admittedly as the leader of a coalition rather than an out-and-out Labour government, who gave diplomatic recognition to the newly declared Soviet Union, and agreed to lend the Soviets £30 million on condition that outstanding debts to British creditors from during and before World War I were acknowledged. This is the 'Russia loan' to which the chattering middle-class denizens of Eliot's prose piece refer. There is a blurring of the enemy without (Russia) and the enemy within (the decadent and fatally weakened English ruling class, their days at the helm of a world empire surely numbered) which is very close to Hesse's analysis of Europe's malaise after World War I in the light of Dostoevsky's *The Brothers Karamazov*. At the same time Turgenev is perhaps a more apt Russian author as a role model. After all, Dostoevsky had been a diehard Slavophile, who asserted Russia's cultural (and almost theological) exceptionalism. While Dostoevsky's emphasis on sin and expiation might come to suit the later Eliot of the 1930s and 1940s, by which time he was producing explicitly Christian poetry (*Four Quartets*) and drama which became ever more neo-classical in a certain sense, in another way he and the Russian novelist are diametrically opposite. It is hard to imagine that Dostoevsky, who was deeply suspicious of the Poles as a Roman Catholic people, undermining the orthodoxy of pan-Slavism, would have been happy to accept Eliot's adoptive Anglo-Catholicism. By contrast 'On the Eve', with its allusion to Turgenev, makes much more sense, as an aspect of Russian culture to be embraced by Eliot. For in many ways Turgenev ought to have been the Russian writer *par excellence* Eliot might have been expected to emulate. Both were cosmopolitans and expatriates, and both were committed to an ideal of universal sophisticated culture rather than any crude nationalism. Yet, as will be seen below, in the longer term it was still Dostoevsky to whom Eliot was to return as his preeminent Russian influence.

The nineteen thirties saw Eliot move away from a central focus upon poetry as he experimented with drama. In their commentary on Eliot's poems, Ricks and McCue indicate that Eliot professed a reverence for Chekhov:

> Dostoevski's *Plan of the novel,* 'The Life of a Great Sinner' was published in the last issue of the *Criterion* in Oct 1922 along with *The Waste Land*. TSE to Enid Faber, 24 Feb 1938 of *The Family Reunion*: 'The tragedy, as with my Master, Tchechov, is as much for the people who have to go on living, as for those who die. And I may urge you ... to go and see St. Denis' superb production of *Three Sisters* ... the best production of a great play that I have seen for a long time.' *Hodin* reported TSE in conversation: 'what Russia has given to the West is a peculiar – peculiar, that is, to Russian – spiritual point of view, which is something one is very much aware of in the great Russian novelists', *Horizon* Aug 1945.[76]

But it has to be said that this reverence for Chekhov does not show prominently in Eliot's own plays. As regards dramatic form and dramatic technique Eliot cannot be said to be following a primarily Russian model here, for Eliot's verse dramas, boasting in at least two cases a chorus (*Murder In the Cathedral* and *The Family Reunion*) are far removed from the greatest Russian dramatist, whom Woolf had praised for eschewing formulaic structure and cultivating an inconclusive mood (see Chapter 7). In all cases after *Murder in the Cathedral* the plays are consciously modelled upon classical originals from the Ancient World – Aeschylus's *Choephori* (*Family Reunion*), Euripides's *Alcestis* (*The Cocktail Party)*, Plautus and Terence in *The Confidential Clerk* and Sophocles's *Oedipus at Colonus* (*The Elder Statesman*). Moreover, all Eliot's plays are written in verse rather than prose. But beyond these formal aspects, in terms of the spiritual experience of the central hero in each of the plays, there persists a clear parallel with Dostoevsky. By the time Eliot produced these plays he had reconverted to Christianity, and this idea of reconversion – so emphatically a part of *Crime and Punishment* and other works of Dostoevsky – is manifestly present in Eliot's plays. Harry (Lord Monchensey), in *The Family Reunion* (1939), returning to his ancestral home after a disastrous marriage which ends in

76 Eliot, *The Poems of T. S. Eliot*, I, p. 647.

the controversial death of his wife, makes his first entry complaining of the difficulty of believing that the world around him is real, and greeting his assembled uncles and aunts with dismay: 'Changed? Nothing changed? How can you say that nothing is changed? You all look so withered and young.'[77]

His uncles' and aunts' conversation at times closely mimics that of the earlier 'On the Eve' piece – for example, in response to a press report of a motor accident involving one of the younger sons , Arthur (who evokes the novels of P. G. Wodehouse) Harry's uncle Charles says; 'This is what the Communists make capital out of.'[78] However, Harry himself is the typically alienated hero of a Dostoevsky novel, and like Raskolnikov he suffers delusions which make him think the world unreal. When, having described the death by drowning of his wife on board ship, he is reassured by his uncle Charles 'Your conscience can be clear.' Harry responds,

> It goes a good deal deeper
> Than what people call their conscience; it is just the cancer
> That eats away the self. I knew how you would take it.
> First of all, you isolate the single event
> As something so dreadful that it couldn't have happened,
> Because you could not bear it. So you must believe
> That I suffer from delusions. It is not my conscience,
> Not my mind, that is diseased, but the world I have to live in.[79]

Also like Raskolnikov, by the end of the play Harry has been reconverted to Christianity. He makes his exit: 'I must follow the bright angels',[80] forswearing the duties of his ancestral home Wishwood, determined to become some sort of Christian missionary, albeit accompanied on his evangelising work by his valet Downing. Celia Copplestone, the heroine of Eliot's next play, *The Cocktail Party*, does something not dissimilar, and we later hear

77 T. S. Eliot, *The Family Reunion* (London: Faber & Faber, 1959), p. 25.
78 Ibid. p. 89.
79 Ibid. p. 29.
80 Ibid. p. 107.

that she has been crucified by those she was seeking to convert.[81] This is all extreme and almost fundamentalist stuff in the manner of Dostoevsky, the scourge of a godless world. The debt to Dostoevsky is made patent in a speech delivered towards the end of *The Family Reunion*, in which Agatha, an Oxbridge academic and Harry's aunt, says,

> What we have written is not a story of detection,
> Of crime and punishment, but of sin and expiation.[82]

Agatha, having once had an affair with the hero Harry Monchensey's father, has spent

> Thirty years of solitude,
> Alone among women in a woman's college,
> Trying no to dislike women.[83]

But although this might suggest that we are far removed from the wistful urbanity of Turgenev, while Eliot may have been inspired by Dostoevsky in theory, perhaps things worked out rather differently in practice. A 1949 review of Eliot's third play *The Cocktail Party* reads as follows: 'The play comes from a mind as acute as Sir Isaac Newton's, that wishes to write like Dostoevsky, and succeeds at its best but not its most ambitious in doing as well as Jane Austen.'[84] Perhaps in that early contrast between Dostoevsky and Austen in the 1917 letter to Eleanor Hinkley, Eliot was closer than he realised to the truth. This is of interest as regards both Eliot's motives for evoking Russian literature and the actual contemporary reception which his drama received in the English-speaking world (admittedly in America rather than Britain), and in consequence gives some indication of the degree which by this later, just post-World War II period, Russia did or did not

81 'From what we know of local practices, it would seem that she must have been crucified' (T. S. Eliot, *The Cocktail Party* (London: Faber, 1950), p. 169).

82 Eliot, *The Family Reunion*, p. 97.

83 Ibid. p. 108.

84 *The Sunday Times* (7 May 1950); quoted in Mildred A. Martin, *A Half Century of Eliot Criticism; An Annotated Bibliography of Books and articles in English 1916–1965* (Pennsylvania: Bucknell University Press, 1973), p. 163.

continue to represent cultural capital. Back in 1895 Edward Garnett could claim Turgenev's superiority to Austen, because she lacked the Russian's 'poetic insight'; in 1919 Virginia Woolf reinforced the Dostoevsky–Austen polarity; now Eliot, though he had consciously endeavoured to fashion 'poetic' drama in the twentieth century, was judged by at least one contemporary reviewer to have tried to emulate Dostoevsky and succeeded only in calling Austen to mind.

The prose piece 'On the Eve' from 1925 shows Eliot at a critical juncture, balancing between the twin Russian influences of Turgenev and Dostoevsky. It is even possible that Eliot was put in mind of these two canonical Russian novelists by the translations which Koteliansky made for the same edition of *The Criterion* from four letters exchanged between Leo Tolstoy and the critic N. N. Strakhov in the 1880s, where the topic of conversation is Dostoevsky. In the first letter Tolstoy praises *The House of the Dead* in the highest terms, 'I do not know a better book in the whole new literature including Poushkin',[85] but by the end, after Dostoevsky's death, Tolstoy reins in his enthusiasm, stating that he was, as a writer, vitiated by a fatal 'kink' by comparison with the more reliable Turgenev, speaking of Dostoevsky's 'exaggerated importance' and saying that by contrast Turgenev 'will outlive Dostoevsky, and not for his artistry, but because he is without a kink'.[86]

In his later work Eliot was to find common ground with Dostoevsky, chiefly for the element of redemption through religion which the latter's novels feature, notably in *Crime and Punishment* and in *The Brothers Karamazov*, but at this date, in the mid-1920s before his own religious reconversion to Christianity in its Anglo-Catholic rather than Unitarian form, he appears to have been equally under the influence of Turgenev, who was a cosmopolitan by contrast with the vision of 'Holy Russia' nationalism to which Dostoevsky was closer. And at this date, in the mid-1920s, it seems clear that Eliot still subscribed to the view, expounded earlier in this paper, that the Russians collectively were a 'picturesque, violent and

85 S. S. Koteliansky, 'A Few Extracts from Letters Exchanged Between Leo Nicolayevich Tolstoy and N. N. Strakhov', *The Criterion* 3.11 (1925), 164–9 (p. 164).

86 Ibid. 169.

romantic people'.[87] But when his career is viewed overall, the Russian influence upon Eliot appears to have fluctuated significantly between the poles represented by Turgenev and Dostoevsky.

As with Woolf and Lawrence (the two writers in this survey closest to him in age and also in terms of technical innovation), Eliot continued to write after coming through a period of intense interest in, and exploitation of, the Russian myth (in *The Love Song of J. Alfred Prufrock*), and, as Woolf was to do a little later, in the 1930s, moved away from the great Russian novelist of alienation and crisis, avoiding Dostoevsky's didacticism, towards Turgenev. Perhaps Eliot might have gone on to make more of Turgenev in the mid-1920s, had he not embraced Christianity at this point. Certainly Turgenev as cosmopolitan émigré (not accidentally, perhaps, a friend of Eliot's precursor as adoptive European, Henry James) should logically have provided Eliot with a plausible model to follow. But in the event, after this brief flirtation, evoking Turgenev in 1925, it was the example of Dostoevsky which was to prove more lasting in his case, and to constitute a renewed source of cultural capital for the American poet. It would be wrong to over-represent the Russian component in Eliot – clearly the allure of writers from other traditions, such as the Classical Greek tragedians and Dante, can be argued to be more sustained. Nevertheless, Eliot definitely responded to the Russophilia movement which coincided with his emergence as a writer, and also returned to those same early themes and approaches found in Russian literature later in his career.

This set Eliot apart in some degree from the other writers covered in this book. For Eliot alone, Russian literature continued to function as cultural capital throughout the period when he was at his most influential as an opinion former (beyond his own creative work) at the helm of *The Criterion*. For Barrie, Wells and Woolf (Lawrence, of course, died in 1930) it is clear that after 1930 the myth of Russia was fading in its power, even as the Soviet State gained an identity wholly at odds with the myth, and the latter thus became an overworked seam. Nonetheless, at a deeper level the years of intense engagement had undoubtedly wrought a fundamental

87 Eliot, 'Light from the East', p. 163.

change in each of them, and this in turn, because of their standing, influenced public opinion in Britain. None of the writers here expresses this more revealingly than Galsworthy, who was acutely aware that the image of Russia projected from the literary classics was 'a Russia of the past', 'perhaps only the crust of that Russia of the past – now split and crumbled beyond repair'. Yet he thought that he, as well as the entire generation of British readers, were 'extremely fortunate to have such a supreme picture of the vanished fabric',[88] for above all it provided an indispensable initiation into the Russian mind-set and Russian aesthetics. By opening up new cultural avenues that surpassed the field of literary conventions, it assisted in introducing the Russian viewpoint to British understanding, and in shaping a new conception of the self, enriched by a different cultural perspective. 'The amazing direct and truthful revelations of the Russian masters', he wrote, have

> let me, I think, into some secrets of the Russian soul, so that the Russians I have met seem rather clearer to me than men and women of other foreign countries. For their construing I have been given what schoolboys call a crib. Only a fool pretends to knowledge – the heart of another is surely a dark forest; but the heart of a Russian seems to me a forest less dark than many.[89]

88 Galsworthy, 'Six Novelists in Profile', p. 159.
89 Galsworthy, 'Englishman and Russian', p. 64.

Bibliography

Alekseev, M. P., 'Shekspir i russkoe gosudarstvo XVI–XVII vv.', in *Shekspir i russkaia kul'tura*, ed. M. P. Alekseev (Moscow and Leningrad: Akademia nauk, 1965), pp. 784–805.

Alston, Charlotte, *Russia's Greatest Enemy?: Harold Williams and the Russian Revolutions* (New York: Tauris, 2007).

Amfiteatrov, Aleksandr V., 'Gorestnye zamety', *Novaia russkaia zhizn'* (Gel'singfors) 221 (27 September 1921), p. 222 (28 September 1921).

Anderson, M. S., *British Discovery of Russia, 1553–1815* (London: St. Martin's Press, 1958).

Archer, William, 'The Theatre', *World*, 11 April 1905, p. 622.

Aristotle, 'Nicomachean Ethics', in *Complete Works of Aristotle*, ed. Jonathan Barnes (Princeton, NJ: Princeton University Press, 1995), II, pp. 729–867.

'Arkay', *The Tatler*, 7 April 1920.

Arnold, Matthew, 'Count Leo Tolstoi', *Fortnightly Review* 42 (1887), pp. 783–99.

Ashton, Rosemary, *Victorian Bloomsbury* (New Haven, CT: Yale University Press, 2012).

Asquith, Cynthia, *Portrait of Barrie* (London: James Barrie, 1955).

Atheling, William [Ezra Pound], 'At the Ballet', *New Age*, 16 October 1919, p. 412.

Baring, Maurice, *Landmarks in Russian Literature* (London: Methuen and Co, 1910).

—— *The Mainsprings of Russia* (London: Thomas Nelson and Sons, 1914).

—— *Maurice Baring: Restored Selections from His Work*, ed. Paul Horgan (London: William Heinemann, 1970).

—— *Russian Essays and Stories* (London: Methuen & Co, 1908).

—— *The Russian People* (London: Methuen and Co, 1911).

Barrie, J. M., *Letters of J. M. Barrie*, ed. Viola Meynell (London: Peter Davies, 1942).

—— 'The Truth of the Russian Dancers', in A. J. Pischl and Selma Jeanne Cohen, eds, *Dance Perspectives* 14 (1962), pp. 12–30.

Bassinsky, Pavel, *Strasti po Maksimu: deviat' dnei posle smerti* (Moscow: Astrel', 2011).

Beasley, Rebecca, and Philip Ross Bullock, eds, 'Introduction: Against Influence: On Writing about Russian Influence in Britain', in *Russia in Britain, 1880–1940: From Melodrama to Modernism*, ed. Rebecca Beasley and Philip Ross Bullock (Oxford: Oxford University Press, 2013) pp. 1–18.

—— *Russia in Britain, 1880–1940: From Melodrama to Modernism* (Oxford: Oxford University Press, 2013).

Beaumont, Cyril W., *The Art of Lydia Lopokova* (London: Beaumont Press, 1920).

—— 'Lydia Lopokova, an appreciation, 1920', in *Lydia Lopokova*, ed. Milo Keynes (London: Weidenfeld and Nicolson, 1983), pp. 224–8.

Becket, Fiona, *D. H. Lawrence: The Thinker as Poet* (Basingstoke: Macmillan, 1997).

Beckson, Karl, Introduction, in *Aesthetes and Decadents of the 1890s: An Anthology of British Poetry and Prose*, ed. Karl Beckson (Chicago: Academy Chicago Publishers, 1981), pp. xxi–xliv.

Behr, Caroline, *T. S. Eliot: A Chronology of His Life and Works* (London: Macmillan, 1983).

Beller, Manfred, 'Perception, Image, Imagology', in *Imagology: The Cultural Construction and Literary Representation of National*, ed. Manfred Beller and Joseph Theodoor (Amsterdam: Rodopi, 2007), pp. 3–16.

—— and Joseph Theodoor Leerssen, *Imagology: The Cultural Construction and Literary Representation of National* (Amsterdam: Rodopi, 2007), pp. xii–xvi.

Benois, Alexander, *Vospominaniia* (Moscow: Nauka, 1980).

Berberova, Nina, *Moura: The Dangerous Life of the Baroness Budberg* (New York: Review Books , 2005).

Besant, Walter, and Henry James, 'Art of Fiction', *Longman's Magazine* 4 (1884), pp. 502–21.

'Bibliographical', *The Academy* 58 (1900), p. 178.

Bingham, Jane, *Popular Culture: 1920–1939* (London: Raintree, 2013).

Bishop, Edward, *A Virginia Woolf Chronology* (London: Palgrave Macmillan, 1989).

Bock, Hans Manfred, 'Nation als vorgegebene oder vorgestellte Wirklichkeit? Anmerkungen zur Analyse fremdnationaler Identitätszuschreibung', in *Nation als Stereotyp: Fremdwahrnehmung und Identität in deutscher und französischer Literatur*, ed. Ruth Florack (Tübingen: Max Niemeyer Verlag, 2001), pp. 11–36.

Bold, Valentina, and Andrew Nash, eds, *Gateway to the Modern: Resituating J. M. Barrie* (Glasgow: Scottish Literature International, 2014).

Booth, Howard J., 'Lawrence in Doubt: A Theory of the "Other" and its Collapse', in *Modernism and Empire*, ed. Howard J. Booth and Nigel Rigby (Manchester: Manchester University Press, 2000), pp. 197–223.

Boulton, James T., and Andrew Robertson, Introduction to *The Letters of D. H. Lawrence*, ed. James T. Boulton and Andrew Robertson (Cambridge: Cambridge University Press, 1979–2001), III, pp. 1–12.

Bourdieu, Pierre, 'Les conditions sociales de la circulation internationale des idées', *Actes de la recherche en sciences sociales* 145.1 (2002), pp. 3–8.

—— *Distinction* (London: Routledge, 1984).

Bracewell, Michael, 'Molotov Cocktails', *Frieze Magazine*, November–December 2004 <http://www.frieze.com/issue/article/molotov_cocktails> [accessed 20 September 2016].

Brewster, Dorothy, *East-West Passage* (London: Georg Allen and Unwin, 1954).

Brome, Vincent, *Six Studies in Quarrelling* (London: Cresset Press, 1958).

Brown, Catherine, 'The Russian Soul Englished', *Journal of Modern Literature* 36.1 (2012), pp. 132–49.

Browning, Robert, 'Ivan Ivanovich', in *The Poems of Robert Browning* (Ware: Wordsworth Classics, 1994), pp. 590–5.

Bruce, Henry James, *Thirty Dozen Moons* (London: Constable, 1949).

Buckle, Richard, *Diaghilev* (New York: Atheneum, 1979).

Bunin, Ivan, 'The Gentlemen from San Francisco', in *Lazarus* by Leonid Andreev and *The Gentlemen from San Francisco* by Bunin, trans. Abraham Yarmolinsky (Boston, MA: The Stratford Company Publishes 1918) pp. 32– 58.

—— *The Gentleman from San Francisco and Other Stories*, trans. S. S. Koteliansky and Leonard Woolf (Richmond: Hogarth Press, 1922), pp. 1–40.

—— 'Some Words to the English Writer', *Obshchee delo* 132 (1920), p. 2.

Burt, Ramsay, *The Male Dancer: Bodies, Spectacle, Sexualities* (London and New York: Routledge, 2003).

Byron, George Gordon, *The Works* (London: John Murray, 1837).

Carter, Huntley, 'About the Theatre in London', *Theatre Arts Magazine* 6 (1920), pp. 217–19.

Caserio, Robert, *Plot, Story, and the Novel* (Princeton, NJ: Princeton University Press, 1979).

'Casts of *The Truth about the Russian Dancers*', *Dance Perspectives* 14 (1962), p. 37.

Chambers, Jessie, *D. H. Lawrence: A Personal Record* (London: Jonathan Cape, 1935).

Chaney, Lisa, *Hide–And–Seek with Angels: The Life of J. M. Barrie* (London: Arrow Books 2006).

Chappelow, Allan, *Shaw – 'The Chucker–out'* (London: George Allen and Unwin Ltd, 1969).

Chekhov, Anton, *Anton Chekhov's Life and Thought: Selected Letters and Commentary*, ed. Simon Karlinsky, trans. Michael Henry Heim (Evanston, IL: Northwestern University Press, 1997).

Chevrillon, André, *Three Studies in English Literature: Kipling, Galsworthy, Shakespeare* (Port Washington, NY: Kennikat Press, 1922).

'Childhood and Youth', *The Saturday Review*, 29 March 1862, pp. 361–2.

Chinitz, D., *T. S. Eliot and the Cultural Divide* (Chicago: University of Chicago Press, 2005).

Chothia, Jean, *English Drama of the Early Modern Period (1890–1914)* (London: Longman, 1996).

Chukovsky, Kornei, *Polnoe sobranie sochinenii. Dnevnik 1901–1921*, ed. E. Chukovskaia (Moscow: Terra, 2013).

Church, Hayden, 'Barrie Writes Play for Russian Ballet Dancer', *The Desert News*, 20 February 1920.

Churchill, William, 'Maurice Baring, *The Russian People* (1911)', *Bulletin of the American Geographical Society* 44.3 (1912), p. 218.

Churchill, Winston, 'H. G. Wells', *Sunday Pictorial*, 23 August 1931, in *The Collected Essays of Sir Winston Churchill*, ed. Michael Wolff, 4 vols (London: Library of Imperial History, 1976), III, pp. 50–4.

—— *A History of the English-Speaking Peoples* (London: Bloomsbury, 2015).

—— 'Mr. Wells and Bolshevism', *The Sunday Express*, 5 December 1920.

'Churchill and Merejkovsky Reply to Wells', *Current Opinion* 70 (1921), p. 217.

Cohen, Harriet, *A Bundle of Time* (London: Faber and Faber, 1969).

Cohen, Selma Jeanne, 'The Text of "The Truth about the Russian Dancers"', *Dance Perspectives* 14 (1962), pp. 31–4.

Cole, Margaret, *The Story of Fabian Socialism* (Stanford, CA: Stanford University Press, 1961).

'Colonel Dunwoddie, and Other Novels', *Atlantic Monthly* 42 (1878), pp. 697–706.

Conan Doyle, Arthur, *His Last Bow* (New York: George H. Doran Company, 1917).

Conrad, Joseph, *The Collected Letters of Joseph Conrad*, ed. Frederick R. Karl and Laurence Davies (Cambridge: Cambridge University Press, 1990).

'Contemporary Life and Thought in Russia', *The Contemporary Review* 47 (1885), pp. 727–36.

'The Cossacks', *The Observer*, 15 September 1878.

'Count Tolstoi's Childhood and Youth', *The Times*, June 20 1862.

'Count Tolstoi's Life and Works', *Westminster Review* 130 (1888), pp. 278–93.

The Criterion 1922–1939 (London: Faber, 1967).

Cross, Anthony, 'British Awareness of Russian Culture (1698–1801)', *Canadian Slavic Studies* 13 (1979), pp. 212–35.

—— 'By Way of Introduction: British Perception, Reception and Recognition of Russian Culture', *A People Passing Rude*, ed. Anthony Cross (Cambridge: Open Book Publishers, 2012), pp. 1–36.

——, *In the Land of the Romanovs: An Annotated Bibliography of First-hand English-language Accounts of the Russian Empire (1613–1917)* (Cambridge: Open Book Publishers, 2014).

——, ed., *A People Passing Rude: British Responses to Russian Culture*, ed. Anthony Cross (Cambridge: Open Book Publishers, 2012).

—— *Peter the Great through British Eyes* (Cambridge: Cambridge University Press, 2000).
—— *The Russian Theme in English Literature from the Sixteenth Century to 1980: an introductory survey and bibliography* (Oxford: W. A. Meeuws, 1985).
Damanskaia, A., 'G. Uells v Petrograde', *Narodnoe delo: Organ Komiteta gruppy sotsi-alistov–revolutsionerov Severo–Zapadnoi oblasti Rossii* 55 (8 October 1920), p. 2.
Defoe, Daniel, *An Impartial History of the Life and Actions of Peter Alexowitz, Czar of Muscovy* (London: W. Chetwood, 1723).
—— *The True Born Englishman* (London: A. Cleugh, 1810).
'Diaghileff Ballet Dances "Carneval"', *New York Times*, 20 January 1916, p. 10.
Dickinson, Thomas H., *Contemporary Drama of England* (Boston, MA: Little Brown, 1931).
Dillon, Emile J. [E. B. Lanin], *The Eclipse of Russia* (New York: George B. Doran, 1918).
—— *Russian Traits and Terrors* (Boston, MA: Benj. R. Tucker 1891); *Fortnightly Review* 52 (1889), pp. 410–32; 573–88; 722–36; 854–68.
Diment, Galya, *A Russian Jew of Bloomsbury: The Life and Times of Samuel Koteliansky* (Montreal: McGill-Queen's University Press 2011).
Dinamov, S., 'M. Gorky i Zapad', *Krasnaia Nov'* 10–11 (1931), p. 225.
Disraeli, Isaac, 'Literary Fashions' (1791), *Curiosities of Literature*, ed. Isaac Disraeli (Boston, MA: Lilly, Wait, Colman and Holden, 1833), III, pp. 35–8.
Donovan, Stephen, Danuta Zadworna-Fjellestad, and Rolf Lundén, eds, *Authority Matters: Rethinking the Theory and Practice of Authorship* (Amsterdam and New York: Rodopi, 2008), pp. 193–222.
Dostoevsky, Fyodor, *Crime and Punishment*, trans. Constance Garnett (New York: P. F. Collier & Son Corp., 1917).
Dunbar, Janet, *J. M. Barrie: The Man Behind the Image* (London: Collins, 1970).
Dupré, Catherine, *John Galsworthy. A Biography* (London: Collins, 1976).
Eagleton, Terry, 'Nudge–Winking', *London Review of Books*, 19 September 2002, p. 7.
Eliot, George, *Adam Bede* (Oxford: Oxford University Press, 2001).
Eliot, T. S., *The Cocktail Party* (London: Faber, 1950).
—— *The Family Reunion* (London: Faber & Faber, 1959).
—— *For Lancelot Andrewes: Essays on Style and Order* (London: Faber and Gwyer, 1928).
—— 'Hamlet and His Problems', *The Sacred Wood: Essays on Poetry and Criticism*, ed. T. S. Eliot (New York: Alfred A. Knopf, 1921), pp. 87–94.
—— *Letters of T. S. Eliot*, ed. Valerie Eliot and Hugh Haughton (New Haven, CT: Yale University Press, 2011).
—— 'Light from the East', *The Criterion* 3.10 (1925), pp. 160–4.
—— 'The Literature of Fascism', *The Criterion* 8.31 (1928), 280–90.

—— *The Love Song of J. Alfred Prufrock*, in *The Poems of T. S. Eliot*, ed. Christopher Ricks and Jim McCue (London: Faber & Faber, 2015).

—— 'On the Eve', *The Criterion* 3.10 (1925), pp. 278–81.

—— *The Poems of T. S. Eliot*, ed. Christopher Ricks and Jim McCue, 2 vols (London: Faber & Faber, 2015).

—— *The Waste Land*, in *The Poems of T. S. Eliot*, ed. Christopher Ricks and Jim McCue (London: Faber & Faber, 2015).

—— *The Waste Land*: a facsimile and manuscript, ed. Valerie Eliot (London: Faber, 1971).

Emeljanow, Victor, Introduction to *Chekhov*: *The Critical Heritage*, ed. Victor Emeljanow (London: Routledge and Paul Kegan, 1981), pp. 1–56.

Farjeon, Annabel, 'Lydia Lopokova and Serge Diaghilev', in *Lydia Lopokova*, ed. Milo Keynes (London: Weidenfeld and Nicolson, 1983).

Ford, Ford Madox, *Portraits from Life* (London: Houghton Mifflin Company, 1937).

Foreman, Lewis, *Bax: A Composer and His Time* (Woodbridge: Boydell Press, 2007).

Forster, E. M., *Aspects of the Novel* (San Diego, New York and London: Harcourt, 1985).

Foster, John Burt (Jr), *Transnational Tolstoy: Between the West and the World* (London: Bloomsbury, 2013).

Foucault, Michel, *The Archaeology of Knowledge*, trans. A. M. Sheridan Smith (London and New York: Routledge, 2002).

France, Hector, *Dictionnaire de la langue verte* (Etoile-sur-Rhône: N. Gauvin, 1990); reprint of the original edn (Paris: Librairie du progrès, 1907).

Fremantle, Anne, *This Little Band of Prophets. The Story of the Gentle Fabians* (London: George Allen & Unwin Ltd, 1960).

Fry, Roger, 'The Scenery of La Boutique Fantasque', *Athenaeum*, 13 June 1919, p. 466.

Galsworthy, John, 'The Apple Tree', in *Five Tales* (London: William Heinemann, 1918), pp. 187–260.

—— 'Englishman and Russian', *Another Sheaf*, ed. John Galsworthy (London: Heinemann, 1919), pp. 64–8.

—— *The Forsyte Saga* (London: Heinemann, 1922).

—— 'Four Novelists in Profile', *English Review* 4 (1932), 485–500.

—— *Glimpses and Reflections* (Leipzig: Tauchnitz, 1937).

—— *The Inn of Tranquillity* (London: Heinemann, 1927).

—— 'Introduction to "Bleak House"', in *Forsytes, Pendyces and Others* (New York: Charles Scribner's Sons, 1935), pp. 199–201.

—— *The Island Pharisees* (London: William Heinemann, 1904).

—— *Jocelyn* (New York: Holt, Rinehart and Winston, 1977).

—— *Letters from John Galsworthy 1900–1932*, ed. Edward Garnett (London: Jonathan Cape, 1934).

—— 'Meditations on Finality', *The Complete Essays of John Galsworthy*, ed. John Galsworthy (Charleston, SC: BiblioBazaar, 2006), pp. 129–33.

—— 'A Note on Edward Garnett', in *Forsytes, Pendyces and Others* (New York: Charles Scribner's Sons, 1935), pp. 185–7.

—— Preface to *The Forsyte Saga* (London: Heinemann, 1922), pp. ix–x.

—— 'Six Novelists in Profile', in *Castles in Spain and other Screeds* (London: Heinemann, 1927), pp. 145–71.

—— 'Twelve Books – and Why?', *The Saturday Review of Literature* 6 (1927), 363–4.

—— 'Vague Thoughts on Art', *The Inn of Tranquillity*, ed. John Galsworthy (New York: Charles Scriber's Sons, 1912).

'Galsworthy's Memories', *The Age*, 29 January 1938, p. 27.

Garafola, Lynn, *Diaghilev, Ballets Russes* (New York: Oxford University Press, 1989).

Garnett, Constance, 'Russian Literature in English', *The Listener*, 30 January 1947, p. 195.

Garnett, David, *Flowers of the Forest* (London: Chatto and Windus, 1955).

—— *The Golden Echo* (London: Chatto & Windus, 1953).

Garnett, Edward, Introduction, *Letters from John Galsworthy 1900–1932*, ed. Edward Garnett (London: Jonathan Cape, 1934).

—— Introduction to Ivan Turgenev, *On the Eve*, trans. Constance Garnett (London: Macmillan Company, 1920), pp. i–xvi.

—— *Turgenev. A Study* (London: W. Collins Sons and Co, 1917).

Garnett, Richard David, *Constance Garnett: A Heroic Life* (London: Sinclair–Stevenson, 1991).

Gel'rot, M., 'Nitsshe i Gorky, *Russkoe bogatstvo* 5 (1903), pp. 24–65.

Gettmann, Royal, *Turgenev in England and America* (Urbana: University of Illinois Press, 1941).

Gindin, James, *John Galsworthy's Life and Art* (London: Macmillan, 1987).

Glendinning, Victoria, *Leonard Woolf: A Biography* (New York and London: Free Press, 2006).

Gold, Arthur, and Robert Fizdale, *Misia: The Life of Misia Sert* (York: Morrow Quill Paperbacks, 1981).

Goldsmith, Oliver, 'Citizen of the World', in *The Works of Oliver Goldsmith*, ed. Peter Cunningham, 4 vols (London: John Murray, 1854), II, pp. 75–487.

Gorky, Maxim, 'Besedy o remesle', *Sobranie sochinenii*, 30 vols (Moscow: Khudozhestvennaia literatura, 1949–55), XXV (1953), pp. 291–359.

—— *Pis'ma*, ed. F. F. Kuznetsov, 24 vols (Moscow: Nauka, 1997).

—— *Untimely Thoughts on Revolution, Culture, and the Bolsheviks 1917–1918*, trans. Herman Ermolaev (New York: Paul S. Eriksson, 1968).

Gould, Gerald, 'New Novels', *New Statesman* 7 (1916), pp. 17–18.

Graham, Stephen, *Undiscovered Russia* (London: John Lane the Bodley Head, 1912).
Graphic, 27 March 1915, p. 412.
Green, Martin, and John Swan, *The Triumph of Pierrot* (University Park: Pennsylvania University Press, 1993).
Guiguet, Jean, *Virginia Woolf and her Works* (London: Hogarth Press, 1965).
Guillory, John, *Cultural Capital: The Problem of Literary Canon Formation* (Chicago: University of Chicago Press, 1993).
'H. G. Wells berates Russian Writers in Preface to Tolstoi', *Chicago Daily Tribune*, 14 August 1929, p. 29.
Hardy, F. E., *The Later Years of Thomas Hardy, 1892–1928* (London: Macmillan, 1930).
Hardy, Thomas, *Tess of the D'Urbervilles* (Peterborough and London: Broadview Press, 1985).
Hargrove, Nancy, 'T. S. Eliot and the Dance', *Journal of Modern Literature* 21.1 (1997), pp. 61–88.
Harrison, Jane Ellen, *Russia and the Russian Verbs: A Contribution to the Psychology of the Russian People* (Cambridge: W. Heffer & Sons, 1915).
Harrison, William, 'H. G. Wells's View of Russia', *Scottish Slavonic Review* 7 (1986), pp. 49–68.
Haycock, David Boyd, *Paul Nash* (New York: Harry N. Abrams, 2002).
Heilbrun, Carolyn G., *The Garnett Family* (London: Allen and Unwin, 1961).
Henley, W. E., 'Count Tolstoi's Novels', *Saturday Review* (1 January 1887).
—— 'New Novels', *The Academy* 329 (1878), pp. 186–7.
Hesse, Hermann, *In Sight of Chaos*, trans. Sydney Schiff (Zurich, Seldwyla and London: A Zwemmer, 1923).
Hill, Aaron, *The Northern-star: A poem* (London: E. Berington, and J. Morphew, 1718).
Hudspith, Sarah, *Dostoevsky and the Idea of Russianness* (London: Routledge, 2004).
Hugo, Leon H., 'Punch: J. M. Barrie's Gentle Swipe at "Supershaw"', *Shaw: Annual of Bernard Shaw Studies* 10 (1990), pp. 60–72.
Humm, Maggie, *The Edinburgh Companion to Virginia Woolf and the Arts* (Edinburgh: Edinburgh University Press, 2010).
Husserl, Edmund, 'The Vienna Lecture. Philosophy and the Crisis of European Humanity' (10 May 1935), in *Phenomenology and the Crisis of Philosophy*, trans. David Carr (Evanston, IL: Northwestern University Press, 1970), pp. 269–300.
Hyde, G. M., *D. H. Lawrence and the Art of Translation* (London: Palgrave Macmillan, 1981). 'An Impertinent Substitution', *New Statesman* 5 (1915), pp. 628–9.
'Ivan Bunin', *The Times*, 17 May 1922, p. 16.
Jack, R. D. C., *The Road to the Never Land: A Reassessment of J M Barrie's Dramatic Art* (Glasgow: Humming Earth, 2010).

James, Henry, *The House of Fiction. Essays on the Novel*, ed. Leon Edel (London: Rupert Hart–Davis, 1957).

—— 'Ivan Turgénieff', *Atlantic Monthly* 53 (1884), pp. 42–55.

—— Preface to *The Portrait of a Lady*, in Henry James, *The Art of the Novel. Critical Prefaces* (New York: Charles Scribner's Sons, 1934), pp. 40–59.

James, William, *Some Problems of Philosophy* (Longmans: Green and Co, New York, 1911), pp. 147–8.

Jefferson, George, *Edward Garnett. A Life in Literature* (London: Jonathan Cape, 1982).

Johnson, A. E., 'The Truth about Karsavina', *Eve*, 1 April 1920, pp. 112–13.

Jones, Susan, *Literature, Modernism, and Dance* (Oxford: Oxford University Press, 2013).

Joyce, James, *Ulysses*, ed. Jeri Johnson (Oxford: Oxford University Press, 1993).

Kabakova, Galina, 'Mangeur de Chandelles. L'image du cosaque au XIX siècle', in *Transferts culturels triangulaires: France–Allemagne–Russie*, ed. Katia Dmitrieva and Michel Espagne (Paris: Editions de la maison des sciences de l'homme, 1996), pp. 207–31.

Karlinsky, Simon, 'Igor Stravisnky and Russian Preliterate Theatre', in *Confronting Stravinsky: Man, Musician, and Modernist*, ed. Jann Pasler (Berkeley: University of California Press, 1986), pp. 3–15.

Karsavina, Tamara, Introduction to 'The Truth about the Russian Dancers', *Dance Perspectives* 14 (1962), pp. 4–10.

—— *Theatre Street* (New York: E. P. Dutton & Co, 1961).

'Karsavina and Barrie', *The Times*, 16 March 1920, p. 14.

Kaye, Peter, *Dostoevsky and English Modernism, 1900–1930* (Cambridge: Cambridge University Press, 1999).

Keynes, Milo, 'Lydia Lopokova', in *Lydia Lopokova*, ed. Milo Keynes (London: Weidenfeld and Nicolson, 1983), pp. 1–38.

Kipling, Rudyard, 'The Man Who Was', in *Life's Handicap* (London: MacMillan and Co, 1891), pp. 84–101.

Koteliansky, S. S., 'A Few Extracts from Letters Exchanged Between Leo Nicolayevich Tolstoy and N. N. Strakhov', *The Criterion* 3.11 (1925), pp. 164–9.

Kovalev, Yurii, 'G Uells v Peterburge i Petrograde', *Vtorzhenie v Persei*, ed. E. Brandis and V. Dmitrievskii (Leningrad: Lenizdat, 1968), pp. 415–34.

Krivokapich, Melitsa, *In Pursuit of the Ideal Society* (Montreal: McGill University Press, 1994).

Kropotkin, Peter, 'Anarchism', in *Encyclopaedia Britannica* (Cambridge: Cambridge University Press, 1910).

—— *Memoirs of a Revolutionist* (London: Smith, Elder and Co, 1899).

Lawrence, D. H., *Aaron's Rod* (New York: Penguin, 1976).

—— *Apocalypse and the Writings on Revelation*, ed. Mara Kalnins (Cambridge: Cambridge University Press, 2002).

—— *A Collier's Friday Night* (London: M. Secker, 1934).

—— *The Complete Poems of D. H. Lawrence*, ed. Vivian de Sola Pinto and Warren Roberts, 2 vols (New York: Viking Press, 1971).

—— Foreword to Lev Shestov, *All Things Are Possible*, trans. S. S. Koteliansky (London: M. Secker, 1920), pp. 7–12.

—— 'Introduction to The Grand Inquisitor', in D. H. Lawrence, *Introductions and Reviews*, ed. N. H. Reeve and John Worthen (Cambridge: Cambridge University Press, 2005).

—— *Kangaroo* (London: Martin Secker, 1923).

—— *Lady Chatterley's Lover* (London: Collector's Library, 2005).

—— *The Letters of D. H. Lawrence*, ed. James T. Boulton et al., 8 vols (Cambridge, Cambridge University Press, 1979–2001).

—— *Movements in European History*, ed. Philip Crumpton (Cambridge; Cambridge University Press, 2002).

—— *Mr Noon*, ed. Lindeth Vasey (Cambridge: Cambridge University Press, 1984).

—— *Phoenix*, ed. Edward D. McDonald (London: Heinemann, 1936).

—— *The Rainbow* (New York: Modern Library, 1915).

—— *Reflections on the Death of a Porcupine and Other Essays*, ed. Michael Herbert (Cambridge: Cambridge University Press, 1988).

—— *Sea and Sardinia*. ed. Mara Kalnins (Cambridge: University Press, 2002).

—— *Selected Critical Writings*, ed. Michael Herbert (Oxford: Oxford University Press, 1998).

—— 'Solitaria, by V. V. Rozanov', in *D. H. Lawrence: Selected Criticism*, ed. Anthony Beal (New York: Viking Press, 1956), pp. 247–9.

—— *Studies in Classic American Literature* (London: Heinemann, 1964).

—— *The White Peacock* (London: Heinemann, 1911).

—— *Women in Love* (New York: The Viking Press, 1920).

Lee, Hermione, *Virginia Woolf* (London: Vintage Books, 1997).

Leerssen, Joep, 'Imagology: History and method', in *Imagology: The Cultural Construction and Literary Representation of National*, ed. Manfred Beller and Joseph Theodoor (Amsterdam: Rodopi, 2007), pp. 17–32.

Levidova, Inna, 'Pervyi priezd G. D. Uellsa v Rossiyu', in *G. D. Uells*, ed. I. M. Levidova and B. M. Parchevskaia (Moscow: Kniga, 1966), pp. 125–9.

Lieven, Peter, *The Birth of the Ballet Russes*, trans. L. Zarine (New York: Dover Publications, 1973).

Lifar, Sergei, *Diaghilev i s Diaghilevym* (Moscow: Vargius, 2005).

Long, R. E. C., 'Anton Tchekhoff', *Fortnightly Review* 72 (1902), pp. 103–18.

Lopukhov, F. V., 'Lydia Vasilievna Lopukhova: A Choreographic portrait', in *Lydia Lopokova*, ed. Milo Keynes (London: Weidenfeld and Nicolson, 1983).

Lotman, Yuri M., 'Siuzhetnoe prostranstvo russkogo romana XIX stoletiia', in Yuri M. Lotman, *Izbrannye stat'I* (Tallinn: Aleksandra, 1993), III, pp. 91–106.

Lowe, Peter, 'Prufrock in St Petersburg', *Journal of Modern Literature* 28.3 (2005), pp. 1–24.

Lunacharsky, Anatolii, 'Bernard Shaw', *Collected Works*, ed. A. V. Lunacharsky (Moscow: Khudozhestvennaia literatura, 1965), VI, pp. 150–3.

Lytton, Edward Bulwer, *Devereux. A Tale* (Chicago and New York: Belford Clarke & Company, 1887).

Macaulay, Thomas Babington, *The History of England from the Accession of James the Second*, in *The Works of Lord Macaulay*, 8 vols, ed. Lady Trevelyan (New York: Longmans, Green and Co, 1897).

McDonald, Jan, 'Barrie and the New Dramatists', *Gateway to the Modern: Resituating J. M. Barrie*, ed. Valentine Bold and Andrew Nash (Glasgow: Scottish Literature International, 2014), pp. 1–16.

Macdonald, Nesta, *Diaghilev Observed by Critics in England and the United States, 1911–1929* (London: Dance Horizons, 1975).

Mackail, Denis, *The Story of J. M. B.* (London: C. Scribner's Sons, 1941).

Mackail, John William, *Russia's Gift to the World* (London: Hodder and Stoughton, 1915).

Mackrell, Judith, *Bloomsbury Ballerina: Lydia Lopokova* (London: Weidenfeld & Nicolson, 2008).

Maĭskiĭ, Ivan Mikhaĭlovich, *The Maisky Diaries: Red Ambassador to the Court of St James's, 1932–1943*, ed. Gabriel Gorodetsky, trans. Tatiana Sorokina and Oliver Ready (New Haven, CT and London: Yale University Press 2015).

Majumdar, Robin, and Allen McLaurin, eds, *Virginia Woolf* (London: Routledge 2003).

Mansuy, Abel, *Le Monde slave et les classiques français aux XVIe–XVIIe siècles* (Paris : Librairie Ancienne Honoré Champion, 1912).

Markovits, Stefanie, *The Crisis of Action in Nineteenth-century English Literature* (Columbus: The Ohio State University Press, 2006).

Marrot, Harold V., *The Life and Letters of John Galsworthy* (London: Heinemann, 1935).

Marsh, Edward, 'Memoir', in *The Collected Poems of Rupert Brooke: with a Memoir* (London: Sidgwick & Jackson, 1918), pp. xi–clix.

Martin, Mildred A., *A Half Century of Eliot Criticism: An Annotated Bibliography of Books and articles in English 1916–1965* (Pennsylvania: Bucknell University Press, 1973).

Maugham, Somerset, *Ashenden* (New York: Doubleday, Doran, Incorporated, 1928).

May, Rachel, *The Translator in the Text: On Reading Russian Literature in English* (Evanston, IL: Northwestern University Press, 1994).

Merezhkovsky, Dmitrii, 'Lettre ouverte à Wells', *Révue hébdomadaire* 1 (1921), p. 132.

—— 'Pis'mo Uellsu', *Svoboda–Varshava* 125 (1920).

Mikhalskaia, N. P., *Obraz Rossii v angliiskoi khudozhestvennoi literature IX–IXX vv.* (Moscow: Moskovskii Gosudarstvennyi, Pedagogicheskii universitet, 1995).

Moore, Harry T., *The Priest of Love: A Life of D. H. Lawrence* (New York: Farrar, Straus and Giroux, 1974).

Moser, Charles A., 'The Achievement of Constance Garnett', *American Scholar* 57 (1988), pp. 431–8.

'Mr Wells Explains himself', *T.P.'s Magazine* 3 (1911), pp. 339–43.

'Mr Wells's Visit to Russia', *The Spectator*, 25 December 1920, pp. 854–5.

Muromtseva–Bunina, Vera, *Ustami Buninykh*, ed. Militsa Grin (Moscow: Posev, 2005).

Nabokov, V. N., 'Uells', *Rech'* 14 (15 January 1914), p. 2.

Nerhood, Harry W., *To Russia and Return: An Annotated Bibliography of Travelers' English-Language Accounts of Russia from the Ninth Century to the Present* (Ohio: Ohio State University Press, 1968).

Neuschäffer, Walter, *Dostojewskijs Einfluss auf englischen Roman Anglistische Forschungen* (Heidelberg: Carl Withers Universitätsbuchhandlung, 1935).

'Notes on Current Books: *Undiscovered Russia* by Stephen Graham', *Russian Review* 1.1 (1912), p. 98.

'Novelists Who May Be Read in A. D. 2029', *Manchester Guardian*, 3 April 1929, p. 16.

Obituary. 'Mr H. G. Wells', *The Times*, 14 August 1946, p. 7.

Orel, Harold, 'English Critics and the Russian Novel 1860–1917', *Slavonic and East European Review* 33 (1954), pp. 457–69.

—— 'The Victorian View of Russian Literature', *Victorian Newsletter* 51 (1977), pp. 1–5.

Ormond, Leonee, *J. M. Barrie* (Edinburgh: Scottish Academic Press, 1987).

Österling, Anders, Presentation Speech of the Nobel Committee of the Swedish Academy, 10 December 1932 <http://www.nobelprize.org/nobel_prizes/literature/laureates/1932/press.html> [accessed 2 September 2016].

'Our London Correspondence', *The Manchester Guardian*, 12 July 1919.

'Our New War', *The Times*, 21 February 1918, p. 7.

Oxford Dictionary of English, 'myth' <http://www.oxforddictionaries.com/us/definition/american_english/myth> [accessed 2 September 2016].

Page, Norman, *D. H. Lawrence: Interviews and Recollections* (London: MacMillan, 1981).

Palmer, Daryl W., 'Jacobean Muscovites: Winter, Tyranny, and Knowledge in *The Winter's Tale*', *Shakespeare Quarterly* 46.3 (1995), pp. 323–9.

—— *Writing Russia in the Age of Shakespeare* (Aldershot: Ashgate, 2004).

Parrinder, Patrick, Introduction to *Reception of H. G. Wells in Europe*, ed. Patrick Parrinder (London: Continuum, 2005), pp. 1–13.

Pease, Edward R., *The History of the Fabian Society* (New York: E. P. Dutton & Company, 1926).

Perl, Jeffrey, *A Dictatorship of Relativism* (Durham, NC: Duke University Press, 2007).

Phelps, Gilbert, *The Russian Novel in English Fiction* (London: Hutchinson's University Library, 1956).

Phelps, William Lyon, *Essay on Russian Novelists* (New York: Macmillan Co, 1911, reprinted New York: Snova Books, 2004).

Piper, Myfanwy, rev. Andrew Causey, 'Nash, Paul (1889–1946)', *Oxford Dictionary of National Biography* (Oxford: Oxford University Press, 2004); online edn, May 2009 <http://www.oxforddnb.com/view/article/35186> [accessed 2 September 2016].

Pope, John, 'Prufrock and Raskolnikov Again', *American Literature* 18.4 (1947), pp. 319–21.

Pound, Ezra, *Pavannes and Divagations* (New York: New Directions, 1958).

Ralston, W. R. S., 'Novels of Count Leo Tolstoy', *Nineteenth Century* 5 (1879), pp. 650–69.

Reed, Christopher, *Roger Fry Reader* (Chicago: University of Chicago Press, 1996).

Reinhold, Natalya, 'The Russian Pigeons in the Groves of Eastwood', *Études Lawrenciennes* 44 (2013), pp. 97–110.

Remnick, David, 'The Translation Wars', *The New Yorker*, 7 November 2005.

Rhondda [Lady], Margaret, 'Shaw's Women', *Time and Tide*, 7 March 1930, pp. 300–1.

Richardson, Ben, unpublished MA Thesis 'Unwrapping the Enigma: Russia in the Works of Wyndham Lewis, T. S. Eliot, and D. H. Lawrence, 1912–1939' (University of Canterbury: New Zealand, 2012).

'Rossiia glazami anglichanina: naivnosti g–na Uellsa', *The New Russia* 38 (1920), p. 250.

Rubenstein, Roberta, *Virginia Woolf and the Russian Point of View* (London: Palgrave, 2009).

Rude and Barbarous Kingdom: Russia in the Accounts of Sixteenth-Century English Voyagers, ed. Lloyd E. Berry and Robert O. Crummey (Madison: The University of Wisconsin Press, 1968).

'Russia as It Is', *New Statesman*, 11 December 1920, pp. 296–7.

'Russia in Literature. Tribute by British Men of Letters', *The Times*, 23 December 1914, p. 10; reprinted in 'Causerie', *New York Times*, 24 January 1915.

'The Russian Ballet. From behind the Scenes', *Manchester Guardian*, 29 July 1919.

'The Russian Ballet. No Public Festivity', *The Times*, 14 May 1919, p. 14.

'The Russian Invasion' (the review of Rosa Newmarch's book *The Russian Opera*), *Spectator*, 27 June 1914, p. 1089.
Said, Edward, *Culture and Imperialism* (London: Vintage, 1994).
—— *Orientalism* (New York: Pantheon Books, 1978).
'St James's Theatre', *The Times*, 2 July 1910, p. 8.
Sarolea, Charles, *Europe's Debt to Russia* (London: Heinemann, 1916).
'Savoy Theatre', *The Times*, 29 July 1926, p. 10.
Sayers, Dorothy, letter to *New Statesman*, 17 February 1937, *Letters of Dorothy Sayers*, 2 vols (Cambridge: Dorothy L. Sayers Society, 1997).
Scott Kathleen, *Self-Portrait of an Artist* (London: John Murray, 1949).
Semino, Elena, 'Blending and Characters' Mental Functioning in Virginia Woolf's Lappin and Lapinova', *Language and Literature* 15 (2006), pp. 55–72.
Seymour-Smith, Carole, *Painted Shadow: a Life of Vivienne Eliot* (London: Constable, 2001).
Shakespeare, William, *The Plays of Shakespeare*, 9 vols (London: William Pickering, 1825).
Sharma, Radhe S., *The Rainbow: A Study of Symbolic Mode in D. H. Lawrence's Primitivism* (Hyderabad: Trust Publishers, 1981).
Sharp, W., 'New Novels', *The Academy* 871 (1889), p. 22.
Shaw, Bernard, et al., 'Assure New Russia of British Regard', *The New York Times*, 1 April 1917, p. 3.
Shaw, G. B., 'The Censor's Revenge', *The Times*, 26 June 1909, p. 10.
—— 'London Music – Jane Annie', *World*, 24 May 1893.
—— *Music in London 1890–1894* (London: Constable and Company, 1932), II, p. 315.
—— *Our Theatre in the Nineties* (London: Constable and Company, 1932).
Sherborne, Michael, *H. G. Wells: Another Kind of Life* (London: Peter Owen, 2010).
Shestov, Lev, *All Things Are Possible*, trans. S. S. Koteliansky (London: M. Secker, 1920).
—— 'Dostoevsky and Nietzsche: The Philosophy of Tragedy', in Lev Shestov, *Dostoevsky, Tolstoy and Nietzsche*, ed. Bernard Martin (Columbus: Ohio State University Press, 1969), pp. 141–322.
'Shestov's Challenge to Civilisation', *New York Times Book Review and Magazine*, 3 October 1920, p. 19.
Shklovsky, E. A., Notes to Fedor Dostoevsky, *Crime and Punishment* (Moscow: Olma–Press, 2005), pp. 744–62.
Sidney, Philip [Sir], *Astrophel and Stella*, in Sir Philip Sidney, *The Last Part of the Countesse of Pembrokes Arcadia: Astrophel & Stella and Other Poems*, ed. Albert Feuillerat (Cambridge: Cambridge University Press, 1922), pp. 241–300.
Sinjohn, John, 'The Salvation of a Forsyte', in John Sinjohn, *A Man of Devon* (Edinburgh and London: W. Blackwood and Sons, 1901), pp. 109–86.

Sitwell, Osbert, *Great Morning* (London: Little and Brown, 1947).

Smith, Alexandra, 'Jane Harrison as an Interpreter of Russian Culture in the 1910s–1920s', in *A People Passing Rude*, ed. Anthony Cross (Cambridge: Open Book Publishers, 2012), pp. 175–88.

Snodin, Michael, and Maurice Howard, *Ornament: A Social History Since 1450* (New Haven, CT: Yale University Press, 1996).

Sokolova, Lidiia, *Dancing for Diaghilev* (London: John Murray, 1960).

Stevens, Hugh, 'From Genesis to the Ring: Richard Wagner and D. H. Lawrence's Rainbow', *Textual Practice* 28.4 (2014), pp. 611–30.

Stokes, Adrian, *Russian Ballets* (London: Faber and Faber, 1934).

Stokes, John, *Oscar Wilde: Myths, Miracles and Imitations* (Cambridge: Cambridge University Press, 1996).

Stout, Felicity, *Exploring Russia in the Elizabethan Commonwealth* (Manchester: Manchester University Press, 2015).

Stephens, Winifred, Preface to *The Soul of Russia*, ed. Winifred Stephens (London: Macmillan, 1916), pp. v–viii.

Surits, E. Ya., 'Malen'kaia Lopukhova: Lidiia Lopukhova (1891–1981), ee zhizn' i tvorchestvo za rubezhom', in *Khudozhestvennaia kul'tura russkogo zarubezh'ia 1917–1939* (Moscow: Indrik, 2008), pp. 366–80.

Swaffer, Hannen, '*Les Noces* filled my cup of bitterness to overflowing', *Daily Express*, 16 February 1926.

Swinburne, Algernon Charles, *The Poems*, 6 vols (London: Chatto & Windus, 1911).

Swinnerton, Frank, *The Georgian Scene* (London: Farrar & Rinehart, 1934).

'T', 'At the Play', *Punch*, 24 March 1920, p. 236.

Taunton, Matthew, 'Russia and the British Intellectuals. The Significance of *The Stalin–Wells Talk*', *Russia in Britain, 1880–1940: From Melodrama to Modernism*, ed. Rebecca Beasley and Philip Ross Bullock (Oxford: Oxford University Press, 2013), pp. 209–24.

Tennyson, Alfred, *Poems and Plays* (London, New York and Toronto: Oxford University Press, 1968).

Thomas, Gareth, 'Modernism, Diaghilev and the Ballets Russes in London, 1911–1929', in *British Music and Modernism, 1895–1960*, ed. Mathew Riley (Farnham: Ashgate Publishing, 2010), pp. 67–92.

Tolstoï, Lyof, 'Two Hussars', in *The Russian Proprietor and Other Stories*, trans. Nathan Haskell Dole (New York: Thomas Crowell, 1887).

Tolstoy, Leo, *Anna Karenina*, trans. Nathan Dole (New York: Thomas Crowell, 1899).

—— *Childhood and Youth* (London: Bell and Dalby, 1862).

—— *Cossacks*, trans. Eugene Schuyler (New York: Scribner's Sons, 1878; London: Sampson Low and Co, 1878).

—— *Polnoe sobranie sochinenii*, ed. V. G. Chertkov, 90 vols (Moscow: Goslitizdat, 1928–1958).

—— *War and Peace*, trans. Louise and Aylmer Maude (Chicago and London: William Benton, 1952).

Toye, Richard, 'The Great Educator of Unlike People: H. G. Wells and the Origins of the Welfare State', in *No Wealth but Life: Welfare Economics and the Welfare State in Britain, 1880–1945*, ed. Roger E. Backhouse and Tamotsu Nishizawa (Cambridge: Cambridge University Press, 2010), pp. 161–88.

A Treasury of War Poetry: British and American poems of the world war, 1914–1917, ed. George Herbert Clarke (Boston, MA and New York: Houghton Mifflin Company, 1917).

Trubetskoi, N. S., Preface to G. D. Uells, *Rossiia vo mgle* (Sofiia, Rossiisko–bolgarskoe kn–vo, 1921), pp. iii–xvi.

Turgenev, Ivan, *A House of Gentlefolk*, trans. Constance Garnett (London: William Heinemann, 1922).

—— *On the Eve*, trans. Constance Garnett (London: William Heinemann, 1920).

Turner, C. E., *Studies in Russian Literature* (London: Kessinger Publishing Company, 1882).

Turner, Frank M., 'The Victorian Crisis of Faith and the Faith that Was Lost', in *Victorian Faith in Crisis*, ed. Richard J. Helmstadter and Bernard Lightman (Stanford, CA: Stanford University Press, 1990), pp. 9–38.

Turner, John C., 'Towards A Cognitive Redefinition of the Social Group', in *Social Identity and Intergroup Relations*, ed. Henri Tajfel (Cambridge: Cambridge University Press, 1982), pp. 15–40.

Turton, Glyn, *Turgenev and the Context of English Literature 1850–1900* (Routledge: London, 1992).

Tyrkova-Williams, Ariadna, *Cheerful Giver* (London: P. Davies, 1935).

'U. S. and the War. New York Journalist on National Awakening', *The Times*, 10 February 1917, p. 5.

Ushakova, Olga, 'Russia and Russian Culture in *The Criterion* 1922–1939', *A People Passing Rude*, ed. Anthony Cross (Cambridge: Open Book, 2012), pp. 231–40.

Uspensky, Leonid, 'The Meaning and Content of the Icon', in *Eastern Orthodox Theology: A Contemporary Reader*, ed. Daniel B. Clendenin (Grand Rapids, MI: Baker, 2000) pp. 33–63.

Vengerova, Zinaida, 'Dzhordzh Uells ego prebyvanie v Peterburge', *Den'* 17 (18 January 1914), p. 3.

Walbrook, H. M., *J. M. Barrie and the Theatre* (London: F. V. White & Co, 1922).

Wallace, Donald Mackenzie, *Russia* (London: H. Holt, 1880).

Wattison, Meredith, 'This Furred Place – the Woolfs' anthropomorphism, bunnies in people suits and the zoomorphic other', *Plumwood Mountain* 2.1 (2015). <https://plumwoodmountain.com/articles-and-essays/> [accessed 8 September 2016].

Watts, Cedric, 'Edward Garnett's Influence on Conrad', *The Conradian* 21.1 (1996), pp. 79–91.

Webb, Beatrice, *Our Partnership* (London: Longmans, Green & Co, 1948).

Webb, Sidney and Beatrice, *The Letters of Sidney and Beatrice Webb*, ed. Norman Mackenzie (Cambridge: Cambridge University Press, 2008).

Wells, H. G., *The Correspondence of H. G. Wells*, ed. David C. Smith, 4 vols (London: Pickering and Chatto, 1998).

—— *Experiment in Autobiography* (London: Faber and Faber, 1934).

—— Introduction to Denis N. Garstin, *Friendly Russia* (London: T. F. Unwin, 1915).

—— Introduction to Leo Tolstoy, *Resurrection* (London: Humphrey Milford, Oxford University Press, 1928), pp. vii–x.

—— *Joan and Peter. The Story of an Education* (York: The Macmillan Company, 1918).

—— 'The Liberal Fear of Russia', *The Nation*, 22 August 1914.

—— 'Liberalism and the Revolutionary Spirit', in H. G. Wells, *After Democracy* (London: Watts and Co, 1932), pp. 1–28.

—— *Meanwhile: the Picture of a Lady* (London: George Doran, 1927).

—— *A Modern Utopia* (London: Chapman & Hall, 1905).

—— 'Mr. Wells and the Bolsheviks. Some Disregarded Aspects', *Daily Mail*, 15 January 1918.

—— *The New Machiavelli* (London: John Lane, 1911).

—— 'The Novels of Mr. George Gissing', *Contemporary Review* 72 (1897), p. 193.

—— *The Outline of History* (London: Cassell, 1951).

—— 'Russia and England: A Study in Contrast', *Daily News*, 21 February 1914.

—— *Russia in the Shadows* (London: Hodder and Stoughton, 1920).

West, Julius, 'Translated from the Russian', *New Statesman* 5 (1915), 447–8.

Williams, Raymond, *Politics of Modernism* (New York: Verso, 1989).

Winsten, S., ed., *G. B. S.* (London: Hutchinson, 1946).

Wolff, Larry, *Inventing Eastern Europe* (Stanford, CA: Stanford University Press, 1994).

Woods, Joanna, *Katerina: The Russian World of Katherine Mansfield* (London: Penguin, 2001).

Woolf, Leonard, *Beginning Again: An Autobiography of the Years 1911 to 1918* (London: Hogarth Press, 1964).

—— Foreword to Virginia Woolf, *A Haunted House and Other Stories* (New York: Harcourt Inc., 1944), pp. v–vi.

Woolf, Virginia, *Books and Portraits* (London: Hogarth, 1977).

—— *The Diary of Virginia Woolf*, ed. Anne Olivier Bell, 5 vols (London: Hogarth Press, 1977–84).
—— *A Haunted House and Other Stories* (New York, Harcourt Inc., 1944).
—— *Jacob's Room* (London: Hogarth Press, 1990).
—— *The Letters of Virginia Woolf*, ed. Nigel Nicolson, 6 vols (London: Hogarth Press, 1975–1980).
—— 'Modern Fiction', in Virginia Woolf, *The Common Reader* (London: Vintage Classics, 2003), I, pp. 146–54.
—— *Mr Bennett and Mrs Brown* (London: Hogarth Press, 1924).
—— *Night And Day* (Harmondsworth: Penguin, 1992).
—— 'The Novels of Turgenev', in Virginia Woolf, *The Captain's Death Bed and Other Essays* (San Diego, New York and London: Harcourt Brace, 1950), pp. 53–61.
—— *Orlando: A Biography* (London: Wordsworth Classics, 1995).
—— 'The Russian Point of View', in Virginia Woolf, *The Common Reader* (London: Vintage Classics, 2003), I, pp. 173–82.
—— *To The Lighthouse* (Harmondsworth: Penguin, 1992).
—— 'Uncle Vanya', in *A Haunted House*, ed. Susan Dick (London: Vintage, 1985), p. 241.
—— *The Voyage Out* (London: Vintage, 2004).
Yeats, W. B., 'The Circus Animals' Desertion', in *The Collected Works of W. B. Yeats*, ed. Richard J. Finneran (New York: Scribner's Sons, 1997), I, p. 356.
Yedlin, Tovah, *Maxim Gorky. A Political Biography* (Westport, CT: Praeger, 1999).
Zashikhin, Andrei N., *Britanskaia rossika vtoroi poloviny XIX–nachala XX veka* (Archangel: Pomorskii pedagogicheskii universitet, 1995).
Zohrab, Irene, 'From New Zealand to Russia to Britain: a comment on the work of Harold W. Williams and his relations with English writers', *New Zealand Slavonic Journal* 1 (1985), pp. 3–15.
Zytaruk, George J., 'D. H. Lawrence's Hand in Translation of Maxim Gorki's "Reminiscences of Leonid Andreev"', *The Yale University Library Gazette* 46.1 (1971), pp. 29–34.
—— *D. H. Lawrence's Response to Russian Literature* (The Hague: Mouton, 1971).
—— Introduction to George J. Zytaruk, *The Quest for Rananim: D. H. Lawrence's Letters to S. S. Koteliansky* (Montreal: McGill-Queen's University Press, 1970).
—— 'The Phallic Vision: D. H. Lawrence and V. V. Rozanov', *Comparative Literature Studies* 4.3 (1967), pp. 283–97.

Index